BESTSELLING BOOK SERIES

iPod® & iTunes® For Dummies 5th Edition

iTunes Keyboard Shortcuts

Function	Mac Shortcut	Windows Shortcut
Play selected song or video from beginning	Return	Enter
Play song or video after pausing	Spacebar	Spacebar
Pause playing the song or video	Spacebar	Spacebar
Play next song or video	→	→
Play previous song or video	←	←
Increase volume	⌘-↑	Ctrl-↑ or Ctrl++
Decrease volume	⌘-↓	Ctrl-↓ or Ctrl+–
Mute volume	⌘-Option-↓ or ⌘-Option-↑	Ctrl-Alt-↓ or Ctrl-Alt-↑
Eject CD	⌘-E	Ctrl-E
Open Info window	⌘-I	Ctrl-I
Show currently playing song or video	⌘-L	Ctrl-L
Create a playlist	⌘-N	Ctrl-N
Shrink to mini-player (Windows)	Not applicable	Ctrl-M
Minimize to Dock (Mac)	⌘-M	Not applicable
Display visuals full-screen	⌘-F	Ctrl-F
Go to next page in iTunes Store	⌘-]	Ctrl-]
Go to previous page in iTunes Store	⌘-[	Ctrl-[

iPod Shortcuts

- **Prevent the iPod from automatically synchronizing.** Press ⌘-Option when connecting to a Mac or press Ctrl-Alt when connecting to a Windows PC.
- **Reset first-, second-, and third-generation iPods.** Toggle the Hold switch on and off, and then press the Menu and Play/Pause buttons simultaneously for five seconds. (For first- and second-generation iPods, you don't need to toggle the Hold switch, but it doesn't hurt.)
- **Reset fifth-generation video iPod and iPod nano; and fourth-generation iPods, including iPod mini, iPod U2 Special Edition, and color-display iPods.** Toggle the Hold switch on and off, and then press the Menu and Select buttons simultaneously for six seconds.
- **Increase volume.** Scroll clockwise while the song is playing. On an iPod shuffle, press the plus (+) button.
- **Decrease volume.** Scroll counterclockwise while the song is playing. On an iPod shuffle, press the minus (–) button.
- **Fast-forward a song.** Press and hold the Next/Fast-Forward button.
- **Rewind a song.** Press and hold the Previous/Rewind button.
- **Turn off the iPod.** Press and hold the Play/Pause button.
- **Turn on the iPod.** Press any button with the Hold switch off.
- **Go to the previous menu.** Press the Menu button.

For Dummies: Bestselling Book Series for Beginners

iPod® & iTunes® For Dummies®, 5th Edition

iPod Shuffle Shortcuts

- **Turn on the iPod shuffle.** Slide the on/off switch away from the Off position.
- **Turn off the iPod shuffle.** Slide the on/off switch to the Off position.
- **Play songs in an iPod shuffle randomly.** Slide the position switch to the crossing arrows icon.
- **Play songs in an iPod shuffle sequentially.** Slide the position switch to the arrows-in-a-loop icon.

Twelve Soundtracks for Travel Experiences

- ***The Joshua Tree,* by U2:** Cruising Death Valley. (If you start the album at the entrance, you hear "In God's Country" at an appropriate spot, no matter how fast or slowly you drive.)
- ***Anthem of the Sun,* by the Grateful Dead:** While you're driving over the Golden Gate Bridge into San Francisco at sunset.
- **"Across the Great Divide" on *The Band,* by The Band:** When you reach the crest of Donner Pass in the California Sierras on I-80, or the crest of Monarch Pass on the Continental Divide on U.S. 50 in Colorado. "Just grab your hat / And take that ride."
- ***Magical Mystery Tour,* by the Beatles:** Taking the Number 77 double-decker out of Liverpool to Grove Street, Dale Street, Smithdown Road, and yes, Penny Lane (where you can walk to Strawberry Fields, if you have the directions in the Notes section on your iPod).
- **"All Aboard" on *Fathers and Sons,* by Muddy Waters:** Taking a train heading north to Chicago, and then following this tune with Junior Parker's "Mystery Train" and John Lee Hooker's "Peavine."
- **"East-West" by the Butterfield Blues Band, or "Eight Miles High" by the Byrds:** Traveling on a plane, heading east or west.
- **The Beach Boys, Fleetwood Mac, or Jan and Dean:** Roller-skating on the Venice, California boardwalk.
- **"Walk on the Wild Side" by Lou Reed, and *Paul's Boutique,* by the Beastie Boys:** Jogging in Central Park.
- **"Wooden Ships" by Crosby, Stills, and Nash; anything by Jimmy Buffett; and "Sail Away" by Randy Newman:** Sailing around the Florida Keys and up the east coast into Charleston Bay.
- **"Feets Don't Fail Me Now" by Little Feat, and "I've Been Everywhere" by Johnny Cash:** Driving an 18-wheeler, rolling through northern New Jersey into New York City.
- **Miles Davis, John Coltrane, McCoy Tyner, or Sonny Rollins:** Hiding backstage in the Green Room at the Village Gate.
- **Pink Floyd:** Hopping around in an astronaut suit on the dark side of the moon.

For more information about Wiley Publishing, call 1-800-762-2974.

iPod® & iTunes®

FOR DUMMIES®

5TH EDITION

by Tony Bove and Cheryl Rhodes

Wiley Publishing, Inc.

iPod® & iTunes® For Dummies®, 5th Edition

Published by
Wiley Publishing, Inc.
111 River Street
Hoboken, NJ 07030-5774

www.wiley.com

Published by Wiley Publishing, Inc., Indianapolis, Indiana

Published simultaneously in Canada

For general information on our other products and services, please contact our Customer Care Department within the U.S. at 800-762-2974, outside the U.S. at 317-572-3993, or fax 317-572-4002.

For technical support, please visit www.wiley.com/techsupport.

Wiley also publishes its books in a variety of electronic formats. Some content that appears in print may not be available in electronic books.

Library of Congress Control Number: 2007936463

ISBN: 978-0-470-17474-6

Manufactured in the United States of America

10 9 8 7 6 5 4 3 2 1

About the Author

Tony Bove (www.tonybove.com) has written more than two dozen books on computing, desktop publishing, and multimedia, including *iLife '04 All-in-One Desk Reference For Dummies* (Wiley), *The GarageBand Book* (Wiley), *The Art of Desktop Publishing* (Bantam), and a series of books about Macromedia Director, Adobe Illustrator, and PageMaker. Tony also founded *Publish* magazine and the *Inside Report on New Media* newsletter, and he wrote the weekly Macintosh column for *Computer Currents* for a decade, as well as articles for *NeXTWORLD,* the *Chicago Tribune* Sunday Technology Section, and *NewMedia.* Tracing the personal computer revolution back to the 1960s counterculture, Tony produced a CD-ROM interactive documentary in 1996, *Haight-Ashbury in the Sixties* (featuring music from the Grateful Dead, Janis Joplin, and Jefferson Airplane). He also developed the Rockument music site, www.rockument.com, with commentary and radio programs focused on rock music history. As a founding member of the Flying Other Brothers (www.flyingotherbros.com), which tours professionally and has released three commercial CDs (*52-Week High, San Francisco Sounds,* and *Estimated Charges*), Tony has performed with Hall of Fame rock musicians and uses his iPod to store extensive concert recordings. Tony has also worked as a director of enterprise marketing for a large software company, and as a communications director and technical publications manager.

Cheryl Rhodes has co-authored more than a dozen books on computing, desktop publishing, and multimedia, including iLife '04 All-in-One Desk Reference For Dummies (Wiley), The Art of Desktop Publishing (Bantam), and a series of books about Macromedia Director, Adobe Illustrator, and PageMaker. Cheryl contributed to the influential Inside Report on New Media newsletter and wrote articles for NeXTWORLD, Computer Currents, the Chicago Tribune Sunday Technology Section, and NewMedia. Cheryl also co-founded and edited Desktop Publishing/Publish magazine. Cheryl recently founded and served as director of a charter school and has worked as a professional courseware designer and an instructor in computer courses at elementary and high schools.

Dedication

This book is dedicated to John and Jimi (the Bove Brothers) for contributing tips and spending considerable time testing iPods.

Author's Acknowledgments

I want to thank John Paul and Jimi for providing technical expertise and performing valuable testing. I also want to thank Rich Tennant for his wonderful cartoons, and Dennis Cohen for technical expertise. And let me not forget my Wiley editors Christopher Morris, Teresa Artman, and Brian Walls for ongoing assistance that made my job so much easier. A book this timely places a considerable burden on a publisher's production team, and I thank the production crew at Wiley for diligence beyond the call of reason.

I owe thanks and a happy hour or three to Carole McLendon at Waterside, my agent. And I have acquisitions editor Bob Woerner at Wiley to thank for coming up with the idea for this book and helping me to become a professional dummy — that is, a Dummies author.

Finally, my heartfelt thanks to members of the Flying Other Brothers (Pete Sears, Barry Sless, Jimmy Sanchez, Bill Bennett, Bert Keely, TBone, Roger and Ann McNamee, and G.E. Smith) for the music that inspired me while writing this book.

Publisher's Acknowledgments

We're proud of this book; please send us your comments through our online registration form located at `www.dummies.com/register/`.

Some of the people who helped bring this book to market include the following:

Acquisitions, Editorial, and Media Development

Sr. Project Editor: Christopher Morris

(Previous Edition: Rebecca Senninger)

Sr. Acquisitions Editor: Bob Woerner

Copy Editors: Brian Walls, Teresa Artman

Technical Editor: Dennis Cohen

Editorial Manager: Kevin Kirschner

Media Project Supervisor: Laura Moss-Hollister

Media Development Associate Producer: Richard Graves

Editorial Assistant: Amanda Foxworth

Sr. Editorial Assistant: Cherie Case

Cartoons: Rich Tennant (`www.the5thwave.com`)

Composition Services

Project Coordinator: Patrick Redmond

Layout and Graphics: Carl Byers, Joyce Haughey, Barbara Moore, Laura Pence, Melanee Prendergast, Ronald Terry

Proofreaders: John Greenough, Toni Settle

Indexer: Slivoskey Indexing Services

Anniversary Logo Design: Richard Pacifico

Publishing and Editorial for Technology Dummies

Richard Swadley, Vice President and Executive Group Publisher

Andy Cummings, Vice President and Publisher

Mary Bednarek, Executive Acquisitions Director

Mary C. Corder, Editorial Director

Publishing for Consumer Dummies

Diane Graves Steele, Vice President and Publisher

Joyce Pepple, Acquisitions Director

Composition Services

Gerry Fahey, Vice President of Production Services

Debbie Stailey, Director of Composition Services

Contents at a Glance

Introduction 1

Part I: Setting Up and Acquiring Media Content 7

Chapter 1: Firing Up Your iPod 9
Chapter 2: Setting Up iTunes and Your iPod 33
Chapter 3: Getting Started with iTunes 43
Chapter 4: Shopping at the iTunes Store 55
Chapter 5: Bringing Content into iTunes 81
Chapter 6: Playing Content in iTunes 99
Chapter 7: Sharing Content Legally 121

Part II: Managing Your Media Content 137

Chapter 8: Searching, Browsing, and Sorting in iTunes 139
Chapter 9: Adding and Editing Information in iTunes 155
Chapter 10: Organizing iTunes Content with Playlists 167
Chapter 11: Managing Photos and Videos 177
Chapter 12: Synchronizing Devices with iTunes 185
Chapter 13: Gimme Shelter for My Media 213
Chapter 14: Baking Your Own Discs with Printed Inserts 225

Part III: Playing Your iPod 239

Chapter 15: Playing iPod Content 241
Chapter 16: Getting Wired for Playback 271

Part IV: Using Advanced Techniques 281

Chapter 17: Fine-Tuning the Sound 283
Chapter 18: Decoding Audio Encoding 299
Chapter 19: Changing Encoders and Encoder Settings 307

Part V: Have iPod, Will Travel 317

Chapter 20: Going Mobile 319
Chapter 21: Sleeping with Your iPod or iPhone 329
Chapter 22: Using Your iPod as a Hard Drive 351
Chapter 23: Synchronizing Personal Info with Your iPod or iPhone 359
Chapter 24: Updating and Troubleshooting 367

Part VI: The Part of Tens 377
Chapter 25: Ten iPod Problems and Solutions 379
Chapter 26: Eleven Tips for the Equalizer.....................................385
Index 389

Table of Contents

Introduction *1*

About This Book 2
Conventions Used in This Book 3
And Just Who Are You? 4
A Quick Peek Ahead 4
Part I: Setting Up and Acquiring Media Content 4
Part II: Managing Your Media Content 5
Part III: Playing Your iPod 5
Part IV: Using Advanced Techniques 5
Part V: Have iPod, Will Travel 5
Part VI: The Part of Tens 5
Bonus Chapters 6
Icons Used in This Book 6

Part I: Setting Up and Acquiring Media Content *7*

Chapter 1: Firing Up Your iPod **9**

Introducing iPods 10
Comparing iPod Models 11
Earlier-generation iPods 11
Sixth-generation iPods 12
Fingering the iPod touch 13
Twirling the iPod classics 14
Mano a mano with iPod nano 14
Doing the iPod shuffle 15
The all-in-one iPhone 16
Thinking Inside the Box 18
Powering Up Your iPod 19
Facing Charges of Battery 21
Maintaining battery life 23
Saving power 24
Replacing your battery 24
Thumbing Through the iPod Menus 25
Touching iPod touch and iPhone displays 25
Scrolling iPod classic and nano wheels 28
Activating iPod Playback Functions 29
Setting the Language 31

Chapter 2: Setting Up iTunes and Your iPod **33**

Installing iTunes on a Windows PC 33
Installing iTunes on a Mac 36

Setting Up Your iPod 38
Downloading and Installing Software Upgrades 41

Chapter 3: Getting Started with iTunes 43

What You Can Do with iTunes 44
Opening the iTunes Window 45
Playing CD Tracks in iTunes 48
- Rearranging and repeating tracks 50
- Skipping tracks 50
- Repeating a song list 50
- Displaying visuals 51

Using the iTunes MiniStore 53

Chapter 4: Shopping at the iTunes Store 55

Visiting the iTunes Store 56
Setting Up an Account 59
Browsing and Previewing Songs 61
- Browsing the charts 63
- Power searching 63
- Browsing celebrity and published playlists 63

Browsing and Previewing Movies, TV Shows, Videos, and Audiobooks 65
Browsing and Subscribing to Podcasts 68
Browsing and Previewing iPod Games 71
Buying and Downloading Content 71
- Using 1-Click 71
- Using the shopping cart 72
- Changing your iTunes Store preferences 73
- Resuming interrupted downloads 74
- Redeeming gift certificates and prepaid cards 76

Managing Your Account 76
- Viewing and changing account information 77
- Viewing your purchase history 77
- Setting up allowances 78
- Sending gift certificates 78
- Setting parental controls 79
- Authorizing computers to play purchased music 80

Chapter 5: Bringing Content into iTunes 81

Adding Music 82
- Setting the importing preferences 82
- Don't fall into the gaps 86
- Ripping music from CDs 88
- Adding music files 89

Adding Audio Books 91
Adding Podcasts 92
- Subscribing to podcasts 93
- Updating podcasts 95
- Scheduling podcast updates 95

Adding Videos 96

Chapter 6: Playing Content in iTunes 99

Changing the Computer's Output Volume 100
    Adjusting the sound on a Mac 100
    Adjusting the sound in Windows.....102
Using AirTunes for Wireless Stereo Playback 103
Playing Songs.....106
    Queuing up tunes with Party Shuffle 106
    Cross-fading song playback 108
Playing Streaming Radio.....109
    Listening to a radio station 110
    Creating a playlist of your radio stations.....111
    Adding a radio station to iTunes.....112
Playing Podcasts 112
Playing Audio Books 115
Playing Videos 115
    Playing a video in a separate window.....116
    Playing a video full-screen.....117

Chapter 7: Sharing Content Legally 121

Sharing Content from the iTunes Store.....122
Sharing Content on a Network 124
    Sharing your library with other computers.....124
    Accessing a shared library.....126
Sharing Content with Your Apple TV.....127
    Setting up Apple TV 128
    Choosing an iTunes library for Apple TV.....129
Copying Media Files.....132
Copying Files between Macs and PCs 133

Part II: Managing Your Media Content.....137

Chapter 8: Searching, Browsing, and Sorting in iTunes 139

Browsing Your Library Content.....140
    Browsing by cover art.....142
    Browsing songs by artist and album.....143
    Browsing audio books 144
    Browsing movies, videos, and TV shows 145
    Browsing iPod games.....146
Displaying Content in List View 146
    Understanding the content indicators 146
    Changing the List view options 147
Sorting Content by the List View Options 148
Searching for Content.....149
Finding the Content's Media File.....151
Showing Duplicate Items.....151
Deleting Content.....151

Chapter 9: Adding and Editing Information in iTunes 155

Retrieving Song Information from the Internet 156
- Retrieving information automatically 156
- Retrieving information manually 156

Entering Content Information 157

Editing the Information 158
- Editing multiple items at once 159
- Editing fields for a single item 160
- Adding a rating 164

Adding Cover Art 164

Chapter 10: Organizing iTunes Content with Playlists 167

Creating Playlists 168
- Song playlists 168
- Album playlists 169
- Podcast playlists 170
- Video playlists 172
- Deleting items from a playlist 173

Using Smart Playlists 173
- Creating a smart playlist 174
- Editing a smart playlist 175

Creating an iMix 176

Chapter 11: Managing Photos and Videos 177

Organizing Photos on Your Computer 178
- Organizing photos with iPhoto 179
- Organizing photos in Photoshop Album 181
- Preparing videos for iTunes and iPods 182
- Exporting your videos 182
- Converting your videos for iPods 183

Chapter 12: Synchronizing Devices with iTunes 185

Copying and Deleting Content Automatically 186
- Synchronizing your iPhone 188
- Synchronizing your Apple TV 190
- If your library won't fit on the device 191

Copying and Deleting Content Selectively 192
- Selecting items to ignore when synchronizing 193
- Choosing playlists to synchronize 194
- Choosing movies to synchronize 196
- Choosing TV shows to synchronize 198
- Choosing podcasts to synchronize 200
- Choosing photo albums to synchronize 201

Copying Content to Your iPod Manually 204
- Copying items directly 205
- Deleting items on your iPod 206

Creating playlists directly on an iPod 207
Editing content information on your iPod 208
Synchronizing an iPod shuffle 208
Using Autofill 209
Copying items manually 210
Managing space on your iPod shuffle 211

Chapter 13: Gimme Shelter for My Media 213

Studying Files in an iTunes Library 214
Finding the iTunes library 214
Changing how files are stored in the library 215
Locating a media file 216
Manipulating an iTunes Library 217
Consolidating the library media files 217
Changing the location of the library 218
Moving your library to another hard drive 219
Exporting iTunes playlists 219
Managing Multiple iTunes Libraries 220
Creating a sub-library of the main library 221
Creating a separate library on a different hard drive 221
Backing Up an iTunes Library 222
Backing up to DVD-Rs or CD-Rs 222
Backing up to another hard drive 223
Backing up from Mac to PC or PC to Mac 224

Chapter 14: Baking Your Own Discs with Printed Inserts 225

Selecting Recordable CDs and DVDs 226
What You Can Fit on a CD-R or DVD-R 226
Creating a Burn Playlist 227
Calculating how much music to use 228
Importing music for an audio CD-R 229
Switching import encoders for MP3 CD-R 230
Setting the Burning Preferences 230
Burning a Disc 233
Printing Song and Album Information 234
Printing inserts 234
Printing song lists and album notes 235
Troubleshooting Burns 237

Part III: Playing Your iPod....................239

Chapter 15: Playing iPod Content 241

Locating Songs on Your iPod 241
By cover art (using Cover Flow) 242
By artist name 244
By album title 245
By playlist 246

Playing a Song....247
Repeating songs....248
Shuffling song order....250
Playing Podcasts....252
Playing Audio Books....253
Playing Movies, TV Shows, and Videos....254
Playing Games on Your iPod....256
iQuiz....257
Vortex....257
Klondike (Solitaire)....257
Brick and Parachute (older iPods)....258
Music Quiz (older iPods)....258
Games from the iTunes Store....258
Viewing Photos....259
Setting up a slide show....259
Playing a slide show....261
Creating an On-The-Go Playlist....262
Selecting and playing items in an On-The-Go playlist....263
Deleting items from an On-The-Go playlist....264
Clearing an On-The-Go playlist....265
Saving an On-The-Go playlist in your iPod classic or nano....266
Transferring an On-The-Go playlist to iTunes....266
Playing an iPod shuffle....267
Adjusting and Limiting the Volume....269

Chapter 16: Getting Wired for Playback....271

Making Connections....271
Connecting to a Home Stereo....273
Connecting to a TV or Video Input....275
Playing an iPod through iTunes....276
Accessories for the iHome....278

Part IV: Using Advanced Techniques....281

Chapter 17: Fine-Tuning the Sound....283

Adjusting the Sound in iTunes First....284
Setting the volume in advance....284
Enhancing the sound....285
Sound-checking the iTunes library....286
Sound-checking the iPod....287
Equalize It in iTunes....288
Adjusting the preamp volume....288
Adjusting frequencies....289
Using the iTunes presets....289
Saving your own presets....290
Assigning equalizer presets....291

Equalize It in Your iPod 293
Choosing an equalizer preset on your iPod 293
Applying the iTunes equalizer presets 294
Modifying Content in iTunes 295
Setting the start and stop points 295
Splitting a track 296

Chapter 18: Decoding Audio Encoding 299

Trading Quality for Space 299
Choosing an iTunes Encoder 300
Manic Compression Has Captured Your Song 304
Selecting Import Settings 304

Chapter 19: Changing Encoders and Encoder Settings 307

Customizing the Encoder Settings in iTunes 308
Changing AAC encoder settings 308
Changing MP3 encoder settings 310
Changing AIFF, WAV, and Apple Lossless encoder settings 313
Importing Voice and Sound Effects in iTunes 314
Converting Songs to a Different Encoder Format in iTunes 315

Part V: Have iPod, Will Travel 317

Chapter 20: Going Mobile 319

Connecting Headphones and Portable Speakers 320
Playing Car Tunes 321
Using cassette and power adapters for your car 322
Integrating an iPod with your car stereo 324
Connecting by Wireless Radio 325
Dressing Up Your iPod for Travel 327
Using Power Accessories 328

Chapter 21: Sleeping with Your iPod or iPhone 329

Using the Clock 329
Displaying multiple clocks 332
Setting the alarm clock 333
Setting the sleep timer 337
Using the stopwatch 337
Choosing Display Settings 340
Backlight timer 340
Brightness and contrast 341
Checking Your Calendar 342
Sorting Your Contacts 342
Setting the Combination Lock 343

Speaking into Your iPod 346
Recording voice memos 347
Playing back voice memos 347
Managing voice memos in iTunes 348
Customizing the Menu and Settings 348

Chapter 22: Using Your iPod as a Hard Drive 351

Enabling an iPod as a Hard Drive 351
Opening iPod Folders 353
Adding Notes and Text 355
Using the Notes folder 355
Adding guides, books, and news feeds 356

Chapter 23: Synchronizing Personal Info with Your iPod or iPhone 359

Synchronizing Contacts and Calendars 360
Adding Calendars Manually to an iPod 363
Adding Contacts Manually to an iPod 364
Using Utilities to Copy Files and Music 364
Mac utilities 365
Windows utilities 366

Chapter 24: Updating and Troubleshooting 367

Taking Your First Troubleshooting Steps 367
Checking the Hold switch 367
Checking the power 368
Resetting an iPod 368
Resetting an iPhone or iPod touch 369
Draining the battery 370
Hitting the iPod panic button (Disk Mode) 370
Updating Your iPod, iPhone, or Apple TV 372
Checking the software version 372
Updating with newer software 373
Restoring to factory conditions 374
Updating an Apple TV 375

Part VI: The Part of Tens 377

Chapter 25: Ten iPod Problems and Solutions 379

How Do I Get My iPod to Wake Up? 379
How Do I Get My Battery to Last Longer? 380
How Do I Keep My Scroll Wheel from Going Crazy? 380
How Do I Get My Computer to Recognize My iPod? 381
What Are These Strange Icons on My iPod? 382
How Do I Restore My iPod to Its Factory Condition? 382

How Do I Update My iPod Software? 383
How Do I Synchronize My iPod When My Library Is Larger Than My iPod's Capacity? 383
How Do I Cross-Fade Music Playback with My iPod? 384
How Do I Decrease Distortion or Set a Lower Volume? 384

Chapter 26: Eleven Tips for the Equalizer 385

Setting the Volume to the Right Level 385
Adjusting Another Equalizer 385
Setting Booster Presets 386
Reducing High Frequencies 386
Increasing Low Frequencies 386
Setting Presets for Trucks and SUVs 386
Setting Presets When You're Eight Miles High 386
Reducing Tape Noise and Scratch Sounds 387
Reducing Turntable Rumble and Hum 387
Reducing Off-Frequency Harshness and Nasal Vocals 387
Cranking Up the Volume to Eleven 387

Index 389

Introduction

You don't need much imagination to see why so many people are so happy with their iPods, or why more than 100 million iPods have been sold as of this writing . . . or why millions of iPhones will also be in circulation by the time you read this.

Imagine no longer needing CDs. You can grab an iPod for a hike or jog and always listen to something different. You can take road trips that last for weeks and never hear the same song twice. Best of all, you can leave your music library safely at home.

Imagine no longer needing DVDs (or, heaven forbid, ancient VHS cassettes). You can take your favorite movies and TV shows with you on the road and watch them on your iPod or connect your iPod to a television to see your programs on a larger screen. The iPod is a convenient video player that holds up to 150 hours of video, which represents many more DVDs than you would probably want to carry with you on the road.

Imagine not waiting for hot new music or a hot TV show. You can be the first in your circle of friends to experience the exclusive new music and videos available from the iTunes Store by purchasing the content and loading it onto your iPod within minutes of discovering it on the Internet.

Imagine not having to buy music and videos more than once — never again having to replace an unplayable CD or DVD. You can purchase a CD or downloadable music and import the music into a digital library that lasts forever. You can also purchase a movie or TV show, or convert your favorite videos, and add them to your everlasting library.

Imagine a musician going backstage after a performance and meeting a promoter who says that he can get him ten more gigs if he can confirm the dates *right now*. This musician calmly scrolls through his calendar for the entire year (conveniently stored on his iPod), finding all the details that he needs about gigs and recording sessions, right down to the minute, including travel directions to each venue. "No problem," he says. And of course, he gets the gigs.

Okay, maybe you're not a rock star whose career depends on the information on your iPod or iPhone. But if rock stars can use them, so can average music lovers.

When we first encountered the iPod, it came very close to fulfilling our dreams as road warriors — in particular, the dream of filling up a car with music as easily as filling it up with fuel. For example, we use iPods with our cars using custom in-vehicle interface adapters with iPod connectors, or cassette adapters, or even FM radio transmitters (see Chapter 20). Whether you want to be *On the Road* with Jack Kerouac (in audio book form) or "Drivin' South" with Jimi Hendrix, just fill up your iPod and go!

iTunes was originally developed by Jeff Robbin and Bill Kincaid as an MP3 player called SoundJam MP, and released by Casady & Greene in 1999. It was purchased by Apple in 2000 and redesigned and released as iTunes. And speaking of mobile, versions of iTunes have been developed for mobile phones, such as the Motorola ROKR, Motorola RAZR, and Motorola SLVR.

iTunes version 7.4, the current version as of this writing, packs in a lot more features. Apple released version 7.0 in September 2006. When the gapless playback feature wasn't quite working right (among other things), Apple updated the program; version 7.0.2 arrived in November 2006. In March 2007, Apple updated the program to version 7.1, providing support for Apple TV and offering a full-screen option for the Cover Flow cover browser, as well as improved sorting options to let you decide how iTunes handles your favorite artists, albums, and songs. Apple also released QuickTime 7.1.5, delivering numerous bug fixes and addressing critical security issues. Then in March 2007, Apple fixed a few more bugs and released version 7.1.1 of iTunes. On May 30, 2007, Apple released version 7.2 and QuickTime Security Update 7.1.6 in order to provide support for purchasing higher-quality audio tracks without the Digital Rights Management (DRM) copy protection. Since then, as everybody knows, Apple introduced the iPhone on June 29, 2007, and newer versions of iTunes (now up to version 7.4) and QuickTime (version 7.2).

Do you need these new features, such as gapless playback? Of course, you do: Concert CDs and albums such as The Beatles' *Sgt. Pepper's Lonely Hearts Club Band* should be played in a seamless fashion. The tracks are separate, but the end of one song merges into the beginning of the next song. With similar albums, you probably don't want an annoying gap between the songs after ripping the CD into iTunes, so you can now set the Gapless Album option. iTunes is getting better all the time.

Gapless playback is one of many new features in iTunes that can improve your music library and your iPod or iPhone experience. You can also manage multiple iTunes libraries, which makes it much easier to keep multiple iPods or iPhones synchronized to different libraries. All these important new features are covered in this book.

About This Book

We designed *iPod & iTunes For Dummies,* 5th Edition, as a reference. You can easily find the information you need when you need it. We organized the information so that you can read from beginning to end to find out how to use iTunes and your iPod from scratch. But this book is also designed so that you can dive in anywhere and begin reading the info you need to know for each task.

We don't cover every detail of every function of the software, and we intentionally leave out some detail so that we don't befuddle you with technospeak when it's not necessary. (Really, engineers can sometimes provide too many obscure choices that no one ever uses; on the other hand, we did need gapless playback.) We write brief but comprehensive descriptions and include lots of cool tips on how to get the best results from using iTunes and your iPod.

If your PC is on the trailing edge rather than the leading edge, don't worry — you won't miss out on the iPod revolution. True, if you don't use Windows 2000 or Windows XP on your PC, you can't use iTunes for Windows. However, if you use Windows Me (Millennium Edition), you can use MusicMatch Jukebox. Please note that if you're using MusicMatch, you can find that content online on this book's companion Web site.

At the time we wrote this book, we covered every iPod and iPhone available and the latest version of iTunes. Although we do our best to keep up, Apple occasionally slips in a new iPod model or new version of iTunes between book editions. If you've bought a new iPod that's not covered in the book or your version of iTunes looks a little different, be sure to check out the companion Web site for updates on the latest releases from Apple.

Conventions Used in This Book

Like any book that covers computers and information technology, this book uses certain conventions:

- **Choosing from a menu:** In iTunes, when you see "Choose iTunes⇨Preferences in iTunes," you click iTunes on the toolbar and then choose Preferences from the iTunes menu.

  With the iPod, when you see "Choose Extras⇨Calendars from the iPod main menu," you highlight Extras in the main menu with the scroll wheel, press the Select button to select Extras, and then highlight and choose Calendars from the Extras menu.
- **Clicking and dragging:** When you see "Drag the song over the name of the playlist," we mean to click the song name, hold the mouse button down, and then drag the song with the mouse over to the name of the playlist before lifting your finger off the mouse button.
- **Keyboard shortcuts:** When you see ⌘-I, press the ⌘ key on a Mac keyboard, along with the appropriate shortcut key. (In this case, press I, which opens the Song Information window in iTunes.) In Windows, the same keyboard shortcut is Ctrl-I (which means press the Ctrl key along with the I key).
- **Step lists:** When you come across steps that you need to do in iTunes or on the iPod, the action is in bold, and the explanatory part follows. If you know what to do, read the action and skip the explanation. But if you need a little help along the way, check out the explanation.

And Just Who Are You?

You don't need to know anything about music or audio technology to discover how to make the most of your iPod and the iTunes software that comes with it. Although a course in music appreciation can't hurt, the iPod is designed to be useful even for air-guitar players who barely know the difference between downloadable music and System of a Down. You don't need any specialized knowledge to have a lot of fun with your iPod and the iTunes software while building up your digital music library.

However, we do make some honest assumptions about your computer skills:

- **You know how to use Mac Finder or Windows Explorer.** We assume that you already know how to locate files and folders and that you can copy files and folders from one hard drive to another on the computer of your choice: a Mac or a Windows PC.
- **You know how to select menus and applications on a Mac or a Windows PC.** We assume that you already know how to choose an option from a menu; how to find the Dock on a Mac to launch a Dock application (or use the Start menu in Windows to launch an application); and how to launch an application directly by double-clicking its icon.

For more information on these topics, see these excellent books, all by Wiley: *Mac OS X Tiger All-in-One Desk Reference For Dummies* (Mark L. Chambers), *Windows Vista All-in-One Desk Reference For Dummies* (Woody Leonhard), or *Windows XP GigaBook For Dummies* (Peter Weverka).

A Quick Peek Ahead

This book is organized into six parts, and each part covers a different aspect of using your iPod. Here's a quick preview of what you can find in each part.

Part I: Setting Up and Acquiring Media Content

This part gets you started with your iPod: powering it up, recharging its battery, using its menus, and connecting it to your computer. You install and set up iTunes on your Mac or your Windows PC. We show you what you can do with iTunes. To acquire music, you can buy music from the iTunes Store or rip audio CDs. You can also find podcasts, audio books, movies, TV shows, and music videos in the iTunes Store or import them into iTunes from other sources. You can even play Web radio stations.

Part II: Managing Your Media Content

This part shows you how to sort the content in your iTunes library by artist, album, duration, date, and other items. You can add and edit iTunes song information. You discover how to arrange songs and albums into iTunes playlists that you can transfer to your iPod. When you have your music, audio books, podcasts, photos, movies, TV shows, and videos organized efficiently, you can transfer them to the iPod. For your peace of mind, we also cover backing up your content library, burning CDs, and printing CD, jewel case inserts with the song information.

Part III: Playing Your iPod

We show you how to locate and play all types of content — music, audio books, podcasts, movies, TV shows, and videos — on your iPod. We also describe how to connect your iPod to your home stereo or speakers, and to a television for a larger video picture. You then discover how to fine-tune the sound playback in iTunes with the iTunes equalizer and on your iPod with the iPod equalizer, and how to modify songs in iTunes for playback on your iPod.

Part IV: Using Advanced Techniques

In this part, you discover digital music encoding and how to change your importing preferences to get the best results with digital audio compression. We also focus on what you can do to improve the sound of your music without sacrificing hard drive space.

Part V: Have iPod, Will Travel

This part covers how to use your iPod on the road with car stereos and portable speakers. You find out all the techniques of an iPod road warrior: setting your alarm clock, sorting your contacts, recording voice memos, entering personal information into your computer (such as calendar appointments, To-Do lists, and contacts), and synchronizing your iPod with all your personal information. We also provide initial troubleshooting steps and details about updating and restoring your iPod.

Part VI: The Part of Tens

In this book's Part of Tens chapters, we outline common problems and solutions for most iPods and provide tips about the iPod equalizer.

Bonus Chapters

This book includes bonus chapters covering:

- Earlier iPod models and the cables for connecting them to your computer
- Creating photo libraries, videos, address books, and calendars
- Using MusicMatch Jukebox on a Windows PC to manage your iPod music library
- Using your iPod for data backup and restore operations
- Resources for information and iPod products and services

You can find these chapters on this book's companion Web.

Icons Used in This Book

The icons in this book are important visual cues for information you need.

Remember icons highlight important things you need to remember.

Technical Stuff icons highlight technical details you can skip unless you want to bring out the technical geek in you.

Tip icons highlight tips and techniques that save you time and energy — and maybe even money.

Warning icons save your butt by preventing disasters. Don't bypass a Warning without reading it. This is your only warning!

On the Web icons let you know when a topic is covered further online at `www.dummies.com/go/ipod5e`, this book's companion Web site.

Part I

Setting Up and Acquiring Media Content

"I could tell you more about myself, but I think the playlist on my iPod says more about me than mere words can."

In this part . . .

Part I shows you how to do all the essential tasks with your iPod and iTunes.

- Chapter 1 gets you started with your iPod. Here you find out how to get the most from your battery, use the menus and buttons, and connect your iPod to your Mac or PC.
- Chapter 2 describes how to install iTunes, including the iPod software, on a Mac or Windows PC.
- Chapter 3 gets you started with iTunes on a Mac or Windows PC.
- Chapter 4 covers purchasing content online from the iTunes Store.
- Chapter 5 describes how to get music, audio books, videos, and podcasts into your iTunes library.
- Chapter 6 describes how to play music, audio books, videos, radio shows, and podcasts in your iTunes library.
- Chapter 7 shows how you can share content (legally) with other iTunes users on your network, use iTunes libraries with Apple TV over a network, and copy items to other computers (even songs, audio books, and videos purchased online).

Chapter 1

Firing Up Your iPod

In This Chapter

- Comparing iPod models
- Powering up your iPod
- Using and recharging your battery
- Scrolling through the iPod main menu

The B-52's sing, "Roam if you want to, roam around the world" through your headphones as you take off. The flight is just long enough to watch Tom Cruise in the movie *Vanilla Sky* and the "Mr. Monk and the Airplane" episode from the first series of the *Monk* TV show, as well as catch up on the latest episodes of *The Daily Show with Jon Stewart* and *The Colbert Report.* It's so easy to hold and watch your iPod that you don't have to put it away when your flight dinner arrives. You even have time to listen to the "NFL Rants and Raves" podcast to catch up on American football.

As the plane lands, you momentarily forget where it is you're going, so you read your destination information on your iPod without even pausing the podcast, and you queue up a playlist of songs to get you through the terminal. If Chicago is your kind of town, you might choose Frank Sinatra. If you're in San Francisco, you might choose anything from Tony Bennett to the Grateful Dead. You have so much content on your iPod (that you can select and play so easily) that you probably could land anywhere in the world with appropriate music in your ear and convenient eye candy in your hand.

iPods changed the way people play music on-the-run. Now, they're changing the way people play TV shows and videos. A full-size video iPod holds so much music that no matter how large your music collection is, you'll seriously consider putting all your music into digital format on your computer, transferring portions of it to an iPod, and playing music from both your computer and your iPod from now on. And why wait for the best episodes of your favorite TV shows to be broadcast, when you can download the shows anytime you want and play them on a video iPod anywhere you want? Albums, music videos, TV shows, and movies — you might never stop buying CDs and DVDs, but you won't have to buy *all* your content that way. And you'll never again need to replace the content that you already own.

As an iPod owner, you're on the cutting edge of entertainment technology. This chapter introduces iPods and tells you what to expect when you open the box. We describe how to power up your iPod and connect it to your computer, both of which are essential tasks that you need to know how to do — your iPod needs power, and it needs audio and video, which it gets from your computer.

Introducing iPods

An iPod is, essentially, a hard drive or flash memory drive as well as a digital music and video player in one device. iPods are such a thing of beauty and style — and so highly recognizable by now — that all Apple needs to do in an advertisement is show one all by itself.

The convenience of carrying music on an iPod is phenomenal. For example, the 160GB sixth-generation iPod Classic can hold around 40,000 songs. That's more than two months of nonstop music played around the clock — or about two new songs per day for the next 54 years. And with iPod's built-in skip protection in every model, you won't miss a beat as you jog through the park or when your car hits a pothole.

A common misconception is that your iPod becomes your music and video library. Actually, your iPod is simply another *player* for your content library, which is safely stored on your computer. One considerable benefit of using your computer to organize your content is that you can make perfect-quality copies of music, videos, movies, podcasts, and audio books. You can then copy as much of the content as you want, in a more compressed format, onto your iPod and take it on the road. Meanwhile, your perfect copies are stored safely on your computer. Your favorite albums, audio books, TV shows, movies, and podcast episodes can be copied over and over forever, just like the rest of your information, and they never lose their quality. If you save your content in digital format, you'll never see your songs or videos degrade, and you'll never have to buy the content again.

The iPod experience includes *iTunes* (for Mac or Windows), which lets you synchronize content with your iPod and other devices, such as the iPhone and Apple TV. You also use it to organize your content, make copies, burn CDs, and play disc jockey without discs. We introduce iTunes in Chapter 2.

Second-generation and third-generation iPod models can also be synchronized with a Windows PC using MusicMatch Jukebox version 7.5, which was provided on CD-ROM with some second-generation models before iTunes became available for Windows. A newer version of this software, renamed MusicMatch, does not work directly with iPods. If you're using MusicMatch, visit this book's companion Web site to find out how to use MusicMatch.

An iPod is also a *data player*, perhaps the first of its kind. As an external hard drive, an iPod serves as a portable backup device for important data files. You can transfer your calendar and address book to help manage your affairs on the road, and you can even use calendar event alarms to supplement your iPod's alarm and sleep timer. You can keep your calendar and address book automatically synchronized to your computer, where you normally add and edit information. We cover using an iPod as a general-purpose hard drive in Chapter 22 and using it to synchronize your computer's calendar and contact information in Chapter 23.

Comparing iPod Models

Introduced way back in the Stone Age of digital music (2001), the iPod family has grown by six generations as of this writing, with custom versions for the band U2 and offshoots such as the popular iPod nano and the tiny $79 iPod shuffle that lets you wear up to 240 songs on your sleeve. Apple has recently introduced sixth-generation iPod models and the iPhone, combining iPod capabilities with a cell phone and wireless PDA. Even from the beginning, iPod models were truly innovative for their times. With the MP3 music players of 2001, you could carry about 20 typical songs (or a single live Phish set) with you, but the first iPods could hold more than 1,000 typical songs (or a 50-hour Phish concert).

Earlier-generation iPods

Today's iPod models and iPhone work with iTunes on either Windows computers or Macs, but that wasn't always the case. The first-generation iPods worked only with Macs. In 2002, Apple introduced the second generation — one version for Windows and another for the Mac, using the same design for both. For the third generation (2003), Apple changed the design once again.

Third-, fourth-, fifth- and sixth-generation iPods — as well as offshoots, such as iPod mini, iPod nano, and iPod shuffle — work with either Windows or Mac and come in a variety of hard drive or flash memory sizes. One way to tell what kind of iPod you have is by its navigational controls. By design, you can hold an iPod in your hand while you thumb the *scroll wheel* (our generic term for scroll wheel, scroll pad, touch wheel, or click wheel). The LCD screen on full-size models offers backlighting so that you can see it in the dark. The iPhone and sixth-generation iPod Touch let you tap the sensitive display with your finger to select items and functions, and flick with your finger to scroll or move the display.

To learn more about previous generations of iPods, including detailed information about cables and connections, visit this book's companion Web site. For a nifty chart that shows the differences between iPod models, see the Identifying Different iPod Models page on the Apple iPod Web site (`http://docs.info.apple.com/article.html?artnum=61688`).

Sixth-generation iPods

Apple shook the world once again in late 2007 by introducing a new generation of iPod models (see Figure 1-1) with attractive enclosures and easier-to-use controls.

The sixth-generation iPod models include:

- **The iPod touch:** This spectacular model, which shares the design characteristics and many of the features of the iPhone, offers a touch-sensitive display and Wi-Fi Internet connectivity so that you can purchase music directly from your iPod and surf the Web. (Wi-Fi, which is short for wireless fidelity, is a popular connection method for local area networks; you can set up your home or office with Wi-Fi using an inexpensive Wi-Fi hub such as Apple's AirPort Extreme.)

Figure 1-1: Sixth-generation iPods include (left to right) the iPod touch, iPod classic, iPod nano, and iPod shuffle.

- **The iPod classic:** The original iPod design is now slimmer and offers more capacity and longer battery life than previous generations, with 80GB and 160GB models.
- **The iPod nano ("the fatty"):** The new fatter, shorter iPod nano now plays video as well as music, podcasts, and audio books.
- **The iPod shuffle:** The tiniest iPod now comes in a variety of colors.

You can put videos on your iPhone or sixth-generation iPod classic or nano models by using iTunes. You can even get some of your favorite TV shows, plus music videos and full-length movies, directly from the iTunes Store. The color display provides crisp definition for the iPod's menus, making them easier to read, even in sunlight.

Like third-, fourth-, and fifth-generation iPods, the sixth generation also uses a dock adapter cable to connect the iPod or iPhone to a computer or power supply. You can also use an Apple or third-party dock with your iPod, and use the dock adapter cable to connect the dock to your computer or power supply. The dock keeps your iPod in an upright position while connected and lets you connect a home stereo or headphones. This makes the dock convenient as a base station when you're not traveling with your iPod because you can slip the iPod into the dock without connecting cables. You can pick one up at an Apple Store or order one online, or take advantage of third-party dock offerings.

Fingering the iPod touch

The iPod touch, like the iPhone, lets you access the Web over a Wi-Fi Internet connection. You can use the built-in Safari Web browser to interact with Web services and applications, and the built-in YouTube application to play videos. Safari even displays a virtual keyboard for typing login entries, passwords, and text of any kind, including numbers and punctuation symbols. The innovative touch-sensitive display provides a rich set of navigation controls and menus controlled by software. You can use the Cover Browser with your finger to browse your music and video collection. You can even access the iTunes Store directly from your iPod touch and purchase content.

Less than a third of an inch thick and weighing only 4.2 ounces, the iPod touch is slightly smaller than an iPhone and offers the same single menu button on the front. Apple offers 8GB and 16GB models as of this writing. The 8GB model holds about 1,750 songs, 10,000 photos, or about 10 hours of video. The 16GB model holds about 3,500 songs, 20,000 photos, or about 20 hours of video. Both models use the same battery that offers up to 22 hours of music playback, or 5 hours of video playback.

Twirling the iPod classics

Sixth-generation iPod classic models use the same click wheel and buttons as the fifth-generation models, combining the scroll wheel with pressure-sensitive buttons underneath the top, bottom, left, and right areas of the circular pad of the wheel. As of this writing, Apple provides a slim, 4.9-ounce 80GB model and a 5.7-ounce 160GB model.

The 80GB model holds about 20,000 songs or about 100 hours of video, and its battery offers up to 30 hours of music playback, or 5 hours of video playback. The 160GB model holds about 40,000 songs or about 200 hours of video, and its battery offers up to 40 hours of music playback, or 7 hours of video playback. Both models hold up to 25,000 photos.

Mano a mano with iPod nano

Nicknamed "the fatty" by Apple fans, the new iPod nano, pencil thin and a little over two inches wide by less than three inches high, weighs only 1.74 ounces but packs a punch: video. This mini marvel offers a 2-inch color LCD display that crisply displays video, iPod menus and album artwork. Apple offers a 4GB model that holds about 1,000 songs, and an 8GB model that holds about 2,000 songs. (See Figure 1-2.)

Each model offers a battery that can play up to 24 hours of music — all day and all of the night — or 5 hours of video.

Figure 1-2: iPod nano is the smallest iPod that can display video.

The iPod nano is the smallest iPod that can serve up videos, podcasts, photos, and musical slideshows as well as your personal calendar and contacts. Unlike the smaller iPod shuffle, iPod nano is a full-featured iPod with loads of accessories tailored specifically for it.

iPod nano uses the same style of click wheel and buttons as the sixth-generation iPod classic models. Like other sixth-generation iPods, iPod nano uses a dock adapter cable to connect to a computer or power supply. A variety of docks for the iPod nano are available from Apple and other companies.

Doing the iPod shuffle

If the regular iPod models aren't small enough to fit into your lifestyle, try iPod shuffle. The 0.55-ounce iPod shuffle, as shown in Figure 1-3, is shaped like a money clip and is about the same size — 1.07 x1.62 inches with a depth of 0.41 inch. In several different flashy colors and convenient for clipping to just about anything, the iPod shuffle is fast becoming a fashion statement.

However, the current iPod shuffle that clips to your clothing is not the first iPod that you could wear. That honor belongs to the original iPod shuffle, which is 3.3 inches long, less than 1 inch wide, and about one-third of an inch thick. It weighs only 0.78 ounce, which is little more than a car key or a pack of gum. You can hang it from your ears with the supplied earbuds and wear it around your neck like a necklace. You can still find them for sale in retail outlets and used ones on eBay, but Apple replaced the original with the much smaller clip-on model.

iPod shuffle models have no display, but that's actually a good thing because this design keeps the size and weight down to a minimum, and you don't need a display to play a couple hundred songs in random or sequential order. You can also use your iPod shuffle to hold data files, just like an external flash memory drive.

The 1GB iPod shuffle holds about 240 songs. The older iPod shuffle, at 512MB, holds 120 songs, assuming an average of 4 minutes per song, using the AAC format at the High Quality setting (as described in Chapter 18). Remember, iPod shuffle is not meant to store music permanently. Instead, you use it just to play selections from your iTunes library on your computer.

With skip-free playback, lightweight design, and no need for a display, you can easily use it while skiing, snowboarding, or even skydiving. That's because it uses flash memory rather than a hard drive: You can shake it as hard as you want without a glitch. An iPod shuffle battery offers up to 12 hours of power between charges.

Figure 1-3: An iPod shuffle weighs less than an ounce and offers skip-free playback.

Unlike other iPods, iPod shuffle can't play tunes in the highest-quality Audio Interchange File Format (AIFF) or Apple Lossless formats, which consume a lot of storage space. See Chapter 18 for more details on encoding formats.

The current iPod shuffle models built to resemble a money clip connect to power and to your computer by using a special mini-dock supplied in the box. The mini-dock includes a cable that links your iPod shuffle to a computer or to an optional power supply and supplies power for recharging its battery. You don't need a separate cable. iPod shuffle charges its battery from your computer, so you don't need the optional power supply. You can also get the optional $29 iPod shuffle External Battery Pack, which provides 20 additional hours of playtime with two AAA batteries.

The all-in-one iPhone

When Apple introduced the iPhone on June 29, 2007, lines formed around the block at the New York and San Francisco stores as eager early adopters bought out all inventories. Hold one in your hands and you'll understand why: the innovative touch-sensitive display provides a rich set of navigation controls and menus, as shown in Figure 1-4, controlled by software — including a full keyboard for entering text, numbers, and special symbols. This iPod can not only phone home; it can monitor all your e-mail and browse the Internet with full page display, utilizing a Wi-Fi network when it senses one.

Figure 1-4: The iPhone offers a touch-sensitive display with rich menus and navigational controls.

The iPhone comes in 4G ($499) or 8G ($599) models and incorporates flash memory just like an iPod touch, iPod shuffle or iPod nano. Its 3.5-inch, widescreen multi-touch display offers 480-by-320–pixel resolution at 160 dots per inch for crisp video pictures, and it can display multiple languages and characters simultaneously. The iPhone's built-in rechargeable lithium ion battery offers up to 8 hours of talk time (250 hours on standby), up to six hours browsing the Internet or seven hours playing video, and up to 24 hours playing music. It also offers Bluetooth for using wireless headphones and microphones. And the iPhone is no slouch when it comes to acting like an iPod: It can play music, audio books, videos (such as TV shows, music videos, and even feature-length movies), and even podcasts. You can also display photos and slideshows set to music.

Thinking inside the Box

Don't destroy the elegantly designed box while opening it; you might want to place it prominently in your collection of Technology That Ushered in the 21st Century. Before going any further, check the box and make sure that all the correct parts came with your iPod or iPhone. Keep the box in case, heaven forbid, you need to return the iPod or iPhone to Apple — the box ensures that you can safely return it for a new battery or replacement.

The sixth-generation iPod classic box includes earphones and a USB dock adapter cable that can connect either the iPod or a dock to a computer or power adapter. You can get accessories, including Apple's Universal Dock and an AC power adapter, separately. For example, the iPod AV Connection Kit offers the adapter, AV cables, Apple Remote, and the Universal Dock with adapters for all models.

The accessories don't stop there. Docks of various sizes, shapes, and functions are available from vendors, such as Belkin, Monster, and Griffin and some docks are combined with home speaker systems. You might also want a carrying case and some other goodies, many of which are describe in this book. They are available at the online Apple Store (`www.apple.com/store`).

You also need a few things that don't come with the iPod:

- **A PC or Mac to run iTunes:** On a PC, iTunes version 7.4 requires Windows XP (with Service Pack 2 to support Apple TV and the iPhone), or 32-bit editions of Windows Vista, running on a 500 MHz Pentium-class processor or faster, and a minimum of 256MB. If you intend to watch video, you need at least a 2.0 GHz Pentium-class processor or faster, and at least 512MB of RAM and 32MB of video RAM.

With a Mac, iTunes version 7.4 requires Mac OS X 10.3.9 or newer or Mac OS X 10.4.7 or newer (version 10.4.10 or newer required for iPhone), a 500 MHz G3 processor or better; and at least 256MB of RAM. If you intend to watch video, you need a 1GHz G4 processor or better, and 16MB of video RAM.

- **USB connection:** PCs must have USB 2.0 (also called a *high-powered USB*) for fifth-generation iPods and iPod nano. However, you can use FireWire (IEEE 1394) with older iPod models. All current-model Macs provide USB 2.0, and all Macs provide FireWire.

  For details about using USB or FireWire cables, visit this book's companion Web site.

- **Internet connection:** Apple recommends a broadband Internet connection to buy content and stream previews from the iTunes Store, although it is possible with a dial-up connection. At minimum, you need some kind of Internet connection to download iTunes itself.
- **CD-R or DVD-R drive:** Without a disc burner, you can't burn your own discs. On a PC, you need a CD-R or DVD-R drive. On a Mac, you need a Combo or Super Drive to burn your own discs.
- **iTunes:** Make sure you have the current version of iTunes — use the automatic update feature, which we describe in Chapter 2. You can also download iTunes for Windows or the Mac from the Apple site (`www.apple.com/itunes/download`); it's free. See Chapter 2 for instructions.

  Older models, still available in stores and online, might include versions of iTunes as old as version 4.5, which is fine because version 4.5 works. (It just doesn't have all the features of 7.4.) You can download a newer version at any time to replace it.
- **QuickTime:** QuickTime (required for video) comes with iTunes. The iTunes installer for the PC installs the newest version of QuickTime for Windows (version 7.2 as of this writing), replacing any older version you might have. Macs have QuickTime preinstalled (version 7.2 as of this writing), and Mac OS X automatically updates QuickTime if you use the Software Update feature of System Preferences in the Apple menu.

Powering Up Your iPod

All iPods come with essentially the same requirement: power. Fortunately, each iPod also comes with a battery and a way of charging it, either directly from your computer or by using a cable and an AC power adapter that works with voltages in North America and many parts of Europe and Asia. (See Chapter 20 for information about plugging into power in other countries.)

Fifth- and sixth-generation iPod models (including the iPod touch) and the iPhone — as well as iPod nano, iPod mini, and third- and fourth-generation iPods — offer a dock connection. You can connect these models to a dock that offers USB 2.0 connections for power and synchronizing (or FireWire for third-generation models). Docks for full-size iPods can also connect to your home stereo through a line-out connection.

Sixth-generation iPods and iPod nanos are supplied with a cable that has a USB connector on one end and a flat dock connector on the other end to connect to a dock or to an iPod itself. You can connect the USB end to either the Apple power supply or the computer's USB 2.0 port. The iPhone is also supplied with a USB cable for connecting the iPhone or its dock to your computer or to the power supply.

The connection on the bottom of the iPod or iPhone is the same as the connection on the back of the iPod or iPhone dock. To connect your iPod or iPhone to your computer, plug the flat connector of the cable into the device or dock (press the buttons on both sides of the flat connector to fit it snugly into the connection), and then plug the USB connector on the other end into the USB port on your computer. (Press the same buttons on both sides of the flat connector to disconnect it.)

Most PCs already have USB 2.0, which is all you need to provide power to your sixth-generation iPod, iPod shuffle, or iPod nano, and to synchronize it with your PC. Although you can use a low-powered USB 1.0 or 1.1 connection, it doesn't supply power to most iPod models.

Fifth- and sixth-generation models and iPod nano can use FireWire connections to charge their batteries but not for synchronizing with a computer. Fifth- and sixth-generation iPods, iPod nano, and iPod shuffle models use USB to connect to the computer and synchronize content, not FireWire. The iPod shuffle is supplied with a mini-dock with a USB cable attached and draws power from the USB port on the computer or from a USB power adapter.

An older USB 1.0 or 1.1 port works for synchronizing your iPod, but it doesn't provide power to the iPod. If all you have is an older USB port, you can use it to synchronize your fifth- or sixth-generation iPod or iPod nano, and then use a FireWire cable (available from the Apple Store) to provide power by connecting it to a FireWire-compatible AC power adapter.

Don't use another USB device in a chain and don't use a USB 2.0 hub to connect your iPod unless the hub is a powered hub. Note that a USB keyboard typically acts like a USB 1.1 hub, but it's not powered, so it can't provide power to the iPod and might slow down performance.

A FireWire or USB connection to a Mac provides power to an iPod and recharges the battery as long as the Mac isn't in sleep mode. A FireWire connection to a FireWire/IEEE 1394 card in a PC might not be able to provide power; to be safe, check with the card manufacturer. The smaller four-pin connections for FireWire/IEEE 1394 cards typically don't supply power to an iPod.

If your iPod shows a display but doesn't respond to your touch, don't panic. Just check the Hold switch on top or bottom of the unit and make sure that it's set to one side so that the orange bar disappears (the normal position). You use the Hold switch for locking the buttons, which prevents accidental activation.

You might notice that your iPod's display turns iridescent when it gets too hot or too cold, but this effect disappears when its temperature returns to normal. iPods can function in temperatures as cold as 50 degrees and as warm as 95° F (Fahrenheit) but work best at room temperature (closer to 68° F).

If you leave your iPod out in the cold all night, it might have trouble waking from sleep mode, and it might even display a low-battery message. Plug the iPod into a power source, wait until it warms up, and try it again. If it still doesn't wake up or respond properly, try resetting the iPod as we describe in Chapter 24.

Facing Charges of Battery

You can take a six-hour flight from New York City to California and listen to your iPod the entire time — and with some models, listen all the way back on the return flight — without recharging. All iPod models use the same type of built-in, rechargeable lithium ion (Li-Ion) battery with the following power specs:

- The first-, second-, and third-generation iPod models offer up to 8 hours of battery power.
- The fourth-generation models and the iPod shuffle offer up to 12 hours.
- iPod mini offers up to 18 hours.
- The color-display fourth-generation models offer 15 hours of music playing time or 5 hours of photo display with music.
- The fifth-generation iPod models offer between 14 and 20 hours of music playing time, between 3 and 6 hours of video playing time, or between 4 and 6 hours of photo display with music.
- The iPod nano offers 24 hours of music playing time or 5 hours of video or photo display with music. (Older models offered 14 hours of music and 4 hours of photo display with music.)

- The sixth-generation iPod classic 80GB model offers 30 hours of music playback or 5 hours of video or photo display with music. The 160GB model offers 40 hours of music playback or 7 hours of video or photo display with music.
- The iPod touch offers 22 hours of music playing time or 5 hours of video or photo display with music.
- The iPhone models offer up to 24 hours of music playing time, 7 hours of video playing time, or between 4 and 6 hours of photo display with music.

However, keep in mind that playback battery time varies with the type of encoder that you use for the music files in iTunes. (Chapter 18 has more information about encoders.) It also varies depending on how you use your iPod or iPhone controls and settings.

The iPod or iPhone battery recharges automatically when you connect it to a power source. For example, it starts charging immediately when you insert it into a dock that's connected to a power source (or to a computer with a powered FireWire or USB connection). It takes only four hours to recharge the battery fully for all models, and only three hours for an iPod nano.

Need power when you're on the run? Look for a power outlet in the airport terminal or hotel lobby — the battery fast-charges to 80-percent capacity in 1.5 hours. After the first hour and a half, the battery receives a trickle charge for the next hour and a half, until fully charged.

Don't fry your iPod or iPhone with some generic power adapter. Use *only* the power adapter from Apple or a certified iPod adapter, such as the power accessories from Belkin, Griffin, Monster, XtremeMac, and other vendors.

A battery icon with a progress bar in the top-right corner of the iPod or iPhone display indicates how much power is left. When you charge the battery, the icon turns into a lightning bolt inside a battery. If the icon doesn't animate, the battery is fully charged. You can also use your iPod or iPhone while the battery is charging or disconnect it and use it before the battery is fully charged.

To check the battery status of an iPod shuffle, press the battery status button on the back (the long button above the Apple logo and below the position switch for setting the iPod shuffle to shuffle songs or play them in order). If the battery status light is

- **Green:** The iPod shuffle is fully charged.
- **Yellow:** The charge is low.
- **Red:** Very little charge is left, and you need to recharge it.

If no light is visible, the iPod shuffle is completely out of power, and you need to recharge it to use it.

Maintaining battery life

The iPod or iPhone built-in, rechargeable battery is, essentially, a life-or-death proposition. After it's dead, it can be replaced, but Apple charges a replacement fee of $59 plus shipping. Some services may charge less, especially for older iPod models. If your warranty is still active, you should have Apple replace it under the warranty program (which may cost nothing except perhaps shipping). Don't try to replace it yourself because opening your iPod or iPhone invalidates the warranty. If your warranty is no longer active, compare Apple's prices and service to others — we have had very good (if more expensive) experiences with Apple's services.

Fortunately, the battery is easy to maintain. We recommend *calibrating* the battery once soon after you get your iPod or iPhone; that is, run it all the way down (a full discharge) and then charge it all the way up (which takes four hours). Although this doesn't actually change battery performance, it does improve the battery gauge so that the gauge displays a more accurate reading.

Unlike nickel-based batteries that require you to fully discharge and then recharge in order to get a fuller capacity, an iPod or iPhone battery prefers a partial rather than a full discharge, so avoid frequent full discharges after the initial calibration. (Frequent full discharges can lower battery life.)

Lithium-ion batteries typically last three years or more and are vulnerable to high temperatures, which decrease their life spans considerably. Don't leave your iPod or iPhone in a hot place, such as on a sunny car dashboard, for very long.

For a complete description of how Apple's batteries work, see the Apple Lithium-ion Batteries page at `www.apple.com/batteries`.

The bottom of an iPod warms up when it's powered on. The bottom functions as a cooling surface that transfers heat from inside the unit to the cooler air outside. An iPod's carrying case acts as an insulator, so be sure to remove the iPod from its carrying case before you recharge it.

Keeping an iPod in its carrying case when charging is tempting but also potentially disastrous. An iPod needs to dissipate its heat, and you could damage the unit by overheating it and frying its circuits, rendering it as useful as a paperweight. To get around this problem, you can purchase one of the heat-dissipating carrying cases available in the Apple Store. Alternatively, MARWARE (`www.marware.com`) offers a variety of sporty cases for about $30 to $40.

Even when not in use, your iPod drinks the juice. If your iPod is inactive for 14 days, you must recharge its battery. Perhaps the iPod gets depressed from being left alone too long.

Saving power

iPod classic models include a hard drive, and whatever causes the hard drive to spin causes a drain on power. Your iPod also has a *cache* — a memory chip holding the section of music to play next. An iPod uses the cache not only to eliminate skipping when something jostles the hard drive, but also to conserve power because the drive doesn't have to spin as much.

If you use the AIFF or WAV formats for importing music into iTunes (or MusicMatch Jukebox version 7.5): Don't use these formats with your iPod. Instead, convert the music first, as we describe in Chapter 19. These formats take up way too much space on the iPod and fill up the iPod cache too quickly, causing skips when you play them and using too much battery power because the drive spins more often. (See Chapter 5 for bringing content into iTunes. Chapter 18 provides detailed information about these encoding formats, and Chapter 19 describes how to convert your music.)

The following are tips on saving power while using your iPod:

- **Pause.** Pause playback when you're not listening. Pausing (stopping) playback is the easiest way to conserve power.
- **Back away from the light.** Use the iPod backlight sparingly. Select Backlight Timer from the iPod Settings menu to limit backlighting to a number of seconds, or to Off, in the iPod's Settings menu. (Choose Settings from the main menu.) Don't use the backlight in daylight if you don't need it.
- **Hold it.** Flip the Hold switch to the locked position (with the orange bar showing) to make sure that controls aren't accidentally activated. You don't want your iPod playing music in your pocket and draining the battery when you're not listening.
- **You may continue.** Play songs continuously without using the iPod controls. Selecting songs and using Previous/Rewind and Next/Fast-Forward require precious energy. Not only that, but the hard drive has to spin more often when searching for songs, using more power than during continuous playback.

Always use the latest iPod software and update your software when updates come out. Apple constantly tries to improve how your iPod works, and many of these advancements relate to power usage.

Replacing your battery

Apple customers aren't always happy campers. Early iPods came with batteries that couldn't be replaced, but all it took were a few premature battery failures and quite a few customer complaints for Apple to institute a battery-replacement service. Apple also offers a special AppleCare warranty for iPods and iPhones.

You shouldn't try to remove or replace the iPod or iPhone internal battery yourself — and certainly not if the iPod or iPhone is still under warranty (because opening it breaks the warranty). You need Apple to replace it if it dies while under warranty, or use Apple or another service to replace it if the warranty period is over.

If your iPod or iPhone isn't responding after a reset, follow the troubleshooting steps in Chapter 24. If these steps don't restore your iPod or iPhone to working condition, you might have a battery problem. Go to the Apple support page for the iPod (`www.apple.com/support/ipod`) or the iPhone (`www.apple.com/support/iphone`) and click the Service FAQ link to read frequently asked questions and answers about support. Then click the Battery Service Request Form link on the support page and follow the instructions to request service and return your iPod or iPhone for a replacement.

Thumbing through the iPod Menus

After you bring content into iTunes and synchronize your iPod, you're ready to play. The design of the iPod classic and iPod nano lets you hold the iPod in one hand and perform simple operations by thumb. Even if you're all thumbs when pressing small buttons on tiny devices, you can still thumb your way to iPod heaven.

The iPod touch, like the iPhone, offers a multi-touch interface that lets you tap your way into iPod heaven even faster. With an iPod touch, your fingers do the walking. You can make gestures, such as flicking a finger to scroll a list quickly, sliding your finger to scroll slowly or drag a slider (such as the volume slider), pinching with two fingers to zoom out of a Web page in Safari, or pulling apart with two fingers (also known as *unpinching*) to zoom in to the page to see it more clearly.

Touching iPod touch and iPhone displays

The first button you see on an iPod touch or iPhone display (besides the time of day and the date) is the message "slide to unlock" — slide your finger across this message to unlock your iPod touch or iPhone.

Your content is now immediately available at the touch of a finger. The iPhone provides an iPod button in the lower right corner of its main menu (refer to Figure 1-4) to provide access to your content. The iPod touch provides Music, Videos and Photos buttons that appear along the bottom row of the iPod touch main menu, as shown in Figure 1-5.

After touching a button on the iPod touch or iPhone display, a new page appears with more selections you can touch. In fact, you can touch every menu or button you see on the display. The iPod touch and iPhone run separate applications (Safari, Contacts, Calendar, YouTube, and so on), and the multi-touch interface changes for each application.

For example, touch the Music button to view a list of artists. After touching Music, buttons appear along the bottom of the display that you can touch to view a list of playlists, artists, songs, albums, and more. With a flick of your finger you can scroll the list, and touch selections to view the albums of an artist or the contents of an album or playlist. Touch any song to start playing it, and control buttons appear to control playback: Previous/Rewind, Play/Pause, Next/Fast-Forward, and a volume slider. All these buttons work by touch, and the only hard button on the front of the iPod returns you to the main menu.

The iPod touch and iPhone applications respond to gestures you make with your fingers. For example, you make the following gestures to perform the following functions:

- **Drag with finger:** Scroll up or down lists slowly.
- **Flick:** Quickly scroll up or down lists.
- **Tap an hold:** While scrolling, tap and hold to stop the moving list.
- **Flick from left to right (swipe):** Change panes on the iPhone (Safari, weather, iPod) and delete items (mail, SMS).
- **Single tap:** Select an item.
- **Double tap:** Zoom in or out with Safari and all other applications; zoom in with Maps on the iPhone.
- **Two-finger single tap:** Zoom out (Maps on the iPhone only).
- **Pinch:** Zoom out of photos, Maps on the iPhone, and Safari Web pages.
- **Unpinch:** Zoom into photos, Maps on the iPhone, and Safari Web pages.

The iPod touch menu (refer to Figure 1-5) offers the following selections:

- **Safari:** Use the Safari Web browser.
- **YouTube:** List and select videos from YouTube.
- **Calendar:** View your calendar.
- **Contacts:** View your contacts.
- **Clock:** View and set the date and time, alarm clock, and timer.
- **Calculator:** A simple calculator for adding, subtracting, multiplying, dividing, and so on.
- **Settings:** Adjust settings for Wi-Fi, sounds, brightness, and Safari usage, as well as other settings for the device.
- **Music:** Select music playlists, artists, songs, albums, and more (including podcasts, genres, composers, audio books, and compilations). The Music button also offers Cover Flow browsing, as we describe in Chapter 15.

Figure 1-5: Touch buttons on the iPod touch main menu.

- **Videos:** Select videos by type (movies, music videos, TV shows, or video podcasts).
- **Photos:** Select photos by photo album or select individual photos in the Photo Library.
- **iTunes:** Go to the iTunes online store to purchase content.

Scrolling iPod classic and nano wheels

The circular scroll wheel on iPod classic and iPod nano models makes scrolling through an entire music collection quick and easy. With your finger or thumb, scroll clockwise on the wheel to scroll down a list, or counter-clockwise to scroll up. As you scroll, options on the menu are highlighted. Use the Select button at the center of the scroll wheel to select whatever is highlighted in the menu display.

In full-size, third-generation models, the touch-sensitive buttons above the scroll wheel perform simple functions when you touch them. (First- and second-generation models aren't touch sensitive, so you need to press them.)

Fifth-generation iPods and sixth-generation iPod classic models, iPod nano, iPod mini, and fourth-generation iPods (including color-display models) provide a click wheel that offers the same functions as the scroll wheel *and* the clickable buttons. The click wheel has pressure-sensitive buttons underneath the top, bottom, left, and right areas of the circular pad of the wheel. These areas tilt as you press them, activating the buttons.

The iPod main menu for sixth-generation iPod classic models and the iPod nano offers the following selections:

- **Music:** Select music playlists, artists, albums, songs, genres, or composers; or select an audio book. You can also select Cover Flow to browse by cover art, or Search to search for a song or album title or artist (as we describe in Chapter 15).
- **Videos:** Select videos by video playlist or by type (movies, music videos, or TV shows).
- **Photos:** Select photos by photo album or select all photos in the photo library.
- **Podcasts:** Select podcasts by title, and then select podcast episodes.
- **Extras:** View the clock, set clocks for time zones, set alarms and the sleep timer, use the stopwatch, view contacts, view your calendar, view notes, and play games.

- **Settings:** Adjust various settings including menu settings, the backlight timer, the clicker, the iPod's EQ, the date and time, and so on.
- **Shuffle Songs:** Play songs from your music library in random order.
- **Now Playing:** This selection appears only when a song is playing — it takes you to the Now Playing display.

The iPod main menu for fifth-generation models offers the following selections:

- **Music:** Select music playlists, artists, albums, songs, podcasts, genres, or composers; or select an audio book.
- **Photos:** Select photos by photo album or select individual photos in the photo library. This selection appears only on color-display models.
- **Videos:** Select videos by playlist or by type (movies, music videos, TV shows, or video podcasts). This selection appears only on fifth-generation models.
- **Extras:** View and set the clock and alarm clock, view contacts, view your calendar, view notes, and play games.
- **Settings:** Adjust display settings, menu settings, the backlight timer, the clicker, and the date and time.
- **Shuffle Songs:** Play songs from your music library in random order.
- **Now Playing:** This selection appears only when a song is playing — it takes you to the Now Playing display.

The iPod main menu for fourth-generation models and iPod nano is the same as fifth-generation models but without the Videos selection.

Activating iPod Playback Functions

The touch buttons on iPod touch and iPhone models do various tasks for playing content items such as songs, audio books, podcasts, and videos:

- **Previous/Rewind:** Tap once to start an item over. Tap twice to skip to the previous item (such as the previous song in an album). Touch and hold to rewind.
- **Play/Pause:** Tap to play the selected item. Tap Play/Pause when an item is playing to pause the playback.
- **Next/Fast-Forward:** Tap once to skip to the next item (such as the next song in an album). Touch and hold Next/Fast-Forward to fast-forward play.

- **Left-arrow button:** Tap to go back to the previous menu.
- **Bullet-list button (playing music):** Tap to view the contents of the album containing the song.
- **Menu button on front:** Press once to go back to the main menu.

The buttons on full-size iPod models do various tasks for song, podcast, audio book, and video playback:

- **Previous/Rewind:** Press once to start an item over. Press twice to skip to the previous item (such as a song in an album). Press and hold to rewind.
- **Menu:** Press once to go back to the previous menu. Each time you press, you go back to a previous menu until you reach the main menu.
- **Play/Pause:** Press to play the selected item. Press Play/Pause when the item is playing to pause the playback.
- **Next/Fast-Forward:** Press once to skip to the next item. Press and hold Next/Fast-Forward to fast-forward.

The buttons and scroll wheel on full-size iPods can do more complex functions when used in combination:

- **Turn on the iPod.** Press any button.
- **Turn off the iPod.** Press and hold the Play/Pause button.
- **Disable the iPod buttons.** To keep from accidentally pressing the buttons, push the Hold switch to the other side so that an orange bar appears (the locked position). To reactivate the iPod buttons, push the Hold switch back to the other side so that the orange bar disappears (the normal position).
- **Reset the iPod.** You can reset the iPod if it gets hung up for some reason. (For example, it might get confused if you press the buttons too quickly.) See Chapter 24 for instructions on how to reset your iPod.
- **Change the volume.** While playing a song (the display reads `Now Playing`), adjust the volume with the scroll wheel. Clockwise turns the volume up; counterclockwise turns the volume down. A volume slider appears on the iPod display, indicating the volume level as you scroll.
- **Skip to any point in a song, video, audio book or podcast.** While playing an item (the display reads `Now Playing`), press and hold the Select button until the progress bar appears to indicate where you are , and then use the scroll wheel to scroll to any point in the song. Scroll clockwise to move forward and counterclockwise to move backward.

Setting the Language

Wiedergabelisten? Übersicht? (Playlists? Browse?) If your iPod classic or iPod nano is speaking in a foreign tongue, don't panic — you're not in the wrong country. You might have purchased one that's set to a foreign language. More likely, someone set it to a different language accidentally or on purpose (as a practical joke). Fortunately, you can change the setting without having to know the language that it's set to.

To set the language, no matter what language the menu is using, follow these steps:

1. **Press the Menu button repeatedly until pressing it doesn't change the words on the display or until you see the word *iPod* at the top.**

   If pressing the Menu button no longer changes the display, you're at the main menu. With fourth-, fifth-, and sixth-generation models and iPod nano, the menu displays the word *iPod* no matter what language is selected — and you know you're at the main menu.

2. **Choose the sixth option from the top on sixth-generation iPods and the iPod nano, or the fifth option on fifth-generation iPods, or the fourth option on fourth-generation iPods, iPod mini, and the older iPod nano. Choose the third option from the top on third-, second-, and first-generation models. (In English, this is the Settings option.)**

   Scroll clockwise until the item is highlighted, and then press the Select button. The Settings menu appears.

3. **Choose the third option from the bottom of the Settings menu (which, in English, is the Language option).**

   The Language menu appears.

4. **Choose the language that you want to use. (English is at the top of the list.)**

If these steps don't do the trick, the menu may have been customized (something you can discover how to do in Chapter 21). Someone could have customized it previously, or perhaps you accidentally pressed buttons that customized the menu. To get around this problem, you can *reset all the iPod settings* back to the defaults (which is not the same as simply resetting your iPod, as described in Chapter 24). Unfortunately, resetting your iPod's *settings* wipes out any customizations that you've made. You have to redo any repeat/shuffle settings, alarms, backlight timer settings, and so on.

Follow these steps to reset all your settings, no matter what language displays:

1. **Press the Menu button repeatedly until pressing it doesn't change the words on the display or until you see the word *iPod* at the top.**

   If pressing the Menu button no longer changes the display, you're at the main menu. With fourth-, fifth-, and sixth-generation models and iPod nano, the menu displays the word *iPod* no matter what language is selected — and you know you're at the main menu.

2. **Choose the sixth option from the top on sixth-generation iPods and the iPod nano, or the fifth option on fifth-generation iPods, or the fourth option on fourth-generation iPods, iPod mini, and the older iPod nano. Choose the third option from the top on third-, second-, and first-generation models. (In English, this is the Settings option.)**

3. **Choose the option at the bottom of the menu (in English, the Reset All Settings option).**

   The Reset All Settings menu appears.

4. **Choose the second menu option (in English, the Reset option; the first menu option is Cancel).**

   The Language menu appears.

5. **Choose the language you want to use. (English is at the top of the list.)**

The language you choose now applies to all the iPod menus. But don't pull that practical joke on someone else!

Chapter 2

Setting Up iTunes and Your iPod

In This Chapter

- Installing iTunes on a Windows PC
- Installing iTunes on a Mac
- Setting up your iPod
- Downloading upgrades to the software

An iPod without iTunes is like a CD player without CDs. Sure, you can use utility programs from sources other than Apple to put music, podcasts, and videos on an iPod. (See Chapter 23 if you don't believe us.) But iTunes gives you access to the vast online iTunes Store, and it's excellent for managing content on your computer and synchronizing your content library with your iPod.

This chapter explains how to set up your iPod with iTunes on a Mac or for Windows. iTunes includes the iPod software, which provides the intelligence inside your iPod. iTunes recognizes the type of iPod you have and installs the correct software for your iPod.

Installing iTunes on a Windows PC

Setting up iTunes is a quick and easy process. The most up-to-date version of iTunes as of this writing is version 7.4. However, software updates occur very rapidly. If you really want the latest version, go directly to the Apple Web site (`www.apple.com/itunes`) to get it. You can download iTunes for free.

The CD-ROMs supplied with older iPods offer older versions of iTunes and iPod software. You should visit the Apple Web site to download the most up-to-date version of iTunes, which recognizes all iPod models.

Before installing iTunes, make sure that you're logged on as a Windows administrator user. Quit all other applications before installing and disable any antivirus software.

The iTunes installer also installs the newest version of QuickTime, replacing any older version you might have. *QuickTime* is the Apple multimedia development, storage, and playback technology. Although Windows users aren't required to use QuickTime beyond its use by iTunes, QuickTime is a bonus for Windows users because it offers digital video playback.

If you're using MusicMatch Jukebox, visit this book's companion Web site to find out how to install it.

To install iTunes for Windows, follow these steps:

1. **Download the iTunes installer from the Apple site.**

   Browse the Apple Web site (`www.apple.com/itunes`) and click the Download iTunes button, as shown in Figure 2-1. Follow the instructions to download the installer to your hard drive. Pick a location on your hard drive to save the installer.

2. **Run the iTunes installer.**

   Double-click the `iTunesSetup.exe` file to install iTunes. The installer displays the License Agreement dialog.

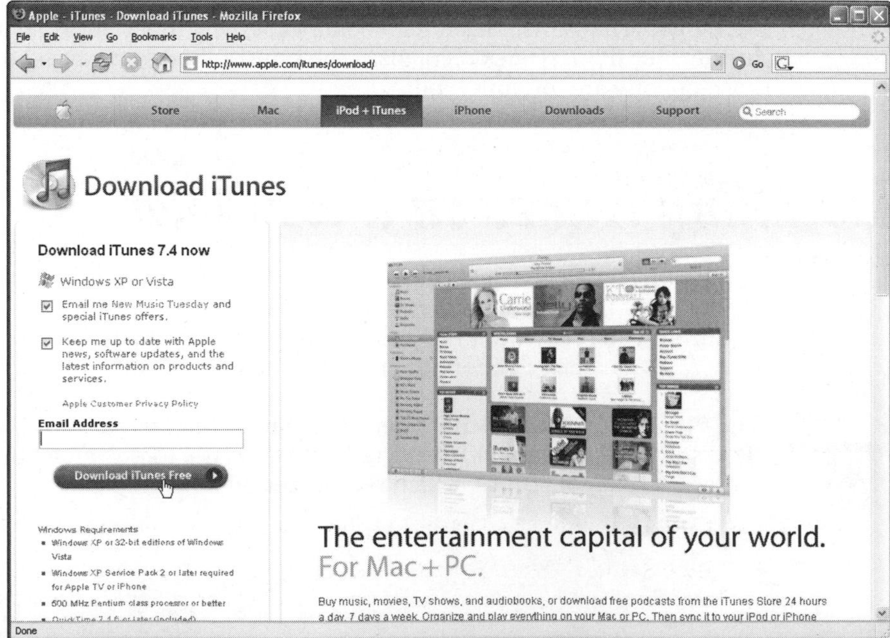

Figure 2-1: Download the newest version of iTunes from the Internet.

3. **Click the option to accept the terms of the License Agreement, and then click Next.**

   Apple's License Agreement appears in the installer window, and you can scroll down to read the agreement. You must choose to accept the agreement, or the installer goes no further.

   After clicking Next (which is active only if you accept), the installer displays the About iTunes information.

4. **Read the About iTunes information and then click Next.**

   The installer might display important Read Me information about the latest iTunes features. Scroll down to read the entire information.

   After clicking Next, the installer displays the iTunes installation options, as shown in Figure 2-2.

5. **Choose iTunes installation options.**

   You can turn the following options on or off (as shown in Figure 2-2):

   - *Install Desktop Shortcuts:* You can install shortcuts for your Windows desktop for iTunes.
   - *Use iTunes as the Default Player for Audio Files:* We suggest turning this option on, allowing iTunes to be the default audio content player for all audio files it recognizes. If you're happy with your audio player, you can deselect this option, leaving your default player setting unaffected.

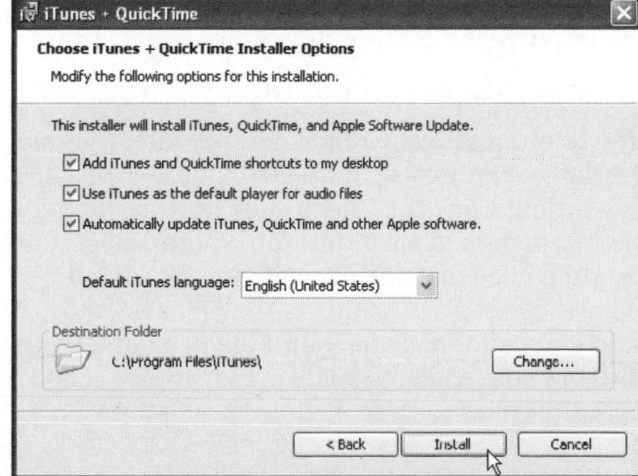

Figure 2-2: Choose iTunes installation options.

6. **Choose the destination folder for iTunes.**

   By default, the installer assumes that you want to store the program in the Program Files folder of your C: drive (which is an excellent place to store it, unless you have other ideas). If you want to use a different folder, click Browse to use Windows Explorer to locate the desired folder.

7. **Click Install to finish.**

   After you click Install, the installer finishes the installation and displays the InstallShield Wizard Complete dialog.

8. **Choose the option to restart your computer and then click Finish.**

   Restarting your Windows PC after installing software is always a good idea.

iTunes (including the iPod software) and QuickTime are now installed on your PC. To start using iTunes, double-click the iTunes program or use your Start menu to locate iTunes and launch it.

Installing iTunes on a Mac

As a Mac user, you probably already have iTunes installed because all Macs sold since 2003 (and many before that time) are preinstalled with iTunes and Mac OS X, and you also get iTunes if you install Mac OS X on an older machine. The most up-to-date version of iTunes as of this writing is version 7.4.

The version of iTunes that's provided with the Mac might be the newest version; then again, it might not be. Software updates occur very rapidly. If iTunes displays a dialog with the message that a new version of iTunes is available and asks whether you would like to download it now, click Yes to download the new version. Mac OS X not only downloads iTunes but installs it automatically.

You can set your Mac to automatically download the latest version of iTunes when it becomes available. Simply use Software Update from the Mac OS X System Preferences window. Click the Check Now button to check for a new version. If one exists, it appears in a window for you to select. Click the check mark to select it and then click Install to download and install it.

If you want to manually install iTunes on your Mac or manually upgrade the version you have, browse the Apple Web site (`www.apple.com/itunes`) to get it. You can download iTunes for free. Follow these steps:

1. **Download the iTunes installer from the Apple site.**

   Browse the Apple Web site (`www.apple.com/itunes`), select the Mac OS X version, and then click the Download iTunes button. (Refer to Figure 2-1.) Your browser downloads the iTunes installer drive image file `iTunes.dmg` to your hard drive. After your browser downloads the file, locate the file in the Finder.

2. **Open the iTunes installer drive image.**

   Double-click the `iTunes.dmg` file to mount the iTunes installation drive.

3. **Read the Read Before You Install iTunes document for up-to-date information.**

   Apple provides important Read Me information about installing iTunes manually.

4. **Double-click the `iTunes.mpkg` file to unpack the installer package.**

   The `iTunes.mpkg` file is a package containing all the elements of the iTunes software and the installation program. After double-clicking this package file, a dialog appears that asks whether the installer can run a special program to check your computer.

5. **Click Continue to run the special program.**

   The installer needs to run a program to check your computer and make sure it's capable of running iTunes. After it runs the program, the installer displays the Introduction page.

6. **Click Continue, read the Read Me page, and click Continue again.**

   The installer displays important Read Me information about the latest iTunes features. If you like, click Save to save the page as a document or click Print to print it. Click Continue to continue to the License Agreement.

7. **Read the License Agreement and click Continue to go to the second page. Click the Agree button and then click Continue again.**

   You can scroll down to read the agreement. You must choose to accept the agreement by clicking the Agree button, or the installer goes no further. After clicking Agree, the installer displays the Select a Destination page.

8. **(Optional) Before you click the Agree button, you can click Save to save the license agreement as a document or click Print to print it.**

   No lawyers are present when you do this; it's all up to you.

9. **Select the destination volume and then click Continue.**

   The installer asks for the *destination* volume (hard drive), which must be a Mac OS X startup drive. Any other drive is marked by a red exclamation point, indicating that you can't install the software there. iTunes is installed in the Applications folder on the Mac OS X startup drive, and the iPod Software Updater is installed in the Utilities folder inside the Applications folder.

10. **Click Install (or Upgrade) to proceed with the installation.**

    As an alternative, you can customize your installation by clicking Customize, selecting each package you want to install, and then clicking Install. The installer skips installing iTunes if you already have a version as current as (or newer than) the one downloaded.

11. **Click Close when the installer finishes.**

You can now launch iTunes by double-clicking the iTunes application or clicking the iTunes icon on the Dock.

Setting Up Your iPod

When you connect a new iPod for the first time, iTunes displays the Setup Assistant. Follow these steps to set up your iPod:

1. **With iTunes open, connect your iPod to the computer with a USB cable (or FireWire cable for an older iPod model).**

   iTunes recognizes your iPod and opens the iPod Setup Assistant to get you started, displaying first the License Agreement. If your iPod isn't recognized in five minutes, see Chapter 24.

2. **Click the option to accept the terms of the License Agreement, and then click Next in Windows, or Continue on a Mac.**

   Apple's License Agreement appears in the Setup Assistant window, and you can scroll down to read the agreement. You must choose to accept the agreement, or the installer goes no further.

   After clicking Next in Windows or Continue on a Mac (which is active only if you accept), the Setup Assistant displays a dialog that lets you enter a name for your iPod.

3. **Give your iPod a name, set automatic options, and then click Next in Windows or Continue on a Mac (or Finish if you have already registered the iPod or are setting up an iPod shuffle).**

   If you plan on sharing several iPods among several computers, give your iPod a unique name.

   If you want to copy your entire iTunes music library, leave the Automatically Choose Songs For My iPod option selected (not provided for the iPod shuffle). This option creates a mirror image of your music library on the iPod, including all playlists and audio files, every time you connect your iPod. (Don't worry. You can always change this setting later; see Chapter 12.) If you want to copy only a portion of your library to the iPod, deselect this option.

The iPhone Setup Assistant provides the option to Automatically Sync Contacts, Calendars, Email Accounts, and Bookmarks. Deselect this option if you want to change these synchronization settings first.

For an iPod shuffle, the Setup Assistant displays an option to copy songs randomly. If you leave the Automatically Choose Songs for My iPod option selected, iTunes copies a random selection of songs to your iPod shuffle. You can always choose to fill your iPod shuffle with a different selection by clicking the Autofill button, as we describe in Chapter 12.

If you have a color-display iPod model, including iPod nano, select the Automatically Copy Photos to My iPod option if you want to copy all the photos in your Pictures folder to your iPod. Leave it deselected if you want to transfer photos later.

If you turn on both the option to copy photos automatically and the option to copy songs automatically, iTunes copies the songs first and then copies photos up to the limit of the iPod's capacity. (See Chapter 12 to find out about transferring photos to your color-display iPod.)

After you click Next in Windows or Continue on a Mac, the Setup Assistant moves on to the dialog for registering your iPod.

4. **Click the Register button to register your iPod online.**

   The Setup Assistant allows you to register your iPod with Apple online, to take advantage of Apple support. Apple displays a dialog for entering your Apple ID; a membership ID for the .Mac service is also valid. If you purchased your iPod directly from Apple and you have an Apple ID or .Mac ID, enter the ID and password to swiftly move through the registration process — Apple automatically recognizes your purchase so that you don't need to enter the iPod's serial number. If you bought your iPod elsewhere or you don't have an Apple ID or .Mac ID, Apple displays a dialog for entering your iPod's serial number and your personal information. Fields marked with an asterisk (*) are required, such as your name and e-mail address. Click Continue to advance through each dialog in the registration process.

   You can find the iPod's serial number of the back of your iPod (use a magnifying glass) or on the side of its packaging.

5. **Click Finish on Windows, or Done on a Mac, to finish setup.**

After finishing setup, your iPod's name appears in the iTunes Source pane (the left column) under the Devices subheading, as shown in Figure 2-3. Information about your iPod, including how much space is available, appears in the main part of the iTunes window. The iPod icon also appears in Windows Explorer on a Windows PC, or on the Finder Desktop on a Mac.

You can also use the Finder on a Mac, or Windows Explorer on a PC, to see how much free space is left on the iPod. On a Mac, click the iPod icon on the Desktop and choose File⇨Get Info. The Finder displays the Get Info window with information about capacity, amount used, and available space. On a PC, select the iPod in Windows Explorer and choose Properties from the shortcut menu to see this information. You can also use the About command on the iPod, which is available on the Settings menu: Choose Settings⇨About. The iPod information screen appears with capacity and available space.

If you selected the automatic update feature in the Setup Assistant, your iPod quickly fills up with the music from your iTunes music library. Of course, if you're just starting out, you probably have no tunes in your library. Your next step is to import music from CDs, buy music online, or import music from other sources (see Chapter 4).

Don't want to add songs now? If you deselect the automatic update feature, you can still add songs later either manually or automatically, as we describe in Chapter 12.

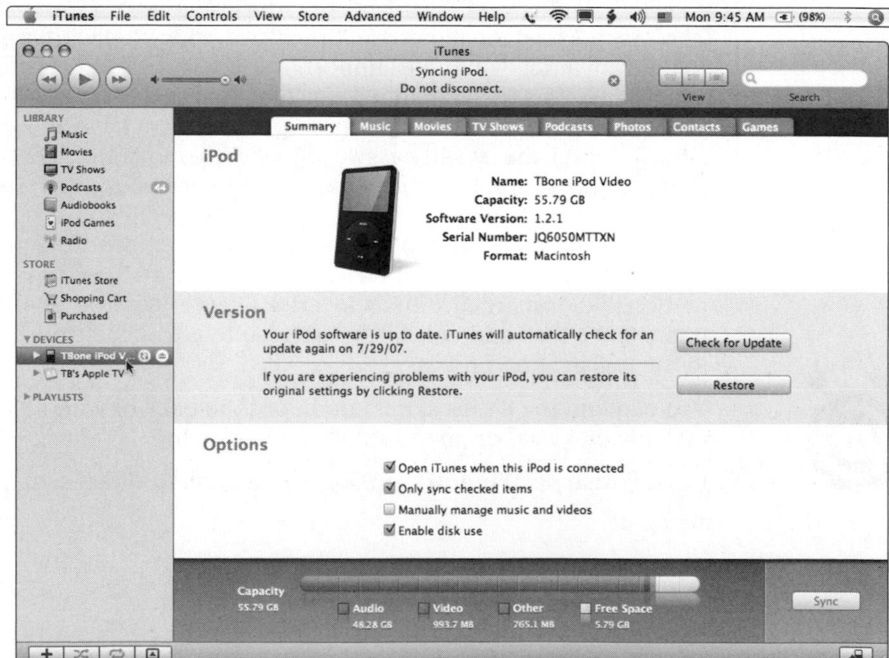

Figure 2-3: Your iPod appears as a device in the Source pane of iTunes, with information about the iPod filling the main window.

You can leave your iPod connected to the computer, using the computer as a source of power — the iPod appears in iTunes whenever you start iTunes. However, you might not want to connect to your iPod every time you start iTunes. If you have an alternate power source for your iPod, disconnect it from iTunes and your computer by *ejecting* it. To eject your iPod, click the eject button next to the iPod name (refer to Figure 2-3) or click the iPod eject button in the lower-right corner of the iTunes window.

After ejecting the iPod, wait for its display to show the main menu or the `OK to disconnect` message. You can then disconnect the iPod from the computer. Don't ever disconnect an iPod before ejecting it because such bad behavior might cause your iPod to freeze up and require a reset. (If that happens, see Chapter 24 for instructions.)

Downloading and Installing Software Upgrades

Apple upgrades iTunes and the built-in iPod software regularly to add new features and fix bugs. The best way to stay updated with the latest version is to get in the habit of downloading upgrades over the Internet. To install the upgrade, follow these steps:

1. **If iTunes displays a dialog with the message that a new version of iTunes is available and asks whether you would like to download it now, click Yes to download the new version.**
   - *On a Windows PC:* iTunes launches your Web browser and takes you right to the iTunes download page (refer to Figure 2-1). Follow the instructions in "Installing iTunes on a Windows PC" in this chapter.
   - *On a Mac:* iTunes automatically downloads and installs the upgrade. When you start iTunes after installing an upgrade, you must click the option to agree to Apple's License Agreement. iTunes then starts as usual.

You can set your Mac to automatically download the latest version of iTunes and iPod Software when they become available. Just use Software Update from the Mac OS X System Preferences window. Click the Check Now button to check for a new version. If one exists, it appears in a window for you to select. Select it and then click Install to download and install it.

2. **After installing the iTunes upgrade, connect your iPod to your computer as you normally do.**

   iTunes automatically detects new iPod software if it is available, as shown in Figure 2-4.

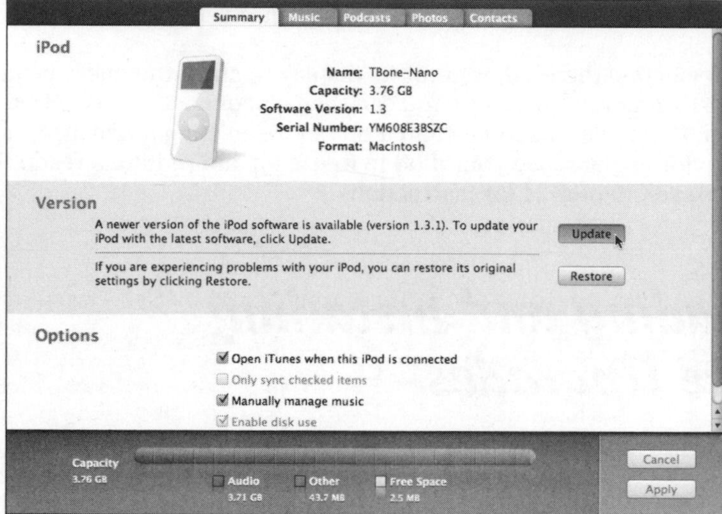

Figure 2-4: iTunes automatically detects new iPod software and lets you update your iPod.

3. **Click the Update button to install the software in your iPod.**

   iTunes displays information about the new iPod software.

4. **Click Next to continue to the Apple License Agreement, and click the option to agree with it.**

   iTunes automatically installs the update into your iPod. After your iPod is set up and updated with the newest version of its software, you are ready to find out what iTunes can do for you.

Chapter 3

Getting Started with iTunes

In This Chapter

- Finding out what you can do with iTunes
- Playing music tracks on a CD
- Skipping and repeating music tracks
- Displaying visuals while playing music
- MiniShopping at the MiniStore

More than half a century ago, jukeboxes were the primary and most convenient way for people to select the music they wanted to hear and share with others, especially newly released music. Juke joints were hopping with the newest hits every night. You could pick any song to play at any time, but you had to insert a coin and pay for each play. Radio eventually supplanted the jukebox as the primary means of releasing new music to the public, and the music was free to hear — but you couldn't choose to play any song you wanted at any time.

Today, using iTunes, you not only have a digital jukebox *and* a radio in your computer, but you also have online access to millions of songs, thousands of podcasts, and hundreds of TV shows, movies, and audio books. Connect your computer to a stereo amplifier in your home or connect speakers to your computer, and suddenly your computer is the best jukebox in the neighborhood. Connect your computer to a television, and you have a full multimedia environment in your home, all controlled by iTunes.

This chapter gives you an overview of what you can do with iTunes, and you get started in the simplest way possible: using iTunes to play music tracks on a CD. You can use iTunes just like a jukebox, only better — you don't have to pay for each song you play, and you can play some or all of the songs on an album in any order.

The most up-to-date version of iTunes as of this writing is version 7.4. However, software updates occur very rapidly. If you really want the latest version, go directly to the Apple Web site to get it, as we describe in Chapter 2.

What You Can Do with iTunes

You can purchase songs or entire albums, audio books, TV shows, movies, and other videos from the iTunes Store and download them directly into your iTunes library (as we describe in Chapter 4), or you can copy these items from other sources (including audio CDs) into your iTunes library. You can also subscribe to *podcasts* that transfer audio or audio/video episodes, such as weekly broadcasts, automatically to your iTunes library from the Internet or through the iTunes Store. You can even use iTunes to listen to Web radio stations and add your favorite stations to your music library. After you store the content in your iTunes library, you can play it on your computer and transfer it to iPod, Apple TV, and iPhone devices. You can also burn the audio content onto an audio CD or make backup copies of audio and video onto other hard drives or DVD data discs.

Transferring songs from a CD to your computer is referred to as *ripping* a CD (to the chagrin of the music industry old-timers who think that users intend to destroy the discs or steal the songs). Ripping an entire CD's worth of songs is quick and easy, and track information, such as artist name and title, arrives automatically over the Internet for most commercial CDs. (You can add the information yourself for rare CDs, custom-mix CDs, live CDs, and others that are unknown to the database.)

You can also add video files to your iTunes library by: choosing content from the iTunes Store (such as TV shows, feature-length movies, music videos, and even free movie trailers); or by downloading standard video files in the MPEG-4 format from other sources on the Internet.

Why not create your own videos? Use a digital camcorder — or use the iSight camera built into every MacBook — and copy the videos to iTunes. You can even convert a television signal (or any analog video signal) for viewing in iTunes by using products such as EyeTV 250 from Elgato Systems (`www.elgato.com`).

Although you can't use iTunes to transfer video content from a DVD, you can use other software to convert DVDs to digital video files, and you can transfer video content from older VHS players by using a digital video camcorder. Visit this book's companion Web site for more details.

iTunes gives you the power to organize content into playlists. You can even set up dynamic, smart playlists that reflect your preferences and listening habits. iTunes offers an equalizer with preset settings for all kinds of music and listening environments, and it gives you the ability to customize and save your own personalized settings with each item of content.

The Mac and Windows versions of iTunes are virtually identical, with the exception that dialogs look a bit different between the two operating systems. There are also a few other differences, mostly related to the different operating environments. The Windows version lets you import Windows Media (WMA) songs; the Mac version, like most Mac applications, can be controlled by AppleScript programs. Nevertheless, as Apple continues to improve iTunes, the company releases upgrades to both versions at the same time, and the versions are free to download.

Opening the iTunes Window

You can run iTunes anytime (with or without an iPod) to build and manage your library of music, audio books, podcasts, Web radio stations, TV shows, and other videos. You don't have to connect your iPod until you're ready to transfer content to it (as we describe in Chapter 12).

When you launch iTunes, your library and other sources of content appear. Figure 3-1 shows the iTunes window on a PC running Windows XP, using the Browse pane to browse by artist. You can click the column headings in the List pane to sort your library by artist, album title, or any of the other view options.

The Mac and Windows versions of iTunes look nearly identical and offer the same viewing options, including the *cover browser* (also known by its older name, Cover Flow). Figure 3-2 shows the iTunes window on the Mac with the cover browser open, displaying the cover art for albums.

iTunes offers a view of your library and your sources for content, as well as controls for organizing, importing, and playing content, as follows:

- **Source pane:** Displays the source of content, now handily divided into the following sections:
    - *Library:* Includes your music, movies, TV shows, podcasts, audio books, iPod games, and all available radio stations
    - *Store:* Includes the iTunes Store and your Purchased list
    - *Devices:* Can include iPods, such as the iPod nano in Figure 3-2 named TBone-Nano, CDs such as the *Sgt. Pepper's* CD in Figure 3-1, iPhones, and Apple TV
    - *Playlists:* Includes Party Shuffle and your playlists

- **Cover browser:** The coolest new feature, also called Cover Flow. The cover browser lets you flip through your cover art to choose songs. You can use the slider to move swiftly through your library, or you can click to the right or left of the cover in the foreground to move forward or backward in your library.
- **List pane and Browse pane:** Depending on the source that's selected in the Source pane under Library, Store, Devices, or Playlists, these two panes (refer to Figure 3-1) display a list of the content in your library or a list of Web radio stations, the content available in the iTunes Store, the tracks of a music CD or the entire library on your iPod, or the Party Shuffle list or any one of your playlists.

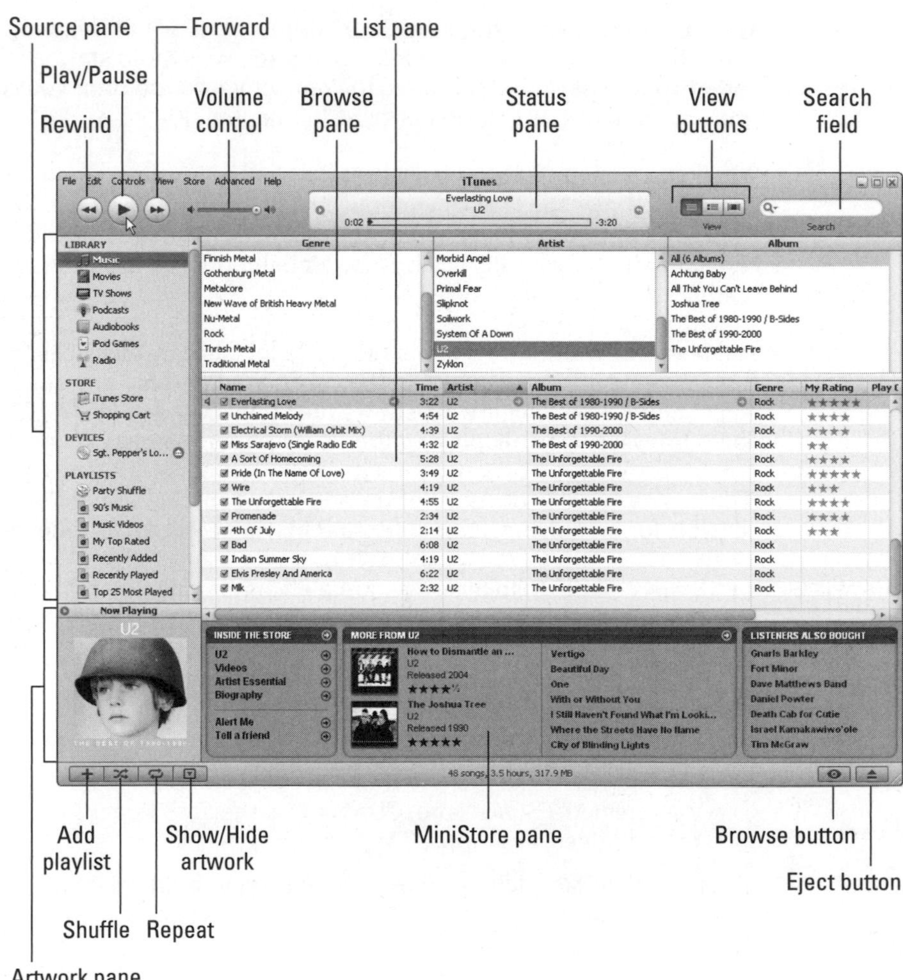

Figure 3-1: The iTunes window on a PC in Browse view.

- **MiniStore pane:** The MiniStore pane (refer to Figure 3-1) makes suggestions for what to get from the iTunes Store based on what you're listening to. There's no obligation to buy anything, and you can dispense with this pane if it bothers you. (See the section, "Using the iTunes MiniStore," later in this chapter.)
- **View buttons:** The three buttons in the upper-right corner change your view of the List and Browse panes to show items in a list, grouped with cover art, or displayed with the cover browser.
- **Browse button:** The Browse button at the lower-right corner of the window toggles between Browse view (with the List pane below and the Browse pane above with genre, artist, and album — refer to Figure 3-1) and the List pane by itself. Browse view isn't available when viewing a playlist, podcasts, Party Shuffle, or the Radio selection.

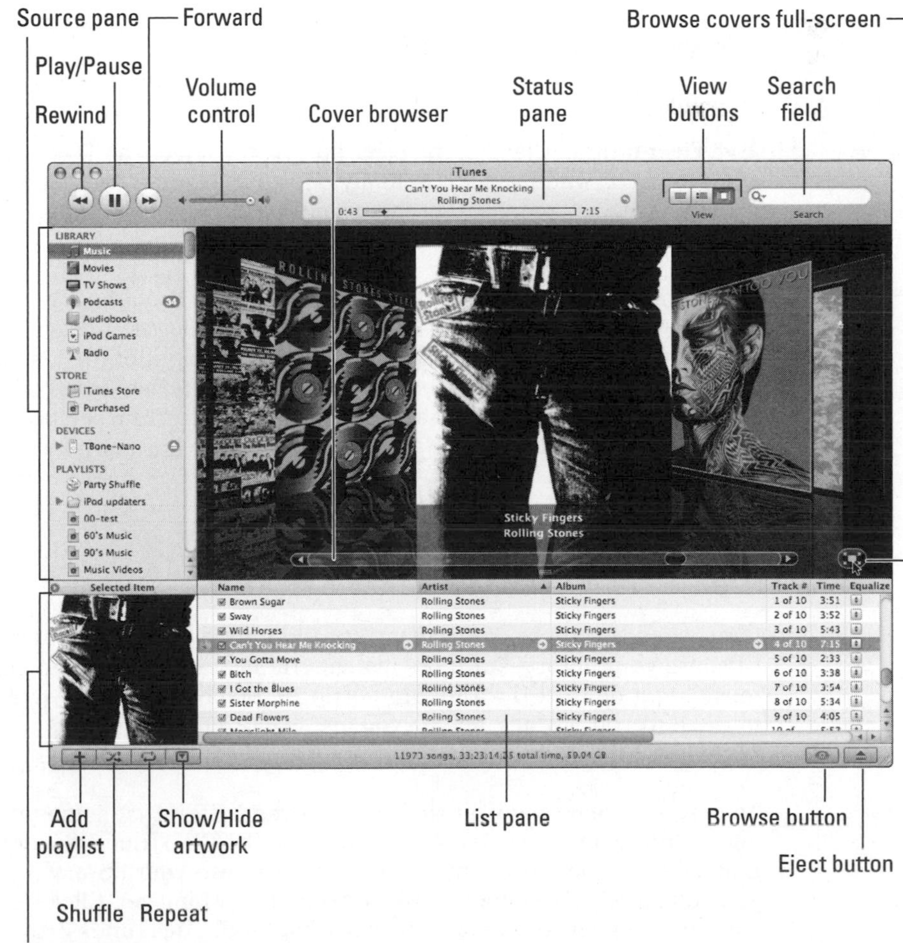

Figure 3-2: The iTunes window on a Mac with the cover browser open.

- **Status pane:** When a song, audio book, radio station, podcast, or video is playing, the artist name, piece title (if known), and the elapsed time display in this pane.
- **Search field:** Type in this field to search your library. You can also use the Search field to peruse a playlist or to look within the iTunes Store.
- **Player buttons — Forward/Next, Play/Pause, and Previous/Rewind:** Use these buttons to control the playback of content in iTunes.
- **Playlist buttons — Add, Shuffle, Repeat:** Use these buttons to add playlists and shuffle or repeat playback of playlists.
- **Volume control:** You can change the volume level in iTunes by dragging the volume control slider in the upper-left section of the iTunes window to the right to increase the volume, or to the left to decrease it. The maximum volume of the iTunes volume slider is the maximum set for the computer's sound.
- **Show/Hide Artwork button:** Use this button to display or hide artwork (either your own or the artwork supplied with purchased songs and videos).
- **Eject button:** Clicking the Eject button, um, ejects a CD or an iPod. However, whereas a CD actually pops out of some computers, iPods are hard drives, and ejecting them simply removes *(unmounts)* the drives from the system so that you can disconnect them.

If you don't like the width of the Source pane, you can adjust it by dragging the shallow dot on the vertical bar between the Source pane and the List pane and Browse pane. You can also adjust the height of the List and Browse panes by dragging the shallow dot on the horizontal bar between them. To resize the iTunes window on a Mac, drag diagonally from the bottom-right corner. In Windows, drag the edges of the window horizontally or vertically.

Playing CD Tracks in iTunes

iTunes needs content. You can get started right away by ripping music from CDs into your library. For more instant gratification, though, you can play music right off the CD without importing it. Maybe you don't want to put the music into your library. Maybe you just want to hear it first, as part of your Play First, Rip Later plan.

To play a CD, insert any music CD — or even a CD-R that someone burned for you — into your computer. After you insert the CD, iTunes displays a dialog that asks whether you want to import the CD into your library right now — you can click Yes to import now, or No to do nothing yet. Click No for now; we show you how to import music in Chapter 5. The iTunes Browse button changes to an Import button in anticipation of ripping the CD at any time.

If you're connected to the Internet, iTunes accesses the Gracenote CDDB for song information while you are answering the import question, so that after you click Yes or No, iTunes presents the track information for each song automatically, as shown in Figure 3-3. (*Gracenote CDDB* is a song database on the Internet that knows the track names of most commercial CDs but not homemade mix CDs. You can read about Gracenote CDDB and editing song information in Chapter 9.)

Figure 3-3: CD track info appears after iTunes consults the Internet.

When you play a CD in iTunes, it's just like using a CD player. To play a CD from the first track, click the Play button. (If you clicked somewhere else after inserting the disc, you might have to click the first track to select it before clicking the Play button.) The Play button then turns into a Pause button, and the song plays.

When the song finishes, iTunes continues playing the songs in the list in sequence until you click the Pause button (which then toggles back into the Play button) or until the song list ends. You can skip to the next or previous song by using the arrow keys on your keyboard or by clicking the Forward button or the Back button (next to the Play button). You can also double-click another song in the list to start playing it.

You can press the spacebar to perform the same function as clicking the Play button; pressing it again is just like clicking the Pause button.

The Status pane above the list of songs tells you the name of the artist and the song title as well as the elapsed time of the track. When you click the artist name, the artist name is replaced by the album name. The time on the left of the slider is the elapsed time; the time on the right is the duration of the song. When you click the duration, it changes to the remaining time; click it again to return to the song's duration.

Eject a CD by clicking the Eject button or by choosing Controls⇨Eject Disc. Another way to eject the CD is to click the Eject icon next to the CD name in the Source pane. You can also right-click the CD name and choose Eject from the contextual menu.

Rearranging and repeating tracks

You can rearrange the order of the tracks to automatically play them in any sequence you want, similar to programming a CD player. When you click the up arrow at the top of the first column in the List pane (refer to Figure 3-3), it changes to a down arrow, and the tracks appear in reverse order.

To change the order of tracks that you're playing in sequence, just click and hold the track number in the leftmost column for the song, and then drag it up or down in the list. You can set up the tracks to play in a completely different sequence.

Skipping tracks

To skip tracks so that they don't play in sequence, deselect the check box next to the song names. iTunes skips deselected songs when you play the entire sequence.

To remove all check marks from a list, press ⌘ on a Mac or Ctrl in Windows while clicking a check mark. Select an empty check box while pressing ⌘ or Ctrl to add check marks to the entire list.

Repeating a song list

You can repeat an entire song list by clicking the Repeat button, which you find below the Source pane on the left side of the iTunes window (or by choosing Controls⇨Repeat All). When it's selected, the Repeat button shows blue highlighting. Click the Repeat button again to repeat the current song (or choose Controls⇨Repeat One). The button changes to include a blue-highlighted numeral 1. Click it once more to return to normal playback (or choose Controls⇨Repeat Off).

The Shuffle button, located to the left of the Repeat button, plays the songs in the list in random order, which can be fun. You can then press the arrow keys on your keyboard or click the Back and Forward buttons to jump around in random order.

Displaying visuals

The visual effects in iTunes can turn your iTunes window into a light show that's synchronized to the music in your library. You can watch a cool display of eye candy while the music plays — or leave it on like a lava lamp.

Choose View⇨Turn On Visualizer to display visual effects (or press ⌘-T on a Mac or Ctrl-T in Windows). An animation appears in the iTunes window and synchronizes with the music. Choose View⇨Turn Off Visualizer (or press ⌘-T on a Mac or Ctrl-T in Windows) to turn off the visual effects.

You can tweak the animation a bit by changing the Visualizer options. Choose View⇨Visualizer⇨Options to open the Visualizer Options dialog, as shown in Figure 3-4.

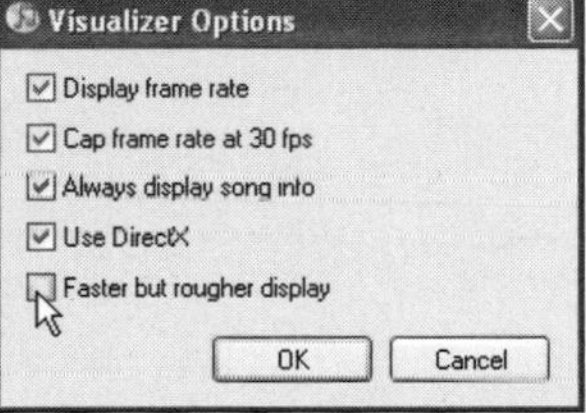

Figure 3-4: Set options for visual effects.

The Visualizer Options dialog offers the following options that affect the animation (but not the performance of iTunes when it's playing music):

- **Display Frame Rate:** Choosing this option displays the frame rate of the animation along with the animation.
- **Cap Frame Rate at 30 fps:** Choosing this option keeps the frame rate at 30 fps (frames per second) or lower, which is roughly the speed of video.
- **Always Display Song Info:** Choosing this option displays the song name, artist, and album for the song currently playing, along with the animation.
- **Use DirectX (Windows only) or Use OpenGL (Mac only):** You can choose to use DirectX on a Windows PC or OpenGL on a Mac to display very cool animation with faster performance. These are the most widely used standards for three-dimensional graphics programming.
- **Faster but Rougher Display:** When you use this option, animation plays faster but with rougher graphics. Select this option if your animation plays too slowly.

Choosing View⇨Full Screen (or pressing ⌘-F on a Mac or Ctrl-F in Windows) while the Visualizer is on sets the visual effects to fill the entire screen. When displaying the full-screen visual effects, you can click the mouse button or press Escape (Esc) to stop the display and return to iTunes.

The Preferences dialog in iTunes gives you a bit more control over the size of the animated effects and density of the visual animation — offering a choice of Small, Medium, or Large animations to suit your tastes. Choose iTunes⇨Preferences on a Mac, or Edit⇨Preferences in Windows, click the Advanced tab, and then click the General tab, which displays the Advanced General preferences. Choose the Visualizer Size — Small, Medium, or Large — in the pop-up menu, as shown in Figure 3-5. You can also select the Display Visualizer Full Screen option to always display the Visualizer in full-screen mode.

While the animated visual effects play, press Shift-/ (as if you're typing a question mark) to see a list of keyboard functions. Depending on the visual effect, you might see more choices of keyboard functions by pressing Shift-/ again.

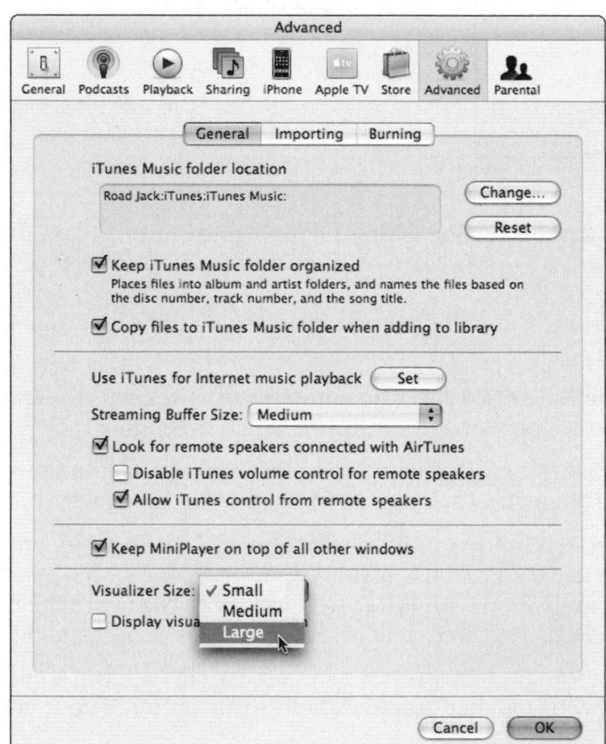

Figure 3-5: Set preferences for the Visualizer.

You can enhance iTunes with plug-ins that provide even better visuals. For example, SpectroGraph from Dr. Lex displays a spectrogram of the music, and Cover Version from imagomat displays the album cover artwork. You can find these and many other enhancements at PluginsWorld.com (`http://itunes.pluginsworld.com`).

After installing an iTunes plug-in, you can switch from one plug-in to another by choosing View⇨Visualizer to see the submenu of plug-ins (including iTunes Visualizer, which is supplied with iTunes). Choose View⇨Visualizer⇨iTunes Visualizer to select the iTunes Visualizer.

Using the iTunes MiniStore

If you turn on the iTunes MiniStore pane, which appears below the List and Browse panes, it makes suggestions for what to buy from the iTunes Store based on what you're listening to. No, celebrity DJs and music historians aren't choosing what shows up here; your peers are. The MiniStore informs the online store about the songs you select whenever the MiniStore pane is open. The store simply shows you music that other listeners purchased when they purchased the music you're playing. You can click any item in the MiniStore pane to go right to the iTunes Store page for that item. See Chapter 4 for details about using the iTunes Store.

The MiniStore operates only if you give it permission. When you first start iTunes, the MiniStore is not yet turned on (refer to Figure 3-2). Choose View⇨Show MiniStore, and the MiniStore pane appears at the bottom of the window (refer to Figure 3-1), offering suggestions as you play the content in your library.

When you have the MiniStore pane open, iTunes transmits information to the store about the selection you're playing. The iTunes MiniStore does not transmit the current song data if the MiniStore pane is hidden. To hide the MiniStore, choose View⇨Hide MiniStore.

If the MiniStore can't find the artist for the song you're playing, it displays `No Match` and offers choices that are simply in the same genre, along with New Releases, Top Songs, and Top Albums. If you select an audio book or TV show in your library, you'll see the top-selling audio books or TV shows in the MiniStore. If you don't have an iTunes Store available for your country, you see the U.S. store, just as Chuck Berry once sang, "Anything you want, we got right here in the U.S.A."

Chapter 4

Shopping at the iTunes Store

In This Chapter

- Setting up an account with the iTunes Store
- Previewing and buying songs, TV shows, movies, and audio books
- Browsing, previewing, and downloading podcasts
- Giving allowances and gift certificates
- Setting parental controls
- Authorizing computers to play purchased music

When Apple announced its online music service, Apple chairman Steve Jobs remarked that other services put forward by the music industry tend to treat consumers like criminals. Steve had a point. Many of these services cost more and add a level of copy protection that prevents consumers from burning more than one CD or using the music (that they bought) on other computers or portable MP3 players.

Record labels drug their feet for years, experimenting with online sales and taking legal action against online sites that allowed free downloads and music copying. Although the free music attracted millions of listeners, the free services were under legal attack in several countries, and the digital music that was distributed wasn't of the highest quality (not to mention the widespread and sometimes intentional misspellings in the song information and artist names). Consumers grew even warier when the Recording Industry Association of America (RIAA; a lobbying organization looking out for the interests of record companies) began legal proceedings (illegal copyright infringement) against people who possibly thought they were downloading free music.

No one should go to jail for being a music junkie. Consumers and the industry both needed a solution. Apple did the research on how to make a service that worked better and was easier to use, and the company forged ahead with the iTunes Store. By all accounts, Apple has succeeded in offering the easiest, fastest, and most cost-effective service for buying content online for your computer and iPod.

When Apple first introduced the online store, it was called the iTunes Music Store. Although the store still has millions of songs and Apple has sold more than two billion songs as of January 2007, the company dropped *Music* from its title because the iTunes Store sells much more. You can now purchase and download feature-length movies as well as TV shows and music videos, and the iTunes Store also offers games you can play on your iPod.

The iTunes Store offers parental controls that let you disable various sections and the purchase of various contents based on PG/TV ratings. It also offers an option to immediately burn a disc backup of the content you purchased. The iTunes Store offers gift certificates that you can e-mail to others and allows accounts that you can set up for others (such as children) with credit limits but without the need to use a credit card. In fact, Apple adds new features to the iTunes Store almost every week.

In this chapter, we show you how to sign in and take advantage of what the iTunes Store has to offer.

Visiting the iTunes Store

You can visit the iTunes Store by connecting to the Internet and using iTunes or America Online (AOL). You can even click an iTunes Store link on Apple's Web site, or a similar link on Web sites that are iTunes affiliates with songs for sale (such as `www.rockument.com`). The link automatically launches your installed copy of iTunes and opens the iTunes Store.

As of this writing, the iTunes Store offers millions of songs, with most songs available for download for 99 cents each and entire albums available for download at less than the CD price. You can play these copy-protected songs on up to five different computers, burn CDs, and use the songs on an iPod. Apple also offers songs and albums in its iTunes Plus section from some record labels (such as EMI) at a higher price and with higher sound quality without copy protection. You can play these songs on just about any music player and on an unlimited number of computers, — and, of course, burn CDs with them.

You can also buy episodes and entire seasons of TV shows and even purchase them in advance, so you see them immediately as they are released. First-run movies are also available along with free movie trailers as well as audio books. iTunes also offers tons of free content in the form of *podcasts,* which are similar to syndicated radio and TV shows, but you can download them into iTunes and play them at your convenience on your computer and iPod.

Like with most online services, the music that you buy online is not as high in audio quality as music on a commercial CD although most people can't tell the difference when playing the music on car stereos or at low volume. In Chapter 18, we explain why there is a quality tradeoff to reduce the space the music occupies on the hard drive or flash memory of your iPod. As we explain in Chapter 18, the quality of the music sold in the iTunes Store is comparable with the quality you get when ripping CDs or importing songs using the MP3 or AAC formats. You also get song information (such as artist, song titles, the album title, and cover artwork), and the iTunes Store provides electronic liner notes for some albums just like the printed notes you sometimes find on a commercial CD. Some albums are provided with the electronic equivalent of a complete jewel case booklet that you can print yourself.

The iTunes Store is part of iTunes version 4 and newer, but you should be using version 7.4 as of this writing. If you're running an older version of iTunes, download the newest version, as we describe in Chapter 2.

You can preview any song or video for up to 30 seconds (and audio books and podcasts up to about 90 seconds). If you have an account set up, you can buy and download songs, audio books, podcasts, TV shows, movies, and videos immediately. We don't know of a faster way to purchase content.

To open the iTunes Store, you have at least four choices:

- **Click the iTunes Store option in the Source pane.** The iTunes Store home page opens, as shown in Figure 4-1.
- **Click any link in the MiniStore pane.** The iTunes Store home page opens and automatically switches your Source pane selection to iTunes Store. The MiniStore pane offers suggestions based on the music you select in your library; see Chapter 3 for details.
- **Follow a content link in iTunes.** Click the *content link* (the gray-circled arrow next to a song or video title, an artist name, or an album title) to go to an iTunes Store page related to the song or video, artist, or album. iTunes searches the iTunes Store based on the item you selected. If nothing closely related turns up, at least you end up in the iTunes Store, and you might even find music you like that you didn't know about.
- **Go to iTunes on AOL and click the iTunes link.** If you use AOL, you can browse or search the AOL music area for songs and click the iTunes link to automatically launch iTunes and go to the iTunes Store.

If you need to fire up your modem and log on to your Internet service to go online, do so *before* clicking the iTunes Store option or following a content link — otherwise iTunes will wait for an Internet connection for a while and eventually give up.

The iTunes Store uses the iTunes List and Browse panes to display its wares. You can check out content to your heart's content although you can't buy content unless you have an iTunes Store account set up. You can use the Choose Genre pop-up menu to specify music genres, or you can click links for new releases, exclusive tracks, and so on.

We use the term *pop-up menu* for menus on the Mac that literally pop up from dialogs and windows; in Windows, the same type of menu actually drops down and is called a *drop-down menu.* We use the term *pop-up menu* for both.

The iTunes Store also provides buttons on a gray bar just above the advertised content in the List pane. The left and right triangle buttons work just like the Back and Forward buttons of a Web browser, moving back a page or forward a page, respectively. The button with the Home icon takes you to the iTunes Store home page. The Browse button in the lower-right corner switches the view between Browse view (with the List and Browse panes both open) and List view (with only the List pane open).

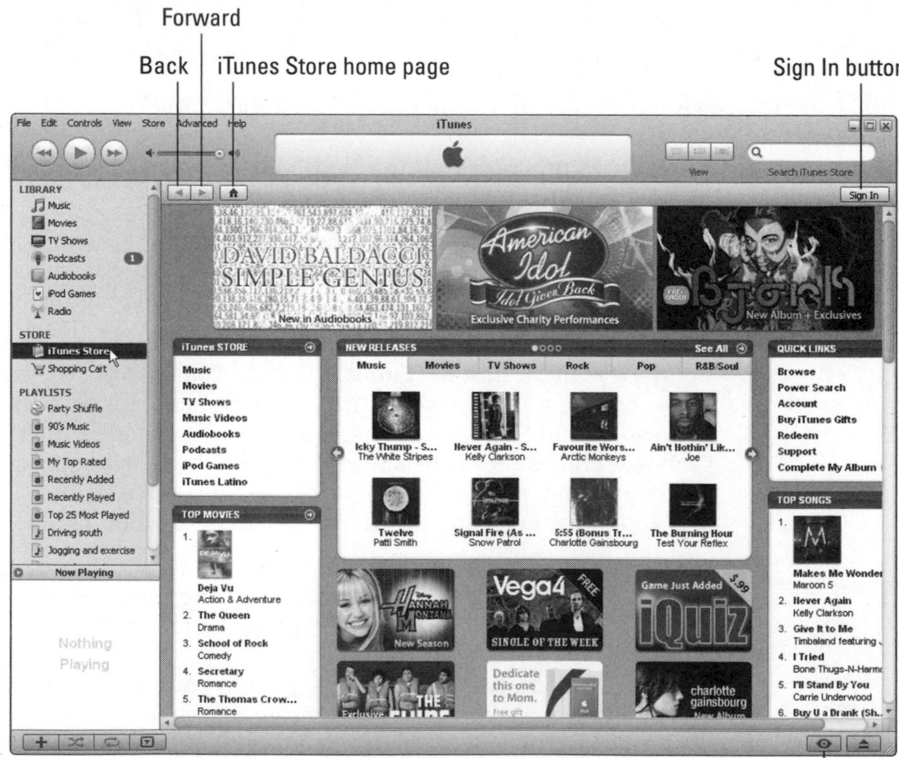

Figure 4-1: The iTunes Store home page.

Setting Up an Account

You need an account to buy music. To create an iTunes Store account, follow these steps:

1. **In iTunes, click the iTunes Store option in the Source pane or click a music link or MiniStore pane link.**

   The iTunes Store home page appears (refer to Figure 4-1), replacing the iTunes List pane and Browse pane.

2. **Click the Sign In button in the upper-right area of the window to create an account (or sign in to an existing account).**

   If you already have an account that you've logged on to before using iTunes, the account name appears in place of the Sign In button.

   After you click the Sign In button, iTunes displays the account sign-in dialog, as shown in Figure 4-2.

   If you already set up an account with the iTunes Store with the .Mac service, with other Apple services (such as the Apple Developer Connection), or with AOL, you're halfway there. Type your ID and password and then click the Sign In button. Apple remembers the personal information that you put in previously, so you don't have to re-enter it every time you visit the iTunes Store. If you forgot your password, click the Forgot Password? button, and iTunes provides a dialog to answer your test question. If you answer correctly, iTunes e-mails your password to you.

3. **Click the Create New Account button.**

   iTunes displays a new page, replacing the iTunes Store home page with the terms of use and an explanation of steps to create a new account.

Figure 4-2: The sign-in dialog for the iTunes Store.

4. **Click the Agree button and then fill in your personal account information.**

   iTunes displays the next page of the setup procedure, shown in Figure 4-3, which requires you to type your e-mail address, password, test question and answer (in case you forget your password), birth date, and privacy options.

5. **Click the Continue button to go to the next page of the account setup procedure, and then enter your credit card information.**

   The entire procedure is secure, so you don't have to worry. The iTunes Store keeps your personal information (including your credit card information) on file, and you don't have to type it again.

6. **Click Continue to finish the procedure.**

   The account setup finishes and returns you to the iTunes Store home page. You can now use the iTunes Store to purchase and download content to play in iTunes and use on an iPod, an iPhone, or an Apple TV.

If you use AOL and the AOL Wallet feature, you can assign payment for your iTunes Store account to your AOL Wallet. AOL Wallet contains your billing and credit card information for purchases. AOL Wallet automatically fills information into the text boxes of the account setup pages so that you don't have to.

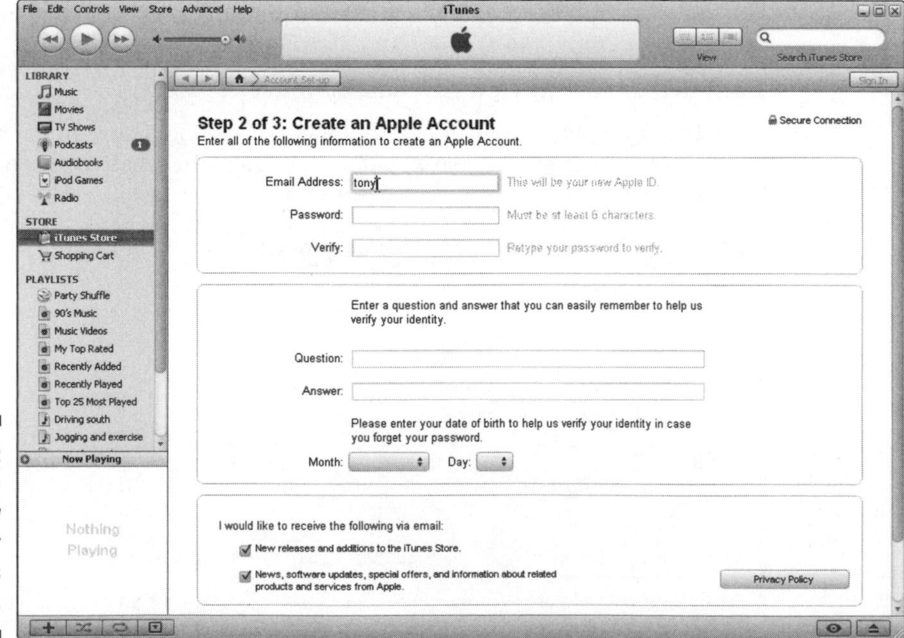

Figure 4-3: Create a new account for the iTunes Store.

Select a country from the My Store pop-up menu at the bottom of the iTunes Store page to choose online stores in other countries. For example, the iTunes Store in France displays menus in French and features hit songs and TV shows for the French market.

Click the flag button next to the My Store pop-up menu to display a page of buttons with flags of other countries; then click one to go to the home page for the iTunes Store for that country.

Browsing and Previewing Songs

The iTunes Store home page is loaded with specials and advertisements to peruse. To look at music in more depth, choose Music from the iTunes STORE menu on the left panel at the top of the home page next to the new releases panel. iTunes displays more panels of advertisements and specials for music lovers. You can then choose a genre from the Genres menu on the left panel next to the advertisements to see only those specials and ads for a particular genre. You can click just about anything to get more information: today's top-ten songs, albums, audio books, TV shows, movies, exclusive offerings, and more.

What if you're looking for particular music in a particular genre? You can browse the iTunes Store by genre and artist name in a method similar to browsing your iTunes library.

To browse the iTunes Store, click the Browse button in the lower-right corner of the iTunes window, or click the Browse link in the Quick Links panel on the right side of the iTunes Store home page.

iTunes displays the store's offerings categorized by type of content (such as Music), and displays music by genre — and within each genre, by artist and album. Select a genre in the Genre column, then a subgenre in the Subgenre column, then an artist in the Artist column, and finally an album in the Album column, which takes you to the list of songs from that album that are available to preview or purchase, as shown in Figure 4-4.

To see more information about a song or the album that it came from, click the content *link* (one of the gray-circled arrow buttons in the List pane):

- Clicking the arrow in the Artist column takes you to the artist's page of albums.
- Clicking the arrow in the Album column takes you to the album page.
- Clicking the arrow in the Name column takes you to album page with the song highlighted.

Figure 4-4: Browsing the iTunes Store for music by genre, artist, and album.

My only complaint about browsing by artist is that artists are listed alphabetically by first name. For example, you have to look up Bob Dylan under *Bob* and not *Dylan*.

To preview a song, click the song title in the List pane and then click the Play button (or press the spacebar).

By default, the previews play on your computer off the Internet in a stream, so you might hear a few hiccups in the playback. Each preview lasts about 30 seconds. Just when you start really getting into the song, it ends. If the song is irresistible, though, you can buy it on the spot.

If you have a slow Internet connection — especially if it's slower than 128 Kbps — the preview might stutter. You can get around this problem by choosing iTunes➪Preferences on a Mac or Edit➪Preferences on a Windows PC and then clicking the Store tab to see the Store preferences. In the Store preferences, click the Load Complete Preview before Playing option to turn it on.

If you know specifically what you're looking for, you can search instead of browse. The Search field in the top-right corner of the iTunes window lets you search the iTunes Store for just about anything. You can type part of a song title or artist name to quickly search the iTunes Store, or use the Power Search feature to narrow your search. (See the "Power searching" section later in this chapter.)

Browsing the charts

What do Louis Armstrong, Roy Orbison, The Beach Boys, Dean Martin, and Mary Wells have in common? Each had a top-ten hit in the charts for 1964 — so says *Billboard,* the weekly magazine for the entertainment industry that has kept tabs on song popularity for more than one-half century. And because the iTunes Store offers pop charts for each year going back to 1946, you can probably find some of the songs that you grew up with.

You can't find *every* song that made the charts — only the songs that the iTunes Store offers.

To find the charts, click the Browse button in the lower-right corner of the iTunes window to browse the iTunes Store (refer to Figure 4-4). Select Charts at the very top of the iTunes Store column. From the Charts column, you can select Billboard Hot 100, Billboard Top Country, or Billboard Top R&B (rhythm and blues).

Power searching

You're serious about music, and you truly desire the power to search for exactly what you want. We know your type — and we have the function right here for you.

Click the Power Search link on the iTunes Store home page in the Quick Links panel to go directly to the Power Search page. At the top of the Power Search page, as shown in Figure 4-5, you can choose the type of content to search through: All (search all types), Music, Movies, TV Shows, Music Videos, Audiobooks, or Podcasts. Click Music to power-search for music.

You can fill in the song title, the artist name, and the album title (refer to Figure 4-5), or just fill in one of those text boxes (for example, if all you know is the song title). You can narrow your search by picking a genre from the Genre pop-up menu or by adding a composer name — or both. After you fill in as much as you know, click the Search button.

Browsing celebrity and published playlists

Do you want to be influenced? Do you want to know what influenced some of today's celebrities and buy what they have in their record collections? Choose Music from the iTunes Store menu to go to the Music page. Scroll down the iTunes Store Music page and click a celebrity name in the Celebrity Playlists pane to go to that celebrity's page with the playlist. A typical celebrity playlist offers about an album's worth of songs from different artists. You can preview or buy any song in the list or follow the music links to the artist or album page.

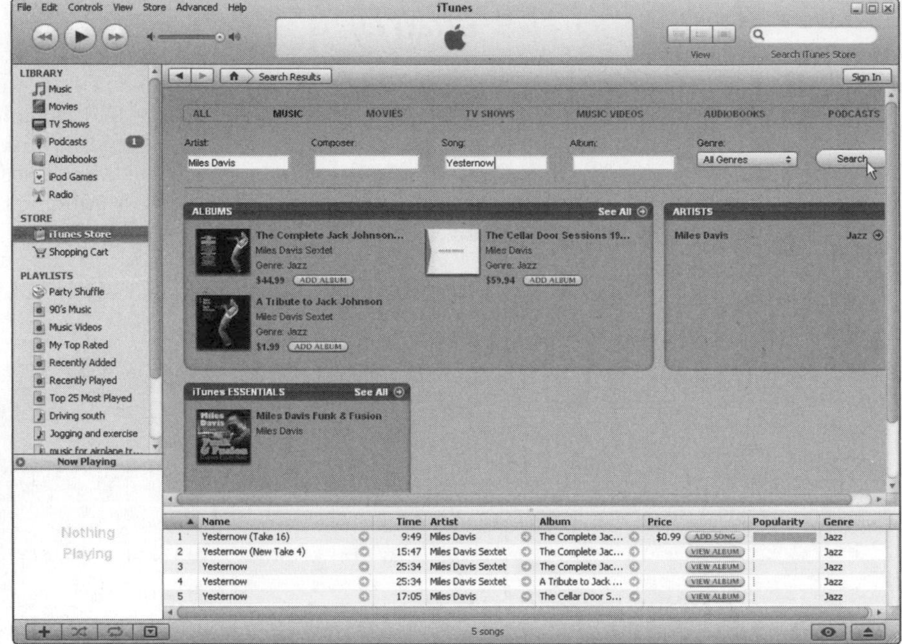

Figure 4-5: Use Power Search to find a song in the iTunes Store.

The Music page lists some of the celebrity playlists, but a lot more aren't listed there (more than 370 the last time we checked). To see all the celebrity playlists, click the Celebrity Playlists link in the More in Music menu on the left side of the Music page.

You can also be influenced by other buyers and do a little influencing yourself. Go to the Music page and click the iMix link in the More in Music menu to check out playlists that have been contributed by other consumers and published in the iTunes Store. iMixes offer 30-second previews of any songs in the playlist. To find out how to publish your own iMix playlist, see Chapter 10.

You can also include a Web link (URL) to an iTunes Store page in an e-mail message or other document so the reader can click the link to go directly to the iTunes Store page. You can drag the last button on the gray bar just above the advertised content that displays the page name — or drag any piece of artwork from the page — to an e-mail message or document you are composing, and iTunes copies the link. You can also Control-click (Mac) or right-click (Windows) the item and choose Copy iTunes Store URL.

Browsing and Previewing Movies, TV Shows, Videos, and Audiobooks

The uncool thing about video stores — besides the weird people who hang out in them — is the lack of any ability to preview videos before you buy them. And the only way to preview TV shows is to watch TV. However, you can use the iTunes Store to preview movies, music videos, and TV shows before you buy them — as long as your computer has a broadband connection to the Internet. Most shows offer 30 seconds of previewing time.

To find TV shows, movies, music videos, or audio books, do one of the following:

- Click the TV Shows, Movies, Music Videos, or Audiobooks link in the iTunes STORE menu on the left side of the iTunes Store home page. The iTunes Store displays advertisements for the most popular items as well as a list of Top Songs, Top Albums, Top TV Show Episodes, and Top Movies.
- Browse the iTunes Store by clicking the Browse link in the Quick Links panel on the right side of the iTunes Store home page (or clicking the Browse button in the lower-right corner of the iTunes window). Select TV Shows, Movies, Music Videos, or Audiobooks from the iTunes Store column, then do one of the following:
    - *For a TV show,* pick a genre in the Genre column, then a TV show in the Shows column, and a season of episodes in the Seasons column.
    - *For a movie,* pick a genre from the Genre column.
    - *For a music video,* pick a genre from the Genre column, then pick an artist from the Artist column.
    - *For an audio book,* pick a genre from the Genre column, then pick an author from the Author/Narrator column.

To preview a TV show or music video, click the title in the list and then click the Play button (or press the spacebar). (Movies are actually videos on the computer, so we use the term *videos* from now on.) The video plays in the Artwork pane in the lower-left corner of the iTunes window, as shown in Figure 4-6. If the Artwork pane isn't visible, click the Show/Hide Artwork button to display it. Click the iTunes Play/Pause, Forward/Next, and Previous/Rewind buttons to control playback, and use the iTunes volume slider to control the volume, just like with songs. For more details about playing videos in iTunes, see Chapter 6.

Figure 4-6: Play a preview of a TV show in the Artwork pane.

You can play the video in a larger, separate window (as shown in Figure 4-7) by clicking inside the Artwork pane while the video is playing. You can then control video playback by using the separate window's controls: Click the right-facing triangle in the window to play the video and click it again to pause the video. Drag the slider to move forward or backward through the video. You can click the Rewind or Fast-Forward buttons in the window to move backward or forward through a video. You can also choose options in the View menu to show the video window half-size, actual size, double-size, fit-to-screen, or full screen.

Movies are also just a click away. The Movies link on the iTunes Store home page takes you to a Movies page. Click an advertisement, thumbnail, or title to go to the specific movie's page, and click the View Trailer button to preview the movie, as shown in Figure 4-8.

Use the iTunes Play button, just as you would for a song, to play the movie trailer. At any time or after the movie trailer plays, click the Close Preview button in the lower-right corner of the iTunes window to return to the movie page.

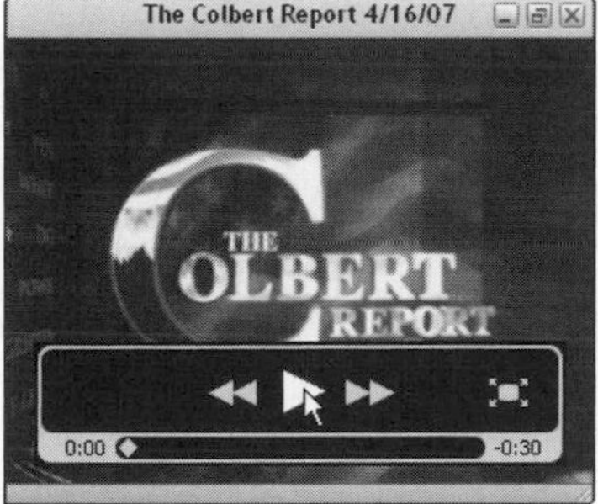

Figure 4-7: Play a preview of a TV show in a separate window.

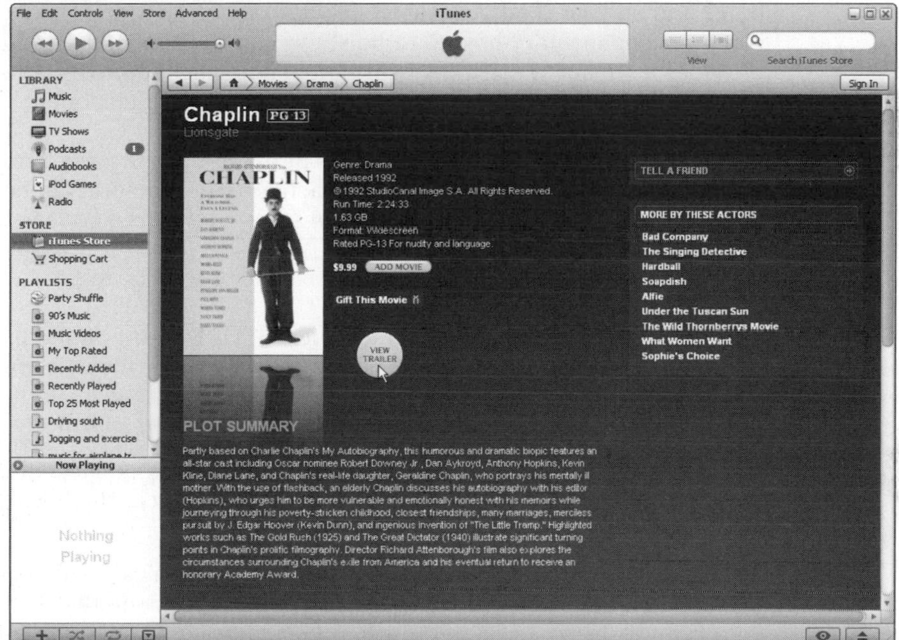

Figure 4-8: Play the movie trailer.

Audio books can be even more entertaining than movies and certainly easier to consume while driving or walking. The Audiobooks link on the iTunes Store home page takes you to the Audiobooks page. Click an advertisement, thumbnail, or title to go to the specific audio booklet page, and click the Preview button to preview the audio book. Use the Play/Pause button to pause and resume playback.

You can play content in your iTunes library while waiting for an iTunes Store page or video to download over the Internet. Double-click the iTunes Store option in the Source pane to open the iTunes Store in a separate window. With two windows, you can use the first window to play content in your library while using the second to browse the iTunes Store and purchase and download a video. The first window stops playing content when you use the second window to play a video or select a song to preview or buy.

Browsing and Subscribing to Podcasts

Podcasting is a popular method of publishing audio and video shows to the Internet, enabling people to subscribe to a feed and receive the shows automatically. Similar to a tape of a radio broadcast, you can save a podcast episode and play it back at your convenience, both in iTunes on your computer and on your iPod. A podcast episode can be anything from a single song to a commentary-hosted radio show; a podcaster, like a broadcaster, provides a stream of episodes over time. Thousands of professional and amateur radio and video shows are offered as podcast episodes.

The iTunes Podcast page on the iTunes Store lets you browse, find, preview, and subscribe to podcasts, many of which are free. You don't need an account to browse the iTunes Store and subscribe to free podcasts.

To find podcasts in the iTunes Store, do one of the following:

- **Click the Podcasts link in the iTunes STORE menu on the home page.** The iTunes Store displays the Podcast page, with advertisements for popular podcasts and a list of Top Podcasts. You can click the Top Podcasts link to see the most popular podcasts in specific categories.

  You can also get to the Podcast page by clicking Podcasts in the iTunes Source pane and then clicking Podcast Directory at the bottom of the List view.
- **Browse all podcasts in a particular category.** Click the Browse button in the lower-right corner and then select Podcasts in the iTunes Store column. Select a category from the Category column and a subcategory from the Subcategory column.
- **Search for a podcast by name or keyword.** You can type a search term into the Search iTunes Store field in the upper-right corner of the iTunes window to find any podcasts or other content items that match. You can also use the Power Search feature, described earlier in this chapter in the section, "Power searching."

After you select a podcast, the iTunes Store displays the podcast's specific page in the iTunes Store, as shown in Figure 4-9, with all available podcast episodes in the List pane. (There are three episodes in Figure 4-9 for the Rockument podcast.)

To select, play, and subscribe to a podcast, follow these steps:

1. **Choose a podcast in the iTunes Store.**

   The iTunes Store offers a description, a Subscribe button to receive new podcasts, and a link to the podcast's Web site for more information. The page also lists the most recent podcast. Some podcasters offer several podcasts in one feed. You can click the lowercase *i* icon on the far-right podcast listing margin to display separate information about the podcast.

2. **To preview the podcast, click the Play button or press the spacebar.**

   You can play a preview of any podcast in the list. iTunes plays the podcast for about 90 seconds just like a Web radio station, streaming to your computer. To jump ahead in a podcast or play the entire podcast episode, you must first subscribe to the podcast. By subscribing, you enable downloading episodes to your computer.

3. **Click the Subscribe button to subscribe to the podcast.**

   In typical Apple fashion, iTunes first displays an alert to confirm that you want to subscribe to the podcast.

4. **Click OK to confirm.**

   iTunes downloads the podcast to your computer and switches to the Podcasts selection in the Source pane. iTunes displays your newly subscribed podcast in the List pane, as shown in Figure 4-10.

Figure 4-9: Play a podcast before subscribing to it.

Figure 4-10: The subscribed podcasts appear in the Podcast List pane as they are downloaded.

5. **(Optional) Get more episodes of the podcast.**

   When you subscribe to a podcast, you get the current episode. However, each podcast can contain multiple episodes. To download previously available episodes, click the triangle next to the podcast name in the List pane (refer to Figure 4-10) to see the individual episodes, and then click the Get button next to an episode to download it. For more information about adding and deleting podcasts and podcast episodes, see Chapter 5.

6. **To play the podcast in full, select it and click the Play button.**

   You can now play the podcast just like any other song in your iTunes library. The blue dot next to a podcast means you haven't yet played it. As soon as you start listening to a podcast, the dot disappears. For more information about playing podcasts, see Chapter 6.

Anyone can create a podcast and then submit it to the iTunes Store by following Apple's published guidelines. (Click the Submit a Podcast link on the Podcast page in the iTunes Store.) In fact, the Rockument and the Flying Other Brothers music podcasts, available in the iTunes Store (and from `www.rockument.com`), are produced by this book's author. You can find out more about creating podcasts in *Podcasting For Dummies,* by Tee Morris and Evo Terra (Wiley).

You can play the podcast, incorporate it into playlists, and make copies and burn CDs as much as you like. See Chapter 5 for details on subscribing to, deleting, and updating podcasts.

Browsing and Previewing iPod Games

Got Pac-Man? How about Ms. Pac-Man? The iTunes Store offers colorful games to play on your iPod — all kinds of games, from Mini Golf and Mahjung to the classic Tetris and Cubis 2. You can even play the wildly popular Japanese game Sudoku. The games play on fifth- and sixth-generation iPods that can play videos — not in iTunes itself. However, you can see a preview of the game while browsing the iTunes Store.

To find the iPod games, click the iPod Games link in the iTunes STORE menu on the iTunes Store home page. iTunes displays the iPod Games page with thumbnail icons for each game. Click the game's icon to go to the games page. Click the Preview button on the game's page to see a preview of the game. Use the iTunes Play button, just as you would for a song, to play the game preview. At any time or after the preview plays, click the Close Preview button to return to the movie page.

Buying and Downloading Content

As you select content, you can purchase the items and download them to your computer immediately. Alternatively, you can gather your selections in a virtual shopping cart first to see your choices and decide whether to purchase them before downloading them all at once.

Depending on how you set up your account, you can buy and download the content immediately with the 1-Click option or place the items in your iTunes Store Shopping Cart temporarily, to purchase and download later. You can change your shopping method at any time.

Each time you buy content, you get an e-mail from the iTunes Store with the purchase information. It's nice to know right away what you bought.

Your decision to download each item immediately or add to a shopping cart and download later is likely based on how your computer connects to the Internet. If you have a slow connection such as a phone line, you probably want to use the shopping cart to avoid tying up the phone with each download.

Using 1-Click

Apple offers 1-Click technology in the iTunes Store so that with one click, your digital content immediately starts downloading to your computer — and the purchase is done.

With 1-Click, you click the Buy button whether the item is a song, an album, a TV show episode, or an audio book. For example, if you select a song in the List pane, click the Buy Song button in the far-right column for the song. (You might have to scroll your iTunes Store window to see the far-right column.) When you select a TV show episode, click the Buy Episode button in the far-right column. You can click the Buy Album button in an album advertisement. With 1-Click, iTunes complies immediately.

The iTunes Store displays a warning dialog to make sure that you want to buy the item, and you can then go through with it or cancel. If you click the Buy button to purchase it, the song, album, audio book, or video download automatically shows up in your iTunes library. The iTunes Store keeps track of your purchases over a 24-hour period and charges a total sum rather than for each single purchase.

1-Click seems more like two clicks. If you really want to use only one click to buy an item from iTunes, select the Don't Warn Me option in the warning dialog so that you never see it again.

Using the shopping cart

You don't have to use the 1-Click technology. Instead, you can add items to the shopping cart to delay purchasing and downloading until you're ready. With the shopping cart, the iTunes Store remembers your selections, allowing you to browse the iTunes Store at different times and add to your total without making any purchases final. You can also remove items from the cart at any time. When you're ready to buy, you can purchase and download the items in your cart in one fell swoop.

If you switch to the shopping cart method (see the following section, "Changing your iTunes Store preferences"), the Buy button changes to an Add button — as in Add Song, Add Album, Add Episode, and so on. After adding items, you can view the selections in your shopping cart by selecting the Shopping Cart option underneath the iTunes Store option in the Source pane (see Figure 4-11).

The shopping cart appears in the List view with your selections listed, and recommendations from the iTunes Store appear along the top of the window. Albums appear with a triangle next to their name, which you can click to open and see the album's songs. As you can see in Figure 4-11, albums, individual songs, music videos, TV episodes, and audio books are listed in alphabetical order by artist name (or TV show name, as in *The Colbert Report*).

Figure 4-11: View your shopping cart before purchasing the items from the iTunes Store.

When you're ready to purchase everything in your shopping cart, click the BUY NOW button in the lower-right corner of the Shopping Cart view to close the sale and download all the items at once. Alternatively, you can click the Buy (for an album) or Buy Song buttons for each item that you want to purchase.

To delete items from your shopping cart, select them and press Delete/Backspace. A warning appears asking whether you're sure that you want to remove the selected items. Click Yes to go ahead and remove the selections from your shopping cart.

You can see the list of all the items that you purchased by selecting the Purchased playlist under the iTunes Store option in the Source pane. The List view and Browse view change to show the items you purchased.

Changing your iTunes Store preferences

You can change your shopping method by choosing iTunes⇨Preferences on the Mac or by choosing Edit⇨Preferences in Windows. In the Preferences window, click the Store button. The Store Preferences window appears, as shown in Figure 4-12.

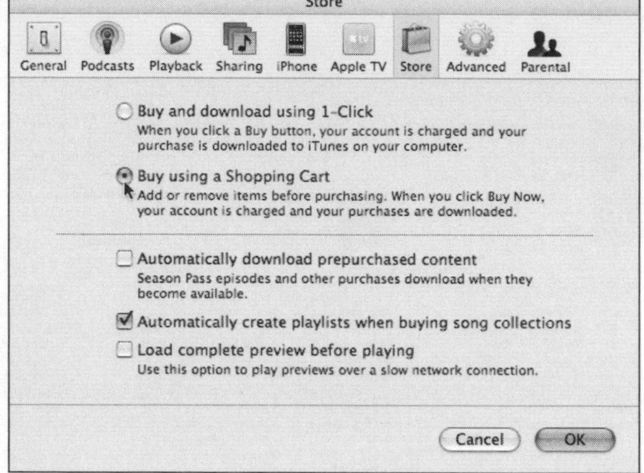

Figure 4-12: Set your iTunes Store preferences.

You can set the following features:

- Change from 1-Click to Shopping Cart or vice versa. 1-Click is the default.
- Automatically download prepurchased content, such as a Season Pass of TV show episodes. As the episodes become available, iTunes automatically downloads them.
- When you purchase a collection of songs, such as an iMix prepared by other iTunes Store visitors or a list of iTunes Essentials chosen by the iTunes Store staff, you can set iTunes to automatically assign the collection to a new playlist by selecting the Automatically Create Playlists When Buying Song Collections option. For details about using playlists, see Chapter 10.
- For better playing performance (fewer hiccups) with previews over slow Internet connections, select the Load Complete Preview before Playing option. (It's deselected by default.)

If you use more than one computer with your iTunes Store account, you can set the preferences for each computer differently and still use the same account. For example, your home computer might have a faster connection than your laptop on a remote connection, so you can set your iTunes preferences accordingly: The home computer could be set to 1-Click, and the laptop could be set to shopping cart.

Resuming interrupted downloads

All sales are final; you can't return the digital merchandise. However, the download must be successful — you have to receive it all — before the iTunes Store charges you for the purchase. If for any reason the download is interrupted or fails to complete, your order remains active until you connect to the iTunes Store again.

iTunes remembers to continue the download when you return to iTunes and connect to the Internet. If, for some reason, the download doesn't continue, choose Store➪Check for Purchases to continue the interrupted download. You can also use this command to check for any purchased music that hasn't downloaded yet.

While downloading from the iTunes Store, you can select Downloads in the Store section of the Source pane, as shown in Figure 4-13, to see the progress of your downloads, and to pause and resume (or cancel) any particular download.

For the impatient viewers, the iTunes Store lets you start watching a video or movie before it finishes downloading. Click Downloads as you're downloading and double-click the item to watch it. The download continues as you watch from the beginning.

If your computer's hard drive crashes and you lose your information, you also lose all your digital content — you have to purchase and download them again. However, you can mitigate this kind of disaster by backing up your content library (which we describe in detail in Chapter 13), including backing up video files. You can also burn your purchases to an audio CD, as we describe in Chapter 14.

Figure 4-13: Check the progress of your downloads.

Redeeming gift certificates and prepaid cards

If you're the fortunate recipient of an iTunes Store gift certificate, all you need to do is go to the iTunes Store (we mean using iTunes online, of course; there are no physical stores as of this writing) and set up a new account if you don't already have one. Recipients of gift certificates can set up new accounts without having to provide a credit card number. As a recipient of a gift, you can simply click None for the credit card option and use the gift certificate as the sole payment method.

You can receive gift certificates on paper (delivered by the postal service) or by e-mail. You can also receive a prepaid card with a fixed balance. To redeem a certificate, click the Redeem link in the Quick Links panel on the right side of the iTunes Store home page to go to the Redeem page. In the Redeem Code section of the Redeem page, type the number printed on the certificate or supplied in the e-mail, and click the Redeem button to credit your account. If you haven't signed into your account yet or you have no account, iTunes displays the sign-in dialog; for information about setting up an account, see the "Setting Up an Account" section, earlier in this chapter.

If you use Apple's Mail program or access your .Mac e-mail through the Safari Web browser, you can redeem a gift certificate that was sent by e-mail by clicking the Redeem Now button at the bottom of the e-mail message. This button launches iTunes with the iTunes Store option selected in the Source pane and displays the Redeem page with the certificate's number automatically filled in. Click the Redeem button to credit your account.

The *balance* of your gift certificate (how much you have left to spend) appears right next to your account name in the iTunes Store window and is updated as you make purchases.

Managing Your Account

Online stores record necessary information about you, such as your credit card number, your billing address, and so forth. You can change this information at any time, and you can also take advantage of iTunes Store account features, such as sending gift certificates, setting parental controls, and setting up allowance accounts.

Viewing and changing account information

Life is unpredictable. As John Lennon sang in "Beautiful Boy (Darling Boy)," "Life is what happens to you while you're busy making other plans." So if your billing address changes, or you need to switch to another credit card, or you need to change your password for any reason, you can edit your account information at any time.

To see your account information in the iTunes Store, click the Account button that shows your account name, or click the Account link in the Quick Links panel of the iTunes Store home page. iTunes displays a dialog for you to enter your account password. Then click the View Account button to see your account in the iTunes Store.

Your account page displays your Apple ID, the last four digits of the credit card that you use for the account, your billing address, your most recent purchase, and your computer authorizations. (See "Authorizing computers to play purchased music," later in this chapter.) You can click buttons to edit your account and credit card information, and also to manage *alerts* (e-mail messages sent by iTunes about new releases from artists that are listed in your purchase history). You can also manage your iMix playlists (see Chapter 10 for details on how to create and manage an iMix), and view your purchase history.

Viewing your purchase history

In the rock 'n' roll lifestyle, you might recall songs from the 1960s but not remember what you bought last week. To view your purchase history, go to your account page by clicking the Account button (top-right corner), or click the Account link in the Quick Links panel of the iTunes Store home page, and then type your password to log into your account. Click the View Account button; on your account page, click the Purchase History button.

The iTunes Store displays the items that you purchased, starting with the most recent. If you bought a lot of content, not all of the items appear on the first page. To see the details of previous purchases, click the arrow to the left of the order date. After viewing your history, click Done at the bottom of the history page to return to your account page.

Setting up allowances

Do you trust your kids with your credit card? You don't have to answer that, but you can sidestep the entire issue by gifting an *allowance account* that lets you set the amount of credit each month, from $10–$200 in increments of $10. You can change the amount of an allowance or stop it at any time. (And if these accounts are for kids, put your mind at rest by reading "Setting parental controls," later in this chapter.)

To use an allowance account, the recipient must be using iTunes version 4 or newer and live in a country where the iTunes Store is available on the Internet (such as the United States).

You can set up the allowance account yourself or define an allowance on an existing account. The recipient signs in to the account and types his or her password — no credit card required. When the recipient reaches the limit of the allowance, that account can't buy anything else until the following month. The iTunes Store saves any unused balance until the next iTunes Store purchase.

To set up an allowance account, click the Buy iTunes Gifts link in the Quick Links panel on the right side of the iTunes Store home page. Scroll the resulting Buy iTunes Gifts page to the bottom to find and click the Set up allowance now link in the Allowances section. iTunes takes you to the Allowance Setup page, where you can enter your name, your recipient's name, the monthly allowance amount (using the Monthly Allowance pop-up menu), and your recipient's Apple ID and password.

Click Continue to proceed with the account setup process, and then follow the instructions to finish setting up the account.

To stop an allowance or change the amount of an allowance account, go to your account page by clicking the Account button (top-right corner), or click the Account link in the Quick Links panel of the iTunes Store home page, and then type your password to log into your account. Click the View Account button and scroll the account page until you see the Setup Allowance button; click this button to go to the Allowance page.

Sending gift certificates

A song is a gift that keeps on giving every time the recipient plays the song. A gift of a music video or TV show might commemorate a special occasion. Besides, you can't go wrong giving an iTunes Store gift certificate to that special person who has everything. You can send a certificate as an e-mail message or print the certificate yourself on your own printer.

Before sending a gift certificate, first make sure that the recipient can run iTunes 4 or newer versions. Also, he or she must be able to run iTunes 6 or newer versions for video. (You might want to subtly suggest to the future recipient in an e-mail that it's time to download the newest version of iTunes, just to find out whether he or she has the requisite system configuration; see Chapter 1.)

To buy a gift certificate to send to someone, click the Buy iTunes Gifts link in the Quick Links panel on the right side of the iTunes Store home page. Scroll the resulting Buy iTunes Gifts page to the Printable Gift Certificates or Email Gift Certificates sections. Click the Buy Now link in either section to start the process of buying a gift certificate. Follow the instructions to enter your name, the recipient's name, the recipient's e-mail or snail mail address (for printed certificates), the amount of the gift, and a personal message.

Setting parental controls

Art may imitate life, but there are times when you might not want life to imitate art — or in this case, your kids' lives to be exposed to entertainment you deem inappropriate. iTunes not only provides a Parental Advisory Label next to explicit items in the online store but also lets you restrict explicit content from displaying in the iTunes Store. You can also disable podcasts, radio content, the iTunes Store itself, and shared music so that these items don't appear in the Source pane.

To set parental controls, choose iTunes⇨Preferences on the Mac or Edit⇨Preferences in Windows. In the Preferences window that appears, click the Parental tab to see the Parental Control preferences.

You can click the options to disable podcasts, radio stations, the iTunes Store, and shared libraries so that they sources of content don't appear in the iTunes Source pane.

To restrict content itself, you can choose a rating system for a specific country in the Ratings For pop-up menu, and then click options to restrict movies and TV shows using the chosen country's rating levels available in pop-up menus. You can also click the option to restrict all explicit content.

After selecting options, click the Lock icon to prevent further changes. iTunes displays a dialog requiring you to type the administrator password for your computer system. Click OK after typing the password, and then click OK again to close iTunes preferences so that the changes take effect.

To make changes later, click the Lock icon to unlock the preferences, and type this administrator password again.

Authorizing computers to play purchased music

The computer that you use to set up your account is automatically authorized by Apple to play the content you buy from the iTunes Store. Fortunately, the content isn't locked to that computer. You can copy your purchased songs, audio books, podcasts, and videos to other computers and play them with iTunes. When you first play them on the other computers, iTunes asks for your iTunes Store account ID and password to authorize that computer. You can have up to five computers authorized at any one time. You can also authorize a computer at any time by choosing Store⇨Authorize Computer.

Purchased songs, audio books, and videos need to be downloaded or copied to one of your authorized computers before you can copy them from the added computer to an iPod using iTunes.

If you want to delete one computer and add another computer, you can remove the authorization from a computer by choosing Store⇨Deauthorize Computer on that computer. If you need to deauthorize a computer that no longer works, you can contact Apple through its iTunes Store support page (`www.apple.com/support/itunes/store/authorization`).

Remember to deauthorize your computer before you upgrade it, sell it, or give it away. Also, we recommend that you deauthorize your computer before upgrading your RAM, hard drive, or other system components. Otherwise, the upgraded system might count as another authorized computer. If you've reached five authorizations due to system upgrades or failed computers, you can reset your authorization count by clicking Deauthorize All on the Account Information screen. You can do this only once per year. The Deauthorize All button appears only if you have five authorized computers and you haven't used the option in the last 12 months.

Chapter 5

Bringing Content into iTunes

In This Chapter

- Setting your music importing preferences
- Ripping music from CDs and adding music files
- Adding audio books and video files to your library
- Subscribing to podcasts on Web sites

Three excellent reasons to bring your music CDs into iTunes, or to download media files from the iTunes Store into iTunes, are

- To preserve the content forever
- To play the content easily from your computer (without having to fumble with discs)
- To take the content in your iPod with you

In this chapter, we show you how to store content in your iTunes library. A song or video in digital format can be kept in that format in a file on any number of digital media storage devices. Even if your CDs, DVDs, and hard drive fail, your backup copy (assuming that you made a backup copy on a safety CD or hard drive) is still as perfect as the original digital file. You may make any number of digital copies with no technical limitations on playing the copies except those imposed by the iTunes Store for content that you purchase.

While you add more content, your iTunes library becomes your entertainment center. With it, you can find any item you want to play faster than you can open a CD jewel case, as we show in Chapter 8. Your iTunes library also manages your content and makes it easy to transfer some, or all of it, to your iPod (see Chapter 12).

Adding Music

Bringing music tracks from a CD into iTunes is *ripping* a CD. We're not sure why it's called that, but Apple certainly took the term to a new level with an ad campaign for Macs that featured the slogan *Rip, Mix, Burn.* Burning a mix CD was the hip thing to do a few years ago. With iTunes, you can still rip and mix, but if you have an iPod, you no longer need to burn CDs to play your music wherever you go.

Ripping, in technical terms, is extracting the song's digital information from an audio CD. In common terms, ripping also includes compressing the song's digital information and encoding it in a particular sound file format. The ripping process is straightforward, but the import settings that you choose affect sound quality, hard drive space (and iPod space), and compatibility with other types of players and computers.

Setting the importing preferences

Although importing music from an audio CD takes a lot less time than playing the CD, it still takes time. To minimize that time, you want your import settings to be correct before starting. To do this

1. **Choose iTunes⇨Preferences–>Advanced on a Mac or Edit⇨Preferences⇨Advanced in Windows.**

   The iTunes Preferences dialog, with the Advanced tab showing, opens.

2. **Click the Importing tab.**

   The Importing preferences appear, as shown in Figure 5-1.

The Importing preferences tab offers the following options, which you set before ripping a CD:

- **On CD Insert:** From this menu, choose from the following to take the appropriate action immediately after you insert an audio CD:
  - *Show the CD:* iTunes does nothing else.
  - *Playing:* See Chapter 3 for details on playing CDs.
  - *Ask to Import CD:* iTunes displays a dialog asking whether you want to import the CD.
  - *Import CD:* iTunes uses the current importing preferences and automatically imports the CD. Don't use this setting unless you're sure that you've set your preferences to your liking for automatic importing.

   - *Import CD and Eject.* iTunes automatically imports and then ejects the CD, making way for the next one. This option is useful for importing a batch of CDs. Don't use this setting unless you're sure that you've set your preferences to your liking for automatic importing.

- **Import Using:** Set this pop-up menu to one of the encoders. For more information that can help you choose the right encoder for your music, see Chapter 18.
- **Setting:** Set this pop-up menu to High Quality or better for most music. You can change this setting to get better quality or use hard drive space more efficiently, as we describe in Chapter 19.
- **Play Songs While Importing or Converting:** Select this check box to play the songs at the same time that you start ripping them. This option slows down the speed of importing, but hey — you get to listen to the music right away.
- **Automatically Retrieve CD Track Names from Internet:** iTunes automatically grabs the song titles, artist names, album titles, and so forth directly from the Internet database of songs, as we describe in Chapter 9. We recommend that you select this option (assuming that you're connected to the Internet, that is).

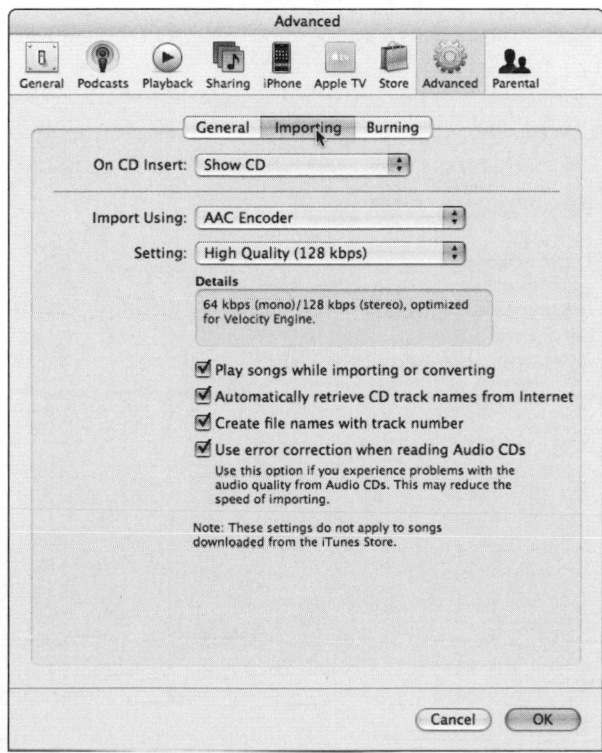

Figure 5-1: Set your importing preferences for ripping CDs.

- **Create Filenames with Track Number:** Select this check box to include the track number in the filenames created by iTunes for the songs that you rip. Including the track number makes it easier to find tracks on an iPod when using a car's audio controls — that is, if you've connected your iPod to a car stereo system, which Chapter 20 covers.
- **Use Error Correction When Reading Audio CDs:** Although you'll reduce importing speed, select this check box to use error correction if you have problems with audio quality or if the CD skips. (Not every skipping CD can be imported even with error correction, but it might help.)
- **The Import Using pop-up menu**: This menu gives you the opportunity to set the type of encoding, and this choice is perhaps the most important.
- **The Setting pop-up menu:** This offers different settings depending on your choice of encoder. For example, in Figure 5-1, we chose the AAC Encoder with the High Quality setting. In Figure 5-2, we switched to the MP3 Encoder in the Import Using pop-up menu, and we're in the process of choosing Higher Quality from the Setting pop-up menu.

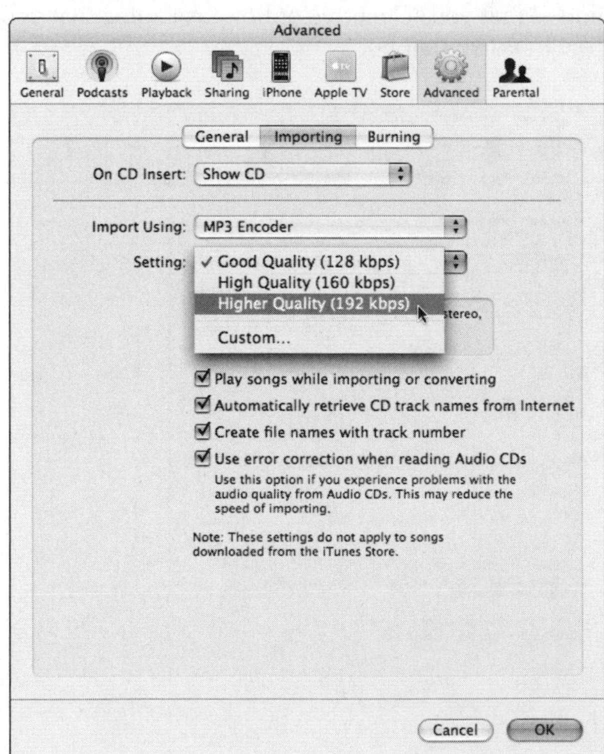

Figure 5-2: Set the quality setting for the encoder you chose for importing.

Encoding is a complicated subject that requires a whole chapter to explain. (In fact, Chapter 18 provides an in-depth look if you want to know more.) For a quick and pain-free ripping session, choose from among the following encoders in the Import Using pop-up menu based on how you plan to use your iTunes library:

- **AAC Encoder:** We recommend AAC for all uses. (However, AIFF or WAV is better if you plan to burn another CD with the songs you ripped and not use them in your iPod.) Choose the High Quality option from the Setting pop-up menu.

  You can convert a song that's been ripped in AIFF, Apple Lossless, or WAV to AAC or MP3. However, ripping a CD with one encoder might be more convenient. After that, you can rip it again with a different encoder. For example, you might import *Sgt. Pepper's Lonely Hearts Club Band* with the AAC encoder for use in your Mac and iPod and then import it again with the AIFF encoder. You might call the album Sgt. Pepper-2, for example, in order to burn songs onto a CD. After burning the CD, you can delete Sgt. Pepper-2 to re-claim the hard drive space.

- **AIFF Encoder:** Use AIFF if you plan to burn the song to an audio CD using a Mac (use WAV for Windows). AIFF offers the highest possible quality, but it takes up a lot of space (about 10MB per minute). Choose the Automatic option from the Setting pop-up menu for best results, or consult Chapter 19 for details on setting custom options. Don't use AIFF format for songs that you intend to transfer to your iPod; convert them first to AAC or MP3.

- **Apple Lossless Encoder:** Use the Apple Lossless encoder for songs that you intend to burn onto audio CDs as well as for playing on iPods. The files are just small enough (about 60–70 percent of the size of the AIFF versions) that they don't hiccup on playback.

- **MP3 Encoder:** Use the MP3 format for songs that you intend to burn on MP3 CDs or that you intend to use with MP3 players or your iPod — it's universally supported. If you use MP3, we recommend choosing the Higher Quality option from the Setting pop-up menu.

- **WAV Encoder:** WAV is the high-quality sound format that's used on PCs (like AIFF), but it also takes up a lot of space (about 10MB per minute). Use WAV if you plan on burning the song to an audio CD or using WAV with PCs. Choose the Automatic option from the Setting pop-up menu for best results, or consult Chapter 19 for details on setting custom options. Don't use WAV for songs that you intend to transfer to your iPod. Convert them first to AAC or MP3, as we describe in Chapter 19.

Don't fall into the gaps

Some CDs — particularly live concert albums, classical albums, rock operas (such as The Who's *Tommy*), and theme albums (such as *Sgt. Pepper's Lonely Hearts Club Band* by The Beatles) — are meant to be played straight through, with no fading between the songs. Although you can cross-fade between songs automatically in iTunes, you can't on your iPod.

Fortunately, you can turn on the Gapless Album option for multiple songs such as Side 1 of an album or an entire album. With the Gapless Album option set in iTunes, songs play seamlessly one to the next. You can also play these songs seamlessly on fifth-generation iPods (and second-generation iPod nanos) that have the latest software update.

To turn on the Gapless Album option for an entire CD before importing it, follow these steps:

1. **Select the CD in the Source pane.**

   The CD title appears in the Source pane under Devices. Click the title to select it.

2. **Choose File➪Get Info.**

   The CD Info dialog opens, as shown in Figure 5-3.

3. **Select the check box next to the Gapless Album option and then click OK.**

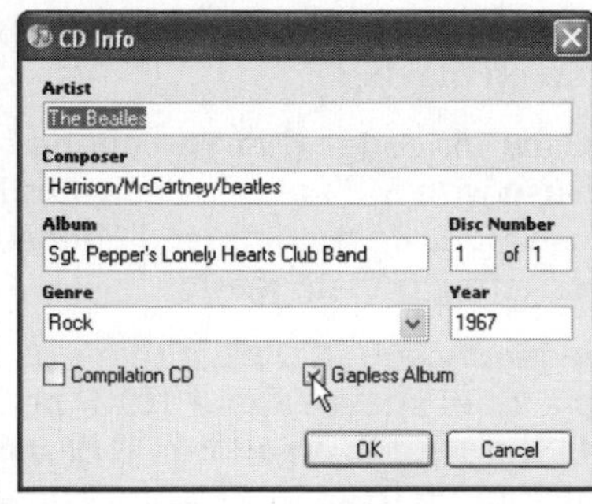

Figure 5-3: Select the Gapless Album option for an entire album.

To turn on the Gapless Album option for multiple songs on the CD but not the entire CD, follow these steps:

1. **Select the songs.**

   From the album, select the songs that you want to play continuously.

2. **Choose File⇨Get Info and then click Yes in the warning dialog about editing multiple items.**

   The Multiple Item Information dialog opens, as shown in Figure 5-4.

3. **Choose Yes from the Gapless Album pop-up menu.**

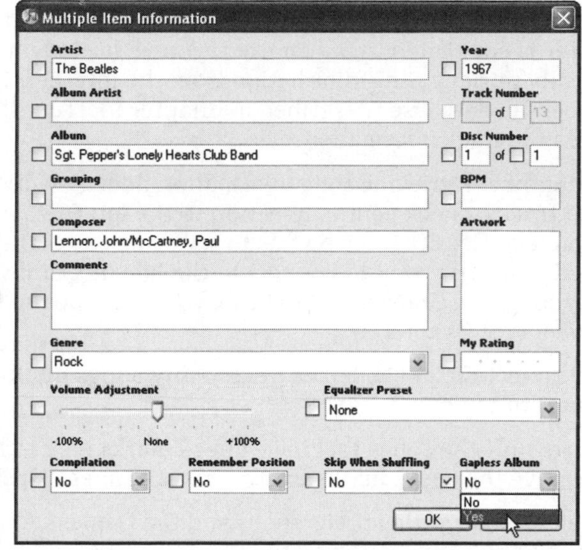

Figure 5-4: Select the Gapless Album option for multiple tracks.

To turn on the Gapless Album option for one song at a time, click the song and choose File⇨Get Info. Click the Options tab and then select the Part of a Gapless Album option for each song.

What happens if you turn on Crossfade Playback for playing songs in iTunes, as we describe in Chapter 6, but you *don't* want to cross-fade between specific songs on an album that has no gaps? You don't have to keep turning Crossfade Playback on and off: Simply deselect the Gapless Album option for those songs.

For older iPod models, or as an alternative to using the Gapless Album option, you can use the Join Tracks option when ripping a CD to join the tracks in your iTunes library so that they play seamlessly on an iPod. To join tracks, select the tracks and choose Advanced⇨Join CD Tracks. You can join tracks only when ripping a CD, not afterward.

To select multiple songs, click the first one, press ⌘ on a Mac or Ctrl in Windows, and click each subsequent song. To select several consecutive songs, click the first one, hold down the Shift key, and then click the last one.

Ripping music from CDs

After checking your importing preferences to be sure that your settings are correct, you're ready to rip. To rip a CD, follow these steps:

1. **Insert an audio CD.**

   The songs appear in the List pane as generic, unnamed tracks at first. If your computer is connected to the Internet, you've turned on the option to automatically retrieve song information from the Internet, and the CD is in the Gracenote database (described in Chapter 9), iTunes automatically retrieves the track information.

   If the first attempt at retrieving song information doesn't work and you see unnamed tracks, check your connection to the Internet and then choose Advanced⇨Get CD Track Names to try again to get the track information. If you don't want to connect to the Internet or if your CD isn't recognized by the Gracenote database, you can type the track information yourself (see Chapter 9).

2. **(Optional) Deselect the check boxes next to any songs on the CD that you don't want to import.**

   iTunes imports only the songs that have check marks next to them; when you remove the check mark next to a song, iTunes skips that song.

   Be sure to set your importing preferences and the Gapless Album option to your liking before actually ripping the CD.

3. **Click the Import button.**

   The Import button is at the bottom-right corner of the iTunes window. The status display shows the progress of the operation. To cancel, click the small *x* next to the progress bar in the status display.

   iTunes plays the songs while it imports them if you previously set the option in the importing preferences to play them while importing. You can click the Pause button to stop playback, but the importing continues. If you don't want to listen to the songs while they import, deselect the Play Songs While Importing check box in the iTunes Preferences dialog. (See the earlier section, "Setting the importing preferences.")

   iTunes displays an orange, animated waveform icon next to the song that it's importing. When iTunes finishes importing each song, it displays a check mark next to the song, as shown in Figure 5-5. (On a color monitor, the check mark is green.) iTunes chimes when it finishes the import list.

4. **When all the songs are imported, eject the CD by clicking the Eject button at the lower-right corner of the iTunes window.**

   You can also choose Controls⇨Eject Disc to eject the disc, or click the Eject icon next to the disc name in the Source pane.

Figure 5-5: iTunes shows a check mark to indicate it's done ripping the song.

Adding music files

The quality of the music that you hear depends initially on the quality of the source. Web sites and services offering music files vary widely. Some sites provide high-quality, legally derived songs that you can download, and some sites provide only streaming audio that you can play — but not save — on your hard drive or on a CD (such as a Web radio station).

The allegedly illegal file-sharing services offering MP3 files might vary in quality. Unauthorized copies of songs might be saved in a lower-quality format to save space and download time, so beware of less-than-high-quality knockoffs.

You can download the music file or copy it from another computer to your hard drive. After you save or copy an MP3 file — or, for that matter, an AIFF or WAV file — on your hard drive, you can simply drag it into the iTunes window to bring it into your library. If you drag a folder or disk icon, all the audio files that it contains are added to your iTunes library. You can also choose File⇨Add to Library as an alternative to dragging.

When you add a song to your iTunes library, a copy is placed inside the iTunes Music folder: that is, as long as you have your iTunes preferences set for Copy Files to iTunes Music Folder When Adding to Library. (This is the default setting, which you can find in the General pane of the Advanced tab of the iTunes Preferences dialog.) See Chapter 13 for details on storing music in your iTunes Music folder.

If you have song files in another folder or another hard drive, and you want to add them to the iTunes library without copying the files to the iTunes Music folder, you can copy a link to the original files without copying the files. To copy only links to song files and not copy the actual files when you add songs, you can turn off the default copy files option by doing the following:

1. **Choose iTunes⇨Preferences (Mac) or Edit⇨Preferences (Windows).**
2. **Click the Advanced tab in the iTunes Preferences dialog.**
3. **Click the General tab under the Advanced tab.**
4. **Turn off the Copy Files to iTunes Music Folder When Adding to Library setting.**

You can check out the contents of your music folder by using the Finder on a Mac or Windows Explorer on a Windows PC. On the Mac, the iTunes Music folder lives in the iTunes folder inside the Music folder in your Home folder. The path to this folder is *`your home folder`*`/Music/iTunes/iTunes Music`. In Windows, the iTunes Music folder resides in the iTunes folder inside the My Music folder of the My Documents folder in your user folder. The path to this folder is *`Your User folder`*`\My Documents\My Music\iTunes\iTunes Music`. These are the default locations; you can change the default folder by following these steps:

1. **Choose iTunes⇨Preferences on a Mac or Edit⇨Preferences in Windows.**
2. **Click the Advanced tab in the iTunes Preferences dialog.**
3. **Click the General tab under the Advanced tab.**
4. **Choose a new location for the music folder.**

When you bring a song file into iTunes, the song is copied into a new file in the iTunes library without changing or deleting the original file. You can then convert the song to another format. For example, you can convert an AIFF file to an MP3 file while leaving the original intact. Find out about converting your songs to a different format in Chapter 19.

MP3 CDs are easy to add because they're essentially data CDs. Simply insert them into your CD-ROM drive, open the CD in the Finder, and drag and drop the MP3 song files into the iTunes window. Downloaded song files are even easier — just drag and drop the files into iTunes. If you drag a folder or CD icon, all the audio files it contains are added to your iTunes library.

Visit the companion Web site to find out how to bring any sound into iTunes, even music from scratchy vinyl records or sound effects recorded through a microphone. You might want to import unusual sounds or digitize and preserve rare music that can't be found anywhere else.

How do you get stuff like that into iTunes? On a Mac, you can use GarageBand, which is part of the iLife suite (available from the Apple Store and preinstalled on all new Macs), or use a sound-editing program such as CD Spin Doctor (about $40) from Roxio (www.roxio.com), or Sound Studio 3 (about $80) from Freeverse (www.freeverse.com/soundstudio). These programs typically record from any analog source device, such as a tape player or even a turntable. Sound Studio 3 lets you record and digitize directly to your hard drive on a Mac running OS X. CD Spin Doctor for Mac OS X provides special features for recording music from vinyl records. Many commercial applications are available to choose from that work with Windows, including RecordNow 9 Music Lab Premier (about $50) from Roxio.

You may also use MusicMatch Jukebox to record sound through a PC's line-in connection. If you're using MusicMatch, visit this book's companion Web site.

AIFF- or WAV-encoded sound files occupy too much space in your music library and on your iPod. Voice recordings and sound effects tend to be low-fidelity and typically don't sound any better in AIFF or WAV format than they do in formats that save hard drive space. Also, sound effects and voice recordings are typically mono instead of stereo. You can save hard drive and iPod space and still have quality recordings by converting these files to MP3 or AAC formats, changing them from stereo to mono in the process, and leaving the original versions intact. We describe converting songs in Chapter 19.

Adding Audio Books

Do you like to listen to audio books and spoken magazine and newspaper articles? Not only can you bring these files into iTunes, but you can also transfer them to an iPod and take them on the road, which is much more convenient than taking cassettes or CDs.

Audible is a leading provider of downloadable, spoken audio files. Audible lets you authorize computers to play the audio files — just like the iTunes Store; see Chapter 4. Audible does require that you purchase the files, and content from Audible is also licensed by Apple to be included in the iTunes Store. Audible content includes magazines and radio programs as well as books.

To import Audible files, follow these steps:

1. **Go to `www.audible.com`.**

   Set up an account if you don't already have one.
2. **Select and download an Audible audio file.**

   Files that end with `.aa` are Audible files.

3. **Drag the Audible file to the iTunes window.**

   If this is the first time that you've added an Audible file, iTunes asks for your account information. You enter this information once for each computer that you use with your Audible account.

To disable an Audible account, open iTunes on the computer that you no longer want to use with the account, and choose Advanced⇨Deauthorize Audible Account. In the Deauthorize Audible Account dialog that appears, enter the user name and password for the account, and then click OK.

You need to be online to authorize a computer or to remove the authorization from that computer.

Adding Podcasts

You can add podcasts to your iTunes library by subscribing to them in the iTunes Store (as we describe in Chapter 4) or by subscribing to them directly from Web sites that host them. Similar to a tape of a radio broadcast, you can save and play a podcast at your convenience — both in iTunes on your computer and on your iPod.

A *podcast* can be anything from a single song or video to a radio or TV show. Audio podcasts are saved in the MP3 format and may be used with any media player, device, or application that supports MP3, including your iPod. Video podcasts are saved in the QuickTime (`.mov`) format or the Moving Pictures Expert Group (MPEG-4) formats, including the standard `.mp4` format and the Apple TV `.m4v` format, which can be used with iPods (that play video), Apple TV, and many other video players.

The podcast producer uses Real Simple Syndication (RSS) technology — the same technology used to distribute blogs and news feeds across the Internet — to publish the podcast. RSS feeds are typically linked to an RSS or an eXtensible Markup Language (XML; the language of RSS) button. With a feed reader, aggregator application, or browser plug-in, you can automatically check RSS-enabled Web pages and display updated stories and podcasts. RSS version 2, the most popular version for podcasting, is supported directly by some Web browsers, including Apple's Safari for Mac OS X.

With iTunes, you can play a podcast, incorporate it into playlists, make copies, and burn it onto CD as much as you like. If you don't like the podcast, simply delete it from your iTunes library and update your iPod to delete it from your iPod.

Subscribing to podcasts

The Podcasts section of the iTunes Store offers access to thousands of podcasts, but more than a million podcasts exist, many of which are available only by visiting their Web sites. You can subscribe to podcasts directly from iTunes without ever visiting the iTunes Store. However, the store makes it easy to subscribe to the podcasts, so check there first. Turn to Chapter 4 to see how to subscribe to podcasts in the iTunes Store.

By *subscribing,* we mean simply listing the podcast in your iTunes Podcasts pane so that new episodes are downloaded automatically. It's like a magazine subscription that's updated with a new issue every month or so. You don't have to register or fill out any form. You don't have to provide an e-mail address or any other information. Your copy of iTunes automatically finds new podcast episodes and downloads them to your computer.

The easiest way to subscribe to a podcast is through the iTunes Store. If you can't find a podcast in the store and you know how to find its Web site, use your browser and then go to that Web site. To subscribe to a podcast on a Web page, follow these steps:

1. **In your browser, Control-click (Mac) or right-click (Windows) the podcast's RSS2 link on the Web page.**

   Look for the RSS version 2 link on the Web page. Many sites use an icon, as shown in Figure 5-6.

2. **Copy the podcast's RSS2 link.**

   - *Safari:* Choose Copy Link.
   - *Firefox or Internet Explorer:* Choose Copy Link Location.

   When you paste it, the link should look something like

   ```
   http://www.rockument.com/blog/?feed=RSS2
   ```

3. **In iTunes, choose Advanced⇨Subscribe to Podcast.**

   The Subscribe to Podcast dialog opens, as shown in Figure 5-7.

4. **Paste the RSS2 link by choosing Edit⇨Paste and then click OK.**

   As an alternative, you can also press ⌘-V on a Mac or Ctrl-V in Windows.

   iTunes downloads the podcast to your computer and switches to the Podcasts selection in the Source pane.

5. **Click the *i* icon to see information about the podcast.**

   You can click the *i* icon on the far-right podcast listing margin, as shown in Figure 5-8, to display separate information about the podcast's newest episode.

Figure 5-6: Browse a Web page and copy the RSS2 link.

Figure 5-7: Paste the RSS2 link into the Subscribe to Podcast dialog.

6. **Select the podcast and then click the Play button.**

   You can now play the podcast just like a song or video in your iTunes library. You can use the iTunes playback controls to fast-forward, rewind, or play the podcast from any point. The blue dot next to a podcast means you haven't played it yet. As soon as you start listening to or watching a podcast, the dot disappears.

Podcasts don't show up in Party Shuffle unless you drag them into the Party Shuffle playlist; see Chapter 6.

If the podcaster embedded a photo in an audio podcast file or included a link to a video from the file, the photo or video content appears in the Artwork pane.

Figure 5-8: Display information about the podcast's current episode.

Updating podcasts

Many podcast feeds provide new material on a regular schedule. iTunes can check these feeds automatically and update your library with new podcast episodes. You can, for example, schedule iTunes to check for new podcast episodes — such as news, weather, traffic reports, and morning talk shows — before you wake up and automatically update your iPod. When you get up, you have new podcast episodes to listen to in your iPod.

To check for updates manually, select Podcasts in the Source pane and then click the Refresh button in the lower-right corner of the Podcasts pane. All subscribed podcast feeds are updated immediately when you click Refresh, and iTunes downloads the most recent (or all) episodes, depending on how you set your podcasts preferences to schedule podcast updates.

Scheduling podcast updates

To set your podcast preferences so iTunes can check for new podcasts automatically, choose iTunes➪Preferences on a Mac or Edit➪Preferences in Windows. In the iTunes Preferences dialog, click the Podcasts tab to display the podcast preferences, as shown in Figure 5-9.

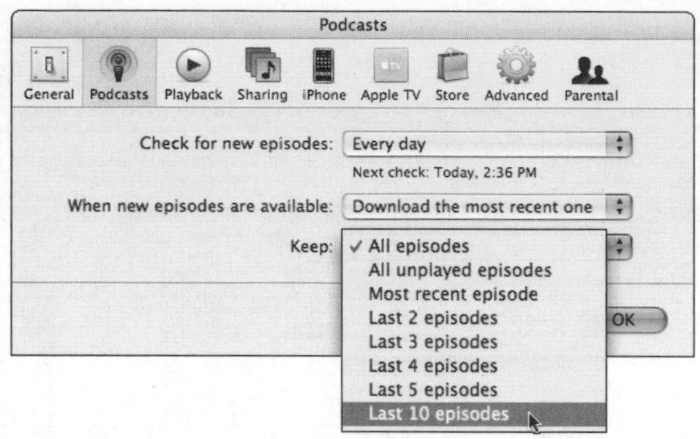

Figure 5-9: Set your podcast preferences to automatically check for new updates.

You can schedule your podcasts with these settings:

- **Check for New Episodes:** Choose to check for podcasts every hour, day, week, or manually — whenever you want.
- **When New Episodes Are Available:** You can download the most recent one (useful for news podcasts), download all episodes (useful for podcasts you might want to keep), or nothing so that you can use the Refresh button to update manually as you need.
- **Keep:** Choose to keep all episodes, all unplayed episodes, the most recent episodes, or previous episodes.

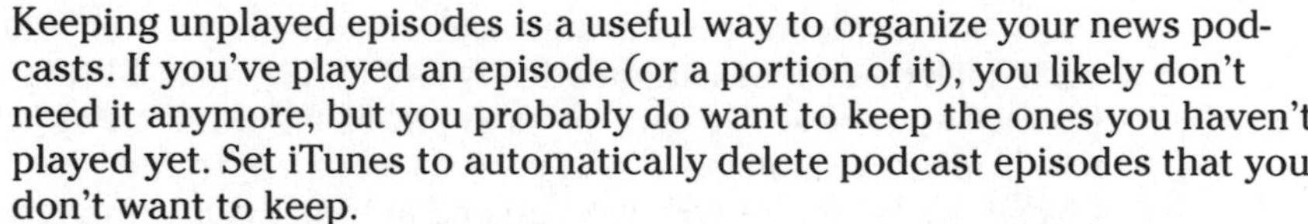

Keeping unplayed episodes is a useful way to organize your news podcasts. If you've played an episode (or a portion of it), you likely don't need it anymore, but you probably do want to keep the ones you haven't played yet. Set iTunes to automatically delete podcast episodes that you don't want to keep.

If you copy podcasts automatically during an update of your iPod, as we describe in Chapter 12, don't set the Keep All Unplayed Episodes option in iTunes. This is why: If you listen to part of a podcast episode on your iPod and then update your iPod, the podcast episode disappears from iTunes (because it is no longer unplayed). But don't worry; the episodes are still out there. You can always recover one by choosing to download all episodes on the Podcasts tab of the iTunes Preferences dialog.

Adding Videos

Besides purchasing and downloading videos from the iTunes Store, as we describe in Chapter 4, you can also download videos from the Internet or copy them from other computers and bring them into iTunes to use with your video-enabled iPod.

You can watch QuickTime and MPEG-4 movies (files that end in `.mov`, `.m4v`, or `.mp4`) in iTunes and use them in a video-enabled iPod and with Apple TV. *QuickTime,* the Apple digital video file format, is installed on every Mac. It's also installed on PCs along with the Windows version of iTunes. QuickTime is used extensively in the digital video production world for making DVDs and movies for the Web. Music videos, movie trailers, and other videos you can buy on the iTunes Store are in the QuickTime format. MPEG-4 is a standard format for digital video that works on just about any computer that plays video.

You can drag the video into iTunes just like a song file. Drag each video file from the Mac Finder or Windows Desktop to the library, directly to a playlist in the iTunes Source pane, or to the Album view on the right side of the iTunes window, as shown in Figure 5-10.

The video files that you drag into iTunes, along with the movies you purchase from the iTunes Store, display in the Movies section of your iTunes library — click Movies in the Source pane (refer to Figure 5-10).

Video files are organized in folders and stored in the music library on your hard drive just like song files. You can find the video file's location on your hard drive and its type by choosing File⇨Get Info.

You can create your own QuickTime or MPEG-4 video files with a suitable video-editing application, such as iMovie for the Mac (part of the iLife software suite that includes iTunes), or Apple QuickTime Pro for Windows, available from the Apple Store.

Figure 5-10: Bring a video file into iTunes.

Chapter 6

Playing Content in iTunes

In This Chapter

- Adjusting your computer volume
- Playing songs on your stereo through a wireless AirTunes connection
- Playing songs, podcasts, and audio books in iTunes
- Playing videos in iTunes

If you like to entertain folks by spinning tunes and playing videos at home or at parties, iTunes could easily become your media jockey console. Imagine how much music you could have at your fingertips with an iTunes library that can grow as large as your hard drive. You can fit more than 20,000 songs, or 64 days of nonstop music, in about 100GB of hard drive space. When we last checked the Apple store, you could buy a 2 terabyte (TB) external drive for either Mac or PC that would probably hold enough music to run a radio station. But that's not all: You can also manage your videos and favorite TV shows and play them in full-screen mode on your computer running iTunes.

Your computer is already a mean multimedia machine with the capability to mix sounds, photos, and videos. You can play music through your computer's built-in speakers or through headphones, but you'll get better results with high-quality external speakers. You can even connect your home computer to an excellent stereo for high-quality sound. The same is true for video: You can use iTunes to play video on your computer's display, or you can send it to a larger television or display monitor — even a video projector — to get a bigger picture.

And if you've integrated Apple TV with your home stereo and television, you can use iTunes to feed music to Apple TV, which has its own hard drive. See Chapter 7 for details on using Apple TV.

Changing the Computer's Output Volume

You can control the volume and other characteristics of the sound coming from your computer's speakers, headphones, or external speakers. Even if you connect your computer to a stereo amplifier with its own volume and equalizer controls, it's best to get the volume correct at the source — your computer and iTunes — and then adjust the output volume as you please on your stereo or external speaker unit.

You control the volume by using your computer system's audio controls. iTunes also controls the volume, but that control is within the limits of the computer's volume setting. For example, if you set your computer's volume to half and set iTunes volume to full, you get half volume because the computer limits the volume to half. If you set your computer volume at half and also reduce the iTunes volume to half, you actually get *one-quarter* volume — half the computer's setting. After the sound leaves your computer, you can adjust it further with the volume controls of your stereo system or external speakers.

The appropriate volume depends entirely on your preferences for hearing music, audio books, or video soundtracks. In general, though, the maximum level of output from your computer is preferable when connecting to a stereo system or speakers with volume controls. After setting your computer to the maximum volume, adjust the iTunes volume or your stereo or speaker volume (or both) to get the best sound. When using the computer's speakers or headphones, the computer's volume and the iTunes volume are the only volume controls that you have, so after adjusting the volume on your computer to the maximum level (or lower if you prefer), adjust the iTunes volume.

Adjusting the sound on a Mac

The Mac was built for sound from the very start. Making and playing music has been part of the Mac culture since the day that Steve Jobs introduced an audience to the original Mac with sound coming from its small speaker. (It played synthesized speech and simple tones, but it was the first personal computer with built-in sound.)

Today's Mac comes with built-in or external speakers and at least one headphone/line-out connection that you can use to connect external speakers or a stereo system. Mac OS X lets you configure output speakers and control levels for stereo speakers and multichannel audio devices.

If you use external speakers, headphones, or a stereo system, make sure that you connect these devices properly before adjusting the volume.

To adjust the volume on your Mac, follow these steps:

1. **Choose System Preferences from the Apple menu or the Dock and then click the Sound icon.**

   Otherwise, press Option and a volume control key simultaneously as a shortcut. You can have iTunes open and playing music while you do this.

2. **In the Sound preferences window that opens, click Output and select the sound output device.**

   If you have headphones or external speakers attached to the headphones connection on your Mac, a Headphones option appears in the list of sound output devices, as shown in Figure 6-1; if not, an External Speakers or Internal Speakers option appears.

3. **Adjust the volume.**

   You can do any of the following:

   - Drag the slider to adjust the volume while you listen to music.
   - Select the Mute check box to silence your Mac.
   - Drag the Balance slider to put more music in the left or right channels.

4. **Close the Preferences window. Choose System Preferences⇨Quit System Preferences, click the red button in the upper-left corner of the window, or press ⌘-Q.**

   The Sound preferences window isn't like a dialog: When you change settings, you can hear the effect immediately without having to click OK. (There isn't an OK button, anyway.)

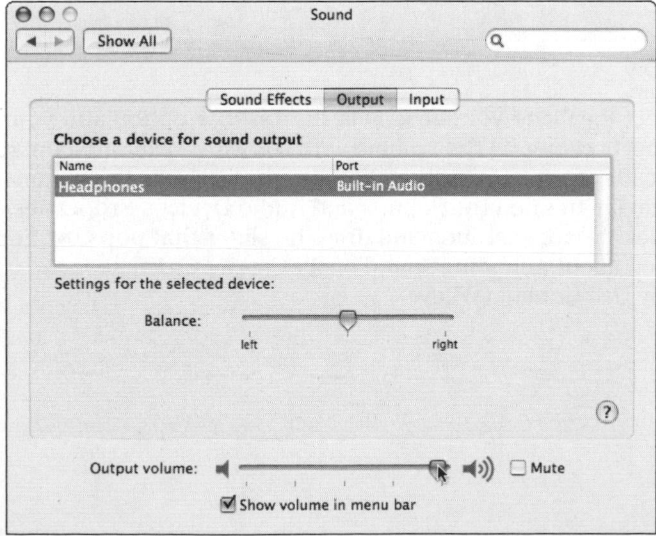

Figure 6-1: Adjust the sound output volume on a Mac PowerBook with headphones attached.

Adjusting the sound in Windows

Windows XP, Windows Vista, and Windows 2000 let you configure output speakers and control levels for stereo speakers and multichannel audio devices.

Use the Sounds and Audio Devices Properties dialog to change the volume. To open this window, choose Start⇨Control Panel, click the Sounds and Audio Devices icon, and then click the Volume tab.

As shown in Figure 6-2, the Sounds and Audio Devices Properties dialog offers the Device Volume slider, which you drag to set the volume. You can also silence your PC by selecting the Mute check box.

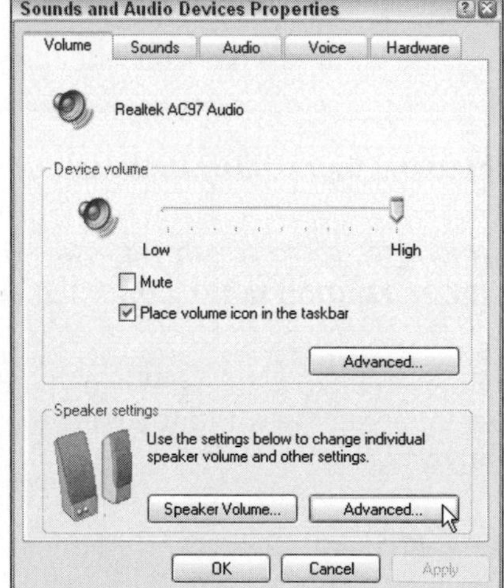

Figure 6-2: Adjust the sound output volume on a PC.

If you select the Place Volume Icon in the Taskbar option and your sound card supports changing the volume with software, a sound icon appears in the notification area of Windows. You can then change the volume quickly without having to open the Sounds and Audio Devices Properties dialog. Simply click the speaker icon and drag the slider that pops up. For more information about adjusting sound on a PC, see *PCs For Dummies,* 11th Edition, by Dan Gookin (Wiley).

Using AirTunes for Wireless Stereo Playback

You want to play the music in your iTunes library, but your stereo system is in another room, and you don't want wires going from one room to the other. What you need is an AirPort in your home — specifically, AirPort Express with AirTunes, which lets you play your iTunes music through your stereo or powered speakers in any room of your house, without wires. The only catch is that your computer must be within range of AirPort Express.

Apple's AirPort technology provides Wi-Fi wireless networking for any AirPort-equipped Mac or PC that uses a Wi-Fi–certified IEEE 802.11b or 802.11g wireless card or offers built-in Wi-Fi. For more about AirPort, see *Mac OS X Tiger All-in-One Desk Reference For Dummies,* by Mark L. Chambers (Wiley).

To use a stereo system or powered speakers with AirTunes, connect the system or speakers to the AirPort Express audio port. iTunes automatically detects the connection.

If you already have a wireless network in place, you can add AirPort Express and AirTunes without changing anything. Connect the AirPort Express Base Station to the stereo system or powered speakers and then plug the Base Station into an electrical outlet. The AirPort Express Base Station wirelessly links to your existing wireless network without requiring any change to the network.

You can use several AirPort Express Base Stations — one for each stereo system or set of powered speakers, in different rooms — and then choose which stereo/speaker system to use from the pop-up menu.

To use AirTunes and AirPort Express, follow these steps:

1. **Install the software supplied with AirPort Express.**

   The CD-ROM includes support for AirTunes.

2. **Connect your stereo or a set of powered speakers to the AirPort Express audio port.**

   You can use an optical digital or analog audio cable. (Both are included in the AirPort Express Stereo Connection Kit available from the Apple Store.) Which cable you use depends on whether your stereo or set of powered speakers has an optical digital or analog connection.

3. **Plug AirPort Express into an electrical outlet.**

   Use the AC plug that came with AirPort Express or the power extension cord included in the AirPort Express Stereo Connection Kit. AirPort Express turns on automatically when connected to an electrical outlet. The status light glows yellow while AirPort Express is starting up. When it starts up completely, the light turns green.

4. **On your computer, set your iTunes preferences to look for speakers connected wirelessly with AirTunes.**

   a. *Choose iTunes⇨Preferences (Mac) or Edit⇨Preferences (Windows).*

   b. *Then click the Advanced button and then click the General tab.*

   c. *Select the Look for Remote Speakers Connected with AirTunes option in the Advanced General pane, as shown in Figure 6-3.*

   In the Advanced General pane, you also have these options:

   - *To control volume from a stereo:* Select the Disable iTunes Volume Control for Remote Speakers option to control speakers separately (a setting you should use if connecting to a stereo with a volume control).
   - *To control volume from iTunes:* Leaving this option deselected (the default) enables you to control the volume from iTunes.

   After turning on the option to look for AirTunes-connected speakers, a pop-up menu appears in the lower-right corner of the iTunes window set to Computer.

5. **Click the Computer pop-up menu and then select the AirTunes-equipped network.**

   The pop-up menu includes the Computer itself and any available wireless AirTunes networks, as shown in Figure 6-4. You can select the AirTunes network to play music ("Little Net Buddy" in Figure 6-4). From that point, iTunes plays music through the AirTunes network rather than the computer. To play music through speakers connected to the computer (or through the computer's built-in speakers), choose Computer from the pop-up menu.

The AirPort Express is small enough to fit in the palm of your hand, and it travels well because all it needs is a power outlet. You can take your laptop and AirPort Express to a friend's house or party, connect the AirPort Express to the stereo system and a power outlet, and then use your laptop anywhere in its vicinity to play DJ. You can even use portable, powered speakers in a hotel room without wires and use a hotel room's LAN-to-Internet access with an AirPort Express to connect your wireless computer and other wireless computers in the room to the Internet.

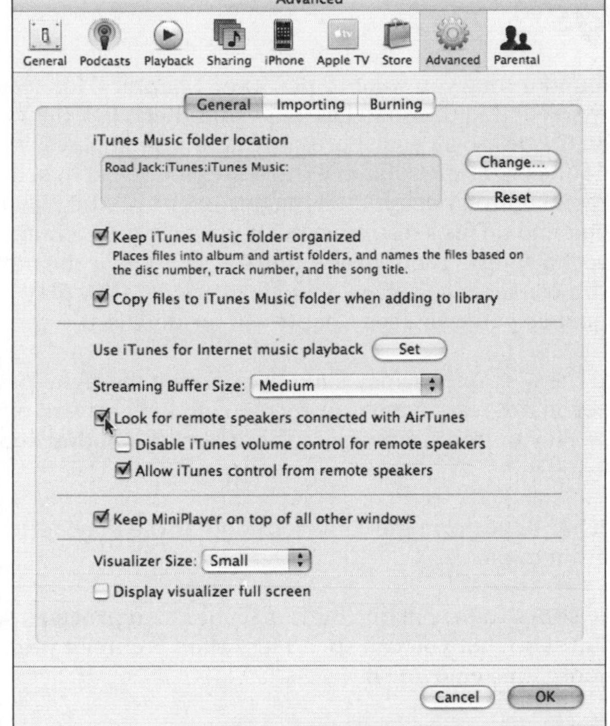

Figure 6-3: Select the option to look for speakers connected wirelessly to your computer using AirTunes.

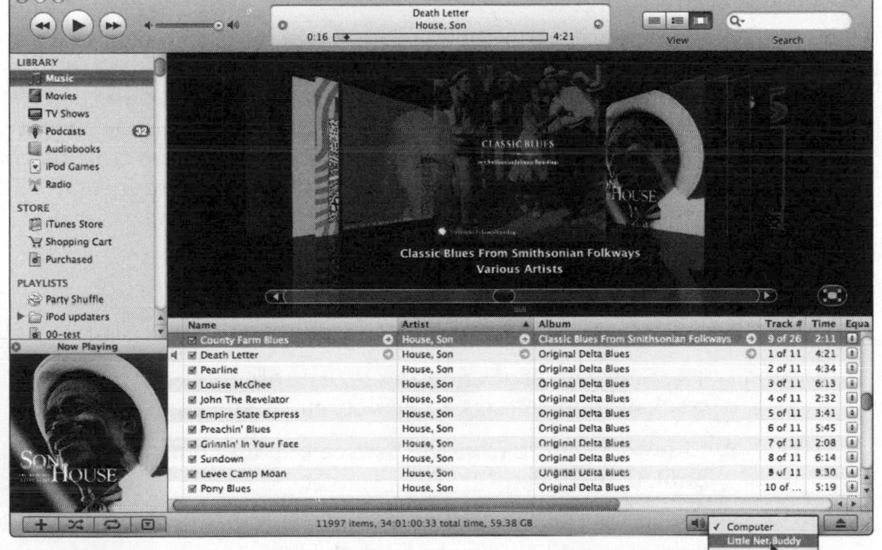

Figure 6-4: Choosing the AirTunes network "Little Net Buddy" to play music.

Playing Songs

When you've found a song you want to play (see Chapter 8 for searching details), simply select it in the Song List pane and then click the Play button. The Play button toggles to a Pause button while the song plays. When the song finishes, iTunes continues playing the songs in the list in sequence until you click the Pause button (which then toggles back into the Play button) or until the song list ends. This setup is useful if you select an album, but not so great if you select a song at random and don't want to hear the next one. (Fortunately, you can arrange songs in playlists so that they play back in exactly the sequence you want; see Chapter 10 for details.)

You can skip to the next or previous song by pressing the right- or left-arrow keys on your keyboard, respectively, or by clicking the Forward or Back buttons next to the Play button. You can also double-click another song in the list to start playing it.

Press the spacebar to perform the same function as the Play button; press the spacebar again to pause.

You can choose songs to play manually, but iTunes also provides several automated features so that you can spend less time prepping your music selection and more time enjoying it.

Queuing up tunes with Party Shuffle

Playlists, as we describe in Chapter 10, are great for organizing music in the order that you want to play it, but you can have iTunes serve up songs at random by using Party Shuffle. Not a dance step or a pub game, *Party Shuffle* is a dynamic playlist that automatically generates a semi-random selection in a list that you can modify on the fly. With Party Shuffle at work, you might even find songs in your library you forgot about or rarely play. Party Shuffle always throws a few rarely played songs into the mix.

To use Party Shuffle, follow these steps:

1. **Click Party Shuffle in the Source pane.**

   The Song List pane and Browse pane are replaced with the Party Shuffle track list and settings at the bottom, as shown in Figure 6-5.

2. **Choose a source from the Source pop-up menu below the Party Shuffle track list.**

   You can select Music (for the entire music portion of your library) or any playlist (including a smart playlist; see Chapter 10 for details) as the source for music in Party Shuffle. If you select a playlist, Party Shuffle limits its choices to songs from that playlist.

Figure 6-5: Adjust the settings for Party Shuffle.

3. **Set the following options:**

   - *Recently Played Songs:* Choose how many songs should remain in the Party Shuffle list after they're played. You can drag already-played songs (even though they're grayed out after playing) to a spot later in the list to play them again.
   - *Upcoming Songs:* Choose how many songs should be listed as *upcoming* (not yet played). By displaying upcoming songs first, you can decide whether to rearrange the list or delete songs from the Party Shuffle playlist before they're played.
   - *Play Higher Rated Songs More Often:* Select this option to have iTunes add more high-rated songs to the random list. Using this option, you weight the randomness in favor of higher-rated songs. See Chapter 9 to find out how to add ratings to songs.

4. **(Optional) If you don't like the order of songs, you can rearrange them. If you dislike any songs, you can eliminate them.**

   You can rearrange the order of songs in Party Shuffle by dragging songs to different positions in the Party Shuffle list. Eliminate songs by selecting them in the Party Shuffle playlist and pressing Delete/Backspace (or choosing Edit⇨Delete). Don't worry — the songs are not deleted from your library, just from the Party Shuffle playlist.

5. **Play Party Shuffle by selecting the first song and then clicking the Play button or pressing the spacebar.**

   You can start playing the first song or any song on the list. (When you pick a song in the middle to start playing, the songs before it are grayed out to show that they won't play.)

6. **Add, delete, or rearrange songs even while Party Shuffle plays.**

   While the Party Shuffle list plays, you can add songs in one of two ways:

   - *Open Party Shuffle in a separate window by double-clicking the Party Shuffle item in the Source pane.* You can then drag songs from the main iTunes window — either from the Music portion of your library or from a playlist — directly into position in the Party Shuffle track list.
   - *Without opening Party Shuffle in a separate window, you can switch to the library or a playlist and drag the song to the Party Shuffle item in the Source pane.* When you add a song to Party Shuffle, it shows up at the end of the track list. You can then drag it to a new position.

You can add one or more albums to the Party Shuffle track list by dragging the albums; the songs play in album order. You can also add all the songs by an artist by dragging the artist's name. Party Shuffle acts like a dynamic playlist — you add, delete, and change the order of songs on the fly.

Cool DJs mix the Party Shuffle window with other open playlist windows. Just double-click the playlist item in the Source pane to open it in a separate window, as shown in Chapter 10. You can then drag songs from different playlist windows to the Party Shuffle window while Party Shuffle plays, adding songs in whatever order you want in real time.

Cross-fading song playback

You can often hear a song on the radio fade out while another song immediately fades in over the first song's ending — a *cross-fade.* With iTunes, you can smoothly transition from the ending of one song to the beginning of the next one. Ordinarily, iTunes is set to have a short cross-fade of one second (the time after the fade-out of the first song to the fade-in of the second).

What's totally cool is that you can cross-fade two songs in iTunes even if they're from different sources. The songs could be in your library, in a shared library, on CD, or even on one (or more) iPods connected to your computer and playing through iTunes (as we describe in Chapter 16). You could play DJ at a party with a massive music library on a laptop and enlarge that library with one or more iPods and any number of CDs, and have the songs cross-fade just like on the radio or at a dance party with a professional DJ.

You can change the cross-fade by choosing iTunes⇨Preferences on a Mac or Edit⇨Preferences in Windows, and then clicking the Playback button. The Playback preferences dialog appears, as shown in Figure 6-6.

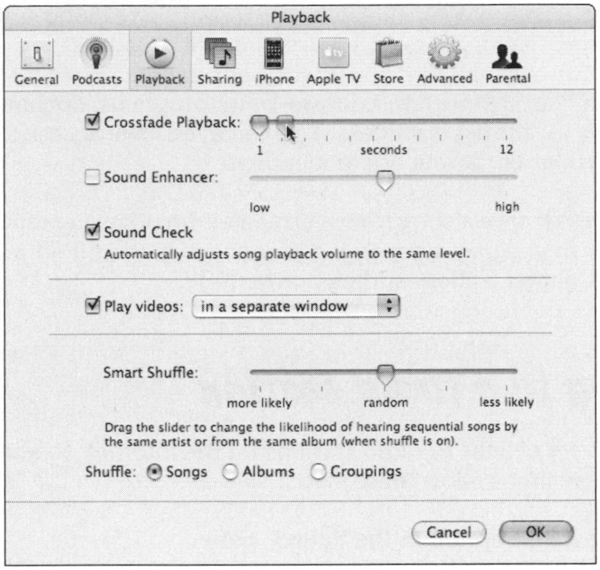

Figure 6-6: Set the cross-fade between songs.

In the Playback preferences dialog, select the Crossfade Playback option and then increase or decrease the cross-fade by dragging the slider. Each notch in the slider represents one second. The maximum amount of cross-fade is 12 seconds. With a longer cross-fade, you get more overlap from one song to the next; that is, the second song starts before the first one ends. To turn off the cross-fade, deselect the Crossfade Playback check box.

Playing Streaming Radio

Radio stations from nearly every part of the world are broadcasting on the Internet. You can tune in to Japan-A-Radio for the top 40 hits in Japan, Batanga Cubanisimo for the best in Cubanismo-Latin jazz, or Radio Darvish for traditional Persian music. You can also check out the local news and sports from your hometown, no matter where you are. You can listen to talk radio and music shows from all over the country and the world.

By *radio,* we really mean a *streaming broadcast.* A streaming broadcast sends audio to your computer in a protected stream of bits over the Internet. Your computer starts playing the stream as soon as the first set of bits arrives, and more sections are transferred while you listen so that you hear it as a continual stream. Broadcasters can use this technology to continually transmit new content, just like a radio station. Of course, real radio stations also make use of this technology to broadcast their programs over the Internet.

In addition, thousands of Web sites offer temporary streaming audio broadcasts all the time. A rock group on tour can offer a broadcast of a special concert, available for only one day. You might want to tune in weekly or monthly broadcasts, such as high-tech talk shows, news programs, documentaries, sporting events . . . the list is endless. You can even have access to private broadcasts, such as corporate board meetings.

You can't record or save a song from a streamed broadcast without special software. Nor can you play a streaming broadcast on your iPod, except as a podcast. (See Chapter 5 about adding podcasts.)

Listening to a radio station

iTunes offers a set of links to radio stations on the Internet, so you might want to try these first. Follow these steps:

1. **Select the Radio option in the Source pane.**

   The iTunes window displays a list of categories of radio stations.

2. **Open a category to see a list of stations in that category.**

   Click the triangle next to a category name to open the list of radio streams in that category, as shown in Figure 6-7. Some large radio stations offer more than one stream. iTunes automatically connects to the Internet to retrieve the latest list of radio stations for each category.

3. **Select a stream and then click the Play button.**

   To select a stream, click its name in the Song List pane. (Actually, it's the Radio Station List pane now because you selected Radio in the Source pane.) Within seconds, you hear live radio off the Web.

If you use a dialup modem connection to the Internet, you might want to choose a stream with a bit rate of less than 56 Kbps for best results. The Bit Rate column (see Figure 6-7) shows the bit rate for each stream.

iTunes creates a buffer for the audio stream so that you hear continuous playback with fewer Internet-related hiccups than most Web radio software. The buffer temporarily stores as much of the stream as possible, adding more of the stream to the end of the buffer while you play the audio in the buffer. If you hear stutters, gaps, or hiccups when playing a stream, set your buffer to a larger size by choosing iTunes⇨Preferences (Mac) or Edit⇨Preferences (Windows). In the Preferences dialog, click the Advanced button and then the General tab, and then choose a size from the Streaming Buffer Size pop-up menu.

Figure 6-7: Open a list of radio streams in the International category.

Creating a playlist of your radio stations

Car radios offer preset stations activated by you pressing a button. Of course, you first need to tune in to the station of your choice to set that button. You can save your radio station choices in an iTunes playlist, and the process is easy:

1. **Select a radio station stream.**
2. **Drag the stream name to the bottom of the list of playlists in the Source pane.**

   iTunes creates a playlist using the stream name. You can add more radio streams to the same playlist by dragging their names over the new playlist name in the Source pane.

Drag as many streams as you like to as many playlists as you like. You can click any playlist name and rearrange that playlist as you want, dragging stream names as you would drag song names. See Chapter 10 to discover how to create and use playlists.

Radio streams in your playlists play only if you're connected to the Internet.

To quickly create a playlist from selected radio streams, first select the streams just as you would select multiple songs and then choose File⇨New Playlist from Selection.

Adding a radio station to iTunes

You can tune in to any broadcast on the Internet. All you need to know is the Web address, also known as the *URL* (Uniform Resource Locator), which is the global address of documents and other resources on the Web. You can find most URLs from a Web site or e-mail about a broadcast.

Follow these steps to add a Web broadcast to your iTunes library:

1. **Choose Advanced⇨Open Stream.**

   The Open Stream dialog appears, with a URL text field for typing a Web address.

2. **Type the exact, full URL of the stream.**

   Include the `http://` prefix, as in

   ```
   http://64.236.34.141:80/stream/1014
   ```

   If you're connected to the Internet, iTunes automatically retrieves the broadcast and places it at the end of your song list.

3. **Click OK.**

As of this writing, iTunes supports only MP3 broadcasts. You can find lots of MP3 broadcasts from SHOUTcast (`www.shoutcast.com`) and Live365.com (`http://live365.com`).

Playing Podcasts

Podcasts that you subscribe to appear in the List pane that appears when you select the Podcasts option in the Source pane. You can add podcast episodes to your library by subscribing to them in the iTunes Store (see Chapter 4) or on a Web site (see Chapter 5). To play a podcast episode, follow these steps:

1. **Select the Podcasts option in the Source pane.**

   The podcasts appear in the Song List pane.

2. **Select the podcast in the Podcasts list and then click the triangle to see its episodes.**

   The triangle rotates, and a list of episodes appears beneath the podcast, as shown in Figure 6-8.

3. **Select the podcast and then click the Play button.**

   You can use the iTunes playback controls to fast-forward or rewind the podcast or play it from any point. The blue dot next to a podcast means you haven't yet played it. As soon as you start listening to a podcast, the dot disappears.

When you play a podcast, iTunes remembers your place when you stop listening to it, just like a bookmark in an audio book. iTunes resumes playing from the bookmark when you return to the podcast to play it.

Some podcasts are enhanced to include chapter marks and photos. When you play an enhanced podcast in iTunes, a Chapters menu appears on the iTunes menu bar. Choose this menu to display the podcast's chapter marks, artwork, and chapter start times, as shown in Figure 6-9.

If the podcaster embedded a photo in an audio podcast file or included a link to a video from the file, the photo or video content appears in the Artwork pane.

While you can drag a podcast into a playlist to include it in a playlist, you can also drag a podcast to the Source pane to create a new playlist, as shown in Figure 6-10, as long as you drag it to an empty space in the Playlist section of the Source pane (and not into another playlist). The new playlist takes on the name of the podcast. (For example, dragging The Flying Other Brothers–Music Podcast to the Source pane in Figure 6-10 creates The Flying Other Brothers–Music Podcast playlist.) For more information about playlists, see Chapter 10.

Figure 6-8: Open a podcast to see its episodes.

Figure 6-9: Enhanced podcasts include a Chapters menu.

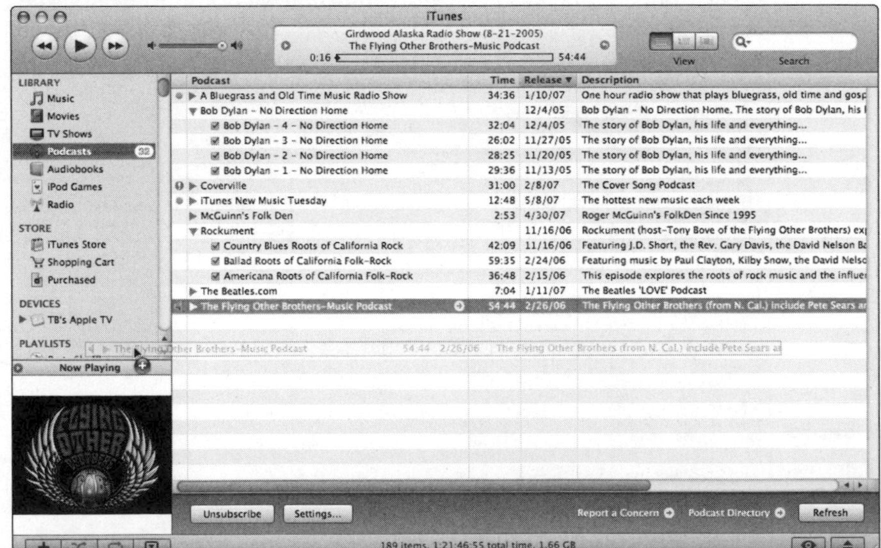

Figure 6-10: Create a new playlist with a podcast.

Playing Audio Books

You can store and play audio books, articles, and spoken-word titles just like songs in iTunes — you can find them by selecting Audiobooks in the Source pane under Library. You can download titles from the iTunes store (as we describe in Chapter 4) or from Audible (`www.audible.com`; as we describe in Chapter 5).

To play an audio book, select it just like you would a song (see details on browsing and listing content in Chapter 8) and then click the Play/Pause button. You can use the iTunes playback controls to fast-forward or rewind the audio book or play it from any point.

Audio books from Audible and the iTunes Store are enhanced to include chapter marks. When you play any of these audio books in iTunes, the Chapters menu appears on the iTunes menu bar, just like a podcast with chapters. Choose the Chapters menu to display and select the audio book's chapter marks (refer to Figure 6-9).

Playing Videos

iTunes is versatile when it comes to playing videos — the TV shows, movies, video podcasts, and music videos you downloaded from the iTunes Store (see Chapter 4) as well as the video files you dragged into iTunes from other sources (see Chapter 5).

To watch a video in iTunes, select it in your library (see details on browsing and listing movies, TV shows, and videos in Chapter 8), and then click the Play/Pause button. Use the iTunes Play/Pause, Forward/Next, and Previous/Rewind buttons to control playback and the iTunes volume slider to control the volume, just like with songs.

The video appears in the Artwork pane in the lower-left corner of the iTunes window, as shown in Figure 6-11. If the Artwork pane isn't visible, clicking the video makes it appear. You can also make the Artwork pane appear or disappear by clicking the Show/Hide Artwork button.

You can view your video in two ways:

- Open it in a separate window at different sizes.
- Fill the entire display with the video.

Figure 6-11: A video appears in the Artwork pane.

Playing a video in a separate window

To watch a video in a separate window, click the video while it plays in the Artwork pane. A separate window appears that includes a transparent QuickTime controls pane with buttons for controlling video playback, as shown in Figure 6-12. Click the right-facing triangle at the center of the QuickTime controls pane to play or pause, and then drag the slider to move forward or backward through the video. Click the rewind or fast-forward buttons on either side of the play button in the controls pane to move backward or forward through a video.

Figure 6-12: Drag the QuickTime playback slider to move forward or backward through a video.

To set your iTunes preferences to always play video in a separate window, choose iTunes⇨Preferences (Mac) or Edit⇨Preferences (Windows). Next, click the Playback button and then choose the In a Separate Window option from the Play Videos pop-up menu, as shown in Figure 6-13. From that point on, videos in your library play in a separate window that offers QuickTime playback controls.

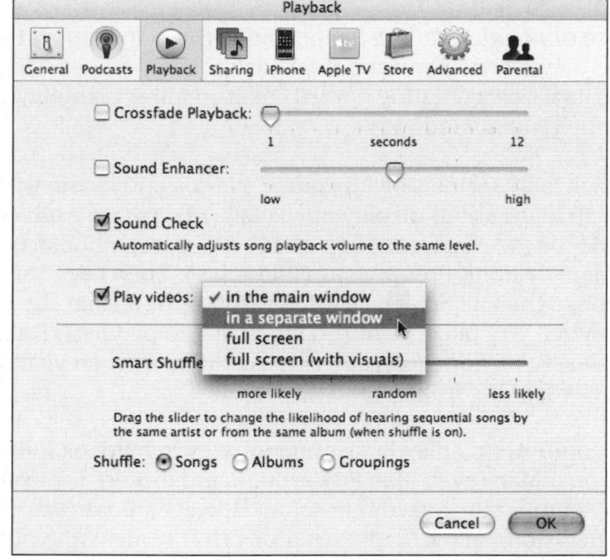

Figure 6-13: Change video playback to a separate window.

The transparent QuickTime control pane disappears while the video plays, but you can make it reappear at any time by moving the cursor to the bottom center of the video window. The control pane also offers a volume control slider to set the audio volume of the video, and the Full-Screen Video button to change the video display to full-screen. (See the following section, "Playing a video full-screen.") You can resize the separate video window by dragging the lower-right corner of the window. You can also choose fixed window sizes by choosing them from the View menu. For example, choose View⇨Half Size to display the video window at half the actual size, or View⇨Double Size to display the window at twice the size. Choose View⇨Actual Size to set the window back to the actual size of the video picture.

Playing a video full-screen

To watch the video on the full screen, click the Full-Screen Video button in the transparent QuickTime control pane (refer to Figure 6-12). This button doesn't appear unless you're playing a video in a separate window. You can also choose View⇨Full Screen.

After clicking the Full-Screen Video button (or choosing View⇨Full Screen), video fills your screen and begins playing. The following controls are available:

- *Esc (Escape):* Press to stop full-screen playback and return to the iTunes window.
- *Spacebar:* Press to pause playback. (Pressing the spacebar again resumes playback.)
- *Your mouse or pointing device:* Simply move these to display the transparent QuickTime control pane and then click the Full-Screen Video button (now with its arrows pointing inward) to stop full-screen playback and return to the iTunes window.

A cool party trick is to seamlessly mix music videos and music with visuals. (See Chapter 3 to learn about displaying visuals.) To create a mixed playlist of music and videos (see Chapter 10 to create playlists), choose iTunes⇨Preferences (Mac) or Edit⇨Preferences (Windows). Then click the Playback button and choose the Full Screen (with Visuals) option from the Play Videos pop-up menu. When you play the mixed music-video playlist, iTunes automatically shows full-screen video for your videos and full-screen visuals for your music, seamlessly moving from one to the other.

For many, the computer display is just fine for viewing videos full-screen. The picture clarity on a Mac (even Mac PowerBook and iBook), for example, is better than any comparably sized television. However, if you want to connect your PC to a television, follow the instructions that came with your PC. (Most likely you'll use the same cables that you would use to connect an iPod to a television; see Chapter 16.)

You can connect a Mac to a television that offers an S-video connection or standard RCA video and audio connections. After connecting to the television, follow these steps:

1. **Choose System Preferences from the Apple menu.**

   The System Preferences window appears with icons for each set of preferences.

2. **Click the Displays icon in the System Preferences window.**

   The Display preferences window appears. Depending on the type of display, you might see tabs for different panes.

3. **Click the Display tab for the Display preferences pane if it isn't already selected.**

   The preferences appear with settings for your display.

4. **Click the Detect Displays button.**

   The Mac detects the television and sets it to the appropriate resolution. For more about setting display resolutions on the Mac, see *Mac OS X Tiger All-in-One Desk Reference For Dummies,* by Mark L. Chambers (Wiley).

If you don't see a picture on your television, be sure your TV is set to the correct input source: Video in (RCA) or S-video in (if you use an S-video cable). You can also use other types of video equipment. For example, a video recorder that accepts RCA or S-video input can record the video and a video projector can display it on a large screen.

Perhaps the easiest way to connect your computer (and other computers in your local network) to your television and stereo system is through Apple TV. Apple TV lets you connect wirelessly (or by wired Ethernet) to any computer running iTunes in the network and store content for playback. See Chapter 7 for details on sharing your iTunes library with Apple TV.

Chapter 7
Sharing Content Legally

In This Chapter

- Sharing content purchased from the iTunes Store
- Using a local area network to share an iTunes library
- Setting up and sharing content with Apple TV
- Copying media files to other drives and computers
- Copying from Macs to PCs and vice versa

Hey, it's your content after you buy it — that is, to the extent that you can make copies for yourself. You want to play your music and videos anywhere and even share them with your friends. It's only natural.

And to help, iTunes lets you share a library over a local area network (LAN) with other computers running iTunes.

If you use a Wi-Fi (wireless) network, consider getting an Apple TV, which connects wirelessly to your network and with high-quality cabling to your television and stereo system. You can then share any iTunes library on any computer on the network with Apple TV to play on your TV and stereo.

You can also copy the content files to other computers without any restrictions on copying although protected content has playback restrictions. You can easily share the music that you rip from your CDs: After the music becomes digital, you can copy it endlessly with no subsequent loss in quality. You can also share the songs, audio books, podcasts, and videos that you download. Of course, if the songs, audio books, and videos are in a protected format (such as content bought from the iTunes Store), the computers that access the shared library must be authorized to play the content. Whether the computers are connected to a LAN by cable (such as Ethernet) or by wireless technology (such as the Apple AirPort), you can share your library with other computers — up to five other computers in a single 24-hour period.

In this chapter, we show you how to bend the rules and share your iTunes library with others. (After all, your parents taught you to share, didn't they?)

Sharing Content from the iTunes Store

To a limited extent, you can share all the content that you buy online from the iTunes Store. Some content — such as free podcasts as well as albums sold at a higher price in the iTunes Plus section of the store with higher audio quality and without copy protection — can be shared without any limitations. However, individual songs and albums sold at lower prices; along with commercial movies, music videos, TV shows, audio books, and paid podcasts; are limited by copy protection, also known as *digital rights management* (DRM).

The songs available in the iTunes Plus section can play on any computer or any digital-audio player. Entire albums and individual songs are now available in this higher-quality, non-DRM format, but they don't replace DRM-protected songs also sold through iTunes at the lower price ($0.99 per song). That way, consumers have a choice. And if you've already purchased DRM-protected EMI songs at 99 cents each, you can upgrade them to the new format for 30 cents each.

I fought the law, and the law won: Sharing and piracy

Apple CEO Steve Jobs gave personal demonstrations of the iTunes Store and the iPod to Paul McCartney and Mick Jagger before introducing the online store. According to Steven Levy at *Newsweek* (May 12, 2003), Jobs said, "They both totally get it." The former Beatle and the Stones' frontman are no slouches: Both conduct music-business affairs personally and have extensive back catalogs of music. They know all about the free music-swapping services on the Internet, but they agree with Jobs that most people are willing to pay for high-quality music rather than download free copies of questionable quality.

Digital Rights Management (DRM), also known as copy protection, is ineffective against piracy because determined pirates always circumvent it with newer technology; only consumers are inconvenienced.

The record labels are finally "getting it" as well. EMI, one of the largest, agreed in the spring of 2007 to sell songs and albums in the iTunes Plus section of the store, at a higher price ($1.29 per song) but without DRM getting in the way. Many of the songs available from free sharing services are low-quality MP3 audio files, which sound only as good as an FM radio broadcast. The iTunes Plus section offers licensed music in a format that offers higher-quality sound, and we prefer the original authorized version of the song — not some knock-off that might have been copied from a radio broadcast.

As for copying songs for personal use, the law is murky at best. You can mix hit songs in with your personal videos, but don't expect to see those videos on MTV or VH1, or even YouTube for very long (as YouTube and other video sharing sites police their sites for unauthorized content). Whether you're interested in obtaining the rights to music to use in semipublic or public presentations or even movies and documentaries for public distribution, you can contact the music publisher or a licensing agent. Music publishing organizations, such as the Music Publishers' Association (`www.mpa.org`), offer information and lists of music publishers as well as explanations of various rights and licenses.

The Apple form of DRM is known as *FairPlay,* and it works with the standard AAC format. (Read all about AAC, MP3, and other audio format encoders in Chapters 18 and 19.) Protected files are keyed to an individual purchaser's identity. Although they can be copied to and from computers, they can't be played on a given computer unless that computer has been authorized.

Apple employs FairPlay protection for the lower-priced songs. These filenames use the `.m4p` extension for protected music rather than `.m4a` for the unprotected AAC format. Apple uses a protected video format for TV shows, music videos, and movies in the online store. These filenames use the `.m4v` or `.mp4` extension for protected video rather than `.mpg` for the standard MPEG-4 format.

Unprotected AAC files are as freely portable and playable as MP3 files are. You can send an unprotected AAC file to anyone else with iTunes or any other software capable of reading AAC files, and the recipient can play it successfully.

To tell whether a song purchased from the iTunes Store is protected with FairPlay or not, select the song and choose File➪Get Info. Next to the Kind heading reads "Protected AAC Audio File" for FairPlay-protected songs or "Purchased AAC Audio File" for non-protected, higher-quality songs bought in the iTunes Plus section.

The FairPlay protection used with iTunes Store content allows you to do the following:

- **Create backups.** You can download the content files and make as many copies as you want (even burn them onto data CDs and DVDs).
- **Copy content to iTunes libraries on other computers.** Play songs and videos on up to five separate computers. See Chapter 4 to find out how to authorize your computers.
- **Copy content to iPods, iPhones, and Apple TV devices.** Copy the music and videos to as many iPods and iPhones as you want as well as to Apple TV devices. See Chapter 12 for automatic and manual device synchronization.
- **Burn up to seven CDs.** Burn seven copies of the same playlist containing protected songs to an audio CD — but no more. You can also burn data CDs and DVDs with content files for backup purposes. See Chapter 14 for tips on CD and DVD burning.
- **Share content over a network.** Up to five computers running iTunes on a LAN can play the content in your shared library in a 24-hour period.

You can also play music in your library over a wireless connection to a stereo amplifier or receiver by using AirTunes and AirPort Express, which we cover in Chapter 6.

You might also want to know where the songs, audio books, podcasts, and videos are stored on your hard drive so that you can copy the content to other computers and hard drives and create a backup of your entire library. You might want to move the library to another computer because computers just keep getting better year after year. To find the location of your content files, see Chapter 13.

Sharing Content on a Network

If you live like the Jetsons — with a computer in every room connected by a wireless or wired network — iTunes is made for you. You can share your iTunes library with other computers in the same network. These computers can be PCs that run Windows or Macs that run OS X — as long as they run iTunes. If they can communicate with each other over the network, iTunes can share a content library with up to five PCs in a single 24-hour period. The restriction to five in a 24-hour period is yet another one of the imposed rules of record labels and video producers.

When you share content on a network, the content is *streamed* over the network from the computer that contains the library (the *library computer*) to the computer that plays it. A stream arrives in the receiving computer bit by bit; the computer starts playing the stream as soon as the first set of bits arrive, and more sections are transferred while you listen. The result is that the recipient hears music and sees video as a continual stream. Broadcasters use this technology to continually transmit new content (just like a radio station). The content isn't copied to the receiving computer's library, and you can't burn the shared library songs onto a CD or copy the songs to an iPod without third-party software — such as WireTap Pro for the Mac (`www.ambrosiasw.com/utilities/wiretap`) or Blaze Media Pro for Windows (`www.blazemp.com`).

Sharing an iTunes library can be incredibly useful for playing content on laptops, such as a PowerBook, that support the wireless AirPort network. You can manage a very large content library on a desktop computer with a large hard drive, and then play content on the laptop or notebook computer with a smaller hard drive without having to copy files to the smaller hard drive.

Sharing your library with other computers

To share your iTunes library — turning your computer into the library computer — follow these steps:

1. **Choose iTunes⇨Preferences (Mac) or Edit⇨Preferences (Windows) and then click the Sharing tab.**

   The Sharing dialog appears, as shown in Figure 7-1, offering options for sharing music.

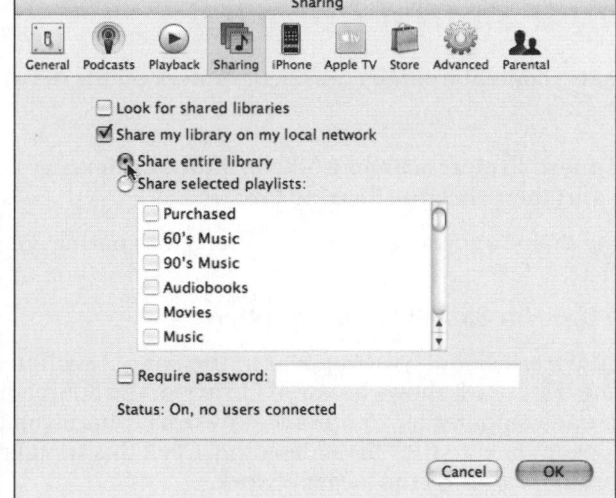

Figure 7-1: Share your iTunes library with other computers on the same network.

2. **Select the Share My Library on My Local Network option.**
3. **Select either the Share Entire Library option or the Share Selected Playlists option and then choose the playlists to share.**
4. **Add a password if you want to restrict access to the shared library or playlists.**

   Pick a password that you don't mind sharing with others; for example, your name is a good password, but your ATM PIN isn't. The password restricts access to only those who know it.

   iTunes displays `Reminder: Sharing music is for personal use only.`

5. **Click OK.**

Shared libraries or playlists appear in the iTunes Source list in the Shared section with the computer's user name (for example, "Tony Bove's Music" is the name of the shared library on the computer where "Tony Bove" is logged in as the user).

You can change the Shared name that iTunes uses for your shared library or playlists. To change the name others see, choose iTunes➪Preferences on a Mac or Edit➪Preferences in Windows, click General, and then type a new name in the Shared Name field. The name that you choose appears in the Shared section of the iTunes Source pane for other computers that share your library.

Before turning off sharing for your library, you must first notify anyone sharing the library to eject the shared library. Otherwise, iTunes displays a warning dialog allowing you to continue (and break off the connection to the shared library) or to leave sharing turned on for the moment.

Accessing a shared library

You can access the content from the other computers on the network by following these steps:

1. **Choose iTunes⇨Preferences on a Mac or Edit⇨Preferences in Windows and then click the Sharing tab.**

   The Sharing dialog appears and offers options for sharing content. Refer to Figure 7-1.

2. **Select the Look for Shared Libraries option.**

   The shared libraries or playlists appear in the Shared section of the Source pane. Figure 7-2 shows a shared library in the Source pane. If more than one computer on your home network is sharing music, a triangle appears next to the Shared heading. Click this triangle to reveal all the shared libraries on the local network.

Figure 7-2: Select the library (shared by iTunes) on a networked computer.

3. **Click the triangle next to a shared library entry in the Source pane, as shown in Figure 7-3, to see shared playlists. Play them as you normally would.**

   iTunes fills the view on the right with the artists and content from the shared library.

4. **When you finish listening, click the tiny Eject button that appears to the right of the shared library name in the Source pane.**

Figure 7-3: Open the list of playlists in the shared library.

Sharing Content with Your Apple TV

Wouldn't it be nice to be able to play the content in your iTunes library on your television and stereo system without having to mess with cables? You can. Just sit back on your couch and let Apple TV offer up a smorgasbord of content from your iTunes library, which can be on your computer in another room and streamed to Apple TV over the network. You can also transfer content to your Apple TV so that you don't have to use your computer to play the content or even have your computer on while playing content.

Apple TV (about $300) is like a large iPod that wirelessly synchronizes with one or more iTunes libraries on Macs and PCs and connects to your high-definition or regular television and stereo system. You can watch movies you download from the online iTunes Store (or anywhere else) on your high-definition television with full surround sound. You can listen to music and podcasts in your iTunes library through your home stereo and show photo slideshows with music. It's the wave of the future — couch potatoes kicking back with Apple consumer gear.

You control Apple TV with the Apple Remote, which uses Apple TV's built-in infrared (IR) receiver. The menus for playing content and changing Apple TV settings appear on your television, so you can sit back on your couch and tune in to anything synchronized from your iTunes library. You can also play all the music in an iTunes library, streamed from the computer running iTunes, without synchronizing the entire library.

Apple TV hardware isn't much different than a low-end laptop computer; it runs a slimmed version of Mac OS X. Apple TV requires a Mac or PC running iTunes version 7.1 or newer. (See Chapter 2 for detailed requirements for running iTunes.) Apple TV works with widescreen, enhanced-definition, or high-definition TVs capable of 1080i, 720p, 576p, or 480p resolutions. As of this writing, the iTunes Store doesn't yet offer HDTV (high-definition television) content — but when it does, Apple TV is ready for it.

The first generation Apple TV includes a 40GB model and a 160GB model for synchronizing with iTunes. With the 40GB model you can synchronize up to 50 hours of movies and TV shows, or fill it up with 9,000 songs (or about 25,000 pictures), and play them on your TV and stereo. And yet, it's so easy to set up that you have to leave your couch for only a few minutes before you're back on it, soaking up the content.

Setting up Apple TV

Apple TV works transparently with a PC or Mac, taking advantage of the broadband connection to the Internet via your wireless network. It supports 802.11 wireless networks, including Apple AirPort networks. Newer AirPort Extreme-enabled Macs let you create a wireless network using only your computer and Apple TV. (If you have a Mac or PC without wireless capability, though, you can connect Apple TV to your network using an Ethernet cable that's sold separately.) You can then synchronize Apple TV with an iTunes library on any Mac or PC within reach of the wireless network. When you change your library in iTunes, Apple TV automatically synchronizes with your library.

To connect the device (only 1.1" thick and 7.7" square) to your TV or audio-video (AV) receiver, use one of the following methods, as shown in Figure 7-4:

- **For TVs with stereo or surround sound that support High-Definition Multimedia Interface (HDMI):** Use an HDMI cable, which provides video and audio to the television/audio system. The Apple Store offers HDMI-to-HDMI cables for TVs and AV receivers that support HDMI.
- **For TVs that support Digital Video Interface (DVI):** Use an HDMI-to-DVI cable or an HDMI-DVI adapter for an HDMI cable, both of which are available from the Apple Store. Then use either an optical audio cable or a standard analog audio cable pair to provide audio to your stereo or surround sound system.
- **For TVs or AV receivers that don't offer HDMI or DVI (or if these ports are used by other devices, such as your cable receiver):** Use a component video cable (with three connectors) and either an optical audio cable or a standard analog audio cable pair.

You should connect Apple TV to your TV and stereo first before proceeding so that when you connect Apple TV to power, you see the menu for Apple TV on your television.

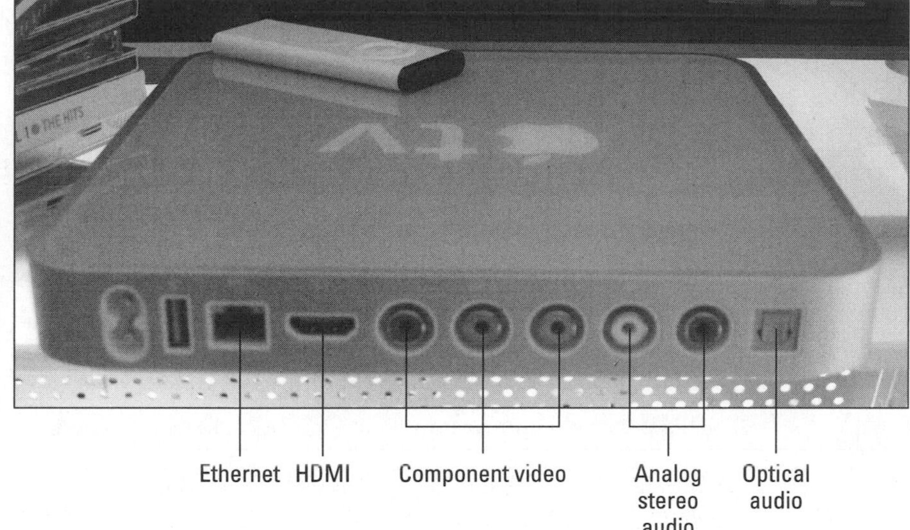

Figure 7-4: Connect Apple TV to your widescreen TV and stereo.

Choosing an iTunes library for Apple TV

When you first connect Apple TV to a power source, it immediately starts its setup procedure, using your television as the display. Grab your Apple Remote (supplied with Apple TV) and follow these instructions — all from the comfort of your couch:

1. **Choose a language.**

   Point the Apple Remote at the Apple TV and use the remote's buttons to navigate up and down the list and select a language. The plus (+) button scrolls up, the minus (–) button scrolls down, and the Play/Pause button selects a menu choice. After choosing a language, Apple TV displays the network screen.

2. **Select a network.**

   Apple TV searches for a wireless network unless you've connected it to an Ethernet network (in which case Apple TV automatically detects it, and that's that). For wireless networks, follow the on-TV instructions to select your network by name, and (if necessary) supply a password by using the Apple Remote to navigate the individual letters of the password. You can even manually configure the IP address, subnet mask, router, and DNS address if your network doesn't allow DHCP connections or you need to for other reasons. (We're assuming here that you know what you're doing — if not, get help from the person who set up your network.)

After setting up your network connection, Apple TV displays a five-digit passcode on your TV that identifies the device for synchronization with a computer.

3. **Remember (or write down) your five-digit passcode.**

   The next step is to get off your couch and go over to your computer — which can be in the next room, as long as it accesses the same network as Apple TV. Then follow these steps:

4. **Start iTunes.**

   Shortly (a minute or less), the Apple TV icon and name appear in the Source pane under Devices.

5. **Select Apple TV in the Source pane (as shown in Figure 7-5) and then enter the five-digit passcode into the digit fields.**

   This passcode appears on your TV; see earlier in this step list.

   The digit fields appear in the iTunes page, to the right of the Source pane. After entering the fifth digit, iTunes displays a page that lets you enter the name for your Apple TV, as shown in Figure 7-6.

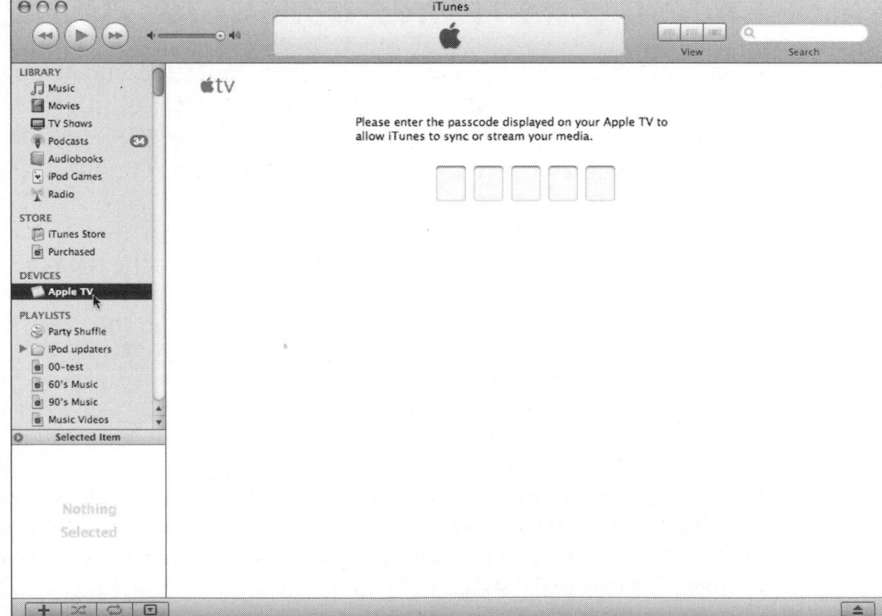

Figure 7-5: Set up Apple TV in iTunes to synchronize with the library.

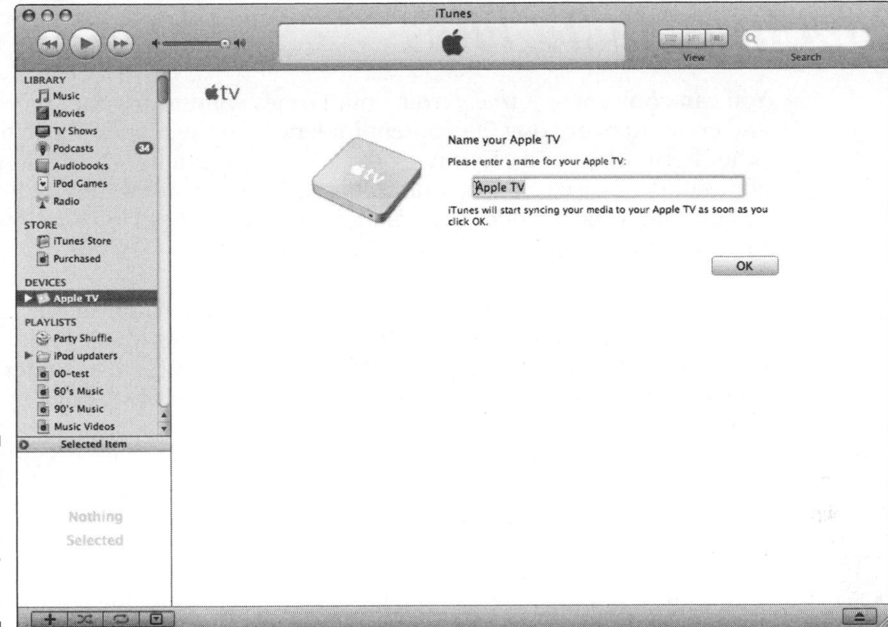

Figure 7-6: Provide a new name for your Apple TV.

6. **Give your Apple TV a new name.**

   Enter a new name that befits the new king of the living room and then click OK. iTunes then displays the registration page for Apple TV.

7. **Register your Apple TV or skip registration if you want.**

   Click Continue to register, Later to register later, or Never Register to skip registration. We recommend registering your Apple TV in order to maintain your warranty (and optionally receive email notices of updates). If you choose to register, follow the instructions to enter your Apple ID and password (or select the option for no ID) and then click Continue. Fill out your personal information and then click Continue to finish the registration process. iTunes then takes you to the online store, so that you can start purchasing content immediately.

Your new Apple TV starts synchronizing automatically with your iTunes library, copying movies, TV shows, music, podcasts, and photos (in that order) until it runs out of space. If your iTunes library is larger than the capacity of your Apple TV, you will want to manage content synchronization — see Chapter 12.

To play content on Apple TV, use the Apple Remote to choose from the Apple TV main menu. You can select Movies, TV Shows, Music, Podcasts, and Photos; or, choose Settings to change your Apple TV settings or choose Sources to change sources of content.

Copying Media Files

You can copy content freely from your iTunes window to other hard drives and computers or copy the content folders from the iTunes Music folder to other hard drives and computers. On a Mac, you can use the Finder to copy content files as well as drag stuff from the iTunes window into folders or hard drives. Windows PCs offer several methods, including using Windows Explorer to copy files.

By default, the files are organized in folders by artist name and by album title (or by book, video, or TV show title) within the iTunes Music folder: that is, unless you change options in the Advanced section of iTunes Preferences; see Chapter 13. For example, copying an entire album, or every song by a specific artist, is easy — just drag the folder to its new-home folder on another hard drive.

You can find out the location of any content item by selecting the item in iTunes and choosing File⇨Get Info. Click the Summary tab in the Get Info dialog to see the Summary options. Although you can change the location of your iTunes library, most people leave the library in its default location, which is inside the iTunes Music folder in the iTunes folder on the startup hard drive.

On a Mac, the iTunes Music folder can be found at its default location:

```
your home folder/Music/iTunes/iTunes Music
```

On a Windows PC, the iTunes Music folder can be found at

```
your user folder/My Documents/My Music/iTunes/iTunes Music
```

Your playlists, including the library itself (which is in some ways a giant playlist), are stored as eXtensible Markup Language (XML) files in the iTunes folder along with your iTunes Music folder.

The easiest way to copy an album from a folder on a hard drive into your iTunes library is to drag the album's folder over the iTunes window and drop the folder there. If you drop it into the Source pane, iTunes creates a playlist of the album's songs using the album name. To copy individual songs, you can drag the song files over the iTunes window and drop them in the Song List pane. When you add a piece of content (song, video, podcast, or audio book) to your iTunes library, a copy is placed inside the iTunes Music folder.

Copying Files between Macs and PCs

Song files are not small: Album folders filled with songs are quite large, and video files are far larger than song files. Copying a library from a Mac to a PC, or vice versa, is not a simple task because of the enormity of these file sizes.

Attaching a file to an e-mail message is the most popular method of transferring a file to someone. However, when you attach a file to an e-mail message, the attached file is encoded in a format that increases the size of the attachment by up to 40 percent. Many e-mail servers won't accept an attachment larger than 5MB; some won't accept attachments larger than 4MB. In cases such as those, don't even think about sending music and video file copies via e-mail. Just remember our little homily: *If the file is over four, it won't go through the door.* (Four megabytes, that is, and the door is the limitation of your Internet service provider's e-mail server.) If you use a .Mac e-mail account, the limitation is 10MB.

Well, heck, just about every jazz tune and Grateful Dead jam we listen to in iTunes is larger than 3MB. A song compressed in the AAC or MP3 format is typically between 2MB and 10MB, so you might get by with one pop song attached to an e-mail, but that's it.

One way to transfer larger amounts of content is by using an external FireWire or a USB hard drive formatted for a PC: For example, an iPod installed for Windows would do nicely. (***Note:*** You need FireWire or USB to connect an external drive.) In such a scenario, the Mac then recognizes that iPod when you plug it in even though the drive is formatted for Windows. You can copy files directly to the hard drive and then take the hard drive over to your PC. (You can find out about using an iPod as a hard drive in Chapter 22.)

On a LAN, you can share forever. If your computers communicate over a LAN, they can share files — even large ones. To copy large files or entire folders between two Macs in a LAN, simply allow personal file sharing on your Mac. Likewise, if someone wants to make a file or folder available to *you* over a LAN, all she has to do is enable personal file sharing.

Allowing personal file sharing perhaps sounds a bit liberal and maybe even a tad dangerous — potentially inviting mischief and voyeurism — but you can indeed control what others can do.

Mac OS X makes it very easy to share files and folders with Windows computers. You can enable Windows file sharing on a Mac, or you can access the Windows computer from a Mac. To access a Windows PC from a Mac, you need a valid user ID and password for an account on the Windows computer.

You can go to that account's Home directory on the Windows computer and use your Mac to copy folders and files to and from the PC. For more information about file sharing on a Mac (specifically between Mac and Windows computers on a network), see *Mac OS X Tiger All-in-One Desk Reference For Dummies,* by Mark L. Chambers (Wiley).

Copying very large song files over the Internet is a bit more complex, involving the use of a communication application such as iChat AV or one that offers the File Transfer Protocol (FTP). Although you can easily download an MP3 song file from a Web page or an FTP site with any browser (all you need is the Web or FTP address, and a user ID and password if the site is protected), you can't send the file to a protected site with most browsers unless the site is set up for this function. One easy way to share your files from a Mac is to use the .Mac service to create a Web page that accommodates anyone with the right password, even Windows-using folks, to visit and download files you put there. For information about setting up a .Mac account, see *iLife '04 All-in-One Desk Reference For Dummies,* by yours truly (Wiley).

To make it easy for others to copy files to and from a Mac at their convenience, enable FTP access for the Mac. To do this

1. **Open System Preferences.**
2. **Click the Sharing icon.**
3. **Click the Services button.**
4. **Select the FTP Access option.**

   A message at the bottom of the Sharing pane provides the address of your FTP server on your Mac, something like

   ```
   ftp://192.168.1.246
   ```

5. **Give the address to those with an account on your computer so that they can access files and folders by using a Web browser, an FTP client (such as Fetch 5), or Mac OS X.**

   If you've turned on the firewall in Mac OS X, click the Firewall button in the Sharing preferences and then select the FTP Access option; this allows FTP access through the firewall.

How about transferring files to other FTP sites, such as a password-protected site that requires the use of an FTP client? You have several options:

- **Use an FTP client,** such as Fetch 5 or RBrowser 4 for Mac OS X or FTP Explorer for Windows. You can find Fetch 5 at `http://fetchsoftworks.com` (for $25, as of this writing). You can use it for 15 days before paying for it. RBrowser 4 (`www.rbrowser.com`) is free to download and use and looks a bit like the Mac Finder. FTP Explorer (`www.ftpx.com`) is shareware you can use for a month before paying $36. (Students and faculty members can use it for free.)

- **Use the FTP function inside another application,** such as Adobe Dreamweaver or Adobe GoLive.
- **Use a free Terminal application,** such as the one supplied with Mac OS X, found in the Utilities folder inside your Applications folder, which offers FTP. For instructions, see *Mac OS X Tiger All-in-One Desk Reference For Dummies,* by Mark L. Chambers (Wiley).

Most FTP utilities and functions within applications provide an easy way to copy files. For example, Fetch 5 provides a drag-and-drop interface for transferring any type of file with FTP servers. After you establish a connection with the FTP server by typing the appropriate information (the FTP server name, your ID, your password, and the directory that you have access to), you can drag files to and from the FTP server window via the Finder, or you can browse folders to select files and then use the Get and Put buttons.

You can send an entire folder of files, such as an album of songs or an artist folder with multiple albums, by stuffing the folder (or even a set of folders) into a compressed *Zip file.* (Zip is a standard compression format.) Select the files or folders and Control-click (Mac) or right-click (Windows) the selection. In Mac OS X, choose Create Archive; in Windows, choose WinZip (or similar Zip utility that installs itself into Windows menus).

You can then transfer the Zip file to the FTP server in one step. Although the Zip file formats compress other types of files, the files won't get any smaller if your music files are already compressed as MP3 or AAC. However, the format offers a compact way of sending an entire folder of files.

Part II
Managing Your Media Content

"Why can't you just bring your iPod like everyone else?"

In this part . . .

Visit this part to find out how to organize the content in your iTunes library, import photos and video, and sync devices with your iTunes library.

- Chapter 8 describes how to browse your iTunes library, change the List view options, sort your content, and search for songs, artists, albums, music videos, movies, and TV shows.
- Chapter 9 describes how to add information, artwork, and ratings for each content item and then edit the info in iTunes.
- Chapter 10 shows you how to build playlists (including smart playlists) of songs and entire albums in iTunes.
- Chapter 11 explains how to import photos from digital cameras and videos from digital camcorders onto your computer to use with your iPod.
- Chapter 12 describes synchronizing your iPod, iPhone, Apple TV, or iPod shuffle with your iTunes library automatically or manually. It also covers how to edit playlists and content information directly on your iPod.
- Chapter 13 shows you how to make backup copies of your iTunes library, manage multiple libraries, and move your library to another hard drive.
- Chapter 14 is a guide to burning audio and MP3 CDs and data DVDs, as well as printing CD jewel-case inserts and song listings.

Chapter 8

Searching, Browsing, and Sorting in iTunes

In This Chapter

- Browsing your iTunes library
- Changing options for viewing your content
- Sorting content by view options
- Searching for content in the library

You rip a few CDs, buy some songs and movies from the iTunes Store, and you're hooked. You keep adding more and more content to your library and forget how to find items you added last month. It's time to discover how to organize your content and navigate your iTunes library.

The iTunes library is awesome, even by everyday jukebox standards. Even though previous versions were limited to a paltry (cough!) 32,000 files per library and you had to create multiple libraries to get around that limit, the current version (actually all versions newer than version 4) can virtually hold an unlimited number of files. Of course, the limit depends entirely on how much space you have on your hard drive.

Consider that an 80GB iPod can hold about 20,000 songs — enough music to last over a month even if played 24 hours each day! If you keep your iTunes library down to the size of what fits on your iPod, though, you still have a formidable collection at your fingertips. If your music collection is getting large, organize it to make finding songs easier. After all, finding U2's "I Still Haven't Found What I'm Looking For" is a challenge even in a library of "only" 32,000 songs.

This chapter shows you how to search, browse, and sort your iTunes library. You can find any song, movie, TV show, audio book, podcast, game, or radio station in seconds. You can also change the viewing options to make your library's display more useful, such as displaying songs sorted by artist, album, genre, or other attributes, or sorting TV shows by season or episode.

Browsing Your Library Content

The iTunes window provides the Browse and List panes on the right side and the Source pane on the left side (refer to Figure 3-1 in Chapter 3). The Browse and List panes offer a view of your library and content, depending on which sources of content you choose in the Source pane on the left side. The choices in the Source pane are as follows:

- **Library section:** Select Music, Movies, TV Shows, Podcasts, Audiobooks, iPod Games, or Radio.
  - *Music:* Lists the entire library of songs and music videos, purchased, ripped, or copied into the library.
  - *Movies:* Lists only the movies purchased in the iTunes Store and movie files you've added to your library.
  - *TV Shows:* Lists only the TV shows purchased in the iTunes Store.
  - *Podcasts:* Lists only the podcasts you've subscribed to. (See Chapter 5 for details on subscribing to and browsing podcasts.)
  - *Audiobooks:* Lists only the audio books purchased in the iTunes Store or from Audible.com or other sources. (See Chapter 6 for details on playing audio books.)
  - *iPod Games:* Lists only the iPod games purchased in the iTunes Store or from other sources.
  - *Radio:* Lists the Web radio stations you can play. Radio station content is streamed to your computer but not stored in your library.
- **Store section:** The iTunes Store. You've likely been there before; see Chapter 4.
- **Devices section:** Your iPod, iPhone, Apple TV, and other devices appear here. When you select a device such as an iPod, iTunes displays the synchronization options for that iPod. See Chapter 12 for details on opening and navigating the library on an iPod.
- **Playlist section:** Smart playlists and regular playlists appear in this section. (See Chapter 10 for information about playlists.) Also appearing in this section is Party Shuffle, which lists the Party Shuffle playlist. (See Chapter 6 for tips on using the Party Shuffle feature.)

Overwhelmed by the long list of content in the List pane? Try browsing: Switch from List view to Browse view, which has browsing columns you can use to easily find items, such as music albums or TV episodes. After selecting a source of content in the Source pane, click the Browse button in the lower-right corner to toggle between Browse view, in which the Browse pane appears above the List pane (refer to Figure 3-1 in Chapter 3), or List view, in which the List pane of songs or other items appears by itself.

In addition to the Browse button, iTunes offers three View buttons in the upper-right corner to change your view of the Browse pane and List pane:

- **The left button** (or choose View➪List View) shows items in a list. Click the Browse button to toggle between the list by itself and the list with browsing columns.
- **The center button** (or choose View➪Album view) shows items in a list grouped with thumbnail cover art images. Click the Browse button to toggle between the album view by itself and the album view with browsing columns, as shown in Figure 8-1.
- **The right button** shows the cover browser, also known as Cover Flow, as described in the upcoming section, "Browsing by cover art." (You can also show the cover browser by choosing View➪Cover Flow View.) The Browse button has no function in this view.

Figure 8-1: Browse music in Album view with thumbnail cover art.

Browsing by cover art

Does viewing an album cover whet your appetite for the music inside? Of course it does. Album covers provide a context for the music that simply can't be put into words or conveyed by sound alone. The box art for a video and the cover of a book help sell the product, but cover art is particularly influential with music.

One fantastic innovation of iTunes (version 7.1.1 or later) is how it integrates cover art from albums, book covers, and video boxes with your library so that you can flip through your content to find items based on the artwork. Figure 8-2 shows the iTunes window (on a Mac) using Cover Flow view to display the Music portion of the iTunes library. (Mac and Windows versions of iTunes look nearly identical and offer the same viewing options.)

Cover Flow lets you flip through your cover art to select music, movies, TV shows, and audio books. (The cover browser doesn't work with podcasts, games, or radio stations.) Just drag the slider to scroll swiftly through your library, or you can click to the right or left of the cover art in the foreground to move forward or backward in your library, respectively. When you scroll or click through cover art, the content items in the List pane also change. Double-click the foreground cover art to start playing the first item — whether it's an album's first song, a movie, the first chapter of an audio book, or the first episode of a TV show.

Figure 8-2: Browse music using Cover Flow view.

Click the Browse Full-Screen button to display Cover Flow, um, full-screen. You can still click a cover to select an album, click within each cover to move forward and backward, and use the cover browser's slider to navigate your library. iTunes also offers a volume control slider to set the audio volume while browsing full-screen cover art. Press Esc (Escape) or click the Browse Full-Screen button (with its arrows pointing inward) in the lower-right corner of the display to stop displaying the cover browser full-screen and return to the iTunes window.

To fill your library automatically with cover art for the CDs you ripped, get yourself an iTunes Store account (if you don't already have one). Log in to your account; then choose Advanced⇨Get Album Artwork. iTunes grabs the cover art not only for iTunes Store purchases but also for CDs you ripped — provided that the albums are also available in the iTunes Store. You can also get your cover art from other places that sell CDs (including Amazon.com) or even scan them from the actual CDs. The optimal size for cover art is 300 x 300 pixels.

Browsing songs by artist and album

To browse music in your library, select Music in the Source pane in the Library section. The List view shows the title of each song in the Name column, the artist or band name in the Artist column, and the title of the album in the Album column. The Browse view organizes songs by Genre, Artist, and Album. (The Genre column appears only if you leave the Show Genre When Browsing option turned on in the General dialog of iTunes Preferences.) You can switch to Album view (refer to Figure 8-1) or to Cover Flow view (refer to Figure 8-2) to show the album cover art.

Select a genre in the Genre column to see artists in that genre or select All at the top of the Genre column to see all artists for all genres. When you select an artist in the Artist column (the middle column; see Figure 8-3), the album titles appear in the Album column (on the right). When you select an album in Browse view, iTunes displays only the songs for that album in the List pane below the Browse pane.

To see more than one album from an artist at a time, press ⌘ (Mac) or Ctrl (Windows) and then click each album name.

When you select different albums in the Album column, the List pane displays the songs from that album. The songs are listed in proper track order, just as the artist, producer, or record label intended (assuming that the correct track information has been downloaded from the Internet or entered into the song's information dialog, as we describe in Chapter 9).

Figure 8-3: Select an artist to see the list of albums for that artist.

If you don't get track information from the Internet for each song (as we show in Chapter 5) or if you add the track information via the content item's information dialog (as we describe in Chapter 9), iTunes displays a blank space for the Artist and Album name along with Track 01 and so on for each track. However, that makes browsing for a song or artist by name difficult.

To see all the songs in the library in Browse view, select All at the top of each of the columns — Genre, Artist, and Album.

Note: iTunes version 7.1.1 and newer versions no longer consider Clash and The Clash to be different music groups, sorting them properly under C. We show you how to edit the artist name and other information in Chapter 9.

Browsing audio books

To browse the audio books in your library, select Audiobooks in the Source pane in the Library section. The List view shows the title of each book with its part number (long books typically have multiple parts) in the Name column, and the author's name in the Artist column. If you add the Album column heading to your List view (as we describe in the section, "Changing the List view options," later in this chapter), the title of the book appears in the Album column. The Browse view organizes audio books by Genre, Artist (the author), and Album (the book). (The Genre column appears only if you leave the Show Genre When Browsing option selected in the General dialog of iTunes Preferences.)

Browsing movies, videos, and TV shows

Any video files you add to your library from sources other than the iTunes Store are classified as movies, and you can find them in the Movies section of the Source pane. You can also find in the Movies section those movies and short films you downloaded from the iTunes Store.

To browse movies, select Movies in the Source pane. The List view shows the title of each movie in the Name column. The Album view (as shown in Figure 8-4) and the Cover Flow view show the first key frame of the movie or the box cover art for the movie. The Browse view organizes movies by Genre, Artist, and Album.

To browse TV shows downloaded from the iTunes Store, select TV Shows in the Source pane. The List view shows the title of each episode in the Name column, the title of the show itself in the Show column, and the season number in the Season column. The Album view and the Cover Flow view show the promotional cover art for the TV show. The Browse view organizes TV shows by Genre, Show, and Season.

Figure 8-4: Browse movies in your iTunes library in Album view.

Browsing iPod games

Your iPod is, in a sense, a pocket game machine. Although they won't give Nintendo, Xbox, or PlayStation models much competition, fifth- and sixth-generation iPods that play video can also play games you can purchase and download from the iTunes Store. And although you can't play the games in iTunes, you can browse the list of games you downloaded from the store.

To browse iPod games downloaded from the iTunes Store, select iPod Games in the Source pane. A scrollable pane appears to the right of the Source pane, displaying thumbnail images of the games. Click a thumbnail image to see a description of the game.

Okay, we know you're a closet gamer, so rush right over to Chapter 15 for details on how to run iPod games.

Displaying Content in List View

To display your content in the List pane as a list, click the left View button (refer to Figure 8-1). You can then click the Browse button in the lower-right corner of the iTunes window to toggle between the list by itself and the list with browsing columns. The column headings in the iTunes List view have different meanings for the following types of content:

- **Songs and music videos:** The Name is the title of the song; the Artist is the band, artist, or performer. The Album is the title of the CD or LP on which the song appeared. For music videos, the Name is typically the title of a song in the music video.
- **Podcasts:** The Name is the title of the podcast episode (as in "Ballad Roots of California Folk-Rock"), the Artist is the name of the podcast author (as in Tony Bove), and the Album is the name of the podcast (as in *Rockument*).
- **Audio books:** The Album is typically the book's title (as in *Fear and Loathing in Las Vegas*), and the Name is typically the title of one of the parts (as in *Fear and Loathing in Las Vegas*–Part 1 of 3).
- **TV shows:** The Name is the name of the TV show episode (as in "Mr. Monk and the Airplane"), the Artist is the name of the show (as in *Monk*), and the Album is the season (as in *Monk,* Season 1).

Understanding the content indicators

When you make choices in iTunes, it displays an action indicator next to each content item in List view — song, movie, TV show episode, music video, audio book, radio station, or podcast episode — to show you what it's doing. Here's a list of the indicators and their meanings:

- **Orange waveform:** iTunes is importing the item.
- **Green check mark:** iTunes finished importing the item.
- **Exclamation point:** iTunes can't find the item.

  If you move or delete the item accidentally, you can move the item back into iTunes by dragging its file from your hard drive into the iTunes window. (To find content files on your hard drive, see Chapter 13.)
- **Broadcast icon:** The item is on the Internet and plays as a stream.
- **Black check mark:** The item is marked for the next operation, such as importing from an audio CD or playing in sequence.

  Click to remove the check mark.
- **Speaker:** The item (song, movie, TV show episode, music video, audio book, radio station, or podcast episode) is playing.
- **Chasing arrows:** iTunes is copying the content item from another location or downloading it from the Internet.

Changing the List view options

iTunes lets you customize the List view in the List pane. The list starts out with the Name, Time, Artist, Album, Genre, My Rating, Play Count, and Last Played categories. You might have to drag the horizontal scroll bar along the bottom of the song list to see all these columns. You can display more, less, or different information in your song list.

Customize your List view in the following ways:

- **Make a column wider or narrower.** While you move your cursor over the divider between two columns, the cursor changes to a vertical bar with opposing arrows extending left and right; you can click and drag the divider to change the column's width.
- **Change the order of columns.** Click a column heading and drag the entire column to the left or right.

  You can't change the position of the Name column and the narrow column to its left, which displays indicators.
- **Add or remove columns.** All columns except Name can be added or removed:

  a. *Choose View⇨View Options.*

  b. *Select the columns that you want to appear in the list from the View Options dialog (as shown in Figure 8-5).*

You can also change the view options by Ctrl-clicking or right-clicking any column heading in the list in either Browse view or List view.

View Options

Music

Show Columns

☑ Album	☐ Episode ID	☐ Show
☐ Album Artist	☑ Equalizer	☐ Size
☑ Artist	☐ Genre	☑ Skip Count
☐ Beats Per Minute	☐ Grouping	☐ Sort Album
☐ Bit Rate	☐ Kind	☐ Sort Album Artist
☐ Category	☐ Last Played	☐ Sort Artist
☐ Comment	☑ Last Skipped	☐ Sort Composer
☐ Composer	☐ My Rating	☐ Sort Name
☑ Date Added	☐ Play Count	☐ Sort Show
☐ Date Modified	☐ Release Date	☑ Time
☐ Description	☐ Sample Rate	☑ Track Number
☐ Disc Number	☐ Season	☐ Year

Cancel OK

Figure 8-5: Change the viewing options for List view.

Browse view includes a Genre column on the left side. If you don't need a Genre column, you can remove it from the Browse view:

1. **Choose iTunes⇨Preferences (Mac) or Edit⇨Preferences (Windows).**
2. **Click the General tab at the top of the Preferences window.**
3. **In the General dialog, deselect the Show Genre When Browsing option, which is on by default.**

Sorting Content by the List View Options

With just a little know-how, you can use the List view options to sort the listing of content items. You can sort items not only by name or album but also by composer, the date the items were added to the library, or other information that you can add to an item (as we describe in Chapter 9).

At the very least, you can sort the content by the column headings you now use in the List view. You can also add other column headings to your List view (as we describe in the earlier section, "Changing the List view options") and sort with them.

For example, clicking the Time heading reorders the items by their duration in *ascending order* (shortest to longest). If you click the Time heading again, the sort is in *descending order* (reversed, starting with the longest item). You can sort by any column heading, such as Artist, Album, Track, Date Added, and Ratings.

You can tell whether the sort is in ascending or descending order by the little arrow indicator in the heading. When the arrow points up, the sort is in ascending order; when pointing down, it's in descending order.

Alternatively, you can sort the list in alphabetical order. Click the Artist heading to sort the items in the list by artist name in alphabetical order (arrow pointing up). Click it again to sort the list in reverse alphabetical order (arrow pointing down).

iTunes also lets you sort the song list via the Album column. Each time you click Album, the heading cycles through each of the following options:

- **Album,** which sorts alphabetically by album title.
- **Album by Artist,** which groups albums by artist and then lists them alphabetically.
- **Album by Year,** which groups albums by artist and then lists them chronologically by year (set in the Song Information dialog).

iTunes keeps track of the songs, audio books, and podcasts you skip — not to be polite, just to be useful. You can use this feature to sort the Music and Audiobooks sections of your library in List view, thereby making it easier to select and delete the items you skip. (The Skip Count doesn't count how many times you skip videos, TV shows, and movies.)

In addition to the usual List view options (which you can change by Ctrl-clicking or right-clicking any column heading in the list, or by choosing View⇨View Options), you can now view and sort by the Skip Count. *Skip Count* keeps track of how many times you skipped the content item within the first 19 seconds, using the Forward/Next button. (Clicking a new item and playing it the first time doesn't count.) You can also view and sort the list by selecting Last Skipped in View Options, which shows the date and time when you last skipped the item. Another way to select and delete items that have a high skip count is to create a smart playlist; see Chapter 10 for details.

Searching for Content

Because your iTunes library will most likely grow, you might find the usual browsing and scrolling methods that we describe earlier in this chapter too time-consuming. Let iTunes find your content for you!

If you want to search the entire library in Browse view, select All at the top of the Genre and Artist columns to browse the entire library before typing a term in the Search field. Or, if you prefer, click the Browse button again to return to the List view.

Locate the Search field — the oval field in the top-right corner — and follow these steps:

1. **Click in the Search field and enter several characters of your search term.**

Use these tips for successful searching:

- *Specify your search* with a specific title, artist, or album.
- *Narrow your search* by typing more characters. Using fewer characters results in a longer list of possible songs.
- *Case doesn't matter.* The Search feature ignores case. For example, when we search for *miles,* iTunes finds "Eight Miles High," "Forty Miles of Bad Road," "She Smiles like a River," and everything by Miles Davis.

2. **Look through the results, which display while you type.**

   The search operation works immediately, as shown in Figure 8-6, displaying, in the song list, any matches in the Name, Artist, and Album columns.

   If you're in Browse view with an artist and a particular album selected, you can't search for another artist or song. Use browsing with searching to further narrow your search.

3. **Scroll through the search results and then click an item to select it.**

To back out of a search so that the full list appears again, you can either click the circled X in the Search field (which appears only after you start typing characters) or delete the characters in the Search field. You then see the entire list in the library's song list, just like before you began your search. All the items are still there and remain there unless you explicitly remove them. Searching manipulates only your view of the items.

Figure 8-6: Search for anything by typing any part of the name, artist, album, or title.

Finding the Content's Media File

Getting lost in a large library is easy. While you browse your library, you might want to return quickly to view the current item playing. While your file plays, choose File⇨Show Current Song (or press ⌘-L on a Mac or Ctrl-L in Windows as a shortcut). iTunes shows you the item that's playing.

You can also show the location of the media file for any content item. This trick comes in handy when you want to copy a song or video file to another hard drive or over a network, or when you want to open it in another application. On a Mac, choose File⇨Show in Finder (or press ⌘-R); in Windows, choose File⇨Show in Windows Explorer (or press Ctrl-R). iTunes gives control to the operating system (Mac or Windows), which displays the folder containing the media file.

You can show the file location if it's on your hard drive but not if it's in a shared library on another computer. See Chapter 13 for more details on looking for media files.

Showing Duplicate Items

Because your library will grow, you'll probably want to check for duplications. Some songs that appear on artist CDs also appear on compilation or soundtrack CDs. If you rip them all, you could have duplicate songs that take up space on your hard drive. You might even have duplicate videos, audio books, or podcast episodes.

On the other hand, maybe you want to find different versions of the same song by the same artist. Even when the songs appear on different albums, iTunes can quickly find all the songs with the same title by the same artist.

To show duplicate items in the list, choose View⇨Show Duplicates. iTunes displays all the duplicate items in alphabetical order in the List pane. If iTunes is in Browse view, you see all the duplicate items in artist order. Click the artist to see the duplicate items specifically for that artist.

To stop showing duplicate items and return to your previous view (either List view or Browse view), click the Show All button below the list of duplicates.

Deleting Content

Deleting content might seem counterproductive when you're trying to build up your iTunes library, but sometimes you just have to do it. For example, you want to delete

- **Versions of songs:** You might have ripped a CD twice — say, once in AIFF format to burn the songs onto another CD and once in AAC format for your library and iPod. You can delete the AIFF versions in your library after burning your CD (as we describe in Chapter 14).
- **Songs from playlists:** You can delete songs from playlists yet keep the songs in your library. When you delete a song from a playlist, the song is simply deleted from the list — not from the library. You can delete entire playlists as well without harming the songs in the library. You have to switch to the Library option in the Source pane to delete songs from the library. (See Chapter 10 for more information about playlists.)
- **Any podcast, video, song, or audio book album, or artist from the library:**
  - *Podcasts:* Select the Podcasts option in the Source pane and then select any podcast or podcast episodes. Press Delete/Backspace (or choose Edit⇨Delete) to delete them. If you delete the podcast, you remove it from your library, and you have to re-subscribe to it to get it back. If you delete an episode, you can get it back by clicking the Get button next to the episode. You can also select a single podcast episode and then choose Edit⇨Delete All to delete all episodes but keep the podcast itself.
  - *Movies or TV shows:* Select the Movies or TV Shows option in the Source pane and then select any movie or TV show episodes or seasons. Press Delete/Backspace (or choose Edit⇨Delete). You can also select a single TV show episode and then choose Edit⇨Delete All to delete all episodes.
  - *Audio books:* Select the Audiobooks option in the Source pane and then select any book section or all the sections of a book (books are typically divided into multiple sections). Press Delete/Backspace (or choose Edit⇨Delete).
  - *Songs (individually, or albums, or artists) or music videos:* Select the Music option in the Source pane and then select the item or items — which can be on or more songs, an entire album, all the works of an artist, or a selection of albums or artists. For example, you can select an album in Browse view to automatically select all the songs on the album. Press Delete/Backspace (or choose Edit⇨Delete).

Deleting a content item from the iTunes library removes the item from your library, but it doesn't remove it from your hard drive until you agree.

In the first warning dialog that appears, click Remove to remove the selected items from the library, or click Cancel.

When iTunes displays a second warning

```
Some of the selected files are located in your iTunes
Music folder. Would you like to move these files to the
Trash?
```

you can click Yes to trash the item, click No to keep it in your music folder, or click Cancel to cancel the operation.

If you choose to move the album or artist folder to the Trash, the album or artist folder is deleted from your hard drive; otherwise, it remains in your iTunes Music folder.

If you leave music files and folders in your iTunes Music folder, you can add them back to your iTunes library by dragging and dropping them into the iTunes window.

You can delete multiple items in one clean sweep. Press Shift while you click a range of items. Alternatively, press ⌘ (Mac) or Ctrl (Windows) when you click individual items to add them to the selection. Then press Delete/Backspace (or choose Edit⇨Delete).

Chapter 9

Adding and Editing Information in iTunes

In This Chapter

- Retrieving information online
- Editing information for each content item
- Adding information, cover art, comments, and ratings

Organization depends on information. You expect your computer to do a lot more than just store a song with *Track 01* as the only identifier. Not only can iTunes retrieve the song's track information from the Internet but it can also find the cover art for you.

Adding all the information for your iTunes content seems like a lot of trouble, but you can get most of the information automatically from the Internet — and without all that pesky typing. Adding track information is important because you certainly don't want to mistakenly play "My Guitar Wants to Kill Your Mama" by Frank Zappa when trying to impress your classical music teacher with the third movement of Tchaikovsky's *Pathétique Symphony,* do you? And because videos you make yourself or convert from other sources don't have this automatic information, you have to enter some description to tell them apart.

This chapter shows you how to add information to your content library in iTunes and edit it for better viewing so that you can organize your content by artist, album name, genre, composer, and ratings. You can then use this information to sort in List view or Browse view by clicking the column headings. This chapter also describes how to add cover art for navigating your library with Cover Flow.

Retrieving Song Information from the Internet

Why bother entering information if someone else has already done it for you? You can easily get information about most music CDs from the Internet (that is, assuming you can connect to the Internet). The online database available for iTunes users holds information for millions of songs on commercial CDs and even some bootleg CDs.

Retrieving information automatically

When you pop a commercial music CD into your computer running iTunes, iTunes automatically looks up the track information for that CD on the Internet and fills in the information fields (name, artist, album, and so on). You don't need to do anything to make this happen. You can also edit the information after iTunes fills in the fields.

If your computer doesn't access the Internet automatically, you might want to turn off this automatic information retrieval (you can always retrieve the information manually as we describe later in this section). To turn off the retrieval of track information, follow these steps:

1. **Choose iTunes⇨Preferences (Mac) or Edit⇨Preferences (Windows).**

   The iTunes Preferences dialog appears with buttons along the top.

2. **Click the Advanced tab.**

   The preferences on the Advanced tab appear.

3. **Click the Importing tab.**

   The Advanced Importing preferences appear.

4. **Deselect the Automatically Retrieve CD Track Names from Internet option.**

   With this option turned on, iTunes connects to the Internet automatically and retrieves the track information. When turned off, iTunes does not retrieve the information, but you can retrieve it manually as we describe in the next section.

Retrieving information manually

You can connect manually to the Internet at any time (for example, by using a modem connection) and retrieve the song information when you're ready to use it. After you connect to the Internet, choose Advanced⇨Get CD Track Names.

Using the Gracenote database

The first time we popped a commercial music CD into a computer, song information appeared like magic. iTunes automatically displayed the song names, album title, and artist names. How did it know? This information isn't stored on a standard music CD in digital form, but iTunes has to recognize the disc somehow.

The magic is that the software knows how to reach out and find the information on the Internet — in the Gracenote CDDB service. CDDB stands for (you guessed it) *CD Database.* The site (`www.gracenote.com`) hosts CDDB on the Web and searches for music CDs by artist, song title, and other methods. The iTunes software already knows how to use this database so you don't have to!

Gracenote recognizes an audio CD by taking into account the number, sequence, and duration of tracks. (This is how the database recognizes CD-Rs that are burned with the identical songs in the same order.) The database keeps track of information for most of the music CDs that you find on the market.

Although the database doesn't contain any information about personal or custom CDs, people can submit information to the database about such CDs. You can even do this from within iTunes: Type the information for each track while the audio CD is in your computer and then choose Advanced➪Submit CD Track Names. The information that you enter is sent to the Gracenote CDDB site, where the good people who work tirelessly on the database check out your information before including it. In fact, if you spot a typo or something erroneous in the information that you receive from the Gracenote CDDB, you can easily correct it. Just use the Submit CD Track Names command to send the corrected version back to the Gracenote site. The good folks at Gracenote appreciate the effort.

Even if you automatically connect to the Internet, the song information database on the Internet (Gracenote CDDB) might be momentarily unavailable, or you might have a delayed response. If at first you don't succeed, choose Advanced➪Get CD Track Names again.

Entering Content Information

You have to enter the information for certain media, including CDs that aren't known by the Gracenote CDDB, custom CD-Rs, and videos and audio books that you bring into iTunes from sources other than the iTunes Store. No big deal, though; just follow these steps:

1. **Click directly in the information field (such as Artist) in either Browse view or List view.**
2. **Click again so that the mouse pointer toggles to an editing cursor.**
3. **Type text directly into the information field.**

After grabbing the song information from the Internet or typing it, iTunes keeps track of the information for the CD even if you just play the CD without importing it. The next time you insert the CD, the song information is automatically filled in.

Editing the Information

Retrieving ready-made song information from the Internet is a great help, but you might not always like the format it comes in. Maybe you want to edit artist and band names or other information. For example, we like to list solo artists by last name rather than by first name. (Gracenote CDDB lists artists by first name.) For example, we routinely change *Miles Davis* to *Davis, Miles.*

Other annoyances sometimes occur when bands feature *The* at the beginning of their names, such as The Who, The Band, The Beatles, and The Beach Boys. Even though these names sort correctly (in alphabetical order, under their proper names), we dislike having *The* before the band name, so we routinely remove it.

You might also want to change the information that is supplied by the iTunes Store for the movies, TV shows, music videos, audio books, and podcasts you download. And if you obtain your content from other sources, you might need to add information for the first time.

In either Browse view or List view, you can edit the content information by clicking directly in the specific track's field (such as the Artist field) and then clicking again so that the mouse pointer toggles to an editing cursor. You can then select the text and type over it — or use the Copy, Cut, and Paste commands on the Edit menu — to move tiny bits of text around within the field. As you can see in Figure 9-1, we changed the Artist field to *Beck, Jeff.*

Figure 9-1: Click inside a field to edit the information.

You can edit the Name, Artist, Album, Genre, and My Ratings fields in the list. However, editing this information by choosing File⇨Get Info is easier. Keep reading to find out why.

Editing multiple items at once

Editing in the content list is fine if you're editing the information for one item, but typically you need to change all the tracks of an audio CD. For example, if a CD of songs by Bob Dylan is listed with the artist as *Bob Dylan,* you might want to change all the songs at once to *Dylan, Bob.* Changing all the information in one fell swoop is fast and clean, but like most powerful shortcuts, you need to be careful because it can be dangerous.

You can change a group of items in either Browse or Song List view. Follow these steps to change a group of items at once:

1. **Select a group of content items by clicking the first item and then pressing Shift while you click the last item.**

   All the items between the first and last are highlighted. You can extend a selection by Shift-clicking other items or add to a selection by ⌘-clicking (Mac) or Ctrl-clicking (Windows). You can also remove items already selected by ⌘-clicking (Mac) or Ctrl-clicking (Windows).

2. **Choose File⇨Get Info or press ⌘-I (Mac) or Ctrl-I (Windows).**

   A warning message displays:

   ```
   Are you sure you want to edit information for multiple
   items?
   ```

   Speed-editing the information in multiple items at once can be dangerous for your library organization. If, for example, you change the name of the item (the song or movie title, for example), the entire selection has that name! Be careful about what you edit when using this method.

3. **Click Yes to edit information for multiple items.**

   The Multiple Item Information dialog appears, as shown in Figure 9-2.

4. **Edit the field you want to change for the multiple items.**

   When you edit a field, a check mark appears automatically in the check box next to the field. iTunes assumes that you want that field changed in all the selected items. Make sure that no other check box is selected except the field that you want.

5. **Click OK to make the change.**

   iTunes changes the field for the entire selection of items.

Figure 9-2: Change the field info for multiple items at once.

You can edit the content information in iTunes immediately after inserting the CD — before importing the audio tracks from the disc. The changes you make to the track information for the CD are imported along with the music. What's interesting is that when you access the library without the audio CD, the edited version of the track information is still there. iTunes remembers the edited song information until the next time you insert that audio CD.

Editing fields for a single item

Although the track information grabbed from the Internet is enough for identifying a song in your iTunes library, some facts — such as composer credits — might not be included. Adding composer credits is usually worth your effort because you can then search and sort by composer and create playlists based on the composer. Videos (movies, TV shows, and music videos), podcasts, and audio books might also have information in their fields that you want to change or have blank fields that could use some helpful information.

To locate a single item — song, video, podcast, or audio book, choose File➪Get Info (or press ⌘-I on a Mac or Ctrl-I in Windows). You see the item's information dialog, as shown in Figure 9-3.

When you select one item, its information dialog appears; when you select multiple items, the Multiple Item Information dialog appears.

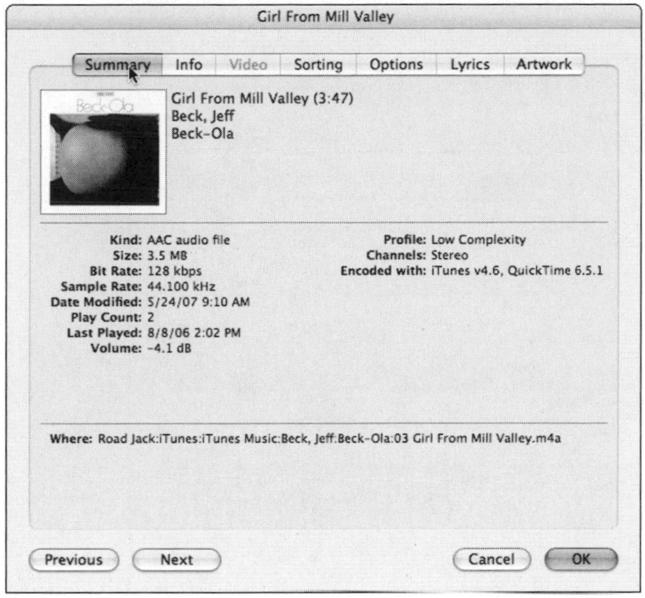

Figure 9-3: A content item's information dialog.

A selection's information dialog offers the following tabs:

- **Summary:** The Summary tab (as shown in Figure 9-3) offers useful information about the media file format and location on your hard drive, the file size, and the information about the digital compression method (bit rate, sample rate, and so on).
- **Info:** The Info tab allows you to change the name, artist, composer, album, genre, year, and other information. You can also add comments, as shown in Figure 9-4.
- **Video:** The Video tab lets you set the type of video — movie, TV show, or music video — in the Kind pop-up menu. For TV shows, you can add show information including the title of the show, episode number and ID, and season number.
- **Sorting:** The Sorting tab allows you to add information to fields for additional choices while sorting your library content. For example, you can add a different name for the artist in the Sort Artist field to the right of the Artist field. Information from the Info tab appears on the left side, and you can add an alternative sort field on the right side. You can even add a Show field for the title of a concert or some other use. Choose View➪View Options to select a sort field as a List view option, and then you can sort your content in List view by using the sort fields.

Girl From Mill Valley

Summary | Info | Video | Sorting | Options | Lyrics | Artwork

Name: Girl From Mill Valley
Artist: Beck, Jeff
Year: 1969
Album Artist:
Track Number: 3 of 7
Album: Beck-Ola
Disc Number: 1 of 1
Grouping:
BPM:
Composer: Nicky Hopkins
Comments: Nicky Hopkins on piano
Genre: Rock
Part of a compilation

Previous | Next | Cancel | OK

Figure 9-4: View and edit information from the Info tab.

- **Options:** The Options tab, as shown in Figure 9-5, offers the following:
  - *Volume Adjustment:* Drag the slider to the right to increase the volume adjustment up to 100%; drag the slider to the left to decrease the volume adjustment up to 100%.
  - *Equalizer Preset:* Choose an equalizer preset for an item. See Chapter 17 for details on how you can use this preset to control how an item sounds on your iPod as well as in iTunes.
  - *Ratings:* Assign up to five stars to an item as a rating. (See how in the upcoming section, "Adding a rating.")
  - *Start Time and Stop Time:* Set the start and stop times for an item.

    Visit this book's companion Web site for details.
  - *Remember Playback Position:* Set this option for an item so that when you select and play the item, iTunes resumes playing it from where you left off. This option is usually turned on for audio books, movies, and TV shows.
  - *Skip When Shuffling:* Set this option for an item to be skipped from Party Shuffle.
  - *Part of a Gapless Album:* Set this option for an item to be played back without a gap between songs. (See Chapter 5 to find out about the gaps between songs.)

Figure 9-5: Add a rating to a song from the Options tab.

- **Lyrics:** The Lyrics tab offers a text field for typing or pasting lyrics (or any text).

  You can view the lyrics on fifth- and sixth-generation iPods and iPod nano models by starting a song, or choosing the Now Playing option from the main menu, and then pressing the Select button three times (once to show the slider, again to show the cover art, and one more time to show the lyrics).

- **Artwork:** The Artwork tab allows you to add or delete artwork for the item. See the upcoming section, "Adding Cover Art."

If you follow the careers of certain guitarists, vocalists, or session musicians, you can sort your music in List view by something other than the given artist for the album. First, provide a new entry for the Sort Artist or Sort Album Artist fields in the Sorting tab, and then choose that field as a view option so that you can sort on it. For example, we like to use the Sort Artist field for the leader, lead guitarist, or lead singer in a band, or a session player or special guest (such as Nicky Hopkins, who played keyboards on a variety of albums by different bands including The Who, The Rolling Stones, and The Beatles). After entering *Nicky Hopkins* into the Sort Artist field for the songs, we can choose View⇨View Options and select Sort Artist for a column heading. We can then sort the List view by clicking the new Sort Artist heading to find all recordings featuring Nicky Hopkins.

You can apply the entry of a sort field in the Sorting tab to all the tracks of the same album, or to all tracks by the same artist, album artist, composer, or show. After changing the sort field for an item in the Sorting tab, select the item in List view, Control-click (right-click in Windows) the item to display the contextual menu, and then choose Apply Sort Field. Click Yes to make the change.

To move through an album one item at a time when using Get Info (without closing and reopening the information dialog), click the Previous or Next buttons in the bottom-left corner of the dialog.

Adding a rating

iTunes also allows you to rate your content. The cool thing about ratings is that they're *yours*. You can use ratings to mean anything you want. For example, you can rate songs based on how much you like them, whether your mother would listen to them, or how they blend into a work environment.

You might have noticed the My Top Rated playlist in the Source pane. This playlist is an example of a *smart playlist* — a playlist that updates when ratings are changed. The My Top Rated playlist plays all the top-rated songs in your library. You can find out more about playlists in Chapter 10. You can also rate videos based on your watching habits as well as audio books and podcasts.

To add a rating to a content item, click the Options tab (refer to Figure 9-5) and drag inside the My Rating field to add stars. The upper limit is five stars (for the best).

Adding Cover Art

iTunes displays the cover art for your albums, videos, movies, podcasts, audio books, and TV shows in the Cover Flow browser (see Chapter 8 for details), and color-display iPods, Apple TV, and the iPhone also display the cover art. So it makes sense to get the art, especially since it's free!

Items that you buy from the iTunes Store typically include an image of the album, book, or box cover art or a photo of the artist that serves as cover art. You can see the artwork in the lower-left corner of the iTunes window by clicking the Show/Hide Artwork button, as shown in Figure 9-6. The artwork changes for each item or album that you select and play.

To fill your library automatically with cover art for the CDs you ripped, get yourself an iTunes Store account if you don't already have one. Log in to your account and then choose Advanced⇨Get Album Artwork. iTunes grabs the cover art not only for iTunes Store purchases but also for CDs you ripped — provided that the albums are also available in the iTunes Store.

Figure 9-6: Show the artwork for a song's album.

To download cover art for ripped CDs automatically after ripping them (without having to manually choose Advanced⇨Get Album Artwork each time), choose Preferences from the iTunes menu on a Mac or the Edit menu in Windows, click the General tab if it is not already selected, and select the Automatically Download Missing Album Artwork option.

You can also get your cover art from other places that sell CDs (including Amazon.com) or even scan them from the actual CDs. The optimal size for cover art is 300 x 300 pixels. Save it in a graphics format that iTunes (and its underlying graphics technology, *QuickTime*) understands — JPEG, GIF, PNG, TIFF, or Photoshop. With a Web browser, you can visit Web pages to scout for suitable art; just Control-click (Mac) or right-click an image (Windows) to download and save the image on your hard drive.

To add artwork to one or more items, select it (or them) in your iTunes library and do one of the following:

- **Drag the artwork's image file from a Desktop folder into the artwork viewing area (the bottom-left corner of the iTunes window).**

  To add artwork for an entire album (rather than just individual songs) or season of TV shows, first select the album or season in Browse view or select all the items in List view. Then drag the image file into the artwork viewing area.

- **Add artwork to a single item through the information window.**

  Choose File⇨Get Info and then click the Artwork tab in the Get Info dialog. Click the Add button, browse your hard drive or network for the image file, select the file, and then click OK.

- **Add artwork for multiple items in the Multiple Item Information dialog.**

  Choose File⇨Get Info after selecting the items, enable the Artwork field (select its check box), and then drag a graphics file for the cover art from a Desktop folder to the Artwork well. Click Yes to the warning message to change the artwork.

  See the "Editing multiple items at once" section, earlier in this chapter, to find out more about using the Multiple Item Information dialog.

To remove the artwork from an item, view the artwork in a larger window or resize the artwork, choose File⇨Get Info, and then click the Artwork tab. You can add a different image (or several images) with the Add button, delete images with the Delete button, or resize images with the size slider.

Chapter 10

Organizing iTunes Content with Playlists

In This Chapter

- Creating a playlist of multiple songs
- Creating a playlist of albums
- Adding podcast episodes and videos to playlists
- Creating and editing smart playlists
- Creating an iMix playlist for the iTunes Store

To organize your content for different operations, such as copying to your iPod or Apple TV, or burning a CD, you make a *playlist* — a list of the items that you want in the sequence that you want to play them.

You can use playlists to organize your music playback experience. For example, you can make a playlist of love songs from different albums to play the next time you need a romantic mood, or you can compile a playlist of surf songs for a trip to the beach. We create playlists specifically for use with an iPod on road trips and generate other playlists that combine songs from different albums based on themes or similarities. For example, we have a jazz playlist for cruising around the city at night, a classic rock playlist for jogging in the morning, a playlist of short films mixed with TV shows for a long airplane ride, and a playlist of rain songs to celebrate rainy days.

You can create as many playlists of songs, audio books, podcast episodes, and videos in any order that you like. The items and their files don't change, nor are they copied: iTunes simply creates a list of the item names with links to the actual items and their files.

You can even create a *smart playlist,* which automatically includes items in the playlist based on the criteria you set up and also removes items that don't match the criteria. The information included in iTunes (see Chapter 9) is very useful for setting up the criteria. For example, you can define the criteria for a smart playlist to automatically include songs from a particular artist or songs that have the highest rating or fit within a particular musical genre.

Creating Playlists

You need to create a playlist to burn a CD, but playlists can also make it easier to play items you like without browsing the entire library looking for them. You can create playlists of individual songs or entire albums. You can also include audio books, TV shows, videos, podcast episodes, and Web radio stations in playlists.

Song playlists

You can drag individual songs into a playlist and rearrange the songs to play in any sequence you want.

To create a playlist, follow these steps:

1. **Click the Add Playlist button or choose File⇨New Playlist.**

   Clicking the Add Playlist button, in the bottom-left corner of the iTunes window under the Source pane, creates a new playlist in the Source pane named *untitled playlist.*

2. **In the Source pane, click *untitled playlist* twice and give it a new descriptive name.**

   After clicking the playlist name once, a text cursor appears, and the playlist name is highlighted. You can begin typing a new name. After you type a new name, iTunes automatically sorts it into alphabetical order in the Source pane (underneath the preset smart playlists and other sources).

3. **Select Music in the Source pane and then drag songs from the library to the playlist.**

   Drag one song at a time (as shown in Figure 10-1) or drag a group of songs, dropping them onto the playlist name in the Source pane. The initial order of songs in the playlist is based on the order in which you drag them to the list. Of course, you can rearrange the songs in any order after dragging them, as we show in the next step.

4. **Select the playlist in the Source pane and then drag songs to rearrange the list.**

   - *To move a song up the list and scroll at the same time:* Drag it over the up arrow in the first column (the song number).
   - *To move a song down the list and scroll:* Drag it to the bottom of the list.
   - *To move a group of songs at once:* Press Shift and select a range of songs (or press ⌘ on a Mac or Ctrl in Windows while clicking to select specific songs) and then drag them into a new position.

Figure 10-1: Drag a song to your playlist.

You can drag songs from one playlist to another. Only links are copied, not the actual files. Besides dragging songs, you can also rearrange a playlist by sorting the list: Just click the column heading Name, Time, or Artist, and so on. When you double-click a playlist, it opens in a new window that displays the song list.

To open a playlist in a new window, double-click the playlist icon next to the playlist name in the Source pane. You can then select the Music option to browse your music library and drag items to the separate playlist window.

To create a playlist quickly, select the group of songs that you want to make into a playlist. Choose File⇨New Playlist from Selection, or drag the selection to the white area underneath the last playlist in the Source pane. You can then type a name for the new playlist that appears.

Album playlists

Making a playlist of an album is simple. Select the Music option in the Source pane and drag an album from the Album list in Browse view to the white area below the items in your Source pane. Or, select the album and then choose File⇨New Playlist from Selection. iTunes automatically creates a new playlist named after the album.

You might want to play several albums of songs without having to select each album when you play them. For example, you might want to use an iPod on that long drive from London to Liverpool to play The Beatles' albums in the order they were released (or perhaps the reverse order, reversing The Beatles' career from London back to Liverpool).

To create a playlist of entire albums in a particular order, follow these steps:

1. **Create a new playlist.**

   Create a playlist by clicking the Add Playlist button under the Source pane or by choosing File➪New Playlist.

   A new playlist named *untitled playlist* appears in the Source pane.

2. **In the Source pane, click *untitled playlist* twice and give it a new descriptive name.**
3. **Select the Music option in the Source pane and then click the Browse button to find the artist.**

   The Album list appears in the right panel.

4. **Drag the album name over the playlist name.**
5. **Select and drag each subsequent album over the playlist name.**

   Each time you drag an album, iTunes automatically lists the songs in the proper track sequence.

You can rename a playlist at any time by clicking its name twice and typing a new one. Also, in case you forget which songs are in which playlists, you can see all the playlists that include a particular song. In Browse view or List view, press Control on a Mac and click the song; in Windows, right-click the song and choose Playlists from the contextual menu. The playlists that include the song are listed in the submenu.

You can organize your playlists into folders in the Source pane. Choose File➪New Folder to create a folder in the Playlists section of the Source pane. Then drag playlist names in the Source pane and drop them over the new folder — just like how you treat folders in your operating system. Folders are useful for grouping playlists that are similar in content — or, in our case, similar in function. For example, we use a folder to organize the playlists we use to synchronize different iPods. (See Chapter 12 to read about iPod synchronization.) You can include smart playlists as well as regular playlists in folders.

Podcast playlists

You can add podcast episodes to your playlists, or you can even create a playlist consisting entirely of podcast episodes. However, podcasts are a slightly different animal than albums or songs. You can drag individual podcast episodes to a playlist. However, if you drag a podcast by its name, iTunes adds to the playlist only the most recent episodes you listened to (even if only for one second). To add episodes that you haven't heard, you have to select the episodes and then drag them to the playlist.

To add a single podcast episode to a playlist, follow these steps:

1. **Click the Add Playlist button or choose File⇨New Playlist.**

   The Add Playlist button is in the bottom-left corner of the iTunes window under the Source pane.

   A new playlist named *untitled playlist* appears in the Source pane.

2. **In the Source pane, click *untitled playlist* twice and give it a new descriptive name.**

   After you type a new name, iTunes automatically sorts it into alphabetical order in the Source pane, underneath the preset smart playlists and other sources.

3. **Select the Podcasts option in the Source pane and then open a podcast by clicking the triangle next to its name.**

   The podcast opens to reveal its episodes. (See Chapter 6 for details on opening podcasts and playing podcast episodes.)

4. **Drag episodes from the Podcasts list to the playlist.**

   Drag one episode at a time or drag a selection of episodes and then drop them onto the playlist name in the Source pane. The initial order of episodes in the playlist is based on the order in which you drag them to the list. Of course, you can rearrange the episodes in any order after dragging them, as we show you in the next step.

5. **Select the playlist in the Source pane and then drag episodes to rearrange the list.**

   - *To move an episode up the list and scroll at the same time:* Drag it over the up arrow in the first column (the item number).
   - *To move an episode down the list and scroll:* Drag it to the bottom of the list.
   - *To move multiple episodes at once:* Press Shift and select a range of episodes (or press ⌘ on a Mac or Ctrl in Windows to select specific episodes) and then drag them into a new position.

You can also create a playlist consisting only of podcast episodes, just like creating a playlist from an album. Follow these steps:

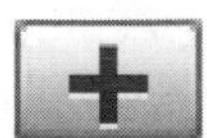

1. **Create a new playlist.**

   Create a playlist by clicking the Add Playlist button under the Source pane or by choosing File⇨New Playlist.

   A new playlist named *untitled playlist* appears in the Source pane.

2. **In the Source pane, click *untitled playlist* twice and give it a new descriptive name.**

3. **Select the Podcasts option in the Source pane and then select a podcast by name.**

4. **Drag the podcast name over the playlist name.**

   iTunes adds the current podcast episode and any other episodes you've already heard to the playlist. Note, however, that episodes you haven't listened to aren't included. You have to drag unheard episodes directly.

Video playlists

You can drag individual videos and TV shows into a playlist and rearrange them to play in any sequence you want.

To create a video playlist, follow these steps:

1. **Click the Add Playlist button or choose File⇨New Playlist.**

   Clicking the Add Playlist button, in the bottom-left corner of the iTunes window under the Source pane, creates a new playlist in the Source pane named *untitled playlist.*

2. **In the Source pane, click *untitled playlist* twice and give it a new descriptive name.**

   After you type a new name, iTunes automatically sorts it into alphabetical order in the Source pane, underneath the preset smart playlists and other sources.

3. **Select the Movies or TV Shows option in the Source pane and then drag videos from the library to the playlist.**

   Drag one video at a time or drag a selection of items, dropping them onto the playlist name in the Source pane. The initial order of videos in the playlist is based on the order in which you drag them to the list.

4. **Select the playlist in the Source pane and then drag videos to rearrange the list.**

   - *To move a video up the list and scroll at the same time:* Drag it over the up arrow in the first column (the item number).
   - *To move a video down the list and scroll:* Drag it to the bottom of the list.
   - *To move a group of videos at once:* Press Shift and select a range of items (or press ⌘ on a Mac or Ctrl in Windows to select specific songs) and then drag them into a new position.

You can mix videos with songs and other items in a playlist. For example, mixing songs and music videos, songs and a video documentary, or just a selection of TV shows, music, podcasts, movies, and audio books for an entire day's worth of entertainment. However, if you transfer the playlist to an iPod that doesn't play video, the iPod skips the videos.

Deleting items from a playlist

You can delete items from playlists while keeping the items in your library. When you delete an item from a playlist, the item is simply deleted from the list — not from the library. You can also delete playlists without harming the content in the library. ***Note:*** Switch to the Library sections (Music, Movies, TV Shows, and so on) in the Source pane to delete items from your library.

To delete an item from a playlist, select the playlist in the Source pane and then select the item. Press Delete/Backspace or choose Edit⇨Delete. In the warning dialog that appears, click Remove to remove the selected item from the list.

You can also completely delete an item from your library from within a playlist by selecting the item and pressing ⌘-Option-Delete (Mac) or Ctrl-Alt-Backspace (Windows).

To delete a playlist, select the playlist in the Source pane and then press Delete/Backspace or choose Edit⇨Delete.

Using Smart Playlists

Under Party Shuffle (near the top of the Playlists section of the Source pane), you can find *smart playlists,* which are indicated by a gear icon. iTunes comes with a few sample smart playlists, such as My Top Rated and Recently Added, and you can create your own. Smart playlists add items to themselves based on prearranged criteria, or *rules.* For example, when you rate your content items, My Top Rated changes to reflect your new ratings. You don't have to set anything up because My Top Rated and Recently Added are already defined for you.

Of course, smart playlists are ignorant of your taste in music or video. You have to program them with rules by using the information in iTunes (see Chapter 9). For example, you can create a smart playlist that uses the Year field to grab all the songs from 1966. This list, in no particular order, might include The Beatles ("Eleanor Rigby"), Frank Sinatra ("Strangers In the Night"), The Yardbirds ("Over Under Sideways Down"), and Ike and Tina Turner ("River Deep, Mountain High") — a far-out playlist, no doubt, but not necessarily what you want. You can use other fields of information that you entered (such as ratings, artist name, or composer) to fine-tune your criteria. You can also use built-in functions, such as *Play Count* (the number of times the item was played) or *Date Added* (the date the item was added to the library).

Creating a smart playlist

To create a new smart playlist, choose File⇨New Smart Playlist. The Smart Playlist dialog appears (as shown in Figure 10-2), offering the following choices for setting criteria:

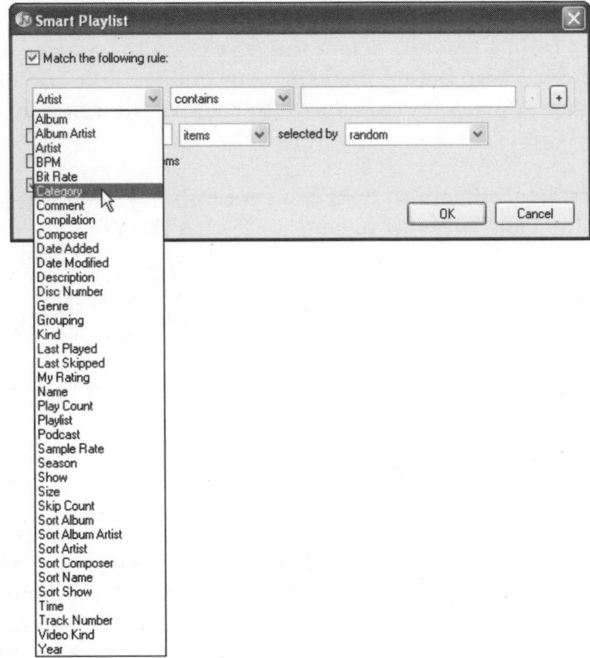

Figure 10-2: Set the first match rule for a smart playlist.

- **Match the Following Rule:** From the first pop-up menu (see Figure 10-2), you can choose any of the categories used for information, such as Composer or Last Played. From the second pop-up menu, you can choose an operator, such as the greater-than or less-than operator. The selections that you make in these two pop-up menus combine to create a rule, such as `Year is greater than 1966`. You can also add multiple conditions by clicking the + button (on the right), and then decide whether to match all or any of these conditions. The Match *xx* of the Following Rules option is enabled by default when you set one or more rules.
- **Limit To:** You can limit the smart playlist to a specific *duration,* measured by the number of songs (items), time, or size in megabytes or gigabytes, as shown in Figure 10-3. You can have items selected by various methods, such as random, most recently played, and so on.
- **Match Only Checked Items:** This option selects only those songs or other items that have a check mark beside them, along with the rest of the criteria. Selecting and deselecting items is an easy way to fine-tune your selection for a smart playlist.

- **Live Updating:** This allows iTunes to continually update the playlist while you play items, add or remove items from the library, change their ratings, and so on.

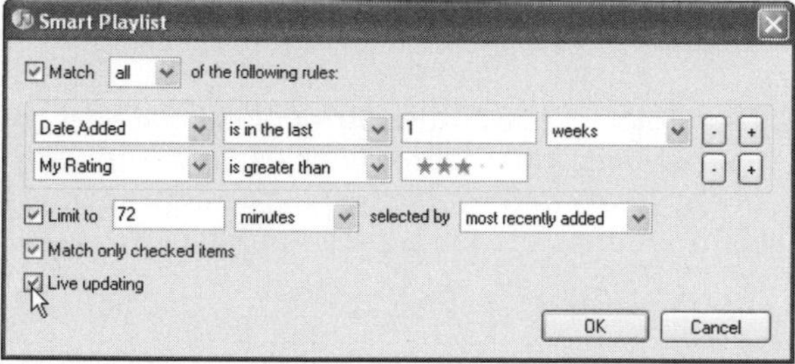

Figure 10-3: Use multiple conditions and a time limit for a smart playlist.

After setting up the rules, click OK. iTunes creates the playlist, noted by a gear icon and the name *untitled playlist* (or whatever phrase you used for the first condition, such as the album or artist name). You can click in the playlist field and then type a new name for it.

Editing a smart playlist

To edit a smart playlist, select the playlist and choose File➪Edit Smart Playlist (or Control-click (Mac) or right-click (Windows) the playlist and then choose Edit Smart Playlist from the pop-up menu). The Smart Playlist window appears with the criteria for the smart playlist.

For example, to modify the smart playlist so that items with a higher rating are picked, simply add another star or two to the My Rating criteria.

A smart playlist for recent additions

Setting up rules gives you the opportunity to create playlists that are smarter than the ones supplied with iTunes. For example, we created a smart playlist with criteria (as shown in Figure 10-3) that does the following:

- Includes any item added to the library in the past week that also has a rating greater than three stars.
- Limits the playlist to 72 minutes to be sure it fits on a 74-minute audio CD, even with gaps between the songs. It also refines the selection to the most recently added if the entire selection becomes greater than 72 minutes.
- Matches only selected items.
- Performs live updating.

You can also choose to limit the playlist to a certain number of items selected by various methods, such as random, most recently played, and so on.

Creating an iMix

Amateur disk jockeys, rejoice! The iTunes Store offers the iMix section for sharing your iTunes playlists with other iTunes users. Although you can submit a playlist of any items to be published in the iMix section of the store, only items available from the store are actually published. Unavailable items are skipped.

Browsers in the iTunes Store can view the playlist by entering the iMix section and clicking any playlist. See Chapter 4 for information about navigating the iTunes Store, playing short preview clips, and buying content.

To create an iMix, follow these steps:

1. **Select the playlist in your iTunes library and choose File⇨Create an iMix.**

   iTunes displays a warning dialog before accessing the iTunes Store to publish your playlist.

2. **Click the Create button in the warning dialog.**

   iTunes displays the iTunes Store sign-in dialog.

3. **Enter your ID and password and then click Publish.**

   iTunes selects the iTunes Store option in the Source pane and displays the iMix page. You see the iMix playlist that will be published, which includes only available items from the store.

4. **Edit the title and description for the iMix playlist and then click the Publish button.**

iTunes publishes the playlist in the iMix section of the store. Others can browse the playlist and buy any items.

Chapter 11

Managing Photos and Videos

In This Chapter

- Organizing photos into albums with iPhoto
- Organizing photos into albums with Photoshop Album
- Exporting video files to use with iTunes
- Converting video files for iPod use

Taking photos has never been easier. Digital cameras and photo-editing software combine to turn computers into digital darkrooms — no need for a real darkroom with smelly chemicals and film-processing equipment. In fact, you no longer even need film. And making videos is also easier than ever before. People use camcorders to record everything from violent weather and police chases to home bloopers, weddings, and school plays. Digital technology makes video editing easy, more cost-effective, and more fun, opening up entirely new possibilities.

Of course, your vacation photos and videos are priceless to you, preserving special memories. Family gatherings, vacations, and weddings don't happen every day. You want to take these pictures and videos with you when you visit friends and relatives. However, you don't want to lug a slide show projector and a carousel loaded with expensive slides, or wait for a video service to transfer your videos from camcorder media to VHS cassettes that you can play in your neighbor's VCR. So why not use your iPod instead?

All color-display iPod models can play photos and slide shows, and the fifth- and sixth-generation iPod, as well as the iPhone and Apple TV can play photo slideshows and videos. The full-size iPod models that display color also connect easily with televisions and video equipment, so you can show slide shows or videos to a larger audience. You can organize your digital photo library on your computer and then transfer the photos directly to a color-display iPod in one easy step — and still keep your color-display iPod synchronized when you add more photos to your library.

In this chapter we describe what you need to know to get your photos and videos organized on your computer and ready for iTunes and your iPod, iPhone, and Apple TV.

To learn more about creating and importing photos and videos into your computer and editing photos and videos, including detailed information about using photo and video applications, visit this book's companion Web site.

Organizing Photos on Your Computer

Using a computer to organize and archive all your digital photos makes sense. You can organize massive quantities of photos in the photo library in your computer. You can also add keywords, titles, and film roll information to each photo automatically, which helps make locating a particular photo very easy. Keep the photos you like and delete the ones you don't like. If you have a color printer, obtaining extra prints is as easy as using the Print command. You can even e-mail the photos to a service for high-quality prints.

Photo library software, such as iPhoto (on a Mac) or Adobe Photoshop Elements 4 or Photoshop Album (on a Windows PC) can organize any number of photos, limited only by available hard drive space. At an average size of 2MB per photo (many photos occupy less space), you can store 10,000 photos on a 20GB hard drive. Of course, you can expand a photo library over multiple hard drives or create multiple libraries. The number of digital photos that you can manage has no practical limit.

Most importantly, you can take your photos with you, safely tucked into your iPod. On a Mac, you can use iPhoto (version 4.0.3 or newer) to import photos into your computer and organize them into albums. You can then use iTunes to transfer photos and photo albums automatically from your iPhoto library.

On a Windows PC, you can use Adobe Photoshop Album (version 1.0 or newer) or Photoshop Elements (version 3.0 or newer) to import photos into your computer and organize your photos into collections. You can then use iTunes to transfer photos automatically from your Photoshop Album or Photoshop Elements library. If you use other photo-editing programs, you can still update your iPod with the photos, as we describe in Chapter 12. However, the collections in Photoshop Album and Photoshop Elements synchronize automatically with your iPod.

After you import the photos, your photo application stores them in its photo library and displays them. For example, when iPhoto finishes importing, it displays a small image for each photo in the photo library, as shown in Figure 11-1. These small versions of your images, which can be reduced to very small, are *thumbnails.*

You've probably seen photo albums with plastic sleeves for holding photographic prints. A *digital photo album* is similar in concept but holds digital photo files instead of prints. In both cases, an album is simply a way of organizing photos and placing them in a proper sequence. You select the photos from your photo library and arrange them in the order you want. iPhoto uses *album* as its term; Adobe Photoshop Elements and Photoshop Album call the album a *collection.* We use the term *album* for both.

Figure 11-1: Imported photos appear as thumbnails in the photo library.

You can use photo albums to assemble photos from special events (say, a vacation) or to display a particular subject (such as your favorite nature photos). If you have more photos in your library than what you want to put on your iPod, consider organizing albums specifically for transfer to the iPod and for automatic updating. The order that your photos appear in the album is important because it defines the order of photos in a slide show on your iPod. You can also use albums to organize photos for a slide show, QuickTime movie, or Web page.

You can make as many albums as you like comprising any images from your photo library. Because the albums are lists of images, they don't use disk space by copying the images. Instead, the actual image files remain in the photo library. Similar to an iTunes playlist, a photo album is a reference list of photos in your library. You can include the same photo in several albums without making multiple copies of the photo and wasting disk space.

Organizing photos with iPhoto

To assign photos to an album in iPhoto, follow these steps:

1. **Select Library in the iPhoto Source pane.**

   The photos in your library appear as thumbnails in the viewer tab.

2. **Click the Add Photo Album button.**

   The + button is underneath the Source pane; refer to Figure 11-1. Alternatively, choose File⇨New Album or press ⌘-N.

   The New Album dialog appears.

3. **Type the album name and then click OK.**

4. **Select photos in your library and then drag them into the album.**

   When you click a photo, you know the photo is selected when an outline appears around it. You can select a block of photos by clicking the first photo and pressing Shift while clicking the last one. The first and last photo — and all the photos in between — are selected automatically. You can also add individual photos to a selection by ⌘-clicking each photo.

   A number appears (see Figure 11-2), showing the number of selected photos in the range.

Click this button to add an album.

Figure 11-2: Add multiple photos at one time to an album.

5. **Click the photo album name in the Source pane to rearrange the photos in the album.**

   When you click an album name in the Source pane, only the photos you dragged to the album — not the entire library — appear in the viewer tab. You can reposition pictures within the album by simply dragging them to a different location.

iPhoto also lets you create *smart albums,* which collect photos based on prearranged criteria. For example, you can set up a smart album that collects only the highest-rated photos taken during the last six months, based on ratings you've assigned to them.

To create a smart album in iPhoto, follow these steps:

1. **Choose File⇨New Smart Album and then type a name for the album in the Name field.**
2. **Set the conditions for including photos in the smart album.**

   Make your choices from the pop-up menus. Choose a condition from the first pop-up menu and then choose a comparison, such as a greater-than or less-than sign, from the second pop-up menu.
3. **Combine conditions for better results.**

   To add additional matching conditions, click the + button. Then decide whether to match any of these conditions by choosing the option you want from the pop-up menu next to Match.
4. **When you finish, click OK to save your smart album.**

iPhoto automatically updates your smart album when any photo that matches the criteria is added to or removed from the library.

Organizing photos in Photoshop Album

Windows users can assign photos to a collection via Adobe Photoshop Album. Follow these steps:

1. **Click the Collections tab.**
2. **Click the Create New Collection button.**

   The Create Collection dialog appears.
3. **Type the collection name and then click OK.**
4. **Select photos and then drag them into the collection.**

   You can select multiple photos by clicking the first one and then pressing Ctrl while clicking more photos.
5. **Select the check box next to the collection name to view the collection and rearrange the photos in the collection.**

   You can reorder pictures within the album by simply dragging them to a different position.

To learn more about creating and importing photos into your computer and editing photos, visit this book's companion Web site.

Preparing videos for iTunes and iPods

Video-editing software allows you to edit and improve your imported video clips, add transitions and special effects, and even edit the soundtrack. The final result is a digital video file on your computer's hard drive, which you can save in a format acceptable to iTunes and your iPod.

To bring a video file into iTunes, simply drag it into the iTunes window or over the iTunes icon, or choose File➪Add File to Library. After the video is in your iTunes library, you can play it just like the videos you buy from the iTunes Store.

iTunes accepts a number of different video file formats, including QuickTime MOV and MPG files as well as files in the MPEG-4 format, including MPEG-4 files encoded with the improved H.264 compression standard. These are typical export options in a number of video-editing programs. H.264, also known as MPEG-4 AVC (Advanced Video Coding), offers significantly greater compression than the current MPEG-4 ASP (Advanced Simple Profile) standard, and provides near DVD quality at under 1 megabits per second, which makes it useful for wireless Internet connections and iPods.

The *QuickTime* video technology comprises a collection of digital video file formats that offer many choices for quality, compression, picture size, and playback format. Since iTunes uses QuickTime, it can play video formats that the iPod won't, such as AVI files, MPEG-1 and MPEG-2, and even MPEG-4 videos in which the aspect ratio or bit rate is not compatible with fifth- and sixth-generation iPods that play video. iTunes won't transfer such videos to these iPods — it skips them during the synchronization process described in Chapter 12.

Exporting your videos

Use your video-editing program to save or export a video project as a video file and then bring your video file into iTunes to play or synchronize it with your iPod (see Chapter 12). For example, in iMovie on a Mac

1. **Choose File➪Share and then click the QuickTime button to export a digital video file.**
2. **Choose Expert Settings from the Compress Movie For pop-up menu.**
3. **Click the Share button to display the Save Exported File As dialog.**
4. **Click the Options button to define your digital video settings.**

   You can set the file format, data rate, image size, and frame rate, which control the picture and audio quality.

Explaining all these digital video settings and formats is beyond the scope of this chapter, but you do need to know which format to use for which purpose. Just about all digital video formats play well on computers, but some formats provide better picture quality on a television or video monitor than others provide. Only two formats — standard MPEG-4 and H.264-encoded MPEG — play on iPods. Here's the difference between the two:

- **Displaying on an iPod:** H.264 encoding for MPEG-4 is better. You can set your video image size to 320 x 240 pixels with a data rate up to 768 Kbps and a frame rate up to 30 frames per second (fps). Although it might not look as good as Standard MPEG-4 encoding on a television, most people don't notice the difference, and the file size is usually smaller.
- **Displaying on a television connected to your iPod:** Standard MPEG-4 is better. You can set your image size to 480 x 480 pixels with a data rate up to 2.5 Mbps and a frame rate up to 30 fps. Although it might not look as good as H.264 on the iPod display, it looks better on a television.

You can easily convert files to an iPod-ready format, but doing so is time-consuming. Predetermined by settings, some computers can take half a day or more to convert a two-hour video file into a format useful for your iPod. Picking the right format and the proper settings in advance in your video-editing software is a good idea; otherwise, you might have to redo your conversions.

To learn more about creating and importing videos into your computer and editing videos, including details about software for converting video files, visit this book's companion Web site.

Converting your videos for iPods

iTunes provides an option for converting videos in the iTunes library into a format that looks better when you play them on an iPod display. To convert a video to H.264 for use in your iPod

1. **Select the video in your iTunes library, and then Control-click (Mac) or right-click (Windows) the selected video.**
2. **Choose Convert Selection for iPod (or choose Advanced⇨Convert Selection for iPod).**

   The selected videos are automatically copied, and the copies are converted to H.264 at a width of 320 pixels. The original versions remain unchanged.

You can also use software utilities to convert video from a variety of sources, including DVDs, into iPod-compatible video formats you can import into iTunes. For details about software for converting video files, visit this book's companion Web site.

Chapter 12

Synchronizing Devices with iTunes

In This Chapter

- Synchronizing your iPod, iPhone, or Apple TV
- Filling up your iPod, iPhone, or Apple TV with selected content
- Copying content directly to your iPod or iPhone
- Managing playlists and editing information on your iPod or iPhone
- Synchronizing an iPod shuffle with Autofill

You use iTunes to put content on your iPod, iPhone, and Apple TV. With iTunes, you can fill these devices very quickly and keep them synchronized every time you connect them. (iTunes can also keep your iPod and iPhone synchronized with contacts and calendars; see Chapter 23.)

iTunes lets you decide whether to copy some or all of your songs and audio books, photos, movies, TV shows, music videos, and podcasts. The choice is easy if your iTunes library and photo library together are small enough to fit in their entirety on your iPod, iPhone, or Apple TV. For example, if your iTunes and photo libraries combined are less than 75GB and you have an 80GB iPod, simply copy everything. (You can see the size of your library in GB, or *gigabytes,* at the bottom of the iTunes window in the center.) Copying your entire library is just as fast as copying individual items (if not faster) because you don't have to select among albums and movies, create special playlists to keep your devices filled, or do anything except connect the devices to your computer. iTunes does the rest.

This chapter shows you how to set up iTunes to automatically synchronize your iPod, iPhone, and Apple TV with everything in your library as well as how to copy content to these devices selectively. You can also copy music, audio books, and podcasts to your iPod manually. (Apple TV models and iPhones synchronize only by playlist.) iTunes is flexible in that you can use separate options to synchronize music, TV shows, movies, and so on. For example, you can copy to your iPod all your songs and audio books but only some of your TV shows, none of your movies, and only the podcasts you haven't heard yet. Or you can automatically copy to your iPod TV shows, movies, music videos, and podcasts, and then manually copy music and audio books to your iPod to fill up the rest of the space, or delete music and audio books directly from your iPod if you need to make more room.

This chapter also explains how to fill an iPod shuffle automatically or manually as well as how to manage space on an iPod shuffle.

Copying and Deleting Content Automatically

You can set your iPod, iPhone, or Apple TV to copy your entire iTunes library automatically — *synchronizing* to your library: The iPod, iPhone, or Apple TV matches your library exactly, item for item, playlist for playlist. If you made changes in iTunes after the last time you synchronized, those changes are automatically made in the device when you synchronize again. If you added or deleted content in your iTunes library, that content is added or deleted in the iPod, iPhone, or Apple TV library.

If you store photos in an iPhoto library (on a Mac) or in a program (such as Adobe Photoshop Album in Windows), you can use iTunes to transfer photos to your iPod, iPhone, or Apple TV automatically and synchronize the device to your library so that any changes you make to the photo library are copied to the device.

iPods can be set by default to automatically synchronize with all music in your iTunes library and all photos in your photo library — see Chapter 2 for details on setting up your iPod. Apple TV models and iPhones synchronize with everything in your iTunes and photo libraries when you click the Sync button, you can transfer photos to your iPod automatically and synchronize your iPod to your library so that any changes you make to the photo library are copied to your iPod.

Content items stored *remotely* (such as songs shared from other iTunes libraries on a network) aren't synchronized because the files aren't physically on your computer. Apple TV can stream content from other iTunes libraries on the same network but synchronizes with only one library. (See Chapter 7 for more info on how to share iTunes files over a network with iTunes as well as how to copy files to different computers and their iTunes libraries.)

To automatically synchronize your iPod with your iTunes library, just follow these simple steps:

1. **With iTunes running, connect the iPod.**

   The iTunes status pane tells you that iTunes is syncing the device. If you select the name of the iPod in the Source pane, as shown in Figure 12-1, you can see on the Summary page of the device's synchronization options how much space on the device is occupied by content and how much is still free.

   When your iPod is set to synchronize automatically (that is, selecting the entire library, or selecting either a playlist or manually selected items), the List view and Browse view for the device's contents are grayed out in the iTunes window. Because you manage the contents automatically, you don't have direct access to the content in the device via iTunes. For direct access, see the later section, "Copying Content to Your iPod Manually."

2. **Wait for the synchronization to finish and then click Eject to eject the iPod.**

   Wait until the iTunes Status pane (at the top) displays that the synchronization is finished. You can then click the Eject button, which appears in the bottom-right corner of the iTunes window.

On a Mac, you can also eject an iPod by dragging its icon on the Desktop to the Trash. (In OS X 10.3, you can click the Eject icon next to the iPod icon in the Finder Sidebar.) In Windows, you can right-click the iPod icon and choose Eject.

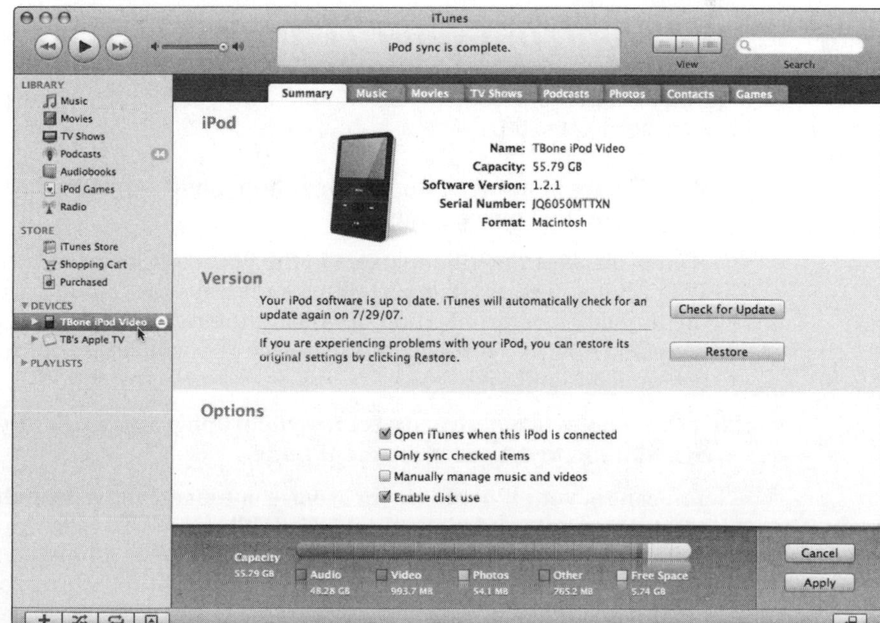

Figure 12-1: Synchronize your iPod automatically with iTunes.

3. **Disconnect your iPod from your computer.**

   Don't disconnect your iPod until its menu appears in its display.

   That's it. Your iPod is now synchronized.

You probably don't need to know anything else in this chapter about synchronizing your iPod unless your iTunes library and additional photo library are too large to fit. (In that case, see the upcoming section, "If your library won't fit on the device.") Or, if you want to be more selective about the content while copying to the device automatically, see the later section, "Copying and Deleting Content Selectively."

iTunes remembers your synchronization settings for each iPod that you connect from the last time when you synchronized the device.

To prevent an iPod from automatically synchronizing, press ⌘-Option (Mac) or Ctrl-Alt (Windows) while you connect the device, and then keep pressing until the iPod name appears in the iTunes Source pane.

If you connect to your computer an iPod previously linked to another computer, iTunes displays a message warning you that clicking Yes replaces the device's content with the content from your computer's library. If you don't want to change the iPod's content, click No. If you click Yes, iTunes erases the iPod and synchronizes the device with your computer's library.

Synchronizing your iPhone

To automatically synchronize your iPhone with your iTunes library, just follow these simple steps:

1. **With iTunes running, connect the iPhone, and select its name when it appears in the Source pane.**

   iTunes displays the iPhone name in the Source pane, as shown in Figure 12-2. After you select its name, iTunes displays the Summary page with the iPhone's synchronization options to the right of the Source pane, including how much space on the device is occupied by content and how much is still free.

2. **If the iPhone is not already set to synchronize automatically, click the Sync button to synchronize the iPhone.**

   You can set your iPhone to synchronize automatically during the iPhone setup process — and if you did so, your iPhone starts synchronizing automatically after you connect it. If you did not set your iPhone to synchronize automatically, click the Sync button to synchronize it to your iTunes and photo libraries. You can also set the iPhone to synchronize automatically from this point on by selecting the Automatically Sync When this iPhone is Connected option on the Summary page (refer to Figure 12-2).

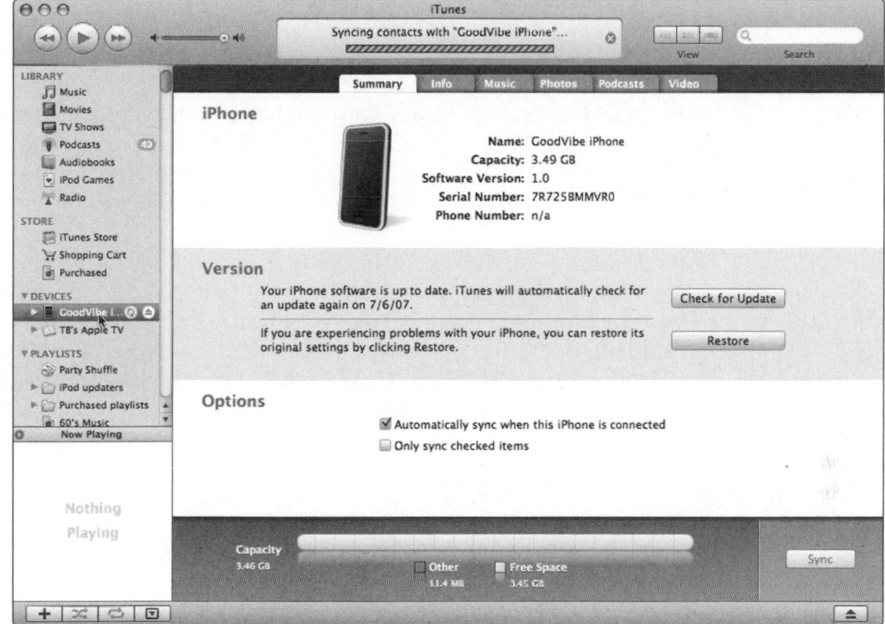

Figure 12-2: Synchronize your iPhone automatically with iTunes.

3. **Wait for the synchronization to finish and then click Eject to eject the iPhone.**

   Wait until the iTunes Status pane (at the top) displays that the synchronization is finished. You can then click the Eject button, which appears in the bottom-right corner of the iTunes window.

   On a Mac, you can also eject an iPhone by dragging its icon on the Desktop to the Trash. (In OS X 10.3, you can click the Eject icon next to the iPhone icon in the Finder Sidebar.) In Windows, you can right-click the iPhone icon and choose Eject.

4. **Disconnect your iPhone from your computer.**

   That's it. Your iPhone is now synchronized.

You probably don't need to know anything else in this chapter about synchronizing your iPhone unless your iTunes library and additional photo library are too large to fit. (In that case, see the upcoming section, "If your library won't fit on the device.") Or, if you want to be more selective about the content while copying to the device automatically, see the later section, "Copying and Deleting Content Selectively."

iTunes remembers your synchronization settings for each iPhone that you connect from the last time when you synchronized the device.

Synchronizing your Apple TV

If you set up Apple TV to connect wirelessly or via Ethernet to your computer running iTunes (as described in Chapter 7), the name of your Apple TV automatically appears in the iTunes Source pane in the Devices section as soon as iTunes detects it on the network. You don't have to do anything — iTunes immediately begins synchronizing the Apple TV device with your library.

The iTunes status pane tells you that iTunes is syncing the device. If you select the name of the Apple TV in the Source pane, as shown in Figure 12-3, you see on the Summary page of the synchronization options how much space on the device is occupied by content and how much is still free. If synchronization doesn't start automatically, click the Sync button on the Summary page to start things rolling.

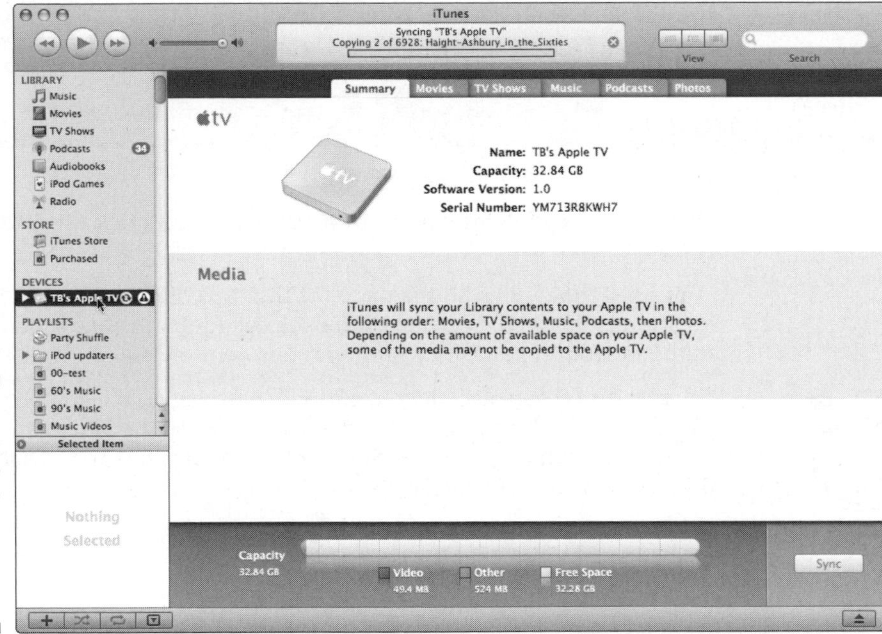

Figure 12-3: Synchronize your Apple TV automatically with iTunes.

When Apple TV and iTunes get together, not only can you smile on your brother and love one another, but

- **You can watch video content (or listen to audio content) on Apple TV while Apple TV is synchronizing.**
- **You can use Apple TV to play anything in your iTunes library on your computer while iTunes is open:**

1. *Choose Sources from the Apple TV main menu.*
2. *Choose the name of your iTunes library in the Sources menu.*

   If the name is grayed out, iTunes isn't connected to your Apple TV. (See Chapter 7 for details on how to set up your Apple TV.)

- **You can enable (or disable) synchronization for an Apple TV device:**

  1. *Choose Sources from the Apple TV main menu.*
  2. *Choose Syncing.*

- **You can also select Change iTunes Library.** To synchronize with a new library, follow the instructions for choosing an iTunes library with Apple TV (see Chapter 7).

  Note: This option erases everything from your Apple TV before synchronizing with the other library, so be sure that's what you want to do.

If your library won't fit on the device

If your iTunes library is too large to fit on your iPod or iPhone, you can still keep your iPod or iPhone automatically synchronized to a subset of your library. You have four options:

- **Create multiple iTunes libraries.** You can create several subsets of your main library (sub-libraries) so that each sub-library could be small enough to fit on a certain type of device. For example, you might create a sub-library for an 80GB iPod, and another sub-library for a 40GB Apple TV, and yet another subset for an 8GB iPod Nano. Before connecting a device, you could switch to its corresponding sub-library and then synchronize automatically. To find out how to manage multiple iTunes libraries, see Chapter 13.
- **Copy content selectively or manually.** You can automatically synchronize your iPod, iPhone, or Apple TV to specific music and music video playlists, TV shows and movies, podcasts, and photo albums. (See the upcoming section, "Copying and Deleting Content Selectively.") You can also copy music and podcasts directly to your iPod. (See the later section, "Copying Content to Your iPod Manually.")
- **Let iTunes decide what goes on the device.** iTunes decides which songs and albums to include by using the ratings that you set for each song, and creates a playlist specifically for synchronizing with that device. We explain this method in this section.

If you synchronized your iPod or iPhone before but your iTunes library has grown larger and won't fit, iTunes first checks for photos on the device. If your iPod or iPhone already has photos on it, iTunes asks whether you want to delete them to gain more space. After clicking Yes or No, iTunes tries its best to fit everything. If it has to cut something, though, it skips the photos and displays the message `Some photos were not copied.`

If you're still short of space even after skipping photos, iTunes displays a warning about the lack of free space, and asks whether you want to disable podcast synchronization for the device, and let iTunes create a selection of songs.

- **If you click Yes,** iTunes creates a new playlist (titled *Your device name* Selection, as in "TBone iPod Video Selection") and displays a message telling you so. Click OK, and iTunes synchronizes your iPod or iPhone using the new playlist. iTunes also sets your iPod or iPhone to synchronize music automatically by playlist, as we describe later in "Copying and Deleting Content Selectively."
- **If you click No,** iTunes updates automatically until it fills your iPod or iPhone without creating the playlist.

Either way, iTunes decides which songs and albums to include by using the ratings that you set for each song. iTunes groups album tracks together and computes an average rating and play count for the album. It then fills the iPod or iPhone, giving higher priority to albums with play counts and ratings greater than zero. You can therefore influence the decisions that iTunes makes by adding ratings to songs or entire albums; see Chapter 9.

The 40GB Apple TV actually holds about 32 gigabytes of iTunes library content; the 160GB model holds about 144GB (the rest is occupied by the system and media files provided by Apple). Your iTunes library could be larger than your Apple TV's capacity, so iTunes synchronizes Apple TV starting with all movies and TV shows before moving on to the music videos, music and audio books, podcasts, and finally photos. See the following section to discover how to copy playlists and items selectively to your Apple TV.

Copying and Deleting Content Selectively

Even if your iTunes library is too large to fit on your iPod, iPhone, or Apple TV, you can still use automatic methods to synchronize your device. Just be selective, choosing which playlists, TV shows, movies, podcasts, and photo albums to automatically copy.

You can automatically keep your device synchronized to a subset of your library, adding new material under your control, in the following ways:

- **Select content items to ignore** during synchronization with iPods and iPhones, as described in the later section, "Selecting items to ignore when synchronizing."

- **Create playlists of the music you want to transfer,** or create a *smart playlist* that selects content for you (as described in Chapter 10) and then synchronize by playlists, as described in the later section, "Choosing playlists to synchronize."
- **Limit the transfer and synchronization of photos** to albums or collections rather than the entire photo library, as we describe in the later section, "Choosing photo albums to synchronize."
- **Select which TV shows to transfer,** as we describe in the upcoming section, "Choosing TV shows to synchronize." TV shows take up considerable space in an iPod, iPhone, or Apple TV device. You can select, for example, to transfer only episodes of shows you haven't watched yet.
- **Select which movies to transfer,** as we describe in the later section, "Choosing movies to synchronize." Movies take up the most space in an iPod, iPhone, or Apple TV device.

By synchronizing selectively, you can still make your iPod, iPhone, or Apple TV match at least a subset of your iTunes library. If you make changes to that subset in iTunes, those changes are automatically made in the device when you synchronize again. For example, if you change your settings to update by certain playlists, any changes you make to those playlists — adding or deleting songs, for example — are reflected in your iPod, iPhone, or Apple TV the next time you synchronize it to your computer.

Selecting items to ignore when synchronizing

You can decide which songs, audio books, music videos, movies, TV shows, or podcast episodes you don't want to synchronize, and simply not include them with your iPod or iPhone (this feature is not available with Apple TV). To use this method, you must first deselect the items in your iTunes library that you don't want to transfer.

To select (or deselect) an item in your iTunes library, select the check box next to the item so that the check mark appears (or disappears). To select (or deselect) a podcast episode, open the podcast first. (See Chapter 6 for information about opening and playing podcasts.)

You can quickly select (or deselect) an entire album by selecting it in Browse view and pressing ⌘ (Mac) or Ctrl (Windows) while making your selections.

After you deselect the items you don't want to transfer and select the items you do want to transfer, connect your iPod or iPhone to your computer. Then follow these steps:

1. **Select the device name in the Devices section of the iTunes Source pane.**

   After selecting the name, the device's synchronization options appear with the Summary page visible. (Refer to Figure 12-1 for an iPod or Figure 12-2 for an iPhone.)

2. **Select the Only Sync Checked Items check box and then click Apply to apply the changes and sync an iPod (click Apply and then Sync to sync an iPhone).**

   iTunes automatically restarts synchronization and copies only the items in the iTunes library that are selected. iTunes also deletes from the device any items in the library that are not selected.

3. **Wait for the updating to finish and then click the iPod or iPhone Eject button.**

   Wait until the iTunes Status pane tells you the sync is complete before ejecting your iPod or iPhone.

Choosing playlists to synchronize

Your music library includes songs, audio books, and music videos. When synchronizing your iPod, iPhone, or Apple TV, you can include all these items or just those items defined in playlists. You can create an infinite number of playlists of any length, as described in Chapter 10. The Music tab of the synchronization options page for the device gives you options for choosing music in playlists.

For example, you can create four playlists that contain all essential rock, folk, blues, and jazz albums, and then select all four, or just one, two, or three of these playlists to synchronize your iPod, iPhone, or Apple TV. You can create sets of playlists specifically for synchronizing different devices, such as your Apple TV set containing movie-related music, or an all-jazz set for your iPod.

Synchronizing automatically by playlists is also an easy way to automatically synchronize an iPod, iPhone, or Apple TV when a large iTunes library won't fit in its entirety. You can also drag songs and albums directly to your iPod just like you do with any other content item, as we describe in the later section, "Copying Content to Your iPod Manually."

Before using this option, create the playlists in iTunes (see Chapter 10) that you want to copy to the device, and then connect your iPod or iPhone to your computer. (If you're synchronizing an Apple TV, it should already be detected and in the Source pane.) Then follow these steps:

1. **Select the device name in the iTunes Source pane.**
2. **Click the Music tab.**

   The Music synchronization options page appears, as shown in Figure 12-4.

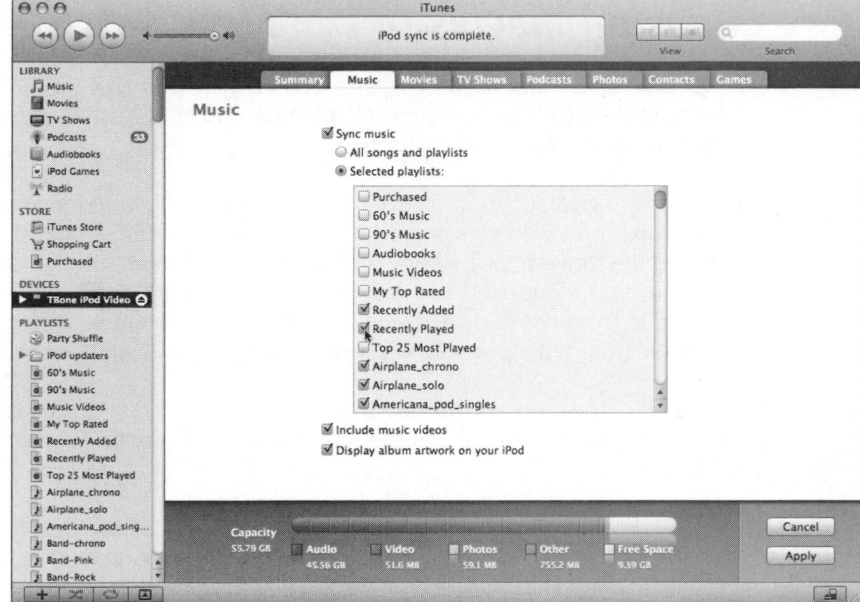

Figure 12-4: Synchronize your iPod with only selected playlists.

3. **Select the Sync Music and the Selected Playlists options.**
4. **From the list box, select each playlist that you want to synchronize with the device.**

   You can scroll the list box to see all your playlists. Mark the check box to select a playlist.
5. **Click Apply to apply the changes and sync an iPod (click Apply and then click Sync to apply changes and sync an Apple TV or iPhone).**

   iTunes automatically synchronizes the device by erasing its contents and copying only the playlists that you select in Step 4.

iTunes copies only the music and audio books in these playlists. If you also select the Include Music Videos option (as in Figure 12-4) on the Music synchronization options page, iTunes includes music videos listed in the playlists. You can also show album cover art on the color display of fifth- and sixth-generation iPods by selecting the Display Album Artwork on your iPod option.

If you select the Only Sync Checked Items option on the Summary page of the device synchronization options (refer to Figure 12-1 for an iPod or Figure 12-2 for an iPhone), only checked items are copied. iTunes ignores items that are unchecked, even if they're listed in the chosen playlists for synchronization.

To select all the music and audio books in your library, select the Sync Music check box and then select the All Songs and Playlists radio button on the Music synchronization options page. To include all music videos, select the Include Music Videos option.

Choosing movies to synchronize

Movies take up a lot of hard drive space, so if you limit the movies you synchronize with your iPhone, Apple TV, or fifth- and sixth-generation video iPod, you gain extra space for more content.

The movies portion of your library includes movies downloaded from the iTunes store and video files copied into the iTunes library from other sources. Any video file that isn't a TV show or music video downloaded from the iTunes store is categorized as a movie in your iTunes library. Music videos downloaded from the iTunes Store are included in the music section of your library; see the earlier section, "Choosing playlists to synchronize."

You can also drag movies directly to your iPod just like you do with any other content item, as we describe in the later section, "Copying Content to Your iPod Manually."

The Movies tab of the synchronization options page for the device gives you options for choosing movies to include. Follow these steps:

1. **Select the device name in the iTunes Source pane.**
2. **Click the Movies tab.**

   The Movies synchronization options page appears, as shown in Figure 12-5.

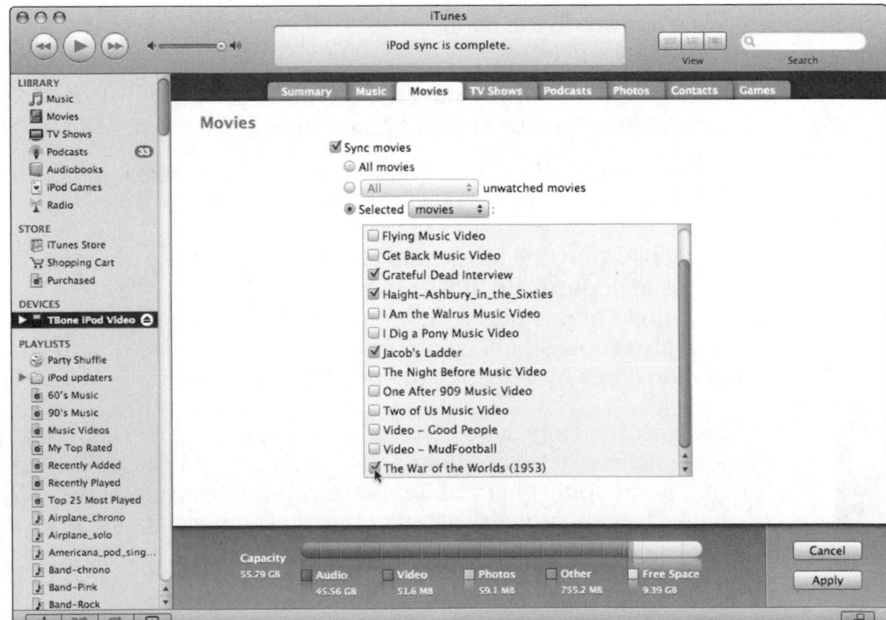

Figure 12-5: Synchronize your iPod with the selected movies only.

3. **Select the movie synchronization options for the device.**

   For fifth- and sixth-generation iPods that play video, as well as the iPhone, select the Sync Movies option (as shown in Figure 12-5), and then select one of the following options:

   - *All Movies:* Synchronizes all movies with your iPod, iPhone, or Apple TV.
   - *Unwatched Movies:* You can select to synchronize all unwatched movies, or choose from the pop-up menu the most recently added unwatched movie (1 most recent), or the three, five, or 10 most recently added unwatched movies (3, 5, or 10 most recent).
   - *Selected:* You can select specific movies or video playlists. Scroll the list box to see all your movies or video playlists. Mark the check box to select a movie or video playlist to synchronize with the device.

   For Apple TV, select these options, as shown in Figure 12-6:

   - *Pop-up menu of unwatched or recent Movies:* You can choose from the pop-up menu to synchronize all movies, all unwatched movies, or the most recently added movie (1 most recent), or the most recently added three, five, or 10 movies (3, 5, or 10 most recent). You can alternatively select *unwatched* recently added movies in the same increments.
   - *Selected:* You can select specific movies or video playlists. Scroll the list box to see all your movies or video playlists. Mark the check box to select a movie or video playlist to synchronize with the device.

   With Apple TV, you can mark both the selected movies option (then selecting movies or playlists to synchronize) and the unwatched movies options in the pop-up menu, to synchronize them as well. For example, in Figure 12-6, we chose 3 Most Recent Unwatched Movies plus the selected movies.

4. **Click Apply to apply the changes and sync an iPod (click Apply and then click Sync to apply changes and sync an Apple TV or iPhone).**

   iTunes automatically synchronizes the device by erasing its contents and copying only the movies that you select in Step 3.

If you select the Only Sync Checked Items option on the Summary page of the device synchronization options for an iPod or iPhone (refer to Figure 12-1 for an iPod or Figure 12-2 for an iPhone), only checked items are copied. iTunes ignores items that are unchecked, even if they're listed in the chosen movies for synchronization.

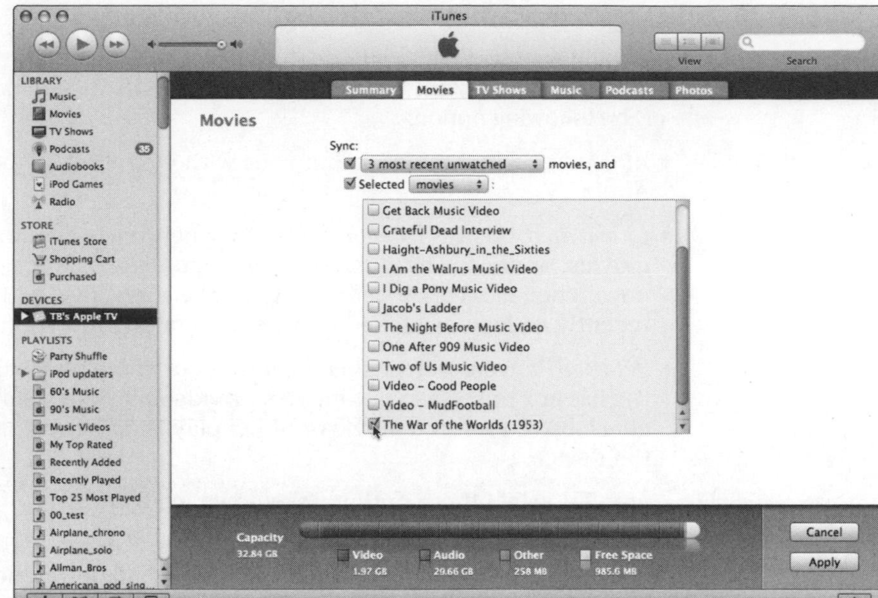

Figure 12-6: Synchronize your Apple TV with only selected movies.

Choosing TV shows to synchronize

TV shows also take up a lot of hard drive space, but you can limit the number of episodes you synchronize with your iPhone, Apple TV, or fifth- or sixth-generation video iPod, you gain extra space for more content.

You can also drag TV show episodes directly to your iPod just like you do with any other content item, as we describe in the upcoming section, "Copying Content to Your iPod Manually."

The TV Shows portion of your library includes only TV shows downloaded from the iTunes store. The TV Shows tab of the synchronization options page for the device gives you options for selecting which TV shows to include. Follow these steps:

1. **Select the device name in the iTunes Source pane.**
2. **Click the TV Shows tab for an iPod or the Videos tab for an iPhone.**

   The TV Shows synchronization options page appears, as shown in Figure 12-7 for an iPod; for an iPhone, the Videos synchronization page appears with separate sections for TV Shows and Movies.

3. **Select the Sync Episodes Of option and choose a modifier from the pop-up menu.**

   You can choose from the pop-up menu to synchronize all unwatched episodes, the most recently added episode (1 most recent), or the three, five, or 10 most recently added episodes (3, 5, or 10 most recent). You can also select unwatched recently added episodes in the same increments.

4. **Select one of the following options below the Sync Episodes Of option:**

   - *All TV Shows:* Synchronizes the episodes selected in Step 3 for all shows with your iPod, iPhone, or Apple TV.
   - *Selected:* Synchronizes the episodes selected in Step 3 for selected TV shows. For example, in Figure 12-7, we're synchronizing all unwatched episodes of *Star Trek: The Original Series* but no other TV shows. You can select specific TV shows or video playlists of TV show episodes. Scroll the list box to see all your TV shows or video playlists. Mark the check box to select a TV show or video playlist to synchronize with the device.

5. **Click Apply to apply the changes and sync an iPod (click Apply and then click Sync to apply changes and sync an Apple TV or iPhone).**

   iTunes automatically synchronizes the device by erasing its contents and copying only the TV show episodes that you selected in Step 4.

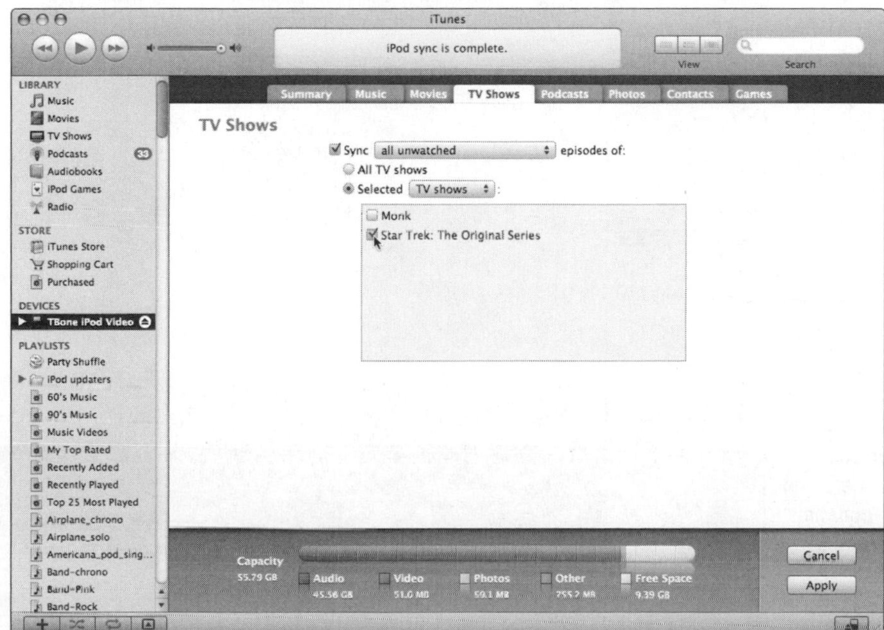

Figure 12-7: Synchronize your iPod with only selected TV show episodes.

Choosing podcasts to synchronize

Although you can listen to an audio podcast or watch a video podcast at any time on your computer, a podcast's real value is that you can take it with you in your iPod or iPhone, or play it on your home TV and stereo with your Apple TV. You can keep your iPod, iPhone, and Apple TV automatically synchronized with the most recent podcast episodes.

You can also drag podcast episodes directly to your iPod just like you do with any other content item, as we describe in the upcoming section, "Copying Content to Your iPod Manually."

The Podcasts tab of the synchronization options page for the device gives you options for choosing podcast episodes to include. Follow these steps:

1. **Select the device name in the iTunes Source pane.**
2. **Click the Podcasts tab.**

   The Podcasts synchronization options page appears, as shown in Figure 12-8.

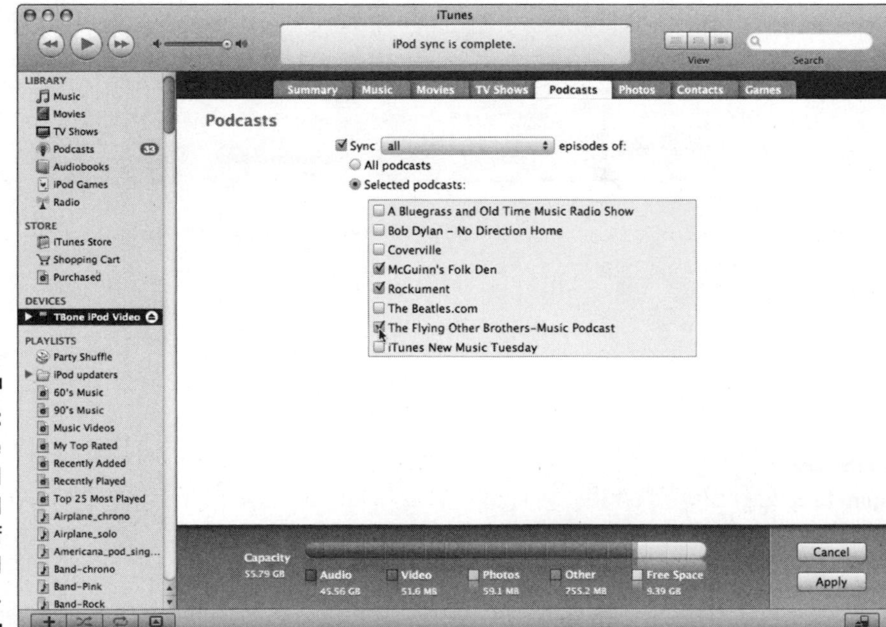

Figure 12-8: Synchronize your iPod with all episodes of selected podcasts.

3. **Select the Sync Episodes Of option and choose a modifier from the pop-up menu.**

   You can choose from the pop-up menu to synchronize all unplayed episodes, the most recently added episode (1 most recent), or the 3, 5, or 10 most recently added episodes (3, 5, or 10 most recent). You can also select unplayed recently added episodes and new episodes in the same increments.

4. **Select one of the following podcast options below the Sync Episodes Of option:**

   - *All Podcasts:* Synchronizes the episodes selected in Step 3 for all podcasts with your iPod, iPhone, or Apple TV.
   - *Selected Podcasts:* Synchronizes the episodes selected in Step 3 for selected podcasts. For example, in Figure 12-8, we're synchronizing all episodes of the selected podcasts (use the pop-up menu to switch from "all" to other choices, such as all unplayed episodes of the selected podcasts). Scroll the list box to see all your podcasts. Mark the check box to select a podcast to synchronize with the device.

5. **Click Apply to apply the changes and sync an iPod (click Apply and then click Sync to apply changes and sync an Apple TV or iPhone).**

   iTunes automatically synchronizes the device by erasing its contents and copying only the episodes of podcasts that you selected in Step 4.

If you set iTunes to keep only your unplayed episodes, listen to part of a podcast episode on your iPod, and then update your iPod, the podcast episode disappears from iTunes.

As described in Chapter 6, iTunes can keep track of the playback position so that when you play a podcast, iTunes remembers your place when you stop listening to it, just like a bookmark in an audio book. iTunes resumes playing from the bookmark when you return to the podcast to play it. You can synchronize podcasts with filenames ending with `.m4b` to any iPod and never lose your bookmarked place, whether you listen on your iPod or on your computer.

Choosing photo albums to synchronize

You can take your pictures with you, safely tucked into your color-display iPod or iPhone, and you can display slide shows at home with your Apple TV. On a Mac, you can use iPhoto (version 4.0.3 or newer) to import photos into your computer and organize them into albums, as we describe in Chapter 11. You can then use iTunes to transfer photos from your iPhoto library automatically.

In Windows, you can use Adobe Photoshop Album (version 1.0 or newer) or Photoshop Elements (version 3.0 or newer) to import photos onto your computer and to organize your photos into collections, as we describe in Chapter 11. You can then use iTunes to transfer photos from your photo library automatically.

If you don't have any of these programs, you can use any other photo-editing or photo-organizing software and store your photos in a folder on your hard drive, or on a CD or server volume. You can then use iTunes to transfer photos from the folder, treating the folder as a photo album. The folder could be on CD-ROM or on a server volume as long as the CD-ROM or volume is mounted.

Whether you transfer photos from a library or from a folder on your hard drive, you can keep your color-display iPod, iPhone, and Apple TV synchronized with the photo library and its albums or with the subfolders and image files in the folder.

If you store photos in a photo library, such as iPhoto (Mac) or Photoshop Elements (Windows), you can synchronize your entire photo library to your color-display iPod, iPhone, or Apple TV automatically. Any changes you make to the library are consequently copied to your iPod, iPhone, or Apple TV. See the earlier section, "Copying and Deleting Content Automatically."

To transfer only photos in specific albums in a library to your iPod and keep your iPod synchronized with these albums (not the entire library), follow these steps:

1. **Select the device name in the iTunes Source pane.**
2. **Click the Photos tab.**

   The Photos synchronization options page appears, as shown in Figure 12-9.
3. **Select the Sync Photos From option and then choose a photo library or a folder from the pop-up menu.**

   You can choose your photo library (such as iPhoto on a Mac, or Adobe Photoshop Album in Windows) from the pop-up menu to synchronize photo albums, or you can choose a folder from the pop-up menu (say, your Pictures folder). You can also choose Folder from the pop-up menu to browse files and folders on your hard drive or other storage media (such as a CD-ROM or a server volume). In Finder or Windows Explorer, browse your hard drive (or other storage media) for the folder containing images and then click Choose (Mac) or OK (Windows).

   If you want photos in a folder to appear in separate photo albums on your iPod, create subfolders inside the folder and organize your photos and image files inside these subfolders. iTunes copies the subfolder assignments as if they were album assignments.

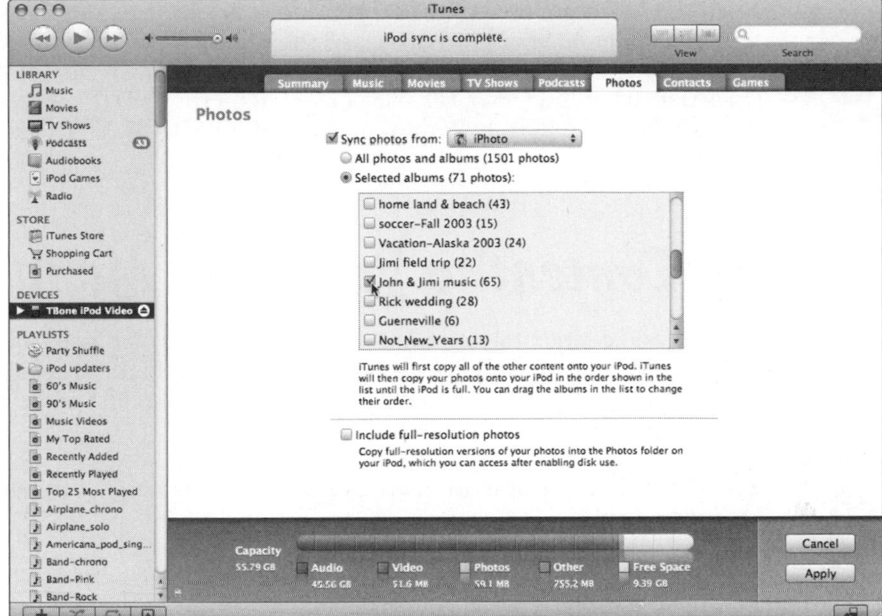

Figure 12-9: Synchronize your iPod with photo albums from your photo library.

4. **Select one of the following photo options below the Sync Photos From option:**

   • *All Photos and Albums:* Synchronizes all photos and albums from the library or folder selected in Step 3 with your iPod, iPhone, or Apple TV.

   • *Selected Albums:* Synchronizes the photo albums from the library (or subfolders from the folder) selected in Step 3. For example, in Figure 12-9, we synchronize from our iPhoto library the selected album "John & Jimi music." Scroll the list box to see all the photo albums in your photo library (or subfolders in your folder). Mark the check box to select a photo album (or subfolder) to synchronize with the device.

5. **Click Apply to apply the changes and sync an iPod (click Apply and then click Sync to apply changes and sync an Apple TV or iPhone).**

   iTunes automatically synchronizes the device by erasing its contents and copying only the photo albums that you selected in Step 4.

iTunes copies all other types of content first, before copying photos, but you can influence the order in which iTunes copies photo albums. When you select photo albums to synchronize in Step 4 above, you can drag the albums in the list into any order you choose — for example, you can select and drag the most important photo albums to the top of the list.

No matter what photo application you use, you can save photos as image files in a folder on your hard drive and then bring them into your iPod whenever you want. It's rare for an iPod to meet an image file format it doesn't like. On a Mac, use JPEG (JPG), GIF, TIFF (TIF), Pict, PNG, PSD (Photoshop), PDF, jpg 2000, SGI, and BMP. In Windows, use JPEG (JPG), GIF, TIFF (TIF), PNG, and BMP.

Copying Content to Your iPod Manually

You can add content to your iPod directly via iTunes, and you can delete content from your iPod as well. The iPod name appears in the iTunes Source pane. When selected, its contents appear in the iTunes List pane, replacing the library contents.

You might have one or more reasons for copying manually, but here are some obvious ones:

- Your entire library is too big for your iPod, and you want to copy individual items directly.
- You want to share a single library with several iPods, and you have different song selections that you want to copy to each iPod directly.
- You share an iPod with others, and you want to copy your content to the iPod without wiping out its existing content.
- You want to copy some songs or videos from another computer's iTunes library without deleting any content from your iPod.
- You want to edit the playlists and content information directly on your iPod without changing anything in your computer's library.
- You want to play your iPod through the computer's speakers and take advantage of iTunes playback features (such as cross-fading between two tracks; see Chapter 6).

When you set your iPod to manually manage music and videos, all contents on your iPod are active and available in iTunes. You can copy items directly to your iPod, delete items on the iPod, and edit the iPod's playlists directly.

To set your iPod to manually manage music and videos, first connect your iPod to your computer. Then follow these steps:

1. **Select the iPod's name in the Devices section of the iTunes Source pane.**

   After selecting the name, the device's synchronization options appear with the Summary page visible. (Refer to Figure 12-1.)

2. **Select the Manually Manage Music and Videos check box and then click OK to the warning.**

   iTunes displays a message warning you that disabling automatic synchronization requires manually ejecting the iPod before each disconnect.

3. **Click Apply to apply the change.**

To prevent an iPod from automatically synchronizing, press ⌘-Option (Mac) or Ctrl-Alt (Windows) while you connect the device, and keep pressing until the iPod name appears in the iTunes Source pane.

If you connect to your computer an iPod previously linked to another computer, iTunes displays a message warning you that clicking Yes replaces the device's content with the content from your computer's library. If you don't want to change the iPod's content, click No. If you click Yes, iTunes erases the iPod and synchronizes it with your computer's library.

Don't disconnect your iPod while managing music and videos manually. You have to eject the device and wait until it displays the message `OK to disconnect` (in first- and second-generation iPods) or the main menu. You risk making the device's hard drive or flash memory unreadable, forcing you to restore it to its original factory condition (see Chapter 24).

Copying items directly

As soon as you set your iPod to manually manage music and videos, you can copy music and video items directly from your iTunes library. Follow these steps (with your iPod connected to your computer):

1. **Select Music in the iTunes Source pane in the Library section (or a playlist).**

   The library's or playlist's songs appear in List view or Browse view.

2. **Drag items directly from your iTunes library or playlist over the iPod name in the Source pane, as shown in Figure 12-10.**

   When you drag a playlist name, all the songs associated with the playlist copy along with the playlist itself. When you drag an album title, all the songs in the album are copied.

3. **Wait for the copying to finish and then click Eject to eject the iPod.**

   Wait until the iTunes Status pane (at the top) tells you that the copying is finished. You can then click the Eject button, which appears in the bottom-right corner of the iTunes window.

   On a Mac, you can also eject an iPod by dragging its icon on the Desktop to the Trash. (In OS X 10.3, you can click the Eject icon next to the iPod icon in the Finder Sidebar.) In Windows, you can use various methods, such as right-clicking the iPod icon and then choosing Eject.

Figure 12-10: Copy an album directly from the iTunes library to an iPod.

4. **Disconnect your iPod from your computer.**

   Don't disconnect your iPod until its menu appears in its display.

Deleting items on your iPod

When you manually manage music and videos, you can delete content from the iPod directly. Manual deletion is a nice feature if you just want to go in and delete a song, video, or album to make room for new content.

To delete any item in your iPod, set the option to manually manage music and videos (if it isn't set that way already), and then follow these steps:

1. **Select the iPod in the iTunes Source pane.**

   The iPod's content appears in List view or Browse view, replacing the view of your computer's library.

2. **Select an item in the List or Browse view and press Delete/Backspace or choose Edit⇨Delete.**

   iTunes displays a warning to make sure you want to do this; click OK to go ahead or Cancel to stop. If you want to delete a playlist, select the playlist and press Delete or choose Edit⇨Delete.

Like in the iTunes library, if you delete a playlist, the items listed in the playlist are not deleted. They're still on your iPod unless you delete the items directly from the iPod in List view or Browse view.

Creating playlists directly on an iPod

Playlists from your iTunes library are automatically copied when you synchronize your iPod. However, you might want to edit the library in your iPod separately, perhaps creating new playlists or changing the song information manually.

To create a new playlist, follow these steps:

1. **Select the iPod in the iTunes Source pane.**
2. **Open the playlists for the iPod.**

   Click the triangle next to the iPod name to open the list of playlists on the device.

3. **Create a new playlist by clicking the Add Playlist (+) button in the bottom-left corner of iTunes under the Source pane or by choosing File⇨New Playlist.**

   Untitled playlist appears in the Source pane under the iPod entry.

4. **Click the Untitled Playlist name twice, and type a new name for the playlist.**

   After you type a new name, iTunes automatically sorts the iPod list into alphabetical order.

5. **Select the iPod name in the Source pane.**

   The iPod's contents appear in the List pane, replacing the computer's library content.

6. **Drag items from the List pane to the playlist.**

The order of items in the playlist is based on the order in which you drag them to the list. You can rearrange the list by dragging items within the playlist.

You can create smart playlists on the iPod exactly the same way as in the iTunes library. A *smart playlist* updates itself when you create it with iTunes and then updates itself every time you connect and select your iPod with iTunes. To read about smart playlists, see Chapter 10.

Editing content information on your iPod

With the iPod selected in iTunes and set for manually managing music and videos, you can edit the content information just like you do in the iTunes library by scrolling down the list and selecting items.

After selecting the iPod in the Source pane, the List pane displays the contents of the iPod.

You can edit song information (such as name, artist, album, genre, and ratings) directly in the columns in the List pane. To edit song information, select the song and then click inside the text field of a column to type new text.

You might find it easier to edit this information by choosing File⇨Get Info and typing the text into the Information dialog that appears.

iTunes grabs song information from the Internet (as we describe in Chapter 9), but this information typically doesn't include composer credits. If you have the inclination to add composer credits, doing so is worth your time because you can then search, sort, and create playlists based on this information. This is particularly important for classical music lovers because the iPod makes it easy to find songs by the performer/artist but not by the composer — and sorting by composer is what many classical music fans prefer.

Synchronizing an iPod shuffle

iPod shuffle is designed for quick and convenient music synchronizing. Just plug it into your computer and then click the Autofill button in iTunes. It also offers automatic compression to fit more songs (or audio books, which are treated as songs) into your iPod shuffle space.

Although Apple proudly advertises its capability to shuffle songs randomly, the key to its success isn't that you can shuffle the songs already there but that you can copy random songs to it every time you connect it to your computer. Eventually, you can shuffle through everything in your library if you so wish, by randomly filling your iPod shuffle every time. On the other hand, you can fine-tune your random selection and even reorder the iPod shuffle's playlist to play back in a specific order.

Although you can add songs to your iPod shuffle manually by dragging a playlist or song, you can also automatically fill it without having to set options for automatic updating. Autofill automatically picks songs from your entire iTunes library or from a playlist you select in the Source pane. You can also manage the playlist for your iPod shuffle directly, after using Autofill, to fine-tune your selection.

Using Autofill

To use Autofill to copy songs to your iPod shuffle, follow these steps:

1. **Connect the iPod shuffle to your computer.**

   When you connect an iPod shuffle to your computer, it shows up in the Source pane.

2. **Select the iPod shuffle in the iTunes Source pane.**

   The Autofill pane appears below the List pane, as shown in Figure 12-11. The songs on the iPod shuffle appear in List view, replacing the view of your library.

3. **Choose your source of music in the Autofill From pop-up menu.**

   Choose either a playlist or Music (for the entire music library). If you choose a playlist, Autofill uses only the playlist as the source of music.

4. **(Optional) To pick random songs, select the Choose Items Randomly option.**

5. **(Optional) To pick only the best songs (if you're choosing them randomly), select the Choose Higher Rated Items More Often option.**

Figure 12-11: Autofill your iPod shuffle from an iTunes playlist.

6. **(Optional) To replace songs already on the iPod shuffle, select the Replace All Items When Autofilling option.**

   If you don't select this option, iTunes adds the songs without replacing existing songs.

7. **Click the Autofill button to start copying songs.**

   iTunes grabs a subset of your music, creates a playlist, and copies the contents of the playlist to your iPod shuffle.

8. **Wait for the copy operation to finish and then click the Eject button.**

   Wait until the iTunes Status pane (at the top) tells you that the copying is finished. You can then click the Eject button, which appears in the bottom-right corner of the iTunes window.

You can click the Autofill button over and over to create different random playlists. When you get one you like, select all its contents and choose File⇨New Playlist From Selection to create a new playlist that contains the songs generated by Autofill. The next time you connect your iPod shuffle, select this new playlist from the Autofill From pop-up menu and then click the Autofill button to load the music from the playlist to your shuffle.

iPod shuffle can play audio books sold by the iTunes Store and by Audible.com. Unfortunately, iTunes won't automatically add them to the iPod shuffle — you have to add them manually. Be sure to play audio book sections on your iPod shuffle in sequential order rather than in random (shuffle) order, or you may hear chapters in the wrong order — see Chapter 15 for details on playing content on an iPod shuffle.

Copying items manually

iPod shuffle is always set for manual management. When you connect an iPod shuffle to your computer, you can copy music (or audio books) directly to it, delete items on it, and edit its playlist.

To copy items to your iPod shuffle directly, connect it to your computer and follow these steps:

1. **Select Music in the iTunes Source pane in the Library section.**

   Your music library's content appears in List view.

2. **Drag and drop items directly from your iTunes library to the iPod shuffle's name in the Source pane.**

   When you copy a playlist, all the songs in the playlist are copied. When you copy an album, all the songs in the album are copied.

3. **Wait for the copy operation to finish and then click the iPod Eject button.**

   Wait until the iTunes Status pane (at the top) tells you that the copying is finished. You can then click the Eject button, which appears in the bottom-right corner of the iTunes window.

To delete any item in your iPod shuffle, follow these steps:

1. **Select the iPod shuffle in the iTunes Source pane.**

   The songs on the iPod shuffle appear in List view, replacing the view of your library.

2. **Select one or more songs on the iPod shuffle and then press Delete/ Backspace or choose Edit⇨Delete.**

   iTunes displays a warning to make sure you want to do this; click OK to go ahead or Cancel to stop.

Managing space on your iPod shuffle

It's a nifty song player! No, it's an external flash drive for data backup! Either way, you can wear the iPod shuffle on your sleeve, around your neck, attached to your belt, or in your pocket — which makes it quite convenient for either music or data. To maximize the data potential of your iPod shuffle, see Chapter 22.

To manage space on your iPod shuffle, connect it, select it in the Source pane, and then click the Settings tab on the iPod shuffle's synchronization options page. Scroll the Settings page to the bottom to see more options, as shown in Figure 12-12.

You can allocate storage for music and data by using the slider at the bottom of the page (as in Figure 12-12) with More Songs on the left side and More Data on the right. Drag the slider to the right to open up space for data, or to the left to open up more space for music. Don't worry — adding more space won't affect any data files already stored on the iPod shuffle.

If the storage allocation slider is as far left as it can go or as far left as you want to take it (leaving space for data), you still have one more method of squeezing music onto the iPod shuffle: the Convert Higher Bit Rate Songs to 128 kbps AAC option. This option does just what it says: It converts songs with higher bit rates in either protected or unprotected AAC files or MP3 files into smaller AAC files by using 128 Kbps as the bit rate. (For more information about these audio formats and bit rates, see Chapter 18.) It performs this conversion on the fly while copying songs to the iPod shuffle, but it doesn't change the songs in your library. Protected AAC songs retain their protection.

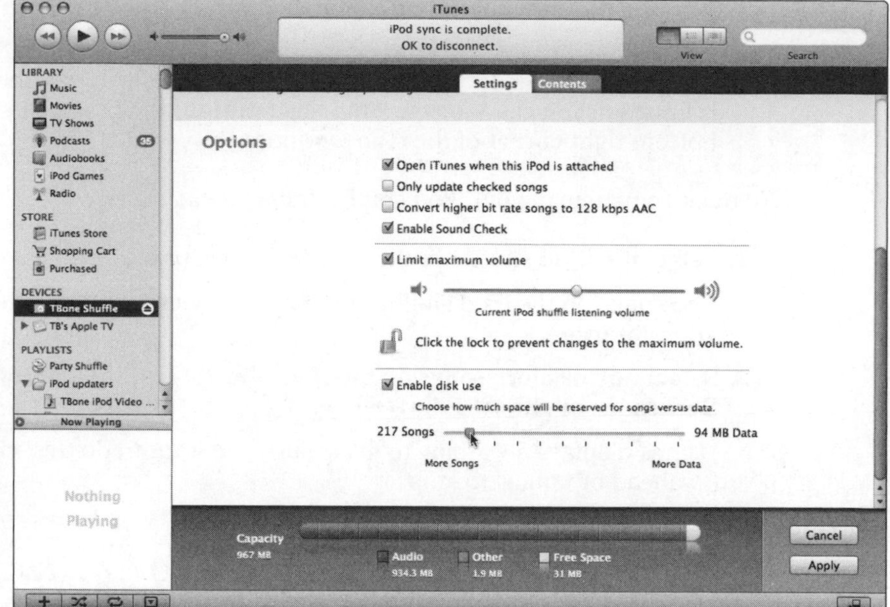

Figure 12-12: Allocate storage on your iPod shuffle for data and music.

You can save considerable space by converting songs to a lower bit rate. An iPod shuffle holding an average of 180 songs encoded at 192 Kbps in MP3 can hold an average of 260 songs via this option. The conversion reduces an uncompressed AIFF file to about 7 percent of its original size.

Chapter 13

Gimme Shelter for My Media

In This Chapter

- Locating the iTunes library
- Exporting playlists from iTunes
- Moving your iTunes library to another hard drive
- Managing multiple iTunes libraries
- Backing up your iTunes library

You might think that your digital content is safe, stored as-is, on your iPod, iPhone, Apple TV, and hard drive. However, demons in the night are working overtime to render your hard drive useless — and at the same time, someone left your iPod out in the rain, your iPhone can't phone home, and your Apple TV is on the fritz.

Copyright law and common sense prohibit you from using copyrighted content and then selling it to someone else. However, with iTunes, you're allowed to make copies of music, videos, audio books, and podcasts that you own for personal use, including copies for backup purposes.

In this chapter, you find out how to make a backup of your entire library. This operation is very important, especially if you've purchased items that don't exist anywhere else in your collection but on your computer. That way, even if your hard drive fails, you still have your iTunes library. You can also manage multiple iTunes libraries, which makes it much easier to keep multiple iPods synchronized to different libraries.

You can't copy content from your iPod, iPhone, or Apple TV to your computer via iTunes. It's a one-way trip from iTunes to your iPod, iPhone, or Apple TV. You can't copy stuff from your player device with iTunes because record labels and video distributors don't want indiscriminate copying, and Apple has complied with these requests. You can, however, use *third-party utility programs* (not supported by Apple) to copy content both ways. (You can read more on this topic in Chapter 23.) This chapter describes how to keep a backup of your iTunes library on your computer, another hard drive, or a backup medium so that you don't rely on your iPod, iPhone, or Apple TV as your sole music storage device.

The iTunes Store uses Apple FairPlay technology, which protects the rights of copyright holders while also giving you some leeway in how you can use the copyrighted content. You can copy the media files freely so that backup is easy and straightforward on either a Mac or a PC.

Studying Files in an iTunes Library

If you're like that guy in the movie *Diner* who couldn't stand to have his records misfiled, you'll love iTunes and its nice, neat file-storage methods. For all content items, iTunes creates a folder named for the artist and also creates folders within the artist folder named for each album. These folders are stored in the iTunes Music folder unless you change your storage preferences.

Finding the iTunes library

The default method of storing content in the iTunes library is to store all media files — including music, videos, podcasts, and audio books — in the iTunes Music folder, which is inside the iTunes folder. With this method, media files that you drag to the iTunes window are copied into the iTunes Music folder without deleting the original files. iTunes keeps iPod games in the iPod Games folder in the iTunes folder and houses cover art in the Album Artwork folder in the iTunes folder. So that's easy — everything is inside the iTunes folder.

iTunes maintains a separate iTunes folder (with a separate iTunes Music folder) in each Home folder (Mac) or user folder (PC). If you share your computer with other users who have Home folders, each user can have a separate iTunes library on the same computer (and, of course, a separate iPod that synchronizes with it). You need only one copy of the iTunes program.

On a Mac, iTunes stores your content library in your Home folder's Music folder. The path to this folder's default location is

```
your home folder/Music/iTunes/iTunes Music
```

On a Windows PC, iTunes stores your content library in your user folder. The path to this folder's default location is

```
your user folder/My Documents/My Music/iTunes/iTunes Music
```

Changing how files are stored in the library

The default method of organizing files in the iTunes library is to store content files in album and artist folders, naming the files according to the disc number, track number, and title.

For example, the song "Here, There and Everywhere" has the track number and song title in the filename (`05 Here, There And Everywhere.mp3`). The filename extension even tells you the type of encoding format — in this case, MP3. ***Note:*** Songs encoded in AAC have the extension `.m4a` (for unprotected songs) or `.m4p` (for protected songs purchased from the iTunes Store). This song is saved in the Revolver folder (for the album), which is in The Beatles folder (for the artist).

Movies, music videos, and TV shows follow the same naming conventions (even if they don't make much sense). Here's an example from the TV show *Monk.* Episode 13 (season 1) is titled "Mr. Monk and the Airplane." This information makes up the filename (`13 Mr. Monk and the Airplane.m4v`), which is stored in the Season 1 folder (the *album*) inside the Monk folder (the *artist*).

What about songs performed by multiple artists, such as movie soundtrack albums and compilations with multiple artists? Compilation and soundtrack albums, and songs designated as part of a compilation, are stored in album folders within the Compilations folder rather than within individual artist folders.

To designate a song as part of a compilation, select the song, choose File⇨Get Info, click the Info tab in the information dialog, and then select the Part of a Compilation check box.

To designate an entire album as a compilation album, select the album, choose File⇨Get Info, and then choose Yes from the Part of a Compilation pop-up menu. Even if Yes is already selected for the album, choose Yes again in order to set the check mark for updating.

The filename and location within artist and album folders change when you change the information for a song (or video, audio book, or podcast episode) in the information fields. For example, if you change the song title, the filename also changes. If you change the artist name, the folder name for the artist might change, or the file might move to a new folder by that name. iTunes organizes the files based on the song information.

To make changes to song information without changing the files on your hard drive, choose iTunes⇨Preferences (Mac) or Edit⇨Preferences (Windows) and then click Advanced. On the Advanced tab, click the General tab and then deselect the Keep iTunes Music Folder Organized option.

Leave the Keep iTunes Music Folder Organized option selected, especially if you plan on copying the music files to an Apple TV or to an iPod or iPhone that will then be used with a car installation. (We describe car installations in Chapter 20.) Most iPod interfaces for car stereos provide a way to navigate the iPod with the car stereo controls but don't display the proper artist, album, and song titles unless the iTunes music folder is organized by the default method.

Maybe you don't want to store copies of your media files in the library — especially if you already have copies stored on your hard drive in another location and need to conserve space. If you want to add content to your iTunes library without copying the files into the iTunes Music folder:

1. **Choose iTunes⇨Preferences (Mac) or Edit⇨Preferences (Windows).**
2. **Click the Advanced tab.**
3. **Click the General subtab in the Advanced pane.**
4. **Deselect the Copy Files to iTunes Music Folder When Adding to Library option.**

The next time you drag a media file into the iTunes window, it stores only a reference in your iTunes library to the file that specifies its actual location. The file isn't copied or moved.

Locating a media file

No matter where you store your iTunes library or your media files, you can find the location of any item by selecting the item, choosing File⇨Get Info, and then clicking the Summary tab of the information dialog that appears. You can see the file type next to the Kind heading of the Summary tab. The Where section tells you where the song is, as shown in Figure 13-1.

If you access shared libraries on a network, you probably have content you can display in iTunes that isn't actually in your library but is part of a shared library or playlist on a network. Thus, when you look at the Summary tab of the information dialog for an item in a shared library, the Where section doesn't appear.

You can also open the folder containing the media file for any content item. Select the item in List, Browse, Album, or Cover Flow view. Then, on a Mac, choose File⇨Show in Finder (or press ⌘-R); in Windows, choose File⇨Show in Windows Explorer (or press Ctrl-R). iTunes gives control to the operating system, which displays the folder containing the media file. You can show the file if it's on your hard drive but not if it's in a shared library on another computer.

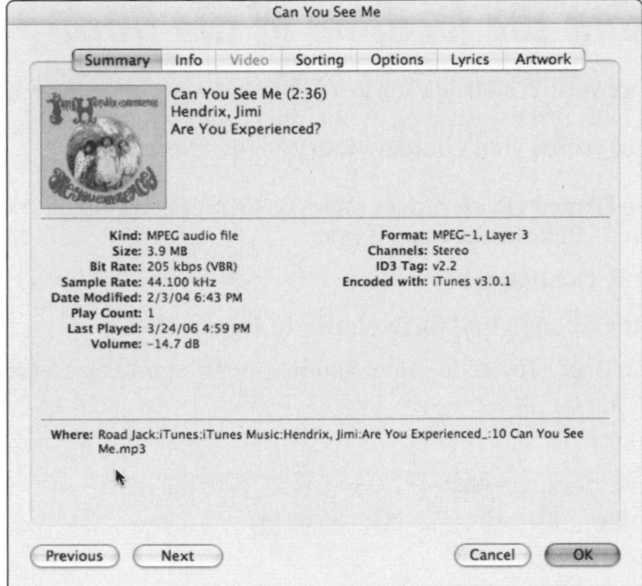

Figure 13-1: Locate a media file from its information dialog.

Manipulating an iTunes Library

If you're like me, your iTunes library is huge. I've nearly filled the internal hard drives of two computers. What do you do if you want to expand your library, but you run out of space? How do you move your library to a higher-capacity hard drive? What if you have media files all over your hard drive and you need to consolidate them all in once place so you can reclaim drive space? You can do all that and more.

Consolidating the library media files

If you have media files that are stored on different hard drives that are connected to the same computer, you can have iTunes consolidate your library by copying everything into the iTunes Music folder. By first consolidating your library, you make sure that any backup operation you perform is complete.

To consolidate your iTunes library, choose Advanced⇨Consolidate Library. The original media files remain where they are, but copies are made in your Music folder.

Changing the location of the library

You can store your iTunes library in a different location on your hard drive or on another hard drive — as long as you tell iTunes where to find it. To change where iTunes stores your content library, follow these steps:

1. **Choose iTunes⇨Preferences (Mac) or Edit⇨Preferences (Windows) and then click the Advanced tab.**
2. **Click the General tab.**
3. **Click the Change button, as shown in Figure 13-2.**

   You can then browse to select another location on any connected hard drive.

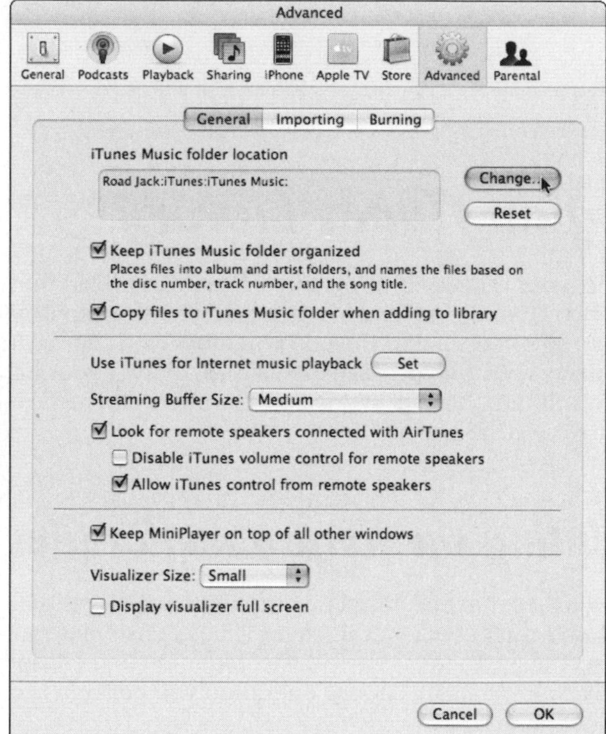

Figure 13-2: Change the location of the iTunes Music folder that contains your entire library.

After selecting a new location, the content you bring into iTunes (by ripping CDs, downloading items from the iTunes Store, or dragging media files) is stored in the new location. However, previously imported media files stay where they are. To move the previously imported files to the new library location, drag the media files into the iTunes window so that iTunes stores them automatically in the new location and updates its library file properly. You can then delete the media files you copied from the old library location.

To change the storage location back to the iTunes folder inside the Music folder, click the Reset button in the Preferences window (refer to Figure 13-2).

Moving your library to another hard drive

To move your entire library to another hard drive (presumably a higher-capacity drive), you can change the location of the library and consolidate the library at the same time. Follow these steps:

1. **Create a folder — name it *iTunes* — on the other hard drive.**

   iTunes is a good name, but you could call it anything, and iTunes can still find it.

2. **Change the location of the iTunes library to the new iTunes folder.**

   To change where iTunes stores the library, see the earlier section, "Changing the location of the library."

   iTunes creates a new iTunes Music folder inside your new iTunes folder.

3. **In the General section of the Advanced pane of the Preferences dialog, select the Copy Files to iTunes Music Folder When Adding to Library and the Keep iTunes Music Folder Organized options and then click OK.**

   These options might already be enabled. Just double-check to make sure that they're selected.

4. **Choose Advanced⇨Consolidate Library.**

   iTunes automatically copies all the media files, along with playlists, into the new iTunes Music folder.

Exporting iTunes playlists

With iTunes, you can export a playlist onto a different computer to have the same playlist in both places.

You must also copy the songs, videos, podcast episodes, and audio books in the playlist for the playlists on the other computer to work. Better yet, copy the entire artist folders containing the items to keep them organized. Exporting a playlist doesn't copy the items in the playlist. You get only a list of the items in *eXtensible Markup Language* (XML) format — not the content of these items. You still need to copy the actual media files to the other computer.

To export a single playlist, select the playlist and then choose File⇨Export. On a Mac, choose the XML option from the Format pop-up menu in the Save: iTunes dialog and then click the Save button. On a Windows PC, choose the XML option from the Save as Type pull-down menu in the Save As dialog.

After exporting a playlist to another computer, you can import the playlist into iTunes on that computer by choosing File⇨Import, selecting the XML file, and then clicking the Choose button. You can also export all the playlists in your library at the same time by choosing File⇨Export Library; then import them into iTunes on the other computer by choosing File⇨Import and selecting the exported XML file.

You can also import M3U playlist files from other applications that manage playlists. The M3U format is supported by media players and streaming servers, such as Winamp (`www.winamp.com`) and VideoLAN Client (`www.videolan.org`).

Managing Multiple iTunes Libraries

You can create more than one iTunes library and manage multiple libraries with one copy of the iTunes application on your computer. You can also create one or more sub-libraries of your main library on the same hard drive. You might want to do this if your main library is too large to fit on an iPod and you don't want to resort to manually managing music and videos. You can set up automatic synchronization with a sub-library that fits entirely on the iPod. Because iTunes can create the sub-library without copying content files, you don't waste hard drive space because sub-libraries share the same files as the main library.

Consider setting up multiple libraries or sub-libraries if you want to do any of the following:

- **Create one or more sub-libraries of your main library on the same hard drive,** sharing the same content folders and files. You can then automatically synchronize different iPods, iPhones, and Apple TVs with each sub-library.
- **Divide a large library into separate libraries on separate hard drives.** You might want to do this to spread a large library over several drives. You can then automatically synchronize different iPods, iPhones, and Apple TVs with each library.
- **Separate your video collection from your music collection** to store the larger video files on a different hard drive.
- **Keep podcasts in a separate library** that's updated more often than your main library.
- **Keep all new content separate from older content.**

Creating a sub-library of the main library

To create a new library, hold down Option (Mac) or Shift (PC) when launching iTunes. Then choose Create a New Library (the other choices are Quit or Choose a Library) to set up a new empty library.

By default, the hard drive location of the iTunes folder for the newly created library is the same as the previously opened library — the folder is named iTunes 1 to distinguish it from the iTunes folder for the pre-existing library. When you add more separate libraries, the folders are named iTunes 2, iTunes 3, and so on.

After you create multiple libraries, remember to hold down Option (Mac) or Shift (Windows) while launching iTunes whenever you want to switch between them. Otherwise, iTunes opens with the library that was previously opened.

You can import playlists and drag content from your iTunes folder into your new library without copying the content files because the files are in the same folder on the same hard drive. This makes it easy to consider your main library to be a Master library that links to the entire contents of the iTunes folder as well as to create sub-libraries for each iPod, iPhone, or Apple TV that share the same content files as the Master library.

Creating a separate library on a different hard drive

You can also create a new library that links to a different iTunes folder on a different hard drive so that the content files are divided (*not* shared) between libraries. For example, you might want to put all video files on a separate hard drive in a separate library. Follow these steps to create a new library on a different hard drive:

1. **Create a new iTunes library by holding down Option (Mac) or Shift (PC) when launching iTunes, and then choose Create a New Library.**

   The new iTunes library is created, empty of content.

2. **Choose iTunes⇨Preferences (Mac) or Edit⇨Preferences (Windows).**

   The Preferences dialog appears with the tabs along the top.

3. **Click the Advanced tab and then click the General tab.**

4. **Click the Change button for the iTunes Music folder location.**

   Your directory browser appears, enabling you to create and then select a folder to locate your iTunes content files. Alternatively, you can click the Reset button to restore the standard location in your user directory (the default setting when you first use iTunes).

5. **Create a folder for your content files and then select it.**

   When starting a new library that links to another hard drive, create a folder somewhere on the other hard drive, call it iTunes Music or something similar, and then select it.

6. **Activate the iTunes folder management options.**

   Make sure the Keep iTunes Music Folder Organized option and the Copy Files to iTunes Music Folder when Adding to Library option are both selected.

7. **Click OK to close Preferences.**

The new library links to the new folder location so that when you add new content to the library, the content is copied to the new folder. If the purpose of your new library is to hold all your videos, you can now copy all your videos from the original library's content folder to the iTunes window, adding the content to the new library. iTunes copies the content files to the new folder. You can then delete the videos from the original library.

Backing Up an iTunes Library

Backups? You don't need no stinkin' backups?

Yes, you do, so think twice about not making them! We know: Backing up your files can be inconvenient and can eat up the capacity of all your external hard drives. Still, it must be done. And fortunately, it's easy to do. With iTunes, you can copy your library to another hard drive on your computer or to another computer. You can burn as many data DVDs as needed to store all the files (see Chapter 14). You can even copy a library from a Mac to a PC and vice versa.

Backing up to DVD-Rs or CD-Rs

Apple provides a handy wizard that walks you through backing up your iTunes library, playlists, and iTunes Store purchases to CD-Rs or DVD-Rs. (*R* means one-time recordable.) You can choose to back up the entire library, perform *incremental backups* (only items added or changed since the last backup), or save only store purchases. Choose File➪Back Up to Disc and then choose one of the following:

- **Back Up Entire iTunes Library and Playlist.** This might take a stack of DVD-Rs (or a truckload of CD-Rs), but it's worth doing if you have no other way to back up your library.

- **Back Up Only iTunes Store Purchases.** This is an essential procedure because if you lose these files, you have to repurchase them. You can use CD-Rs or DVD-Rs.
- **Only Back Up Items Added or Changed Since Last Backup.** Use this method to copy only items that were added or changed.

To restore your iTunes library from a stack of backup DVD-Rs or CD-Rs, open iTunes and insert the first disc. Then follow the instructions to restore your library.

Backing up to another hard drive

To copy your entire library to another hard drive, locate the iTunes folder on your computer. Drag this entire folder to another hard drive or backup device, and you're all set. This action copies everything, including the playlists in your library.

The copy operation might take some time if your library is huge. Although you can interrupt the operation anytime, the newly copied library might not be complete. Finishing the copy operation is always best.

If you restore the backup copy to the same computer with the same names for its hard drive, the backup copy's playlists work fine. *Playlists* are essentially XML lists of songs with pathnames to the song files: If the hard drive name is different, the pathnames won't work. However, you can import the playlists into iTunes by choosing File⇨Import, which realigns the playlist pathnames to the new hard drive. Alternatively, you can use the method described in the upcoming section, "Backing up from Mac to PC or PC to Mac."

If you copy just the iTunes Music folder and not the entire iTunes folder, you're copying the files but not your playlists. You still have to export your playlists; see the earlier section, "Exporting iTunes playlists."

If you use a Mac and subscribe to the Apple .Mac service, you can download and use the free Backup software. This software lets you save the latest versions of your files regularly and automatically so that you never have to worry about losing important files. With Backup, you can quickly and easily store files on your *iDisk* (a portion of an Internet hard drive hosted by .Mac) or on CD or DVD as data files — not as CD songs. (See Chapter 14 to read how to burn an audio or MP3 CD.) The iDisk is perhaps the least convenient even though you do get some free space with a .Mac membership. Copying to the iDisk is slow even over a high-speed connection. We use iDisk to transfer individual songs and large files to other people and to back up very important documents. However, you're better off using data DVDs as a backup medium for data and audio CDs for your songs and albums.

Backing up from Mac to PC or PC to Mac

Maybe you use a Mac but you want to transfer your iTunes library to a PC that runs iTunes, or the other way around. Or perhaps you want a foolproof method of copying your entire library to another computer, whether it's a Mac, a PC running Windows, or just a computer that uses a different name for its hard drive (or a different path to the Home folder or user folder).

To back up your iTunes library no matter what the situation is, follow these steps:

1. **Locate your iTunes Music folder on your old computer.**

   Locate your iTunes Music folder as described in the earlier section, "Finding the iTunes library." Consider the first computer as the *old* computer and the one receiving the copied library as the *new* computer.

2. **Download and install iTunes on the new computer.**

   See Chapter 2 for instructions on installing iTunes. If the new computer already has an iTunes Music folder with music that you want to preserve, move that iTunes Music folder to another folder on the hard drive or copy it to another hard drive or storage medium.

3. **Copy the iTunes Music folder from the old computer to the newly installed iTunes folder on the new computer.**

   If you have multiple users on the new computer, make sure that you choose the appropriate Home folder (Mac) or user folder (Windows). The copy operation for a large music library takes a while.

4. **Choose File⇨Export Library on the old computer, browse to a location on your hard drive or network, and then click Save.**

   When you export your entire library, iTunes creates the XML file `iTunes Music Library.xml` that links to music files and stores all your playlists.

5. **Start iTunes on the new computer.**

6. **Choose File⇨Import on the new computer and then import the `iTunes Music Library.xml` file.**

   The music library is now available on the new computer.

The iTunes Music Library file (`iTunes Music Library.xml`) must be located within the iTunes folder where iTunes can find it.

Chapter 14

Baking Your Own Discs with Printed Inserts

In This Chapter

- Choosing the right format for burning a disc
- Creating a burn playlist
- Setting burn preferences
- Burning an audio CD, an MP3 CD, or a data DVD
- Printing CD jewel case inserts and song lists
- Troubleshooting tips

Once upon a time, when vinyl records were popular, rock radio disk jockeys (who didn't like disco) held disco-meltdown parties. People were encouraged to throw their disco records onto a pile to be burned or steamrolled into a vinyl glob. We admit having participated in one such meltdown. However, this chapter isn't about that (nor is it about anything involving fire or heat). Rather, *burning* a disc is the process in which the CD drive recorder's laser heats up points on an interior layer of the disc to record information.

You burn CDs for a lot of reasons. Reason *numero uno* for us is to make safety copies of songs we buy from the iTunes Store — in addition to backup copies of song files on other hard drives. We also like to custom-mix songs from different artists and albums onto a CD. (Don't confuse a *custom mix* with *mixing:* The latter is a production technique for combining tracks into a single song.) And from iTunes, you can print CD jewel case inserts with the song list. You can even burn data DVDs to back up your files.

This chapter boils down everything about disc recording for you. You can find out here what kind of discs to use, which devices play the discs, how to get your playlist ready, and what settings to use for burning. Read on to discover what you need to make sure your burns aren't meltdowns — where the only melting is the music in your ears.

Do not violate copyright law. You are allowed to copy content to disc for your own use, but you cannot legally copy content for any other purpose. Consult a lawyer if you're in doubt.

Selecting Recordable CDs and DVDs

You can arrange any songs in your library into a playlist and then burn a CD from that playlist. (See Chapter 10 for more on creating playlists.) If you have a CD-R, CD-RW, or DVD-R drive (such as the Apple SuperDrive for a Mac) and a blank CD-R (*R* stands for *recordable*), you can create your own music CDs that play in most CD players. You can also include audio books and podcast episodes in a playlist and burn them onto CDs.

Blank CD-Rs (I'm talking discs now and not drives) are available in most electronics and computer stores — even in supermarkets. You can also get them online from the Apple Store (not the music store — the store that sells computers and accessories). Choose iTunes➪Shop for iTunes Products (Mac) or Help➪Shop for iTunes Products (Windows) to reach the Apple Store online.

The discs are called *CD-R* because they use a recordable format related to commercial audio CDs (which aren't recordable, of course). You can also create a CD-R of songs in the MP3 format, which is useful for backing up a music library or making discs for use in MP3 CD players.

Many CD burners, such as the Apple SuperDrive, also burn *CD-RWs* (recordable, *read-write* discs) that you can erase and reuse. However, CD players don't always recognize CD-RWs as music CDs. Some burners can also create data DVD-Rs and DVD-RWs, which are useful for holding data files, but you can use these discs only with computers that have DVD drives. Some commercial DVD players won't recognize a data DVD-R or DVD-RW but might still recognize an MP3 DVD-R.

You can play MP3 files burned on a CD-R in MP3 format on any MP3 disc player, on combination CD/MP3 players, on many DVD players, and (of course) on computers that recognize MP3 CDs (including computers with iTunes).

What You Can Fit on a CD-R or DVD-R

You can fit up to 74 minutes of music on a high-quality CD-R; most can go as high as 80 minutes. The sound files on your hard drive might take up more space than 650MB if they're uncompressed, but you can still fit 74 minutes (or 80 minutes, depending on the disc) because the CD format stores information without error-correction data.

The little Red Book that launched an industry

The typical audio CD and CD-R uses the Compact Disc-Digital Audio (CD-DA) format Mode 2 Form 2, better known as *Red Book.* This book isn't something from Chairman Mao: It's a document (published in 1980) that provides the specifications for the standard CD developed by Sony and Philips. According to legend, this document was in a binder with a red cover.

Here's another legend: In 1979, Norio Ohga, honorary chairman and former CEO of Sony (and a maestro conductor), overruled his engineers and insisted that the CD format be able to hold Beethoven's *Ninth Symphony.* This symphony is 74 minutes and 42 seconds long — now the standard length of a Red Book audio CD.

CD-DA defines audio data digitized at 44,100 samples per second (44.1 kHz) and in a range of 65,536 possible values (16 bits). The format for the audio is called *pulse code modulation* (PCM).

To import music onto the computer from an audio CD, you have to convert the music to digital sound files by a program, such as iTunes. When you burn an audio CD, iTunes converts the sound files back into the CD-DA format while it burns the disc.

If you burn music to a CD-R in MP3 format, the disc can hold more than 12 hours of music. You read that right — *12 hours on one disc.* This is why *MP3 discs* are popular: because they are essentially CD-Rs with MP3 files stored on them.

If you have a DVD burner, such as an Apple SuperDrive, you can burn data DVD-Rs or DVD-RWs to use with other computers. This approach is suitable for making backup copies of media files (or any data files). A DVD-R can hold about 4,700,000,000 bytes (more than 4GB).

Creating a Burn Playlist

To burn a CD (actually a CD-R, but most people refer to recordable CD-R discs as *CDs*), you must first define a playlist for the CD. (See Chapter 10 to find out how to create a playlist.) You can use songs encoded in any format that iTunes supports; however, you get higher-quality music with the uncompressed AIFF and WAV formats or with the Apple Lossless format.

If your playlist includes music purchased from the iTunes Store in the protected AAC-encoding format, some rules might apply. For example, as of this writing, the iTunes Store allows you to burn seven copies of the same playlist containing protected songs to an audio CD, but no more.

You can get around this limitation by creating or using a new playlist, copying the protected songs to the new playlist, and then burning more CDs with the new playlist.

Calculating how much music to use

When you create an audio CD playlist, you find out how many songs can fit on the CD by totaling the durations of the songs. You can see the size of a playlist by selecting it; the bottom of the iTunes window shows the number of songs, the amount in time, and the amount in megabytes for the selected playlist, as shown in Figure 14-1.

Figure 14-1: Check the duration of the playlist below the song list.

In Figure 14-1, the selected playlist takes about 1.1 hours (exactly 1:08:54) to play, so it fits on a standard audio CD. (The 15 songs take up only 65.3MB of hard drive space; they were purchased from the iTunes Store and encoded in the compressed and protected AAC format.)

A one-hour playlist of AIFF-encoded music, which might occupy over 600MB of hard drive space, also fits on a standard audio CD. The amount you can fit on a standard audio CD depends on the duration, not the hard drive space occupied by the music files. Although a CD holds between 650MB and 700MB (depending on the disc), the music is stored in a special format known as CD-DA (or Red Book) that fills byte sectors without error-correction and checksum information. (You can read about CD-DA and Red Book in the sidebar, "The little Red Book that launched an industry.") Thus, you can fit about 90MB more — 740MB total — of AIFF-encoded music on a 650MB disc. We typically put 1.1 hours (about 66 minutes) of music on a 74-minute or an 80-minute CD-R, leaving minutes to spare.

Always use the actual duration in hours, minutes, and seconds to calculate how much music you can fit on an audio CD — either 74 or 80 minutes for blank CD-Rs. We recommend leaving at least one extra minute to account for the gaps between songs.

You do the *opposite* for an MP3 CD or a data DVD. Use the actual megabytes to calculate how many song files can fit on a disc — up to 700MB for a blank CD-R. You can fit lots more music on an MP3 CD-R because you use MP3-encoded songs rather than uncompressed AIFF songs.

If you have too many songs in the playlist to fit on a CD, iTunes burns as many songs in the playlist as will fit on the CD (either audio or MP3). Then it asks you to insert another CD to continue burning the remaining songs in the playlist.

If you include in a burn playlist a very long song that you purchased from the iTunes Store, you see a dialog telling you to put that long song in its own playlist. Then burn that single-song playlist separately.

Importing music for an audio CD-R

Before you rip an audio CD of songs, as we describe in Chapter 5, that you want to burn to an audio CD-R, you might want to change the import settings. (Check out Chapter 19 if you need to do this.) Use the AIFF, WAV, or Apple Lossless encoders for songs from audio CDs if you want to burn your own audio CDs with music at its highest quality.

AIFF is the standard digital format for uncompressed sound on a Mac, and you can't go wrong with it. *WAV* is basically the same thing for Windows. The Apple Lossless encoder provides CD-quality sound in a file size that's about 55 to 60 percent of the size of an AIFF- or WAV-encoded file. Both the AIFF encoder and the WAV encoder offer the same custom settings for sample rate, sample size, and channels, which you can set by choosing Custom from the Settings pop-up menu in the Importing section of the Advanced pane of iTunes Preferences. You can choose the automatic settings, and iTunes detects the proper sample rate, size, and channels from the source. Apple Lossless is always set to automatic.

Many songs you can purchase from the iTunes Store are supplied in an unprotected format encoded in AAC that carries no restrictions, but others — notably the lesser-priced songs — are sold in a protected AAC format. You can't convert the protected format to anything else, but you can still burn the songs onto CDs, and the quality of the result on CD is acceptable. Audio books also come in a protected format that can't be converted, but you can burn them onto CDs with acceptable quality.

The AAC encoder creates an audio file that is similar in audio quality to one created by the MP3 encoder, but takes up less space; both are acceptable to most CD listeners. We think AAC offers a decent trade-off of space and quality and is suitable (although not as good as AIFF or Apple Lossless) for burning to an audio CD. For a complete description of these encoders, see Chapter 18.

Switching import encoders for MP3 CD-R

MP3 discs are essentially CD-Rs with MP3 files stored on them. Consumer MP3 CD players are readily available in consumer electronics stores, including hybrid models that play both audio CDs and MP3 CDs.

You can fit 8–12 hours of stereo music on an MP3 CD with the MP3 format — the amount varies depending on the encoding options and settings you choose. For example, you might be able to fit up to 20 hours of mono (monaural) recordings because they use only one channel and carry less information. On the other hand, if you encode stereo recordings at high bit rates (above 192 bits per second), you may fit up to 9 hours. If you rip an audio CD, you can set the importing options to precisely the type of MP3 file you want; see Chapter 19.

You can use only MP3-encoded songs to burn an MP3 CD-R. Any songs not encoded in MP3 are skipped and not burned to the CD-R. Audible books and spoken-word titles are provided in an audio format that uses security technologies, including encryption, to protect purchased content. You can't burn an MP3 CD-R with Audible files; any Audible files in a burn playlist are skipped when you burn an MP3 CD-R.

Setting the Burning Preferences

Burning a CD is a simple process, and getting it right the first time is a good idea because when you burn a CD-R, it's done one time — right or wrong. You can't erase content on a CD-R like you can with a CD-RW. Because you can't play a CD-RW in as many CD players, we recommend using a CD-R if you want to burn an audio CD. Fortunately, CD-Rs are inexpensive, so you won't be out more than a few cents if you burn a bad one. (Besides, they're good as coasters for coffee tables.)

Set the following options to ensure that you burn your CD right the first time. You can access these options by choosing iTunes⇨Preferences (Mac) or Edit⇨Preferences (Windows), clicking the Advanced tab, and then clicking the Burning tab:

- **Use Sound Check:** Musicians do a sound check before every performance to check the volume of microphones and instruments and their effect on the listening environment. The aptly named Use Sound Check option in the Burning preferences dialog (see Figure 14-2) turns on the Sound Check feature to balance your tunes, volume-wise.

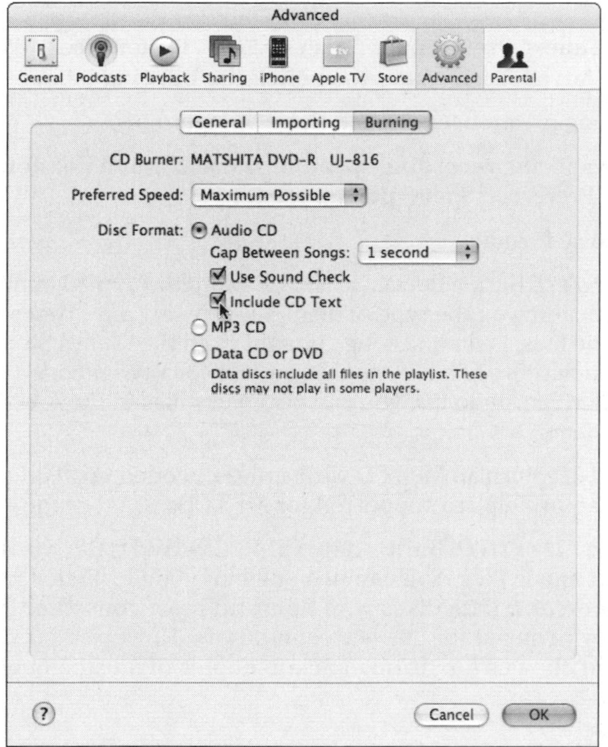

Figure 14-2: Set burning preferences here.

- **Gap between Songs:** Another professional touch is to add an appropriate gap between songs, just like commercial CDs. With this option enabled, you can set the gap time as well.
- **Include CD Text:** Selecting this option adds the artist and track name text to the CD for certain CD players (often, in car players) that can display the artist and track name while playing a CD.
- **Disc Format:** Choosing the appropriate disc format is perhaps the most important choice. Decide whether you're burning an audio CD (CD-R), an MP3 CD (CD-R), or a Data CD (CD-R) or DVD (DVD-R or DVD-RW). Your choice depends on what type of player you're using, or whether you're making a data backup of files rather than a disc that plays in a player.

- **Preferred Speed:** iTunes typically detects the rating of a blank CD-R and adjusts the recording speed to fit. However, if your blank CD-Rs are rated for a slower speed than your burner or if you have problems creating CD-Rs, you can change the recording speed setting to match the CD's rating.

Follow these steps to set the preceding options:

1. **Choose iTunes⇨Preferences (Mac) or Edit⇨Preferences (Windows), click the Advanced tab, and then click the Burning tab.**

   The burning preferences appear. Refer to Figure 14-2.

2. **Choose a specific recording speed or the Maximum Possible option from the Preferred Speed pop-up menu.**

3. **Select a disc format:**

   - *Audio CD:* Burn a normal audio CD of up to 74 or 80 minutes (depending on the type of blank CD-R) using any iTunes-supported music files, including songs bought from the iTunes Store. Although connoisseurs of music might use AIFF- or WAV-encoded music to burn an audio CD, you can also use songs in the AAC and MP3 formats.
   - *MP3 CD:* Burn an MP3 CD with songs encoded in MP3 format. No other formats are supported for MP3 CDs.
   - *Data CD or DVD:* Burn a data CD-R, CD-RW, DVD-R, or DVD-RW with music files. You can use any encoding formats for the songs. ***Important:*** Data discs won't play on most consumer CD players: They're meant for use with computers. However, data discs are good choices for storing backup copies of music bought from the iTunes Store.

4. **(Optional, audio CDs only) Select the Use Sound Check option.**

   Note: This option, for audio CDs only, works regardless of whether you're already using the Sound Check option in the Playback preferences for iTunes playback. You can select this option for burning without ever changing the preferences for iTunes playback.

5. **(Audio CDs only) Choose a duration from the Gap between Songs pop-up menu.**

   You can choose from a gap of 0 to 5 seconds, or None. We recommend leaving the menu set to the default setting of 1 second.

6. **(Optional, audio CDs only) Select the Include CD Text option to include artist and track names for CD players that can display text.**

7. **Click OK.**

Burning a Disc

After you set the burning preferences, you're ready to start burning. Follow these steps to burn a disc:

1. **Select the playlist and then click the Burn Disc button.**

   The Burn Disc button replaces the Browse button in the lower-right corner of the iTunes window whenever you select a playlist (refer to Figure 14-1).

   A message appears telling you to insert a blank disc.

2. **Insert a blank disc (label side up).**

   iTunes immediately checks the media and begins the burn process, displaying a progress bar and the names of the songs burning to the disc.

   When iTunes finishes burning the disc, iTunes chimes, and the disc is mounted on the Desktop.

3. **Eject the newly burned disc from your drive and then test it.**
4. **Don't delete your burn playlist yet.**

   You can read why in the following section.

Burning takes several minutes. You can cancel the operation at any time by clicking the X next to the progress bar, but canceling the operation isn't like undoing the burn. If the burn has already started, you can't use that CD-R or DVD-R again.

If the playlist has more music than can fit on the disc using the chosen format, iTunes burns as much as possible from the beginning of the playlist and then asks you to insert another disc to burn the rest. To calculate the amount of music in a playlist, see the earlier section, "Calculating how much music to use."

Spoken word fans: Audible audio books with chapter markers are burned onto a CD with each chapter as a separate track.

If you choose the MP3 CD format, iTunes skips over any songs in the playlist that aren't in this format.

Printing Song and Album Information

Putting music on a blank CD-R doesn't change the disc's look in any way, so how do you know the disc isn't just another blank? Put it inside a case and include something in print that identifies it.

You can print the CD jewel case insert, song list, and album notes for the CD you just burned. (That's why you didn't delete the burn playlist yet.) You can even print the cover art. If you have a color printer, you can print gorgeous color inserts for your CDs. If you don't have a suitable printer, you can save the printed version as a Portable Document Format (PDF) file that you can print at a Kinko's or similar copy shop.

Select the playlist and choose File⇨Print to see the iTunes Print dialog (as shown in Figure 14-3). You can see all the choices you have for jewel case inserts, song listings, and album notes as well as a preview of how they look when printed.

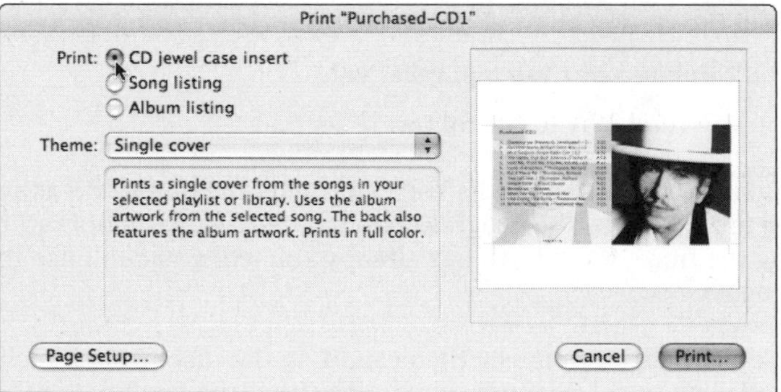

Figure 14-3: Print a jewel case insert directly from iTunes. It can include cover art provided with songs.

Printing inserts

Everyone calls the standard CD case a *jewel case* even though the only precious element in the package is the music. Jewel cases have slots for inserting a printed insert or booklet. You can print your own insert directly from iTunes via the burn playlist.

To print a CD insert, select the album for which you want to print the artwork and then follow these steps:

1. **Choose File⇨Print.**
2. **From the iTunes Print dialog, select the CD Jewel Case Insert option.**

3. **Choose a theme from the Theme pop-up menu.**

   Themes include: Text Only (without song artwork), Mosaic (with artwork from songs arranged in a mosaic), and Single Cover (with one song's artwork). Figure 14-4 shows Mosaic (Black & White) in the preview.

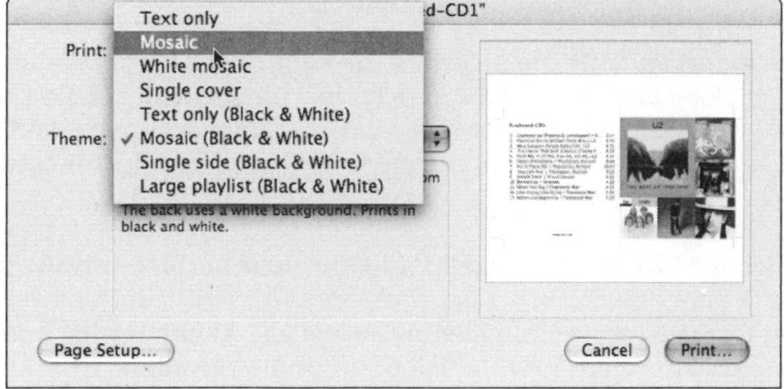

Figure 14-4: Choose a theme for a jewel case insert.

4. **(Optional) Click the Page Setup button to set page layout options, such as landscape or portrait orientation.**

   The CD insert themes automatically set the proper orientation, but you can change them in the Page Setup dialog.

5. **Click the Print button and then follow your normal printing procedures.**

Printing song lists and album notes

Cover art for an insert is a nice decoration, but if you choose an art-based theme rather than one that lists the songs, you might still want another sheet with a song list to tell which track is which. You might also want a more detailed song list that includes information for each song, such as the composer, duration, original album, and perhaps even the rating you assigned in iTunes.

To print a song list, follow these steps:

1. **Choose File➪Print.**
2. **Select the Song Listing option.**
3. **Choose one of the following themes for the song listing from the Theme pop-up menu:**
   - *Songs:* This theme prints a column for each song name, duration, artist, and album title.

- *User Ratings:* This theme prints the same columns as the Songs theme and adds a column with the ratings that you assign in iTunes. This theme prints in landscape orientation.
- *Dates Played:* This theme prints the same columns as the Songs theme and adds columns for the play count and the date last played, set by iTunes when you play songs. This theme prints in landscape orientation.
- *Custom:* This theme prints the columns as they're set in the iTunes Song List pane. You can print any piece of information about the songs that iTunes stores, such as composer, genre, and year. See Chapter 8 to add or change the viewing options for columns in the Song List pane.

4. **Click the Print button and then follow your normal printing procedures.**

To print a catalog-style album listing, select the Album Listing option in the dialog. (Refer to Figure 14-3.) This option prints the album title, artist, song names, and song lengths.

Need a printed list of the music in your library? You can use the Song Listing or Album Listing options to print all the content in your iTunes library (including audio books and music videos) rather than just a playlist. Select the Music option in the Source pane. Then choose File⇨Print and select your printing options. If you want to save paper and create an electronic version, create a PDF file via the Print dialog (Mac or Windows).

If you want to print more extensive notes or use a CD jewel case insert layout that iTunes doesn't offer in its printing themes, you can export the song information to a text file and then edit that information in a word processor or page layout program to make liner notes for the CD. iTunes exports (as a text file) all the song information for a single song, a playlist, an album, songs by an artist, or songs in the library. To export song information, follow these steps:

1. **Select the album, songs, or playlist.**
2. **Choose File⇨Export.**
3. **Browse your hard drive and choose a location to store the song list.**
4. **In the Export dialog, select the Plain Text option from the Format pop-up menu.**

   The Plain Text option is the right choice for you unless you use a double-byte language, such as Japanese or Chinese, for which the Unicode option is the right choice.
5. **Click the Export button.**

To print high-quality inserts from an exported song list, try the Discus Labeling Software (`www.magicmouse.com`), which also allows you to print labels for your CD-Rs and DVD-Rs. Discus supports more than 2,600 different sheet-fed paper labels including labels for CDs and DVDs, mini-CDs, mini-CD jewel cases, business card CDs, jewel case covers and inserts, DVD cases, VHS spine and face labels, audiocassette labels, and business/calling cards.

Mac users can take advantage of Disc Cover from Belight Software (`www.belightsoft.com`), which can import content and images from iTunes, iPhoto, iDVD and other sources and lets you experiment with styles and graphic tools. Disc Cover offers a library of label and paper layouts from popular manufacturers such as Avery, Neato, and Memorex, and supports direct-on-CD printers.

Troubleshooting Burns

Murphy's Law applies to everything, even something as simple as burning a CD-R. Don't think for a moment that you're immune to the whims and treacheries of Murphy (no one really knows who Murphy is) who, in all his infinite wisdom, pronounced that anything that *can* go wrong *will* go wrong (and usually at the least convenient time). In this section, we cover some of the most common problems that you might encounter when burning discs.

The best way to test your newly burned disc is to pop it right back into your computer's drive — or, if it's an audio CD, try it on a consumer CD player. On most CD players, an audio CD-R plays just like any commercial audio CD. MP3 CDs play fine on consumer MP3 CD players and also work in computers with CD-ROM and DVD drives.

If the disc works on the computer but not on a commercial CD player, you might have a compatibility problem with the commercial player and CD-R. For example, we have a ten-year-old CD player that doesn't play CD-Rs very well, and car players sometimes have trouble with them.

The following list gives some typical problems, along with the solutions, that you might run into when burning a CD:

Problem: The disc won't burn.

Solution: Perhaps you have a bum disc. Hey, it happens. Try using another disc or burning at a slower speed.

Problem: In a consumer CD player, the disc doesn't play or stutters while playing.

Solution: This happens often with older consumer players that don't play CD-Rs well, and with some players that are fussy about reading less-expensive CD-Rs or certain brands. Try the disc in your computer's CD-ROM or DVD drive. If it works there and you set the format to Audio CD, you probably have a compatibility problem with your consumer player.

Problem: The disc doesn't show tracks on a consumer CD player or ejects immediately.

Solution: Be sure to use the proper disc format. The Audio CD format works in just about all consumer CD players that can play CD-Rs. MP3 CDs work in consumer MP3 CD players and computer CD-ROM and DVD drives. Data CDs or DVDs work only in computer drives.

Problem: Some songs in your playlist were skipped and not burned onto the disc.

Solution: Audio CD-Rs burn with songs encoded in any format, but you can use only MP3-encoded songs to burn an MP3 CD-R. Any songs not encoded in MP3 — including songs purchased from the iTunes Store in protected AAC format — are skipped when burning MP3 CDs. (Any Audible files are also skipped, which can't be put onto an MP3 CD.) If your playlist for an audio CD-R includes music purchased from the iTunes Store, some rules might apply — see the earlier section, "Creating a Burn Playlist."

Part III

Playing Your iPod

"Okay, the view's just up ahead. Everyone switch to 'America the Beautiful' on your iPhone playlist."

In this part . . .

Part III focuses on playing content with your iPod, connecting it to a stereo or TV, and fine-tuning the sound.

- Chapter 15 shows you how to locate and play songs, audio books, podcasts, and videos on your iPod. You also find out how to create playlists on the fly and adjust an iPod's volume.
- Chapter 16 covers playing music over home stereos and portable speakers with your iPod, connecting your iPod to a television or video equipment to display video and photos, and using cool accessories for the iPod at home.

Chapter 15

Playing iPod Content

In This Chapter

- Locating items by artist, album, or playlist
- Repeating and shuffling a song list
- Playing podcasts, audio books, videos, and games
- Creating, clearing, and saving On-The-Go playlists
- Playing songs in the iPod shuffle
- Changing the volume level and volume limit

For a music lover, nothing compares with the feeling of having a lot of song choices at your fingertips. Rather than sitting back and soaking up the preprogrammed sounds of radio or CDs, you can control your iPod playback to pick any song that you want to hear at any time. Or, shuffle through songs to get an idea of how wide your music choices are or just to surprise yourself or others. You can even follow a thread of musical ideas, such as The Kingsmen's version of "Louie Louie" through "All Day and All of the Night" by The Kinks, "Dirty Water" by The Standells, "Little Bit of Soul" by The Music Explosion, The Troggs' "Wild Thing," all the way to the version of "Wild Thing" by Jimi Hendrix.

With your full-size iPod or iPod nano, you can locate and play music easily, browsing by artist and album — even by composer. Selecting a playlist is simple, but if you don't have playlists from iTunes (or you don't want to hear those playlists), you can create a temporary On-The-Go playlist. In this chapter, you discover how to locate and play content on any iPod. ***Note:*** If you have an iPod shuffle, see the later section, "Playing an iPod shuffle."

Locating Songs on Your iPod

With so many songs on your iPod, finding a particular one by its song title can take longer than finding it another way — like finding a needle in a haystack or even trying to find "Needle in a Haystack" by The Velvelettes in a Motown catalog. It may be faster to locate albums by cover art, or songs by searching for artist (or composer), genre, album, or playlist.

You can also search for audio books and podcasts by artist (author name) or album (title).

By cover art (using Cover Flow)

Sixth-generation iPods, including the iPod nano and the iPod touch, can display the cover art for albums. The Cover Flow browser lets you flip through your cover art to select music on your iPod.

To browse music by cover art with an iPod touch or iPhone model, choose Music from the iPod touch main menu or iPod from the iPhone main menu, and then quickly switch to holding the device horizontally, in order to display a landscape-mode display. The iPod touch or iPhone automatically switches to landscape display and offers the Cover Flow browser, as shown in Figure 15-1.

Figure 15-1: The iPhone displaying iPod music with the Cover Flow browser.

Slide your finger across the album covers to scroll swiftly through the iPod's music library, or you can tap to the right or left of the cover art in the foreground to move forward or backward, respectively. Tap the play button in the lower left corner to start playing the first song in the foreground album; the play button turns to a pause button so that you can tap it again to stop playback. Tap the "i" button in the lower right side, or tap the foreground cover art, to list the songs in that album, and then tap a song to start playing it.

The Cover Flow browser is also available on sixth-generation iPod classic and iPod nano models. Choose Music from the main menu, and then choose Cover Flow from the Music menu as shown in Figure 15-2.

The Cover Flow browser appears in the iPod display as shown in Figure 15-3. To browse by cover art, scroll the click wheel clockwise to move forward, or counterclockwise to move backward through album covers. You can also press the Fast Forward or Rewind buttons to move forward or backward in your library, respectively. Press the Select button in the middle of the click wheel to select the album in the foreground, and a list of songs appears. Use the click wheel to scroll the list of songs, and press the Select button to select a highlighted song.

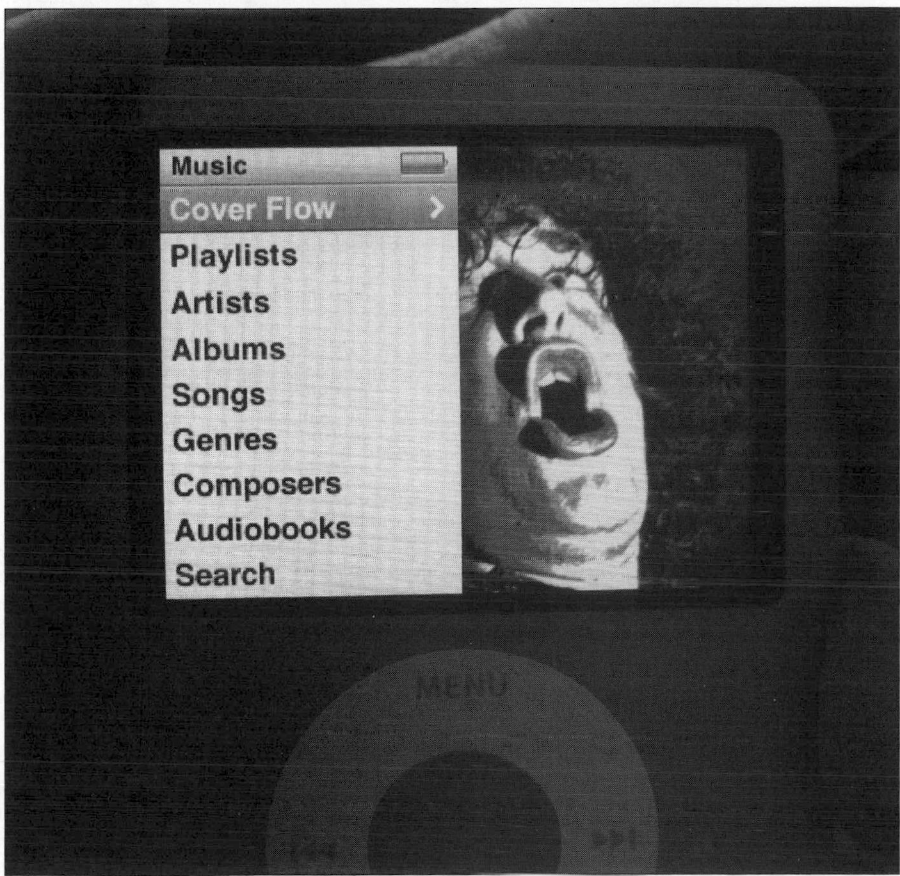

Figure 15-2: The Music menu on an iPod nano.

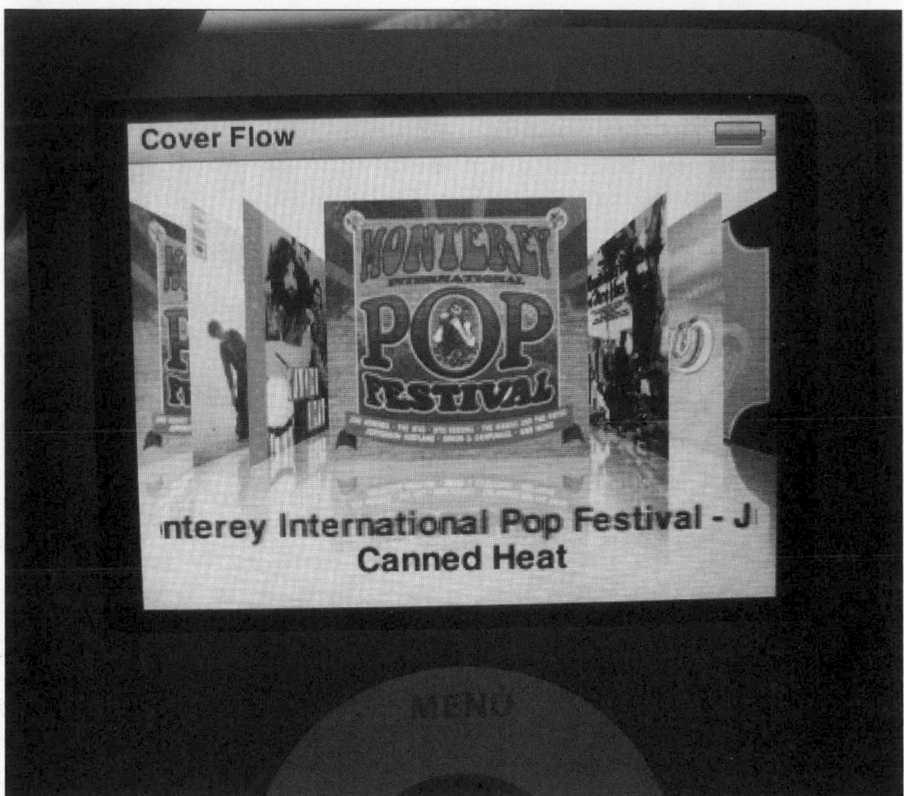

Figure 15-3: The Cover Flow browser on an iPod nano.

By artist name

Your iPod organizes music by artist, and then within each artist by album. To browse music by artist with an iPod touch or iPhone model, choose Music from the iPod touch main menu or iPod from the iPhone main menu, and tap the Artists button along the bottom row of the display. A scrollable list of artists appears with an alphabet listed vertically along the right side. Tap any letter in the alphabet to scroll the list directly to that letter. Tap an artist name to see a list of albums or songs by that artist (you see multiple albums if more than one album is available — tap the album name to select the album). Tap a song title to start playing the song.Follow these steps with an iPod classic or iPod nano (or earlier models) to locate a song by artist and then by album:

1. **Choose Music from the iPod main menu.**
2. **From the Music menu that appears (refer to Figure 15-2), choose the Artists item.**

   To be more selective you can browse by genre first. Choose Genres, then choose a genre from the Genres menu to get a list of artists that have songs in that genre (in alphabetical order by artist name).

3. **Select an artist from the Artists menu.**

   The artists' names are listed in alphabetical order by last name or the first word of a group. ***Note:*** Any leading *The* is ignored, so *The Beatles* appears where *Beatles* is in the list. Scroll the Artists menu until the artist name (such as *Radiohead* or *Bowie, David*) is highlighted and then press the Select button.

   The artist's menu of albums appears. For example, the Radiohead menu in my iPod includes the selections All, *OK Computer,* and *The Bends.* The menu for Bowie, David includes All, *Heroes, Space Oddity, Ziggy Stardust,* and many more.

4. **Choose All or the name of an album from the artist's menu.**

   You can find All at the top of the artist's menu; it should already be highlighted. Press the Select button to choose it or scroll until an album name (or podcast or audio book title) is highlighted; then press the Select button.

   Note: Albums are listed in alphabetical order based on the first word of the album title. A leading *A* or *The* isn't ignored, so the album *The Basement Tapes* is listed *after* the album *Stage Fright.*

   A song list appears after you choose either an album choice or All.

5. **Select a song from the list.**

   The songs in the album list are in *album order* (the order that they appear on the album); in the All list, songs are listed in album order for each album.

By album title

To browse music by album title with an iPod touch, choose Music from the iPod touch main menu, and tap the Albums button along the bottom row of the display. A scrollable list of albums appears with an alphabet listed vertically along the right side. Tap any letter in the alphabet to scroll the list directly to that letter. Tap an album title to see a list of songs in the album. Tap a song title to start playing the song.

Follow these steps with an iPod classic or iPod nano (or earlier models) to directly locate a song by album:

1. **Choose Music from the iPod main menu.**
2. **From the Music menu, choose the Albums item.**

   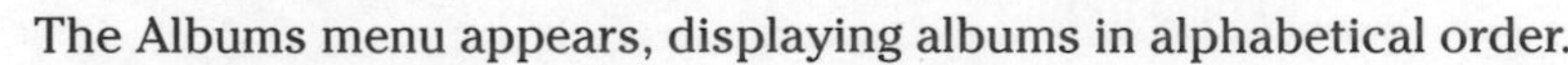

   The Albums menu appears, displaying albums in alphabetical order.

   Choose Composers to choose a composer and then choose a composer from the Composers menu to get a list of songs for that composer.
3. **Choose an album from the Albums menu.**

   The albums are listed in alphabetical order (without any reference to artist, which might make identification difficult). The order is by first word; a leading *A, An,* or *The* isn't ignored, so the album *The Natch'l Blues* is listed after *Taj's Blues* in the T section rather than the N section. Scroll the Albums menu until the album name is highlighted and then press the Select button.

   A song list appears.

   You can also find podcasts and audio books in the Albums menu. The album name is the podcast name or audio book title. After selecting a podcast, a list of the podcast's episodes appear by date of release; after selecting an audio book, a list of the audio book episodes (as in Part 1, Part 2, and so on) are listed in the order that they should be heard.
4. **Select a song from the list.**

   The songs in the album list are in the order that they appear on the album. Scroll the list to highlight the song name and then press the Select button.

   The artist and song names appear.

To browse music by album title with an iPhone, choose iPod from the iPhone main menu, and tap the More button along the bottom row of the display. A scrollable list of options appears, including Albums. Tap Albums to view a list of albums with an alphabet listed vertically along the right side. Tap any letter in the alphabet to scroll the list directly to that letter. Tap an album title to see a list of songs in the album. Tap a song title to start playing the song.

By playlist

When you automatically synchronize your iPod or iPhone with your entire iTunes library, all your playlists in iTunes are copied to the iPod or iPhone. You can choose to synchronize your iPod or iPhone with only specified playlists, as we describe in Chapter 12.

Playlists make playing a selection of content in a specific order easy. The playlist plays from the first item selected to the end of the playlist. You can combine songs, podcast episodes, audio books, and videos in a playlist. Understandably, videos are skipped on iPods that can't play video.

To browse music by playlist with an iPod touch or iPhone model, choose Music from the iPod touch main menu or iPod from the iPhone main menu, and tap the Playlists button along the bottom row of the display. A scrollable list of playlists appears. Tap a playlist title to see a list of songs in the playlist. Tap a song title to start playing the song.

Follow these steps to locate a playlist on your iPod classic or iPod nano (or earlier models):

1. **Choose Music from the iPod main menu.**
2. **From the Music menu, choose Playlists.**
3. **From the Playlists menu that appears, choose a playlist.**

   Playlists are listed in alphabetical order. Scroll the Playlists menu to highlight the playlist name and then press the Select button.

   A list of songs in the playlist appears.
4. **Select a song from the list.**

   The songs in the playlist are in *playlist order* (the order defined for the playlist in iTunes). Scroll up or down the list to highlight the song you want.

Playing a Song

After scrolling the song list until the song name is highlighted, press either the Select button or the Play/Pause button on an iPod classic or iPod nano (or earlier model) to play the selected song. On an iPod touch or iPhone, tap the song title to play the song. When the song finishes, the iPod plays the next song in the song list.

While a song is playing, the artist name and song name appear. On an iPod touch or iPhone, you see the album cover and the touch buttons for playback control — Previous/Rewind, Play/Pause, and Next/Fast-forward. The bullet-list touch button in the upper right corner displays a list of the album's contents, and the left arrow touch button in the upper left corner returns you to the previous menu. Slide your finger along the volume slider at the bottom of the display to change the volume.

Color-display iPods also display the album cover, and you can use the scroll wheel to adjust the volume. See the later section, "Adjusting and Limiting the Volume."

To pause playback, press the Play/Pause button while a song is playing.

Repeating songs

If you want to drive yourself crazy repeating the same song over and over, your iPod is happy to oblige. (You might want to try repeating "They're Coming to Take Me Away, Ha-Haaa" by Napoleon XIV, a favorite from the old *The Dr. Demento Show* radio broadcasts — and perhaps they will come.) More than likely, you'll want to repeat a sequence of songs, which you can easily do.

You can set your iPod classic or iPod nano (or older models) to repeat a single song by following these steps:

1. **Locate and play a song.**
2. **While the song plays, press the Menu button repeatedly to return to the main menu and then choose the Settings item.**
3. **Scroll the Settings menu until Repeat is highlighted.**

   The Repeat setting displays `Off` next to it.
4. **Press the Select button once (`Off` changes to `One`) to repeat one song.**

   If you press the button more than once, keep pressing until `One` appears.

You can also press the Previous/Rewind button to repeat a song.

To repeat all the songs in the selected album or playlist, follow these steps with an iPod classic or iPod nano (or older models):

1. **Locate and play a song in the album or playlist.**
2. **While the song plays, press the Menu button repeatedly to return to the main menu and then choose the Settings item.**
3. **Scroll the Settings menu until Repeat is highlighted.**

   The Repeat setting displays `Off` next to it.
4. **Press the Select button twice (`Off` changes to `All`) to repeat all the songs in the album or playlist.**

The iPod touch and iPhone provide touch buttons to control repeating and shuffling. To access these touch buttons, tap underneath the left arrow button or the album title while a song is playing (if you are viewing another menu, tap Now Playing to go directly to the "now playing" display). The Repeat and Shuffle touch buttons appear, along with the song duration slider, directly below the top row of buttons as shown in Figure 15-4.

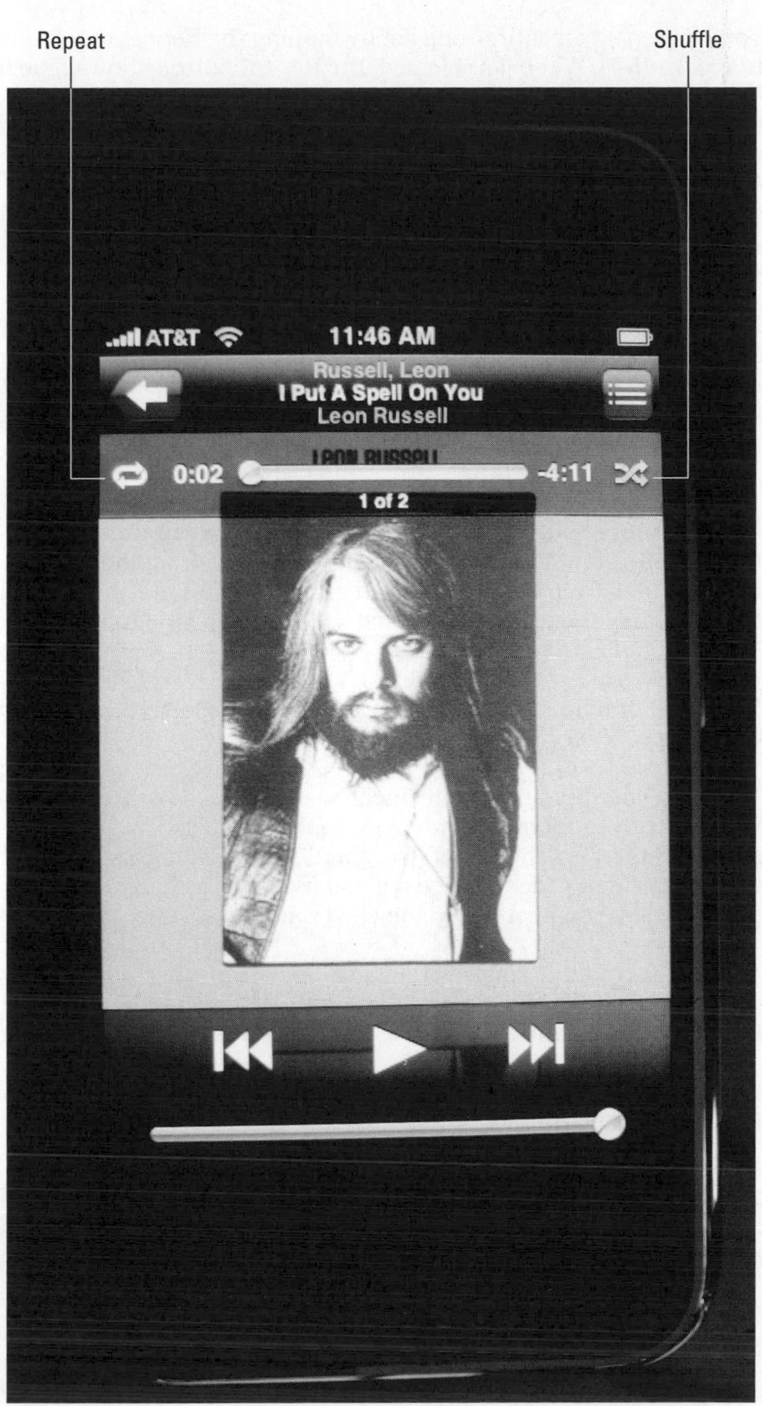

Figure 15-4: The repeat and shuffle touch buttons on an iPhone.

You can repeat an entire song list by tapping the Repeat touch button (refer to Figure 15-4). When it's selected, the Repeat button shows blue highlighting. Touch the Repeat button again to repeat only the current song — the button changes to include a blue-highlighted numeral 1. Touch it once more to return to normal playback.

Shuffling song order

Maybe you want your song selections to be surprising and unpredictable, and you want your iPod to read your mind, as the Apple ads suggest. You can *shuffle* song playback to play in random order, just like an automated radio station without a disk jockey or program guide. See for yourself whether your iPod knows how to pick good tunes without your help.

To turn your iPod classic or iPod nano (or older model) into a random song player, choose Shuffle Songs from the main menu. To turn your iPod touch or iPhone into a random song player, choose Music from the iPod touch main menu or iPod from the iPhone main menu, and tap the Songs touch button at the bottom of the display. The song list appears, with Shuffle at the top of the list. Tap Shuffle to turn on Shuffle.

Your iPod or iPhone then plays all the songs randomly — yup, no repeats — until it plays every song.

Although your iPod or iPhone might seem to play favorites, the shuffle algorithm is truly random, according to Apple. When an iPod or iPhone creates a shuffle, it reorders the songs (like shuffling a deck of cards), and then it plays them in the new order. Trust us: If you listen for as long as it takes to complete the list, you hear every song just once.

You can also shuffle songs within an album or playlist, which gives you some control over random playback. For example, you could create a smart playlist for all jazz songs and then shuffle the songs within that jazz playlist.

Follow these steps to shuffle songs in an album or a playlist with an iPod classic or iPod nano (or older model):

1. **Locate and play a song in the album or playlist.**
2. **While the song plays, press the Menu button repeatedly to return to the main menu and then choose Settings.**
3. **Scroll the Settings menu until Shuffle is highlighted.**

   The Shuffle setting displays `Off` next to it.
4. **Press the Select button once (`Off` changes to `Songs`) to shuffle the songs in the selected album or playlist.**

The iPod touch and iPhone provide touch buttons to control repeating and shuffling. To shuffle songs in an album or playlist, start playing a song in the album or playlist, and then tap underneath the left arrow button or the album title while a song is playing. The Repeat and Shuffle touch buttons appear, along with the song duration slider, directly below the top row of buttons (refer to Figure 15-4). Tap the Shuffle button to shuffle songs within the currently playing album or playlist.

You can set an iPod touch or iPhone to shuffle any album or playlist before playing it. First, select the playlist or album, and then choose Shuffle at the top of the list of songs for that playlist or album.

You can set your iPod to repeat an entire album or playlist but still shuffle the playing order each time you hear it. Start playing a song in the album or playlist, and then set your iPod or iPhone to repeat all the songs in the album or playlist as described in "Repeating songs" in this section. Then set the iPod or iPhone to shuffle the songs as described above.

Say you want to play albums randomly, but you don't like when the songs in an album aren't played in proper album order. To shuffle all the albums in your iPod classic or iPod nano (or older models), but play the songs in normal album order, follow these steps:

1. **Press the Menu button repeatedly to return to the main menu and then choose Settings.**
2. **Scroll the Settings menu until Shuffle is highlighted.**

   The Shuffle setting displays `Off` next to it.
3. **Press the Select button twice (`Off` changes to `Albums`) to shuffle the albums without shuffling the songs within each album.**

When the iPod is set to shuffle, it won't repeat a song until it plays the entire album, playlist, or library.

By default, only songs are included in iPod shuffling. However, you can select podcast episodes, audio books, and videos in iTunes and set an option to include them in shuffles. To do this in iTunes

1. **Select the video, podcast episode, or audio book episode.**
2. **Choose File⇨Get Info.**
3. **Click the Options tab.**
4. **Deselect the Skip When Shuffling option.**

   The next time you synchronize your iPod, any items with this option turned off are included in shuffles.

If you want to exclude a song from shuffles, select the song in iTunes, choose File➪Get Info, click the Options tab, and then select the Skip When Shuffling option.

Playing Podcasts

Podcasts, naturally, have their own menu on an iPod. Podcasts are organized by podcast name (which is like an album name), and podcast episodes are listed within each podcast in the order that they were released (by date).

To play a podcast episode, follow these steps:

1. **Choose Music from the iPod main menu, or iPod from the iPhone menu.**
2. **Choose Podcasts from the iPod classic or iPod nano Music menu. On an iPhone or iPod touch, touch the More button, then touch Podcasts.**

   The More button appears in the lower right corner of the display on an iPhone or iPod touch when selecting music. After touching the More button, more choices appear including the Podcasts choice.
3. **Choose a podcast from the Podcasts menu that appears.**

   Podcast names are listed in alphabetical order by first word. ***Note:*** Any leading *The* is recognized, which is why *The Flying Other Brothers-Music Podcast* appears after the *Rockument* podcast. Scroll the Podcasts menu until the podcast name is highlighted and then press the Select button.
4. **Choose and play an episode from the podcast's menu.**

   The podcast's menu of episodes appears. Scroll the episode list until the episode name you want is highlighted; then press the Select button to play the episode on an iPod classic or iPod nano (or older model), or touch the episode title on an iPod touch or iPhone.

While a podcast episode is playing, the podcast name and episode title appear. On a color-display iPod, the podcast's graphic image — similar to an album cover — appears. To pause playback, press the Play/Pause button when a podcast episode is playing.

Podcast episodes are automatically set to remember the playback position when you pause an episode. This feature lets you pause an episode in iTunes while you synchronize your iPod (as described in Chapter 12). After synchronization, you can continue playing the episode on your iPod from where you left. This feature also works in the opposite way: If you pause an episode on your iPod, the podcast episode resumes the playback position so that you can continue playing it in iTunes (after synchronization) from where you left.

To disable the playback feature

1. **Select a podcast episode in iTunes.**
2. **Choose File⇨Get Info.**
3. **Click the Options tab.**
4. **Deselect the Remember Playback Position option.**

   This option works with any track in your library, letting you resume playback on any song or video as well.

When you synchronize your iPod, any played episodes are deleted if you set iTunes to keep only your unplayed episodes. To make sure that a particular episode stays on your iPod, select it in iTunes, Control-click (Mac) or right-click (Windows) the episode, and then choose Mark as New. You can also change your iPod's synchronization options for podcasts. See Chapter 12 for details.

Playing Audio Books

Audio books also have their own menu on an iPod. Audio books are organized by title (which also appears in the Albums menu), and sections, or *episodes*, of the audio book are listed in the order that they should be read (Part 1, Part 2, and so on).

To play an audio book episode, follow these steps:

1. **Choose Music from the iPod main menu, or iPod from the iPhone menu.**
2. **Choose Audiobooks from the iPod classic or iPod nano Music menu. On an iPhone or iPod touch, touch the More button, then touch Audiobooks.**

   The More button appears in the lower right corner of the display on an iPhone or iPod touch when selecting music. After touching the More button, more choices appear including the Audiobooks choice.

3. **Choose an audio book episode from the Audiobooks menu.**

   The audio book episodes are listed in proper order for each book, with each book title in alphabetical order. ***Note:*** Like song titles, any leading *The* is recognized, which is why *The Hitchhiker's Guide to the Galaxy: The Tertiary Phase* by Douglas Adams would appear below *Mao II* by Don DeLillo. Scroll the Audiobooks menu until the episode title is highlighted.

4. **Press the Select button on an iPod classic or iPod nano (or older model) to play the highlighted episode, or tap the episode title on an iPhone or iPod touch.**

While an audio book episode is playing, the book and episode titles appear on the iPod display. Color-display iPods also show the book's graphic image — similar to a book cover.

To pause the playback, press the Play/Pause button when an audio book episode is playing.

Audio books are automatically set to remember the playback position when you pause an episode. This feature lets you pause an episode in iTunes while you synchronize your iPod. After synchronization, you can continue playing the episode on your iPod from where you left. This feature also works the opposite way: If you start playing an episode on your iPod and then pause, the audio book episode resumes the playback position so that you can continue playing it in iTunes from where you left.

To disable the playback feature

1. **Select the audio book episode in iTunes.**
2. **Choose File⇨Get Info.**
3. **Click the Options tab.**
4. **Deselect the Remember Playback Position option.**

   This option works with any track in your library, letting you resume playback on any song or video as well.

Playing Movies, TV Shows, and Videos

Fifth- and sixth-generation iPods, the iPod nano, the iPod touch, and the iPhone can all play videos from your iTunes library if you convert them for iPod use (see Chapter 11 for details). You can watch your favorite TV show anytime, anywhere. Check out the NCAA March Madness Basketball Championship while waiting in line for tickets to the next game. Watch Disney animations with your children while waiting for the bus. Get your dose of *The Daily Show with Jon Stewart* while taking the subway to work. Or watch one of my favorites, "Mr. Monk and the Airplane" from the *Monk* TV series, on your next flight.

Video is incredibly portable on an iPod classic, iPod nano, iPod touch, or iPhone. People are amazed by the crisp, clear picture quality. And because videos have their own menu, you can easily distinguish between music videos, TV shows, movies, and video podcasts.

To play a video, follow these steps:

1. **Choose Videos from the iPod main menu, or iPod from the iPhone menu.**
2. **Choose Movies, TV Shows, Music Videos, or Video Playlists from the Videos menu on an iPod classic or iPod nano (or fifth-generation models), or scroll the list of videos that appears on an iPod touch or iPhone.**

   The Videos menu on an iPod classic, iPod nano, or fifth-generation iPod offers these genres:

   - *Movies:* The Movies menu lists any videos categorized as Videos.
   - *TV Shows:* The TV Shows menu lists any videos categorized as TV Shows, sorted alphabetically by show title. Scroll to highlight a show title and then press the Select button to see a list of the TV show episodes.
   - *Music Videos:* The Music Videos menu lists any videos categorized as Music Videos, sorted alphabetically by artist. Scroll to highlight a music video artist and then press the Select button to see a list of music videos by that artist.
   - *Video Playlists:* The Video Playlists menu lists any video playlists that you created in iTunes and that you enabled for synchronization with your iPod.

   Scroll the menu until the genre of video you want is highlighted and then press the Select button. A menu or content list appears for each selection.

   On an iPod touch or iPhone, the video titles are listed in alphabetical order divided into the following genres:

   - *Movies:* Any videos categorized as Videos.
   - *TV Shows:* Any videos categorized as TV Shows, sorted alphabetically by show title. Scroll the list and then touch a TV show title to see a list of the TV show episodes.
   - *Music Videos:* Any videos categorized as Music Videos, sorted alphabetically by artist. Scroll the list of music video artists and then touch an artist name to see a list of music videos by that artist.
   - *Podcasts:* Any videos categorized as Podcast, sorted alphabetically by podcast name. Scroll the list of podcasts and then touch a podcast title to see a list of the podcast episodes.

   If you need to change the genre of an item, see Chapter 9.

3. **Press the Select button on an iPod classic or iPod nano (or fifth-generation iPod) to play the highlighted playlist item, movie, music video, or TV episode. On an iPod touch or iPhone, touch the title of the item.**

   The video playback controls work the same way as with songs.

4. **Press the Play/Pause button when a video is playing to pause the playback.**

   Videos are automatically set to remember the playback position when you pause. This feature lets you pause a video or TV episode in iTunes while you synchronize your iPod. After synchronization, you can continue playing the video or episode on your iPod from where you left. This feature also works the opposite way: If you start playing a video on your iPod and then pause, the video resumes the playback position so that you can continue playing it in iTunes from where you left.

To disable the playback feature, do the following:

1. **Select the video in iTunes.**
2. **Choose File⇨Get Info.**
3. **Click the Options tab.**
4. **Deselect the Remember Playback Position option.**

   This option works with any track in your library, letting you resume playback on any song as well.

Playing Games on Your iPod

The sixth-generation iPod models and the iPod nano are supplied with three new games: iQuiz, Klondike, and Vortex. These games, and the games that you can purchase from the iTunes Store (my faves: Pac-Man, Mini Golf, and Sudoku), are as sophisticated as those found on handheld, color-display game machines.

Of the four games supplied with older iPods, three of them — Brick, Parachute, and Solitaire — are a bit dorky for the information age, but hey, they're extras. On the other hand, the fourth, Music Quiz, is a cool way to test your knowledge of your music library.

To find the games, choose Extras⇨Games. (On older iPods, choose Extras⇨Game.) And of course you can listen to music while you play.

iQuiz

Choose iQuiz from the Games menu (sixth-generation iPods). The point of this game is obviously to choose the correct answer before time runs out. Too many wrong answers and that's it — game over! The game displays a timer, the number you've answered wrong, and your score, as well as the number of remaining questions.

iQuiz is supplied with four question packs, three with preset questions: TV Show Trivia, Music Trivia, Movie Trivia. The fourth, Music Quiz 2, uses the music on your iPod to create custom-tailored multiple-choice and true-false queries. You might hear a snippet from a song and have to answer with the album it came from, or what year it was released. Or you might need to figure out if a certain tune came out in a specific year. The quiz may even incorporate your album art.

Vortex

Choose Vortex from the Games menu (sixth-generation iPods). Inspired by the original version of Breakout (from Atari), Vortex lets you bash bricks in three dimensions, using the click wheel to play in 360 degrees. You move your bat around the edge of the Vortex to block the ball as it smashes bricks that rotate inside. Clearing the Vortex of bricks enables you to enter the Vortex and advance to higher levels. As you rotate the click wheel, the bat moves in the direction of your rotation, and you fire your weapon by pressing the Select button or double-tapping the click wheel.

Klondike (solitaire)

Rather than playing the card game (*'til one, with a deck of 51,* with the Statler Brothers), try Klondike, the iPod version of solitaire. Choose Klondike from the Games menu (or Solitaire from the Game menu on older iPods) and press the Select button to start the game. To move cards, scroll the hand pointer over a card and then press the Select button to select the card. Then scroll the hand pointer to the new location for the card and press Select to place it at that position. To deal another round of three cards, scroll the hand pointer over the card deck in the top-left corner of the display and press the Select button. After going through an entire deck, the game places the remaining cards into a new deck so that you can continue dealing cards. The game improves considerably in a smoke-filled room with take-out pizza nearby; gangsters are optional.

Brick and Parachute (older iPods)

Brick is like the original version of Breakout (from Atari). Choose Brick from the Games menu on fifth- and fourth-generation iPods (Game menu on older iPods) and press the Select button to start the game. Move the paddle from side to side, along the bottom of the display, with the scroll wheel. You get a point for each brick you knock out. If you *break out* — knock out all the bricks — you move up a level in the game.

Parachute is a crude shoot-'em-up game where you play anti-aircraft gunner. Choose Parachute from the Games menu on fifth- and fourth-generation iPods (Game menu on older iPods) and press the Select button to start the game. With the scroll wheel, you pivot the gun at the bottom. Then press the Select button to fire at helicopters and paratroopers. Don't let the paratroopers reach the ground, or they'll heave grenades at you. War is hell, ya know.

Music Quiz (older iPods)

Music Quiz (probably the greatest time-waster iPod game of them all) tests your knowledge of your music library by playing the first few seconds of a song picked at random from your iPod. Choose Music Quiz from the Games menu on fifth- and fourth-generation iPods (Game menu on older iPods), put on your headphones or connect your iPod to speakers, and press the Select button to start the game. While the song plays, you have ten seconds to pick the song title from a list of five titles. If you choose the wrong title, the game displays `Incorrect!` and moves on to the next song. If you choose the right title, you gain points and move on to the next one. ("Life's a Long Song" by Jethro Tull would be appropriate.)

Games from the iTunes Store

Games that you purchase from the iTunes Store also show up in the Games menu on sixth- and fifth-generation iPods and the iPod nano. For example, Pac-Man for the iPod (from Namco Networks America) is an excellent version of the best-selling, coin-operated game in history. Pac-Man suits the iPod well because you use the scroll wheel to navigate.

Many popular games are available in iPod format at the iTunes Store; see Chapter 4 for details.

Viewing Photos

You might remember the old days when you carried fading, wallet-sized photo prints that sported creases, rips, and tears the more you showed them around. You can now dispense with carrying prints because all you need is your color-display iPod, which can hold up to 25,000 photos. That's a lot!

Assuming that you've already organized your photos into albums (Chapter 11) and synchronized your iPod with photos (Chapter 12), you can see the photos on your iPod by following these steps:

1. **On the iPod or iPhone, choose Photos from the main menu.**

   The iPod classic and iPod nano displays the Photos menu with All Photos and Settings choices at the top, followed by a list of photo albums in alphabetical order. The iPhone displays the Camera Roll choice at the top, followed by Photo Library and a list of photo albums. The iPod touch displays Photo Library and a list of photo albums. Older iPod models with color displays show a Photos menu with Photo Library and Slideshow Settings choices at the top, followed by a list of photo albums.

2. **On an iPod classic or iPod nano, choose All Photos or an album name; on an iPod touch or iPhone (or older iPod models), choose either Photo Library or the album name.**

   The All Photos or Photo Library choice displays thumbnail images of all the photos in your iPod or iPhone. Selecting an album displays thumbnail images of only the photos assigned to that album.

3. **Use the scroll wheel on an iPod classic or iPod nano (or older iPod) to highlight the photo thumbnail you want and then press the Select button to select the photo; on an iPhone or iPod touch, flick your finger to scroll the thumbnails, and tap a thumbnail to select the photo.**

   You might have several screens of thumbnails. Use the scroll wheel on an iPod classic or iPod nano (or older models) to scroll through the thumbnails or use Next/Fast-Forward and Previous/Rewind to skip to the next or previous screen. Flick your finger to scroll the thumbnails on an iPod touch or iPhone. When you select a photo thumbnail, your iPod displays it.

Setting up a slide show

Slide shows are a far more entertaining way of showing photos because you can include music as well as transitions between photos. You can display your slide show on the iPod or on a television. (See Chapter 16 for details on connecting your iPod to televisions, stereos, video monitors, and video equipment.) Your slide show settings work with any photo album (or with the entire photo library) on your iPod.

To set up a slide show with an iPod classic or iPod nano (or fifth-generation iPod with color display), follow these steps:

1. **Choose Photos from the main menu and then choose Settings from the Photos menu (on fifth-generation iPods, choose Slideshow Settings).**
2. **Choose Time per Slide from the Settings menu (as shown in Figure 15-5) to set the duration of each slide.**

   You can select ranges from 2 to 20 seconds. Or, you can select Manual to set the slide show to advance to the next slide when you click the Next/Fast-Forward button.

Figure 15-5: The Slideshow Settings menu.

3. **Pick your music: Choose Music from the Settings menu and then choose a playlist.**

   You can choose any playlist in your iPod for your slide show, including On-The-Go or Now Playing. iPhoto lets you assign an iTunes playlist to an iPhoto album, and that assignment is saved in your iPod. If you copy the playlist to your iPod, it's automatically assigned to the slide show.
4. **Select a transition to use between photos in the slide show; choose Transitions from the Settings menu.**

   Wipe Across is my favorite, but you can select Cross Fade, Fade To Black, Zoom Out, or Wipe Center. Choose Random if you want to use a different (and random) transition for each photo change. Choose Off for no transition. After choosing a transition, the Settings menu appears again.
5. **Set the iPod to display the slide show by choosing TV Out from the Settings menu.**

   You have three choices for TV Out:

- *On* displays the slide show on a television. (See Chapter 16 for details on the video-out connection.) While the slide show plays on your TV, you can also see the slides as large thumbnails on your iPod, along with the photo number within the album or library, and the Next and Previous icons.
- *Ask* displays a screen requesting that you select TV Off or TV On; you make the choice each time you play a slide show.
- *Off* displays the slide show with full-size images on the iPod.

6. **(Optional) Select other preferences from the Settings menu:**
   - *Repeat:* Repeats the slide show.
   - *Shuffle Photos:* Shuffles photos in the slide show in a random order.
   - *TV Signal:* Changes your television signal to PAL (Phase Alternating Line) for European and other countries that use PAL as their video standard. NTSC (National TV Standards Committee, also referred to humorously as "never the same color") is the U.S. standard.

To set up a slide show with an iPod touch or iPhone, follow these steps:

1. **Choose Settings from the main menu, and then tap Photos at the bottom of the Settings menu.**

   The settings for photos menu appears on your iPod touch or iPhone.
2. **Touch the Play Each Slide For option to set the duration of each slide.**

   You can select ranges from 2 to 20 seconds.
3. **Touch the Transition option to pick a transition to use between photos in the slide show.**

   Wipe Across is my favorite, but you can select Cube, Dissolve, Ripple, or Wipe Down. Touch the Photos button to return to the photo settings menu.
4. **Select other preferences as appropriate for your slide show:**
   - *Repeat:* Repeats the slide show.
   - *Shuffle:* Shuffles photos in the slide show in a random order.
5. **Touch the Settings button to return to the Settings menu, or press the menu button to return to the main menu.**

Playing a slide show

If you want to display the slide show on a television, connect your iPod classic, iPod nano, or fifth-generation color display iPod to the television first, before starting the show. See Chapter 16 for details on connecting your iPod to a television.

To play a slide show, follow these steps:

1. **On your iPod, choose Photos from the main menu.**
2. **Choose an album in the Photos menu, or choose All Photos (or Photo Library on the iPod touch, iPhone, or older iPods).**

   Choosing All Photos or Photo Library includes the entire library in the slide show; choosing an album includes only the photos in that album.
3. **To start the show, press the Play/Pause button on an iPod classic or iPod nano (or older iPod), or touch the Play/Pause button at the bottom of the thumbnail display on an iPod touch or iPhone.**

   You can also start a slide show when viewing a single photo by pressing the Select button on an iPod classic or iPod nano, or touching the Play/Pause button on an iPod touch or iPhone.
4. **If you previously set TV Out to Ask (as described in "Setting up a slide show" in this section), choose TV On or TV Off for your slide show.**
   - *TV On* displays the slide show on a television (through the video-out connection). You can also see the slides as large thumbnails on the iPod.

     TV Off displays the slide show with full-size images on the iPod.
5. **Use the iPod buttons to navigate your slide show.**

   If you set Time per Slide to Manual, press (or touch) Next/Fast-Forward to move to the next photo and press (or touch) Previous/Rewind to return to the previous photo.

   If you set Time per Slide to a duration, use Play/Pause to pause and play the slide show.
6. **Press the Menu button to stop the slide show.**

   On an iPod classic or iPod nano (or older iPod), pressing the Menu button returns to the Photos menu. On an iPod touch or iPhone, you return to the main menu. You can also stop a slideshown on an iPod touch or iPhone by touching outside the photo image.

Creating an On-The-Go Playlist

If you don't want to hear the iTunes playlists already in your iPod (or if you haven't created playlists yet), you can create temporary — *On-The-Go* — playlists. (***Note:*** This particular playlist feature isn't available in first- and second-generation iPods.) You can create one or more lists of songs, entire albums, podcast episodes, audio books, and videos to play in a certain order, queuing the items right on the iPod. This option is particularly useful for picking songs to play right before driving a car. (Hel-*lo!* You shouldn't be messing with your iPod while driving.)

Queued items that you select appear automatically in a playlist, appropriately called *On-The-Go,* on the Playlists menu. (To navigate the Playlists menu, see the earlier section, "By playlist.") This temporary playlist remains defined in your iPod until you delete it or save it as a new iPod playlist. If you synchronize your iPod with new music and playlists, the On-The-Go playlist is copied to your iTunes library and cleared automatically. You can also save any new playlist you create on your iPod in your iTunes library.

Selecting and playing items in an On-The-Go playlist

To select and then play items in your On-The-Go playlist, follow these steps for an iPod classic, iPod nano, or older iPod:

1. **Locate and highlight a song, album title, audio book, podcast episode, or video.**
2. **Press and hold the Select button until the title flashes.**
3. **Repeat Steps 1 and 2, adding items in the order you want them played.**

   You can continue to add items to the list of queued items in the On-The-Go playlist at any time. Your iPod keeps track of the On-The-Go playlist until you clear it, save it, or synchronize your iPod automatically.
4. **To play the On-The-Go playlist, scroll the Music menu until Playlists is highlighted and then press the Select button.**
5. **On the Playlists menu that appears, scroll to highlight On-The-Go, which you can always find at the very end of the list in the Playlists menu, and press the Select button.**

   A list of songs in the On-The-Go playlist appears.
6. **Select a song from the list and press the Select button.**

   The songs in the playlist are in *playlist order* (the order you added them). Scroll up or down the list to highlight the song you want, and press the Select button to play the playlist starting from that song.

To select and then play items in your On-The-Go playlist, follow these steps for an iPod touch or iPhone:

1. **Choose Music from the iPod touch menu or iPod from the iPhone menu.**

   The music list appears with the Playlists and other touch buttons along the bottom of the display.

2. **Tap the Playlists button and choose On-The-Go from the Playlists list.**

   The Songs list appears with a plus (+) sign next to each song, and the option Add All Songs at the top.

3. **Tap the plus (+) sign next to a song you want to add to the On-The-Go playlist.**

   As you tap the plus (+) sign for each song, the song is included in the On-The-Go playlist, and turns gray in the list so that you know it has already been selected. You can choose Add All Songs as an alternative if you want to add all the songs in the library.

4. **Repeat Step 3, adding songs in the order you want them played.**

   You can continue to add songs to the list. Your iPod touch or iPhone keeps track of the On-The-Go playlist until you clear it or synchronize your iPod automatically.

5. **Tap the Done button when finished adding songs.**

   The Done button appears in the upper right corner while you select songs, just waiting for you to finish. After touching Done, you return to the list of songs in the On-The-Go playlist.

6. **To play the On-The-Go playlist, touch any song to start.**

   The songs in the playlist are in *playlist order* (the order you added them). Scroll up or down the list to choose a song, and touch the song title to play the playlist starting from that song. You can choose Shuffle to shuffle the songs in the playlist.

You can also add entire playlists, entire albums, or everything by an artist to the On-The-Go playlist on an iPod touch or iPhone. In Step 2 above, touch the Edit button in the upper right corner of the display, then touch the Playlists, Artists, or Songs button to select from those menus. Then repeat Step 3 for each item in each menu.

Deleting items from an On-The-Go playlist

To delete an item from an On-The-Go playlist in your iPod classic or iPod nano, follow these steps:

1. **Select the On-The-Go playlist.**

   If you don't see the iPod main menu, repeatedly press the Menu button to return to the main menu. Choose Music from the main menu, scroll the Music menu until Playlists is highlighted, and then press the Select button. The Playlists menu appears. Scroll to the On-The-Go item, which you can always find at the very end of the list in the Playlists menu. Press the Select button, and the list of items in the playlist appears.

2. **Locate and highlight the item you want to delete.**
3. **Press and hold the Select button until the title flashes.**
4. **Repeat Steps 2 and 3 for each item you want to delete from the playlist.**

   When you delete items, they disappear from the On-The-Go playlist one by one. The items are still in your iPod; only the playlist is cleared.

To delete an item from an On-The-Go playlist in your iPod touch or iPhone, follow these steps:

1. **Select the On-The-Go playlist.**

   If you don't see the main menu, press the menu button on the iPod touch or iPhone to return to the main menu. Choose Music from the main menu, and then touch Playlists. The Playlists menu appears with On-The-Go at the top. Touch the On-The-Go playlist name and the list of items in the playlist appears.
2. **Touch the Edit button in the upper right corner of the display.**

   Minus (-) signs appear in front of each song title.
3. **Scroll the list to find the item you want to delete.**
4. **Touch the minus (-) sign next to the song to delete, then touch the Delete button.**

   The red Delete touch button appears after you touch the minus (-) sign.
5. **Repeat Steps 3 and 4 to find and delete each item from the playlist.**

   When you delete items, they disappear from the On-The-Go playlist one by one. The items are still in your iPod; only the playlist is cleared.

Clearing an On-The-Go playlist

To clear the list of queued items in an On-The-Go playlist, follow these steps:

1. **Select the On-The-Go playlist.**

   See "Deleting items from an On-The-Go playlist" in this section for instructions on how to select it.
2. **On an iPod classic or iPod nano (or older iPod), select the Clear Playlist item at the end of the list. On an iPod touch or iPhone, tap the Edit button in the upper right corner, and then tap Clear Playlist.**

   The Clear menu appears, showing the Clear Playlist and Cancel options.

3. **Select the Clear Playlist option.**

   All the items disappear from the On-The-Go playlist. The items are still in your iPod; only the playlist is cleared. If you don't want to clear the playlist, select the Cancel option.

Saving an On-The-Go playlist in your iPod classic or nano

You might want to create more than one On-The-Go playlist in your iPod classic or iPod nano (or older iPod), and temporarily save them for transferring to your iTunes library. To temporarily save your On-The-Go playlist, follow these steps:

1. **Select the On-The-Go playlist.**

   Choose Music from the main menu, scroll the Music menu until Playlists is highlighted, and then press the Select button. The Playlists menu appears. Scroll to the On-The-Go item. Press the Select button, and the list of items in the playlist appears.

2. **Scroll to the very end of the list and select the Save Playlist item.**

   The Save menu appears, showing the Cancel and Save Playlist items.

3. **Choose Save Playlist.**

   The On-The-Go playlist is saved with the name *New Playlist 1* (and any subsequent playlists you save are named *New Playlist 2,* and so on). These appear at the very end of the Playlist menu, not in alphabetical order — just above the On-The-Go Playlist item. If you don't want to save the playlist, select the Cancel item.

On-The-Go playlists saved as *New Playlist 1, New Playlist 2,* and so on, are stored temporarily in your iPod until you automatically synchronize the iPod with your iTunes library. The On-The-Go playlist is cleared each time you save it as a new playlist, so you can start creating another On-The-Go playlist.

Transferring an On-The-Go playlist to iTunes

Although most transfer operations are one way from iTunes to your iPod, you can transfer the On-The-Go playlists to your iTunes library — just not the content itself (which must already be in your iTunes library).

When you automatically synchronize your iPod (as we describe in Chapter 12), the current and saved On-The-Go playlists (called *New Playlist 1, New Playlist 2,* and so on) are copied to your iTunes library, saved as regular playlists, and cleared from the iPod. The automatic synchronization also places the newly created playlists on your iPod. ***Hint:*** They'll be in alphabetical order on the Playlist menu, named *On-The-Go 1, On-The-Go 2,* and so on.

To change an On-The-Go playlist name, rename it in your iTunes library. The next time you automatically synchronize your iPod, the playlist names in your iPod change to match your iTunes library.

When managing music and videos on your iPod manually, you can drag the On-The-Go playlist and any saved playlists from your iPod library directly to the iTunes library.

Playing an iPod shuffle

The *iPod shuffle* is a special iPod with no display or any controls to select specific songs or albums. The idea behind an iPod shuffle is to load it with songs in the order you want them to play (like a long playlist) and then play the songs in that order or in shuffle (random) order.

Apple has introduced two iPod shuffle models but has discontinued the first model. The current model, shown in its dock in Figure 15-6, offers two switches on its side for controlling power and playback mode as well as the familiar Play/Pause, Previous/Rewind, Next/Fast-Forward, and volume control buttons. The older iPod shuffle offers one three-position switch on the back for playing songs in order, for shuffling songs, and for turning off the unit. On the older iPod shuffle, the Play in Order position is in the middle of the switch, and the Shuffle position is at the bottom.

To play songs in the order they were copied, set the position switch to the Play in Order position, which is marked by an icon with arrows in a closed loop. To play songs in random order, set the position switch (see Figure 15-5) to the Shuffle position — marked by the crossing arrows icon.

To play songs on a shuffle, press the Play/Pause button. To stop (or pause) playback, press the Play/Pause button again. When you stop playback, the iPod shuffle status light blinks green for a minute.

To navigate through the songs in your iPod shuffle, press the Previous/Rewind button (skip backward) or the Next/Fast-Forward button (skip forward). Press and hold these buttons to skip more than one song forward or backward (as if you were fast-forwarding or rewinding a tape). You can start a song over by pressing Previous/Rewind while the song is playing.

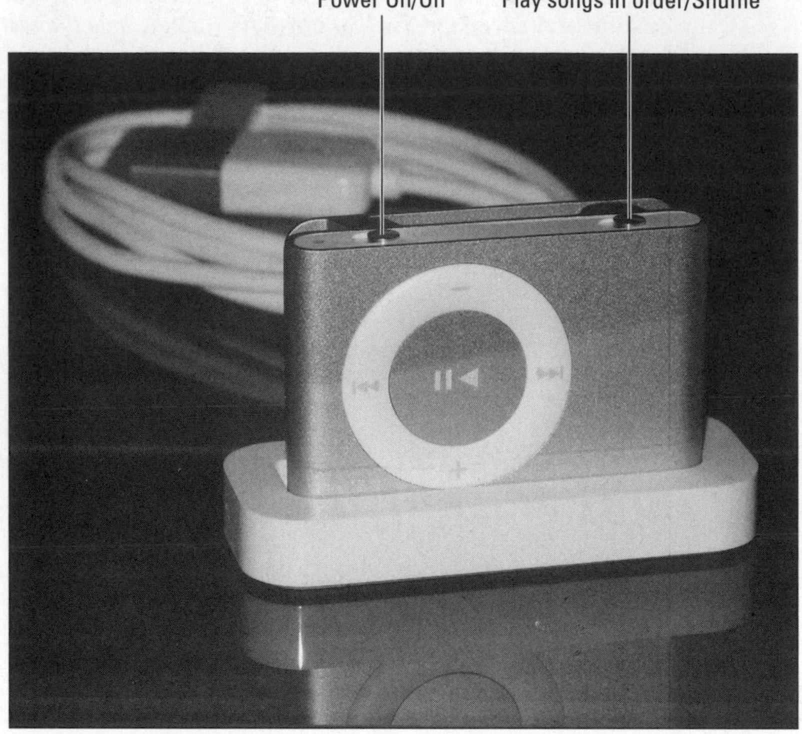

Figure 15-6: The iPod shuffle offers two switches on its side: power on/off, and play songs in order/ shuffle.

If you set the position switch to Play in Order, the Previous/Rewind button skips backward and the Next/Fast-Forward button skips forward in the order the songs were copied to the iPod shuffle. However, if you set the position switch to Shuffle, the playing order is randomized first. Then the Previous/ Rewind button skips backward within the shuffle order, and the Next/Fast-Forward button skips forward within the shuffle order. For example, suppose your iPod shuffle plays the 14th song, then the 5th song, and then the 20th song. In that case, pressing the Previous/Rewind button during the 20th song takes you back to the 5th song, and pressing it again takes you back to the 14th song. From there, pressing the Next/Fast-Forward button skips through the songs in the same order again: the 14th song, the 5th song, and then the 20th song.

To go immediately to the beginning of an iPod shuffle playlist, press the Play/Pause button three times quickly (within a second).

Adjusting and Limiting the Volume

Because an iPod or iPhone can be quite loud when set to its highest volume, we recommend turning down the volume before using headphones. You can read at the end of this section how to control the volume for an iPod shuffle, but here's how to set the volume for an iPod or iPhone.

To adjust volume for an iPod classic or iPod nano (or older iPod), follow these steps:

1. **Play something on the iPod.**
2. **While the content is playing, change the volume with the scroll wheel.**

   A volume bar appears in the iPod display to guide you. Scroll with your thumb or finger clockwise to increase the volume, and counterclockwise to decrease the volume.

To adjust volume for an iPod touch or iPhone, follow these steps:

1. **Play something on the iPod touch or iPhone.**
2. **While the content is playing, touch the lower portion of the display and slide your finger on the volume slider.**

   After touching the lower portion of the display while playing something, the volume slider with a silver knob appears in the iPod touch or iPhone at the bottom of the display underneath the playback controls (refer to Figure 15-4). Slide the knob with your finger to the right to increase the volume, or to the left to decrease the volume.

You can also limit the highest volume for your iPod or iPhone to be lower than the actual maximum. This can help protect your hearing while listening to content from sources with different volume levels.

To limit the volume to be lower than the actual maximum volume on an iPod classic or iPod nano, follow these steps:

1. **Choose Settings from the main menu.**
2. **Choose Volume Limit from the Settings menu.**
3. **Scroll the volume bar with the click wheel to limit the volume.**

   A volume bar appears in the iPod display to guide you. Scroll clockwise to increase the volume or counterclockwise to decrease the volume. While you scroll, a triangle below the volume bar indicates the new limit.
4. **Press the Select button to set the limit, or press Play/Pause to optionally lock the volume limit.**

Press the Select button to accept the new limit without locking it, and skip the next step; or press the Play/Pause button to lock the volume limit.

5. **(Optional) Set the combination lock for locking the volume limit.**

   If you pressed the Play/Pause button to lock the volume limit, your iPod displays the combination lock.

   For more details about setting your iPod combination lock, see Chapter 21.

   The combination lock is useful for locking the volume limit so others can't change it (such as your children). However, it also means that you have to enter the combination to unlock the iPod in order to change the volume limit.

To limit the volume to be lower than the actual maximum volume on an iPod touch or iPhone, follow these steps:

1. **Choose Settings from the main menu.**
2. **Choose iPod from the Settings menu.**
3. **Choose Volume Limit from the iPod menu.**

   A volume slider appears with a silver knob.

4. **Slide your finger on the volume slider to limit the volume.**

   Slide the knob with your finger to the right to increase the volume, or to the left to decrease the volume. While you slide your finger, a triangle below the slider indicates the new limit.

5. **Touch the iPod button to set the limit and return to the iPod menu, or touch the Lock Volume Limit button to optionally lock the volume limit.**

   Touch the iPod button in the upper left corner to accept the new limit without locking it, and skip the next step; or touch the Lock Volume Limit button to lock the volume limit.

6. **(Optional) Set the Volume Limit Code for locking the volume limit.**

   If you touched the Lock Volume Limit button to lock the volume limit, your iPod touch or iPhone displays four squares for entering a code number. Touch the calculator-style number pad to type numbers for your code, and be sure to make up a code that you will remember! (If you don't want to enter a code, touch the Cancel button in the upper left corner.)

   The lock is useful for locking the volume limit so others can't change it (such as your children). However, it also means that you have to enter the volume limit code to unlock the iPod touch or iPhone in order to change the volume limit.

To adjust the volume of an iPod shuffle, press the Volume Up (+) or Volume Down (–) buttons.

Chapter 16

Getting Wired for Playback

In This Chapter

- Finding your iPod's connections
- Connecting your iPod to home stereos
- Connecting to televisions and video equipment
- Playing your iPod through iTunes on any computer
- Using home accessories

The sound quality coming from your iPod is excellent, so why not use it with your home stereo system? Better yet, why not build an excellent home stereo around your iPod — one that truly provides advantages for iPod owners? That's what part of this chapter is about: connecting your iPod to an audio system for your home, office, patio, den, bathroom, or wherever. The other part shows you how to connect a color-display iPod to a television, video monitor, or other video equipment (such as a video projector) to maximize the quality of the picture. It describes the physical connections needed for your iPod to show videos and photo slide shows as if they were playing on a DVD player (only they're actually playing from the palm of your hand).

You can also play your iTunes content wirelessly, using either AirTunes or an Apple AirPort Express wireless network hub connected to a stereo, as described in Chapter 6. Additionally, you can connect your iTunes library wirelessly (or over an Ethernet network) to Apple TV, which connects to your high-definition or regular television and stereo system, as described in Chapter 7.

Making Connections

All iPod models enable you to connect your iPod to headphones or to your home stereo with standard audio cables, as well as to your computer via either FireWire or USB cables. Here's a quick summary:

- **USB/FireWire dock connector:** Sixth-, fifth-, fourth-, and third-generation models, including iPod mini and iPod nano, have a dock connection. You can use the connection to insert your iPod into a dock, or use the iPod with a dock connector cable, as shown in Figure 16-1. The dock connector cable has a dock connector on one end (the same type of connection used in docks) and a FireWire or USB connector (or both FireWire and USB connectors with a split cable) on the other.
- **Headphone/line-out:** You can connect headphones or a 3.5mm stereo mini-plug cable to the headphone/line-out connection. On a color-display iPod, the headphone/line-out connection also serves as an AV (audio-video) connection for displaying slide shows and photos.
- **Docks:** Docks from third parties come in many sizes and shapes. Apple provides a special dock in the box with iPhones and iPod shuffles; for other iPods you can use Apple's optional Universal Dock (available in the optional iPod AV Connection Kit, which you can find in Apple stores and in the online Apple Store) with these connections:
    - A *dock connector* for a FireWire or USB cable connection
    - A *headphone/line-out connection* for a stereo mini-plug cable or AV cable (or headphones)

Figure 16-1: A fifth-generation video iPod with a dock connector cable attached.

Older iPod models offer the following connections:

- **Headphone/line-out and control socket (third- and fourth-generation iPods):** You can connect headphones or a 3.5mm stereo mini-plug cable to the headphone/line-out connection. The combination headphone and control socket connection on top of third- and fourth-generation iPods allows you to plug in accessories, such as remote control devices and voice recorders. The headphone/line-out connection on second-generation models includes an outer ring for connecting the Apple Remote supplied with those models.
- **FireWire (six pin):** First- and second-generation iPods have a six-pin, FireWire-only connection on the top that works with any standard six-pin FireWire cable.
- **Dock:** For fourth- and third-generation iPod models, the dock supplied with the iPod offers two connections: a FireWire connection for the dock connector cable, and also a headphone/line-out connection for a stereo mini-plug cable (or headphones).

You can connect the FireWire or USB end of the dock connector cable to the computer for synchronizing with iTunes, as we describe in Chapter 12, and playing the iPod through iTunes, as we describe in this chapter. You can also connect to the power adapter to charge the iPod battery. The FireWire or USB connection to the computer provides power to the iPod (as long as the computer's USB hardware supplies power, and the computer is powered on and not in sleep mode — for information on powering your iPod, see Chapter 1).

Connecting to a Home Stereo

Home stereo systems come in many shapes and sizes, from an audiophile's monster component racks to a kid's itty-bitty boombox. We're not talking about alarm clock radios. We're talking about stereos with speakers that allow you to add another input device, such as a portable CD player.

Component-style stereo systems typically include a *receiver* that contains a preamp/amplifier (with a volume control) and an FM radio tuner. Some systems separate these functions into separate components, such as a preamp, an amplifier, and a tuner. To connect your iPod or computer to a home stereo, look for RCA-type connections that are marked AUX IN (for auxiliary input), CD IN (for connecting a CD player), or TAPE IN (for tape deck input). All-in-one stereos and boomboxes typically don't have connections for audio input although you can find exceptions. Look at the back and sides of the unit for any RCA-type connections.

You can connect a CD or tape player to most stereos with RCA-type cables — one (typically red or black) for the right channel, and one (typically white if the other is black, or white or black if the other is red) for the left channel. All you need is a cable with a stereo mini-plug on one end and RCA-type connectors on the other, as shown in Figure 16-2. Stereo mini-plugs have two black bands on the plug, but a mono mini-plug has only one black band.

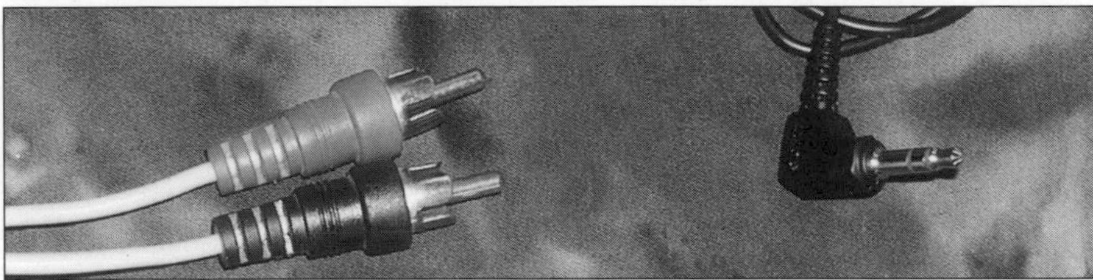

Figure 16-2: RCA-type connectors (left) and a stereo mini-plug (right).

Follow these steps to connect your iPod to your stereo:

1. **Connect the stereo mini-plug to either the headphone/line-out connection on a dock or the headphone/line-out connection on the iPod, depending on whether you want to control the volume from your iPod.**

   With the dock connection, you have no control over volume on the iPod. Instead, you use your stereo system or speakers to control the volume.

2. **Connect the left and right connectors to the stereo system's audio input.**

   Use whatever connections are available, such as AUX IN, TAPE IN, or CD IN.

   Don't use the PHONO IN (phonograph input) connection. On most stereos, these connections are for phonographs (turntables) and aren't properly matched for other kinds of input devices. If you use the PHONO IN connection, you might get a loud buzzing sound that could damage your speakers.

If you use your iPod's headphone/line-out connection, you can control the volume from the iPod via the scroll wheel; see Chapter 15. This controls the volume of the signal from the iPod. Stereo systems typically have their own control to raise or lower the volume of the amplified speakers. For optimal sound quality when using a home stereo, set the iPod volume at less than half the maximum output and adjust your listening volume by using your stereo controls.

Connecting to a TV or Video Input

You can connect your fifth-generation iPod to any television, video projector, or video recorder or player that offers standard RCA video and audio connections, or an S-video connection.

Apple offers the optional iPod AV Cable, which is a special cable that you can plug in to the headphone/line-out connection of the iPod. The cable offers RCA video (yellow) and stereo audio (red and white) connectors as well as an S-video connector, as shown in Figure 16-3, to plug in to your television or video equipment.

While Apple warns that you must use the AV Cable supplied with your iPod (implying others don't work), Belkin (`www.belkin.com`) offers its AV Cable for 4G/5G iPod (Color LCD) for $20, which works fine.

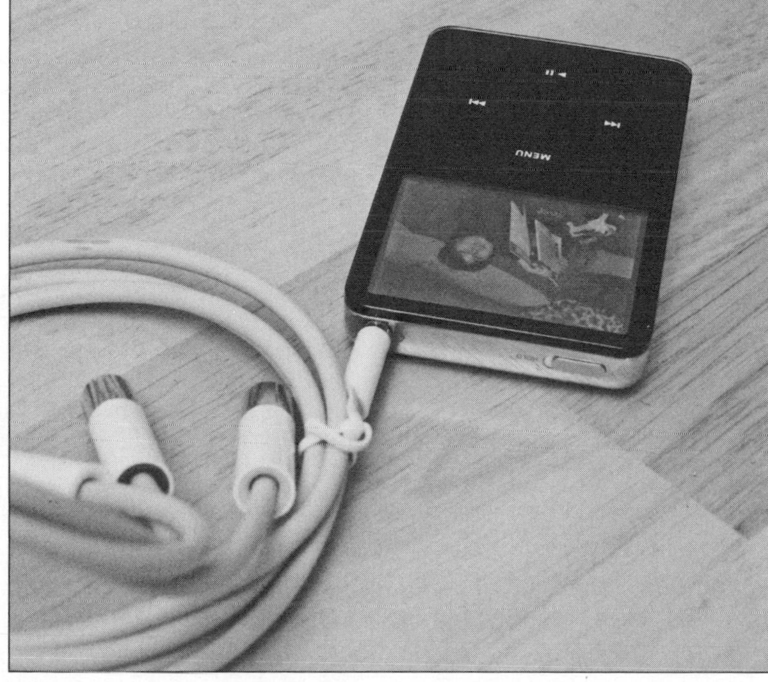

Figure 16-3: The iPod AV Cable provides a yellow video RCA-type connector as well as red and white audio RCA-type connectors.

For even better picture quality, use a television or video monitor that supports component (Y, Pb, and Pr) video, and use your sixth-generation iPod or iPod nano with the Apple Component AV Cable. The Component AV Cable connects to your iPod or Universal Dock via the 30-pin dock connector. On the other end, connect its component cables to the component connections on your TV, home theater receiver, or stereo receiver, and the audio cables to the stereo audio connections in your receiver or speaker system.

If you don't see a picture on your television, check that your television is set to the correct input source — Video In (RCA) or S-video In (if you use an S-video cable and a fifth-generation iPod dock). You can also use other types of video equipment. For example, a video recorder that accepts RCA or S-video input can record the video, and a video projector can display it on a large screen.

Playing an iPod through iTunes

With the exception of content purchased from the iTunes Store, you can't copy the content from your iPod into your iTunes library via iTunes, but you can use iTunes on your computer to play the content directly from the iPod. You can even connect your friend's iPod to your computer and include your friend's iPod songs in your Party Shuffle. Not only can you do that, but when you play songs from different iPods or from your library, you can cross-fade them (see Chapter 6).

If your computer is connected to a home stereo, the iPod content plays through iTunes and on the stereo. You can connect your computer to a stereo wirelessly with an FM radio accessory, such as the Aurius from Engineered Audio (`www.engineeredaudio.com`, $40), which connects to your computer with a USB cable and wirelessly transmits your iTunes content (or any audio and video on your computer) to the FM radio tuner of your home stereo system.

To play the content on your iPod in iTunes, follow these steps:

1. **Connect the iPod to your computer and then press ⌘-Option (Mac) or Ctrl-Alt (Windows) to prevent automatic synchronization.**
2. **Set the iPod to manually manage music and videos.**

   To set the iPod to manage music and videos manually, see Chapter 12. (The iPod synchronizes automatically by default, but you can change that.)

3. **Select the iPod name in the iTunes Source pane in the Devices section.**

   After selecting the iPod in the iTunes Source pane, the device summary page appears in List view or Browse view.

4. **Click the triangle next to the iPod name to see its playlists and contents; then select Music (underneath the iPod name).**

   The list of songs on the iPod appears in the List pane. You can scroll or browse the iPod's library just like you can in the main iTunes library.

5. **(Optional) View the iPod playlists.**

   Scroll the iTunes window to view the iPod's playlists in the Source pane.

6. **Select an item in the iPod song list and then click the iTunes Play button.**

What if you want to connect your iPod to a computer other than your own? Or friends arrive with an iPod filled with songs that you'd like to hear, and you want to hear them on your stereo system that's already connected to your computer?

You can either connect your iPod to another computer or connect someone else's iPod to your computer. Either way, iTunes starts and recognizes that the iPod isn't matched to the iTunes library (because it's matched to another computer's iTunes library). iTunes then displays a message asking whether you want to change the link to this iTunes library and replace all existing songs and playlists; it also asks if you want to change the photos. This is important — *click No for each change request.*

Unless you want to change the contents of your iPod to reflect this computer's library, click No. If you click Yes, iTunes erases the library of your iPod and then updates your iPod with the library on that computer, including photos and videos. If you're using a public computer with no content in the iTunes library, you end up with an empty iPod. If you're using a friend's computer, your friend's library copies to your iPod, erasing whatever was on your iPod. So don't click Yes unless you really want to completely change the content on your iPod. You've been warned.

With color-display iPods, you also get a similar warning message about changing the link to the photo library and replacing all photos in the iPod. Again, click No to prevent this from happening.

If you connect a Mac-formatted iPod to a Windows computer, you get a warning message about reformatting it. *Don't do it!* Click Cancel. Otherwise, you reformat the iPod and clear all music from it. Then click the Safely Remove Hardware icon and safely eject the iPod from the computer. See Chapter 23 for details on how to make a Windows PC recognize a Mac-formatted iPod. Mac users don't have this problem — a Mac can recognize and synchronize with Windows-formatted iPods.

Accessories for the iHome

Many of the thousands of accessories for the iPod are designed for travel. However, companies also provide docks, speaker systems, and stands for iPods for when you're home again.

To see our idea of the best travel accessories, visit this book's companion Web site.

For an extremely powerful, single-cabinet, portable speaker system that offers iPod docking and exceptional sound, the stylish, high-quality iPod Hi-Fi from Apple (www.apple.com/ipodhifi) is hard to beat. Housed in a single unit with a dock for the iPod, the iPod Hi-Fi takes up very little space. It runs on D-cell batteries for boombox portability. And you can use the included wireless Apple Remote to control playback. When you plug in your fifth- or sixth-generation iPod or iPod nano, the iPod Hi-Fi adds a Speakers option to the iPod main menu. Select Speakers to see the Speakers menu, which includes a Tone Control option offering Normal, Bass Boost, and Treble Boost settings to tweak the iPod Hi-Fi sound. The Speakers menu also offers a Backlight option to set your iPod's backlighting while it's connected to the iPod Hi-Fi, and the Large Album Art option to show full-screen art associated with the content.

If you're running iPod Software 1.0 on a fifth-generation iPod or fourth-generation iPod Photo, the Speakers menu offers a Room Size option instead of Tone Control. You should update your iPod Software for these models, as we describe in Chapter 23.

What if you have multiple iPods from different generations and need to organize your docks and cables? The Belkin Tunesync (www.belkin.com) offers a unique USB cradle that not only offers a place for recharging and syncing your iPods but also adds five additional USB ports.

Need a blast of music for the barbecue out on your patio? The iBoom from Digital Lifestyle Outfitters (www.dlo.com) is a 20 watts-per-channel, four-speaker, boombox system with a dock for a full-size iPod, iPhone, or iPod mini. iBoom also includes a digital FM radio and an auxiliary input jack for connecting another music source. It draws power from an AC adapter or six D-cell batteries (not included). While connected to AC power, the iBoom can recharge your iPod's battery.

If you need a more portable solution, check out the battery-powered Portable Folding Speaker System for iPod/MP3, available from Overstock (www.overstock.com) for about $13.

For more solutions that can work in planes, trains, and automobiles — or anywhere for that matter — visit this book's companion Web site.

Perhaps the coolest home outfit for your iPod turns your living room into a juke joint for $700. The Jukebox Station from Saffire-USA (www.saffire-usa.com) houses a universal docking cradle for any iPod along with an FM radio and a CD player. It offers an 80-watt stereo amplifier and a five-speaker system (two magnetically shielded tweeters, two midrange drivers, and a six-inch subwoofer).

The Jukebox Station comes with an infrared (IR) remote to control volume and iPod functions from across the room. It has RCA-type and 3.5mm mini-plug inputs to accept other music players and sources, an RCA-type output connection for another stereo or recording device, and a 3.5mm mini-plug output for headphones. An RCA-type video output is also provided to play your iPod videos and photo slide shows on a television.

When your iPod is tethered to a dock and connected to your home stereo, you don't have to be within reach to change the track or the settings. Instead, you can control it remotely. The wireless Apple Remote (see the Apple Web site) provides the usual CD player controls: Play/Pause, Next Track, Previous Track, and Volume. It works with Apple's Universal Dock and iPod Hi-Fi. The Apple Remote is supplied with current Mac models and with Apple TV, and is also available separately at an Apple Store (including the online store).

Engineered Audio (www.engineeredaudio.com) provides a wireless remote control — the *Aerolink* — for $45. It features an operating range greater than 200 feet. Like its predecessor (the RemoteRemote 2, $40), the Aerolink works around corners and through walls because it uses radio frequency (RF) rather than IR. With these remote controllers, you can control your living room iPod from the bedroom, or deejay a party from another room.

Part IV
Using Advanced Techniques

"The sensor in my running shoe is transmitting information and encouragements to my iPod. Right now, Lance Armstrong is encouraging me to stop running like a girl."

In this part . . .

This part focuses on what you can do to improve the sound of your music.

- In Chapter 17, you discover the iTunes and iPod equalizers for fine-tuning music playback.
- Chapter 18 gives you the info you need to make the right decisions for encoding and compressing sound files to make appropriate trade-offs of space for quality.
- Chapter 19 describes how to change your encoder and importing settings to get the best results with digital audio compression.

Chapter 17

Fine-Tuning the Sound

In This Chapter

- Equalizing the sound in iTunes
- Adjusting the preamp volume and frequencies
- Using the iPod equalizer and iTunes presets
- Defining start and stop times for tracks
- Separating a long track into multiple tracks

Sound is difficult to describe. Describing how to adjust sound to your liking is harder still. Maybe you want more oomph in the lows, or perhaps you prefer highs that are as clear as a bell. Even if you've never mastered a stereo system beyond adjusting the bass, treble, and volume, you can use this limited knowledge to quickly fine-tune the sound in iTunes by using the equalizer settings, as you discover in this chapter.

Sound studio engineers try to make recordings for typical listening environments, so they have to simulate the sound experience in those environments. Studios typically have home stereo speakers as monitors so that the engineers can hear what the music sounds like on a home stereo. In the 1950s and early 1960s, when AM radio was king, engineers working on potential AM radio hits purposely mixed the sound with low-fidelity monaural speakers so that they could hear what the mix would sound like on the radio. (Thank goodness that those days are over, and that cars offer higher-quality FM radio as well as very high-quality audio systems.)

Engineers did this because the quality of the sound is no better than the speakers you play it on. When you find out how to adjust and fine-tune the sound coming from your computer running iTunes and out of your iPod, use your everyday listening environment as a guide. If you tweak the sound specifically for your computer speakers or for your home stereo and speakers, though, remember that with an iPod you have other potential listening environments — different headphones, car stereo systems, portable boomboxes, and so on.

Fortunately, iTunes gives you the flexibility of using different equalization settings for different songs, audio books, podcasts, and videos. You can also use presets on your iPod. In this chapter, you discover how to make presets for songs in your library so that iTunes remembers them. What's more, you can use the standard iTunes presets on your iPod or use other iPod settings in tandem with the iPod's equalizer. This chapter shows you how. You also learn how to modify the starting and stopping points within songs, audio books, podcast episodes, and videos, and how to split a track.

Adjusting the Sound in iTunes First

Some songs are just too loud. We don't mean too loud stylistically, as in thrash metal with screeching guitars; we mean too loud for your ears when you're wearing headphones or so loud that the music sounds distorted in your speakers. And some songs are just too soft; you have to increase the volume to hear them and then lower the volume to listen to louder songs. To remedy instances like these, you can set the volume in advance in several ways.

Setting the volume in advance

With songs, audio books, podcast episodes, and videos that you already know are too loud (or too soft), consider setting the volume for those items (or even entire albums or podcasts) in advance so that they always play with the desired volume adjustment.

To adjust the overall volume of a particular item in advance so that it always plays at that setting, perform the following steps:

1. **Click an item to select it.**

   To set the volume in iTunes for multiple songs, you can select an entire album in Browse view or you can select all the songs. To set the volume for a whole podcast, select it instead of individual episodes.

2. **Choose File⇨Get Info.**

   The information dialog appears.

3. **Click the Options tab.**

   Drag the Volume Adjustment slider left or right to adjust the volume lower or higher, as shown in Figure 17-1. You can do this while playing the file.

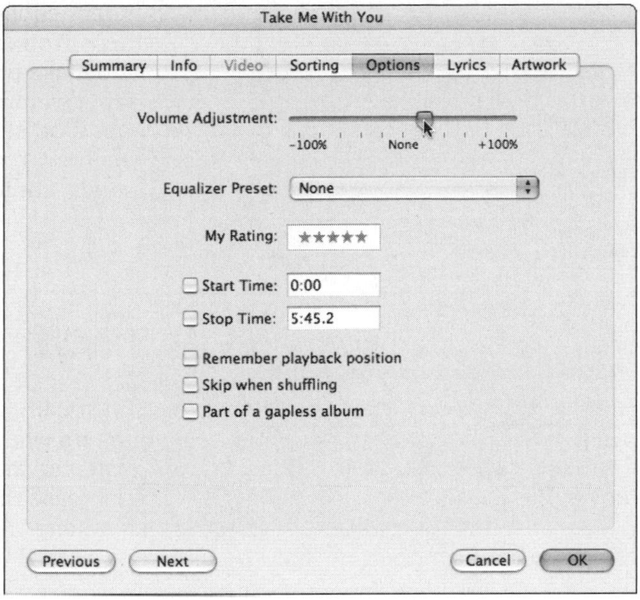

Figure 17-1: Adjust the volume setting for a song here.

Enhancing the sound

Some home or car stereos offer a sound enhancer button to improve the depth of the sound. iTunes offers a similar option — *Sound Enhancer* — that enhances high and low frequencies. Audiophiles and sound purists would most likely use the equalizer to boost frequencies, but you can use this brute-force method to enhance the sound.

To enable Sound Enhancer, follow these steps:

1. **Choose iTunes⇨Preferences (Mac) or Edit⇨Preferences (Windows).**
2. **In the iTunes Preferences dialog that appears, click the Playback tab.**

   The Playback preferences appear, as shown in Figure 17-2.
3. **Adjust the Sound Enhancer slider:**
   - *Increase the sound enhancement.* Dragging the Sound Enhancer slider to the right (toward High) is similar to pressing the loudness button on a stereo or the equivalent of boosting the treble (high) and bass (low) frequencies in the equalizer. (See the upcoming section, "Equalize It in iTunes.")
   - *Decrease the high and low frequencies.* Drag the slider to the left toward Low.

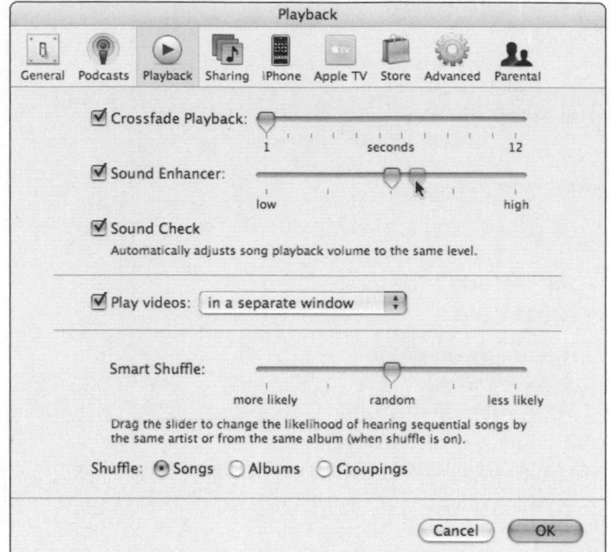

Figure 17-2: Use the Sound Enhancer.

The middle setting is neutral, adding no enhancement — the same as disabling Sound Enhancer by clearing its check box.

Sound-checking the iTunes library

Because music CDs are manufactured inconsistently, discrepancies occur in volume. Some CDs play louder than others; occasionally, even individual tracks on a CD might vary.

You can standardize the volume level of all the songs in your iTunes library with the Sound Check option. (Think of musicians, who do sound checks to check the volume of microphones and instruments and the effect on the listening environment.) The aptly named Sound Check option in iTunes allows you to do a sound check on your tunes to bring them all into line, volume-wise. This option has the added benefit of applying the same volume adjustment when you play the songs back on your iPod, as described in the upcoming section, "Sound-checking the iPod."

Sound Check scans the audio files, finds each track's peak volume level, and then uses this peak volume information to level the playing volume of tracks so that they have the same peak volume. The sound quality isn't affected, nor is the audio information changed: The volume is simply adjusted at the start of the track to be in line with other tracks.

To enable Sound Check, follow these steps:

1. **Drag the iTunes volume slider to set the overall volume for iTunes.**

   The volume slider is located in the top-left corner of the iTunes window, to the right of the Play button.

2. **Choose iTunes⇨Preferences (Mac) or Edit⇨Preferences (Windows).**
3. **In the iTunes Preferences dialog that appears, click the Playback tab.**

   The Playback preferences appear; refer to Figure 17-2.

4. **Select the Sound Check check box.**

   iTunes sets the volume level for all songs according to the level of the iTunes volume slider.

5. **Click OK.**

   The Sound Check option sets a volume adjustment based on the volume slider on all the songs so that they play at approximately the same volume.

The operation runs in the background while you do other things. If you quit iTunes and then restart it, the operation continues where it left off when you quit. You can switch Sound Check on or off at any time.

Sound-checking the iPod

You can take advantage of volume-leveling in your iTunes library with the Sound Check option and then switch Sound Check on or off on your iPod by choosing Sound Check from the iPod Settings menu.

This feature is useful especially when using your iPod in a car or when jogging while listening to headphones because you don't want to have to reach for the volume on the iPod or on the car stereo every time it starts playing a song that's too loud.

The Sound Check option on your iPod works only if you've also set the Sound Check option in your iTunes library. If you need to enable this setting in iTunes, check out the preceding section.

On your iPod, choose Settings⇨Sound Check⇨On from the main menu to enable Sound Check. To disable it, choose Settings⇨Sound Check⇨Off.

Equalize It in iTunes

To open the iTunes equalizer, choose View⇨Show Equalizer. The iTunes equalizer allows you to fine-tune sound spectrum frequencies in a more precise way than with the typical bass and treble controls you find on home stereos and powered speakers. (See the sidebar on equalizers, elsewhere in this chapter.) You can use the equalizer to improve or enhance the sound coming through a particular stereo system and speakers. With the equalizer settings, you can customize playback for different musical genres, listening environments, or speakers.

If you want to pick entirely different equalizer settings for car speakers, home speakers, and headphones, you can save your settings, as described in the upcoming section, "Saving your own presets."

Adjusting the preamp volume

The *preamp* in your stereo is the component that offers a volume control that applies to all frequencies equally.

Volume knobs generally go up to 10 — except, of course, for Spinal Tap's Marshall preamps, which go to 11.

The iTunes equalizer, as shown in Figure 17-3, offers a Preamp slider on the far-left side. You can increase or decrease the volume in 3 decibel (dB) increments up to 12 dB. *Decibels* are units of measure for the intensity (or volume) of the frequencies. You can adjust the volume while playing the music to hear the result right away.

If you want to make any adjustments to frequencies, you might need to adjust the preamp volume first if volume adjustment is needed and then move on to the specific frequencies.

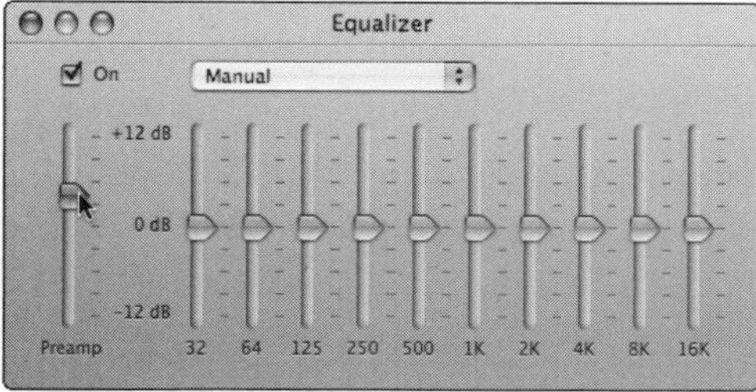

Figure 17-3: Use the Preamp slider to adjust the volume across all frequencies.

What's the frequency, Kenneth? The equalizer opportunity

The Beach Boys were right when they sang "Good Vibrations" because that's what music is — the sensation of hearing audible vibrations conveyed to the ear by a medium, such as air. Musicians measure pitch by the *frequency* of vibrations. The waves can oscillate slowly and produce low-pitched sounds, or they can oscillate rapidly and produce high-pitched sounds. *Amplitude* is a measurement of the amount of fluctuation in air pressure — therefore, amplitude is perceived as loudness.

When you increase the bass or treble on a stereo system, you're actually increasing the volume, or intensity, of certain frequencies while the music is playing. An equalizer lets you fine-tune the sound spectrum frequencies in a more precise way than with bass and treble controls. It increases or decreases specific frequencies of the sound to raise or lower highs, lows, and midrange tones. The equalizer adjusts the volume with several band-pass filters all centered at different frequencies, and each filter offers controllable *gain* (the ability to boost the volume).

On more sophisticated stereo systems, an equalizer with a bar graph display replaces the bass and treble controls. An *equalizer* (EQ in audio-speak) enables you to fine-tune the specific sound spectrum frequencies, which gives you far greater control than merely adjusting the bass or treble controls.

Adjusting frequencies

You can adjust frequencies in the iTunes equalizer by clicking and dragging sliders that look like mixing-board faders.

The horizontal values across the equalizer represent the spectrum of human hearing. The deepest frequency ("Daddy sang bass") is 32 hertz (Hz); the midrange frequencies are 250 Hz and 500 Hz; and the higher frequencies go from 1 kilohertz (kHz) to 16 kHz (treble).

The vertical values on each bar represent decibels. Increase or decrease the frequencies at 3 dB increments by clicking and dragging the sliders up and down. You can drag the sliders to adjust the frequencies while the music is playing so that you can hear the effect immediately.

Using the iTunes presets

iTunes offers *presets,* which are equalizer settings made in advance and saved by name. You can quickly switch settings without having to make changes to each frequency slider. iTunes comes with more than 20 presets of the most commonly used equalizer settings, including ones for specific music genres, such as classical and rock. You can assign these presets (or your own presets) to a specific item or set of items (songs, audio books, podcast episodes, and videos) in your iTunes library.

These preset settings copy to your iPod along with the content when you update your iPod.

To choose an equalizer preset, click the Equalizer's pop-up menu as shown in Figure 17-4, which by default is set to Manual (refer to Figure 17-3). If something is playing, you hear the effect in the sound immediately after choosing the preset.

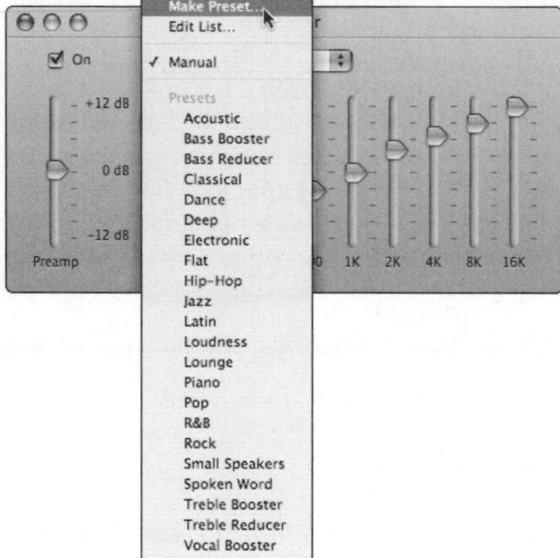

Figure 17-4: Choose a built-in equalizer preset here.

Saving your own presets

You don't have to settle for the built-in equalizer presets — create your own! (Unfortunately, you can't transfer custom presets to an iPod as of this writing.)

Follow these steps to save your own presets to the iTunes equalizer:

1. **Make the frequency changes that you want by dragging the individual sliders up and down.**

   The pop-up menu automatically switches to Manual.

2. **Choose Make Preset from the pop-up menu (refer to Figure 17-4) to save your changes.**

   The Make Preset dialog appears, as shown in Figure 17-5.

3. **Enter a descriptive name for your preset in the New Preset Name text box and then click OK.**

   The name appears in the pop-up menu from that point — your very own preset.

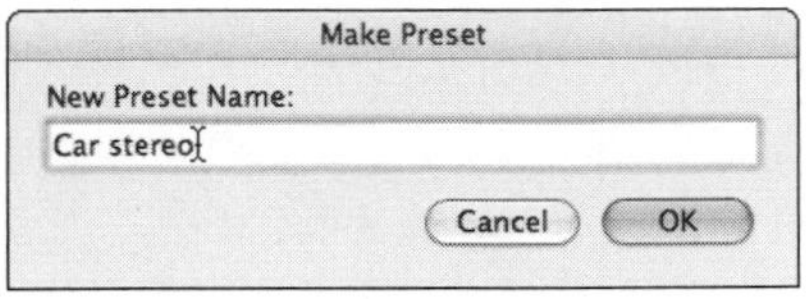

Figure 17-5: Save your own preset here.

You can rename or delete any preset, including those supplied with iTunes (which is useful if you want to recall a preset by another name). Choose the Edit List option from the pop-up menu. The Edit Presets dialog opens, as shown in Figure 17-6. Click Rename to rename a preset, click Delete to delete a preset, and then click Done when you finish editing the list.

Figure 17-6: Rename or delete presets here.

Assigning equalizer presets

One reason why you go to the trouble of setting equalizer presets is to assign them to your iTunes content. The next time you play the item, iTunes uses the equalizer preset that you assigned.

When you transfer content to your iPod, the standard iTunes presets transfer with it; you can choose whether to use these assignments when playing the content on your iPod. However, custom presets don't transfer to the iPod.

Assign an equalizer preset to a content item or set of items by following these steps:

1. **Choose View⇨View Options.**

   The View Options dialog appears, as shown in Figure 17-7.

View Options

Music

Show Columns

☑ Album	☐ Episode ID	☐ Show
☐ Album Artist	☑ Equalizer	☐ Size
☑ Artist	☐ Genre	☑ Skip Count
☐ Beats Per Minute	☐ Grouping	☐ Sort Album
☐ Bit Rate	☐ Kind	☐ Sort Album Artist
☐ Category	☐ Last Played	☐ Sort Artist
☐ Comment	☑ Last Skipped	☐ Sort Composer
☐ Composer	☐ My Rating	☐ Sort Name
☑ Date Added	☐ Play Count	☐ Sort Show
☐ Date Modified	☐ Release Date	☑ Time
☐ Description	☐ Sample Rate	☑ Track Number
☐ Disc Number	☐ Season	☐ Year

Cancel OK

Figure 17-7: Show the Equalizer column to assign presets to songs.

2. **Select the Equalizer check box and then click OK.**

   The Equalizer column appears in the List pane in the iTunes window.

   You can combine Steps 1 and 2 by Control-clicking (Mac) or right-clicking (Windows) on any column heading in List view and then choosing Equalizer.

3. **Locate an item and scroll the list horizontally (if necessary) to see the Equalizer column, as shown in Figure 17-8.**

4. **Choose a preset from the pop-up menu in the Equalizer column.**

   The Equalizer column has a tiny pop-up menu that allows you to assign any preset to a song, audio book, podcast episode, or video.

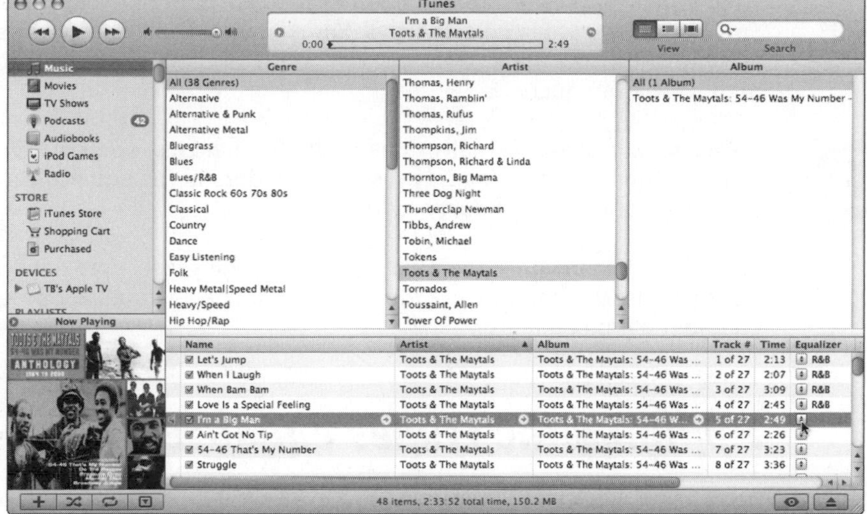

Figure 17-8: Select a song and scroll the List pane to see the Equalizer column.

Equalize It in Your iPod

You leave the back-road bliss of the country to get on the freeway, and now the music in your car doesn't have enough bass to give you that thumping rhythm you need to dodge other cars. What can you do? Without endangering anybody, you can pull over and then select one of the iPod equalizer presets, such as Bass Booster.

Yes, your iPod also has a built-in equalizer. Similar to the iTunes equalizer, the iPod built-in equalizer modifies the volume of the frequencies of the sound. And although you don't have sliders like the iTunes equalizer, you do get the same long list of presets (except for Loudness) to suit the type of music or environment.

The iPod equalizer uses a bit more battery power when it's on, so you might have less playing time.

You can also use the iTunes equalizer to improve or enhance the sound, assigning presets to each song and then updating your iPod.

Choosing an equalizer preset on your iPod

To select an iPod equalizer preset, choose Settings➪EQ from the main menu. The equalizer is set to Off until you select one of the presets.

Each equalizer preset offers a different balance of frequencies designed to enhance the sound in certain ways. For example, Bass Booster increases the volume of the low (bass) frequencies; Treble Booster does the same to the high (treble) frequencies.

To see what a preset actually does to the frequencies, open the iTunes equalizer and then select the same preset. The faders in the equalizer show you exactly what the preset does.

The Off setting disables the iPod equalizer — no presets are used, not even ones you assigned in iTunes. You have to choose an equalizer preset to enable the iPod equalizer.

Applying the iTunes equalizer presets

After assigning a standard preset to a content item in iTunes, enable the iPod equalizer by choosing any equalizer setting (other than Off) so that the iPod uses the item's equalizer preset for playback. To assign standard presets to items with the iTunes equalizer, see the earlier section, "Assigning equalizer presets."

No matter what equalizer preset you choose on your iPod, any item that has an assigned preset uses the assigned preset. That's right — the assigned equalizer preset from iTunes takes precedence over the preset in the iPod.

If you want items that have assigned presets to play with those presets while the rest of the content plays without any equalizer adjustment, choose the Flat EQ preset in your iPod.

If you know in advance that you need to use specific presets for certain songs, assign standard presets to the songs in iTunes *before* copying the songs to the iPod (but not custom presets, which don't transfer to the iPod). If, on the other hand, you don't want the songs fixed to a certain preset, *don't* assign presets to the songs in iTunes. You can then experiment with the presets in the iPod to get better playback in different listening environments.

You can temporarily play an item with an assigned preset via one of your iPod's other equalizer settings. Start playing the item on your iPod, and while the item is playing, press the Menu button until you return to the main menu. Choose Settings⇨EQ and then select a setting you want to try. The content plays to the end with the new equalizer setting. The next time that item is played, it uses the assigned preset as usual.

Modifying Content in iTunes

Although iTunes was never meant to be a media-editing application, it does offer a simple control over the starting and stopping points for playing back media. You can use this feature to cut unwanted intros and outros of a song, such as announcers and audience applause, or to skip opening credits or commercials of movies. You can also use it in conjunction with the Convert feature to split an item (or, in the parlance of record label executives and artists, *split a track*).

To do more significant modifications or editing, use the recording and editing applications described on this book's companion Web site.

Setting the start and stop points

iTunes can play only a portion of a song, video, audio book, or podcast episode — that is, if you specify start and stop times for the item. To set the start and/or stop points, select the item, choose File⇨Get Info, and then click Options, as shown in Figure 17-9.

Figure 17-9: Set the start time.

Click inside the Start Time field to set the start time; in Figure 17-9, we set the Start Time to 0:30 (30 seconds). Then click inside the Stop Time field to set the stop time. The start and stop times are in minutes, seconds, and hundredths of a second: for example, 8:15.93 is 8 minutes and 15.93 seconds.

To determine with accuracy the time for the start and stop points, play the file and look in the Status pane at the top-center part of the iTunes window for the Elapsed Time. You can drag the slider in the Status pane to move quickly and find the exact times for the start and stop points you want to set. ***Note:*** If you click Elapsed Time in the Status pane, it toggles to Remaining Time; click it again for Total Time, and click it once more to see Elapsed Time again.

iTunes plays only the part of the content between the start and stop times. You can use this feature to your advantage because when you convert a song to another format (such as AIFF to MP3), iTunes converts only the part of the song between the start and stop times.

Splitting a track

You might have a CD that was created with all the songs combined into one track, or you might have recorded an entire side of a record or cassette tape onto one sound file. Either way, you probably want to separate the songs into tracks in iTunes.

The best way to split a long track is to open the sound file in a sound-editing program that lets you select sections and them save them separately.

To learn more about using sound recording and editing applications, see this book's companion Web site.

However, you can also separate a track into smaller tracks in iTunes as long as you use the AIFF format at first. Follow these steps:

1. **Before ripping a CD or importing a sound file, set the encoder in your importing preferences to AIFF.**

   See Chapter 5 to find out how to import music with an AIFF encoder.

2. **Rip the CD track into iTunes or import an AIFF sound file into iTunes.**

   Because you set the importing preferences to AIFF, the CD track is imported into iTunes as AIFF at full quality. You want to do this step because you're going to convert it in iTunes, and you need the uncompressed version to convert. Use a song name to identify this track as a long track with multiple tracks — for example, call it something like *side one.*

3. **Change your importing preferences to AAC or MP3.**

   See Chapter 19 for more about changing your importing preferences and converting songs.

4. **Select the song in iTunes and then choose File⇨Get Info.**

   The song information dialog appears.

5. **Click Options to show the Start Time and Stop Time fields.**

   You can set the start and stop times for the song (refer to Figure 17-9).

6. **Define the Start Time and Stop Time for the first song in the long track and then click OK.**

   Play the song and look in the Status pane at the top-center part of the iTunes window for the Elapsed Time. You can drag the slider in the Status pane to move quickly through the song and find the exact times for the start and stop points you want to set. For example, if the first song is exactly 3 minutes and 12 seconds, define the first section to start at 0:00 and stop at 3:12. After setting the start and stop times, click OK to close the song information window.

7. **Convert the defined segment of the long track from AIFF to AAC or MP3.**

   For example, select the long track *(side one)* and then choose Advanced⇨Convert Selection to AAC (or Advanced⇨Convert Selection to MP3 if you chose the MP3 encoder in Step 3). iTunes converts only the section of the song defined by the Start Time and Stop Time fields that you set in Step 6, and creates a new song track in the AAC or MP3 format (depending on your choice in Step 3). iTunes converts the uncompressed AIFF segment into the compressed AAC or MP3 format.

8. **Change the song name of the newly converted track to the actual song name.**

   The converted section of the long track still has the same name *(side one)*. Change its name by clicking inside the song name in the iTunes song list or by choosing File⇨Get Info, clicking the Info tab, clicking in the Name field, and entering the new name. You can also enter a track number in the Track field.

9. **Repeat Steps 4–8 for each song segment.**

   Repeat these steps, selecting the long track *(side one)* each time and setting a new start and stop time for each new song, converting the song to MP3 or AAC, and then changing each newly converted song's name.

10. **When you finish, delete the long track in AIFF format.**

    Delete the long track *(side one)* by selecting it and pressing Delete/Backspace. You don't need it anymore if you converted all the segments to separate songs.

Chapter 18

Decoding Audio Encoding

In This Chapter

- Discovering what MP3, AAC, and Lossless audio encoders do to your music
- Minimizing audio quality tradeoffs when using encoders
- Understanding how encoders use compression
- Choosing the appropriate encoder and import settings

The more you discover more about digital audio technology, you find that you have more decisions to make about your music than you previously thought. This chapter is here to help you make those decisions. For example, you might be tempted to trade quality for space, importing music at average-quality settings that allow you to put more songs on your hard drive and iPod than if you chose higher-quality settings. This choice might make you happy today, but what about tomorrow, when iPods and hard drives double or triple in capacity?

On the other hand, you might be very picky about the sound quality. With an eye toward future generations of iPods and inexpensive hard drives, maybe you decide to trade space for quality, importing music at the highest-possible quality settings and then converting copies to lower-quality, space-saving versions for iPods and other uses. Of course, you'd need more hard drive space to accommodate the higher-quality versions.

This chapter explains which music encoding and compression formats to use for higher quality as well as which ones to use for cramming more songs onto your hard drive.

Trading Quality for Space

The encoding format and settings that you choose for importing music when ripping a CD affect sound quality, iPod space, and computer hard drive space. The format and settings you choose might also affect whether the music files can play on other types of players and computers.

Audio compression methods best for reducing space have to throw away information. In technospeak, such compression methods are *lossy* (the opposite of *lossless*) compression algorithms. For example, AAC and MP3 encoding formats compress the sound via lossy methods. Lossy compression algorithms reduce the sound quality by throwing away information to make the file smaller, so you lose information and some quality in the process. Comparatively, the Apple Lossless encoder compresses sound files without any loss in quality or information, but the resulting file is only a bit smaller than the uncompressed version. The main reason to use Apple Lossless is to maintain quality for burning CDs while also playing the songs on iPods. Because AIFF and WAV encoders don't compress the sound, they are the best choices when burning CDs.

With lossy compression formats, such as MP3 or AAC, the amount of compression depends on the bit rate that you choose as well as the encoding format and other options. *Bit rate* determines how many bits (of digital music information) can travel during playback in a given second. Measured in kilobits per second (Kbps), a higher bit rate (such as 320K) offers higher quality than a bit rate of 192K because the sound isn't compressed as much. Thus, the resulting sound file is larger, taking up more iPod and hard drive space.

Using more compression (a lower bit rate) means that the files are smaller, but the sound quality is poorer. Using less compression (a higher bit rate) means that the sound is higher in quality, but the files are larger. Here's the deal: You can trade quality for space and have more music of lower quality, or you can trade space for quality and have less music of higher quality.

Power consumption is also an issue with the iPod when making compression choices. Playing larger files takes more power because the hard drive inside the iPod has to refresh its memory buffers frequently to process information as the song plays. You might even hear hiccups in the sound.

We prefer a higher-quality sound overall, and we typically don't use the lower-quality settings for encoders except for voice recordings and music recorded in ancient times (cough: before 1960). (Older recordings are already low in quality, so you don't hear that much of a difference when they're compressed.) And because we can hear differences in music quality at the higher compression levels, we just buy another hard drive for storage to accommodate larger files.

Choosing an iTunes Encoder

Your iPod music software gives you a choice of encoders. This choice is perhaps the most important to make before starting to rip music CDs and building your library. Here, we leapfrog years of technospeak about digital music file formats and get right to the ones that you need to know.

If you're using MusicMatch Jukebox, visit this book's companion Web site to choose an appropriate encoder.

Choose iTunes⇨Preferences (Mac) or Edit⇨Preferences (Windows), click the Advanced tab, and then click the Importing tab to see the Importing preferences. You can choose one of five encoders from the Import Using pop-up menu:

- **AAC:** All music purchased from the iTunes Store comes in MPEG-4 *Advanced Audio Coding* (AAC) format. (*MPEG* — the Moving Picture Experts Group — is a committee that recognizes compression standards for video and audio.) AAC is a higher-quality format than MP3 at the same bit rate, meaning that AAC at 128 Kbps is higher quality than MP3 at 128 Kbps. We recommend using AAC for most import operations except when ripping your CDs to burn new audio CDs.

  We think the AAC encoder offers the best tradeoff of space and quality for iPod users. It's suitable for burning to an audio CD (although not as good as AIFF or Apple Lossless), and it's excellent for playing songs on an iPod or from a hard drive. However, it is not suitable for burning MP3 CDs or for playing songs on players other than iPods.

- **AIFF:** *Audio Interchange File Format* is the standard digital format for uncompressed sound on a Mac, and it provides the highest-quality digital representation of sound. Similar to a WAV encoder for Windows, an AIFF encoder uses a platform-specific version of the original Pulse Code Modulation (PCM) algorithm required for compliance with audio CDs.

  Use AIFF if you plan to burn songs onto an audio CD or to edit the songs with a digital sound-editing program. Mac-based sound-editing programs import and export AIFF files, and you can edit and save in AIFF format repeatedly with absolutely no loss in quality. The downside is that AIFF files take up enormous amounts of hard drive and iPod space — 10MB per minute — because they're uncompressed. Don't use AIFF for songs that you want to play on an iPod. Use the Apple Lossless encoder, AAC, or MP3 instead.

- **Apple Lossless:** The *Apple Lossless encoder* is a compromise between the lower-quality encoding of AAC or MP3 (which results in lower file sizes) and the large file sizes of uncompressed, high-quality AIFF or WAV audio. The Apple Lossless encoder provides CD-quality sound in a file size that's about 60 to 70 percent of the size of an AIFF- or WAV-encoded file. The virtue of this encoder is that you can use it for songs that you intend to burn onto audio CDs *and* for playing on iPods. The files are just small enough that they don't hiccup on playback, but they're still much larger than their MP3 or AAC counterparts.

Using the Apple Lossless encoder is the most efficient method of storing the highest-quality versions of your songs. You can burn the songs to CD without any quality loss and still play them on your iPod. You can't store as many songs on your iPod as with AAC or MP3, but the songs that you do store have the highest-possible quality.

- **MP3:** The MPEG-1, Layer 3 format (also known as *MP3*) is supported by most computers and some CD players. Use the MP3 format for songs that you intend to use with MP3 players other than your iPod (which also plays MP3 songs, obviously). Or, use MP3 with applications that support MP3, or when burning to an MP3 CD. (AIFF, WAV, or Apple Lossless formats are better for regular audio CDs.) The MP3 format offers quite a few compression and quality settings, so you can fine-tune the format, sacrificing hard drive (and iPod) space while improving the quality. Use MP3 format for a song that you intend to use with MP3 players, MP3 CDs, and applications that support MP3.
- **WAV:** *Waveform Audio File Format* is a digital audio standard that Windows PCs can understand and manipulate. Like AIFF, WAV is uncompressed and provides the highest-quality digital representation of the sound. Similar to what the AIFF encoder does for a Mac, a WAV encoder uses a Windows-specific version of the original PCM algorithm required for compliance with audio CDs.

  Use WAV if you plan to burn a song to an audio CD or use the song with Windows-based digital sound-editing programs, which import and export WAV files. (AIFF and WAV files are the same except that AIFF works with Mac applications, and WAV works with Windows applications.) WAV files take up enormous amounts of hard drive and iPod space — 10MB per minute — because they're uncompressed. Don't use WAV for songs that you want to play on an iPod: Use the Apple Lossless encoder, AAC, or MP3 instead.

If you want to share your music with someone who uses an MP3 player other than an iPod, you can import or convert songs with an MP3 encoder. As an iPod user, you can use the higher-quality AAC encoder to produce files that are either the same size as their MP3 counterparts but higher in quality, or the same quality but smaller in size.

For the best possible quality, consider not using compression at all (like with AIFF or WAV) or using Apple Lossless. You can import music at the highest quality, burn it to audio CDs, and then convert it to a lesser-quality format for use on an iPod or other devices. If you use Apple Lossless for songs, you can use those songs on an iPod, but they take up much more space than AAC- or MP3-encoded songs. We describe how to convert music in Chapter 19.

The past, present, and future of music

Our suggestions for encoder choice and importing preferences for ripping CDs are mostly subjective. Your listening pleasure depends entirely on your taste and how the song was recorded. Some people can hear qualitative differences that others don't hear or don't care about. Some people can also tolerate a lower-quality sound in exchange for the convenience of carrying more music on their iPods. And sometimes the recording is so primitive sounding that you can get away with using lower-quality settings to save more hard drive space.

Formats for recording sound have changed considerably from brittle 78 rpm records of the early 1900s and the scratchy 45 rpm and 33 rpm records of the mid-1900s to today's CDs. Consumers had to be on the alert then, as you do now, for formats that die off as better ones come along. Think of the ill-fated 8-track cartridge or the legendary quadraphonic LP. You want your digital music to last forever yet still play at high quality — and not get stuck with technology that doesn't evolve with the times.

Digital music has evolved beyond the commercial audio CD, and computers haven't yet caught up to some of the latest audio formats. For example, iTunes can't yet import sound from these formats:

- **DVD-audio:** DVD-audio is a relatively new digital audio format developed from the DVD video format. DVD-audio is based on PCM recording technology but offers improved sound quality. Neither iTunes nor MusicMatch Jukebox support the DVD-audio format, but you can import a digital video file containing DVD-audio sound into iMovie, extract the sound, and export the sound in AIFF or WAV format, which you can use with iTunes. You can also use Toast 8 Titanium from Roxio (`www.roxio.com`) to import and burn DVD-audio. You can maintain its sampling frequency of 48 kHz (which is higher than the 44.1 kHz sampling rate of audio CDs) by setting the Sample Rate pop-up menu in the custom settings for AIFF or WAV to 48.0 kHz.
- **Super Audio CD (SACD):** Super Audio CD is a new format developed from the past audio format for CDs. The SACD format is based on *Direct Stream Digital* (DSD) recording technology that closely reproduces the shape of the original analog waveforms to produce a more natural, higher-quality sound. Originally developed for the digital archiving of priceless analog masters tapes, DSD is based on 1-bit, sigma-delta modulation and operates with a sampling frequency of 2.8224 MHz (64 times the 44.1 kHz used in audio CDs). Philips and Sony adopted DSD as the basis for SACD, and the format is growing in popularity among audiophiles. However, neither iTunes nor MusicMatch Jukebox supports SACD. If you buy music in the SACD format, choose the hybrid format that offers a conventional CD layer and a high-density SACD layer. You can then import the music from the conventional CD layer.

You might also want to take advantage of the compression technology that squeezes more music onto your iPod. Although the Apple-supported AAC format offers far better compression and quality than MP3 format (at the same bit rates), the MP3 format is used more, supported by other players and software programs as well as iPods and iTunes. Sticking with AAC or Apple Lossless as your encoder might make you feel like your songs are stuck inside iTunes with the MP3 blues again. However, with iTunes and your iPod, you can mix and match these formats as you please.

Manic Compression Has Captured Your Song

Every person hears the effects of compression differently. You might not hear any problem with a compressed song that someone else says is tinny or lacking in depth.

Too much compression can be a bad thing. Further compressing an already-compressed music file — say, by converting a song — reduces the quality significantly. Not only that, but after your song is compressed, you can't uncompress the song to its original quality. Your song is essentially locked into that quality, at best.

The lossy-style compression of the MP3 and AAC formats loses information each time you use it, which means that if you compress something already compressed, you lose even more information. This is bad. Don't compress something that's already compressed from a lossy method.

The Apple Lossless encoder doesn't use a lossy method, which is why it's called *lossless* — information is not thrown away. While Lossless compresses to about 60–70 percent of the original sound file, that's not enough of a reduction in space for most people; MP3 and AAC compress sound files to about 10 percent of the original size.

MP3 and AAC use two basic lossy methods to compress audio:

- **Removing non-audible frequencies:** The compression removes what you supposedly can't hear (although this subject is up for debate). For example, if a background singer's warble is totally drowned out by the intensity of a rhythm guitar chord, the compression algorithm loses the singer's sound while maintaining the guitar's sound.
- **Removing less important signals:** Within the spectrum of sound frequencies, some frequencies are considered to be less important in terms of rendering fidelity, and most people can't hear some frequencies. Removing specific frequencies is likely to be less damaging to your music than other types of compression, depending on how you hear things. In fact, your dog might stop getting agitated at songs that contain ultra-high frequencies that only dogs can hear (such as the ending of "Day in the Life" by The Beatles).

Selecting Import Settings

AAC and MP3 formats compress sound at different quality settings. iTunes lets you set the bit rate for importing, which determines the audio quality.

You need to use a higher bit rate (such as 192 Kbps or 320 Kbps) for higher quality, which — all together now! — *increases the file size.*

Variable Bit Rate (VBR) encoding is a technique that varies the number of bits used to store the music, depending on the complexity of the sound. Although the quality of VBR is endlessly debated, it's useful when set to the highest setting because VBR can encode at up to the maximum bit rate of 320 Kbps in those rare cases where the sound requires it, but it keeps the majority of the sound at a lower bit rate.

iTunes also lets you control the *sample rate* during importing, which is the number of times per second the sound waveform is captured digitally *(sampled).* Higher sample rates yield higher-quality sound and large file sizes. However, never use a higher sample rate than the rate used for the source. CDs use a 44.100 kHz rate, so choosing a higher rate is unnecessary unless you convert a song that was recorded from Digital Audio Tape (DAT), DVD, or directly onto the computer at a high sample rate, and you want to keep that sample rate.

Another setting to consider during importing is the Channel choice. Stereo, which offers two channels of music for left and right speakers, is the norm for music. However, mono — monaural or single-channel — was the norm for pop records before the mid-1960s. (Phil Spector was known for his high-quality monaural recordings. And early Rolling Stones records are also recorded in mono.) Monaural recordings take up half the space of stereo recordings when digitized. Most likely, you want to keep stereo recordings in stereo and mono recordings in mono.

Chapter 19

Changing Encoders and Encoder Settings

In This Chapter

- Changing settings for the encoders in iTunes
- Changing your importing preferences in iTunes
- Converting songs to a different encoding format in iTunes

You might want to change your import settings before ripping CDs depending on the type of music, the source of the recording, or other factors, such as whether you plan to copy the songs to your iPod or burn an audio or MP3 CD. Encoders offer general quality settings, but you can also customize encoders and change those settings to your liking. Whether you use iTunes or MusicMatch Jukebox, the software remembers your custom settings until you change them again.

If you're using MusicMatch Jukebox, visit this book's companion Web site to find out what type of encoders it offers.

This chapter provides the nuts and bolts for changing your import settings to customize each type of encoder, importing sounds other than music, and converting songs from one format to another. With the choice of settings for music encoders, you can impress your audiophile friends — even those who doubted that your computer could reproduce such magnificent-sounding music.

You can also convert songs to another format, as we describe in the later section, "Converting Songs to a Different Encoder Format in iTunes." However, you can't convert copy-protected songs that you buy from the iTunes Store to another file format because they're encoded as protected AAC files. (If you could, they wouldn't be protected, would they?) You can convert and share the unprotected AAC music available in the iTunes Plus section of the store (as we describe in Chapter 7), but if you convert a compressed song into another compression format you will lose audio quality, as we describe in Chapter 18. You also can't convert Audible audio books and spoken-word content to another format; you can burn them to an audio CD and re-import them, but that might cause a noticeable drop in quality.

Customizing the Encoder Settings in iTunes

To change your encoder settings, quality settings, and other importing preferences before ripping an audio CD or converting a file in iTunes, follow these steps:

1. **Choose iTunes⇨Preferences (Mac) or Edit⇨Preferences (Windows), click the Advanced tab, and then click the Importing tab.**

   The Importing preferences appear, allowing you to make changes to the encoding format and its settings.

2. **From the Import Using pop-up menu, choose the encoding format that you want to convert the song into and then select the settings for that format.**

   The Setting pop-up menu will differ depending on your choice of encoder from the Import Using pop-up menu. See the sections on each encoding format later in this chapter for details on settings.

3. **Click OK to accept changes.**

   After changing your importing preferences — and until you change them again — iTunes uses these preferences whenever it imports or converts songs.

AAC, MP3, AIFF, and WAV encoders let you customize the settings. The Apple Lossless encoder is automatic and offers no custom settings.

Changing AAC encoder settings

We recommend using the AAC encoder for most types of music — except songs that you intend to burn to an audio CD or an MP3 CD — because AAC offers the best trade-off of space for hard drives and iPods as well as quality.

The Setting pop-up menu for the AAC encoder offers four choices: High Quality (128 kbps), Higher Quality (256 kbps), Spoken Podcast, and Custom, as shown in Figure 19-1. The Spoken Podcast setting is useful for converting podcasts exported from GarageBand (or a similar audio-editing application) into iTunes. We recommend using the Higher Quality setting for most music you rip from CDs. For very intense music (such as complex jazz or classical music, recordings with lots of instruments, or your most favorite songs), you might want to fine-tune the settings. To customize your AAC encoder settings, choose Custom from the Setting pop-up menu to see the AAC Encoder dialog, as shown in Figure 19-2.

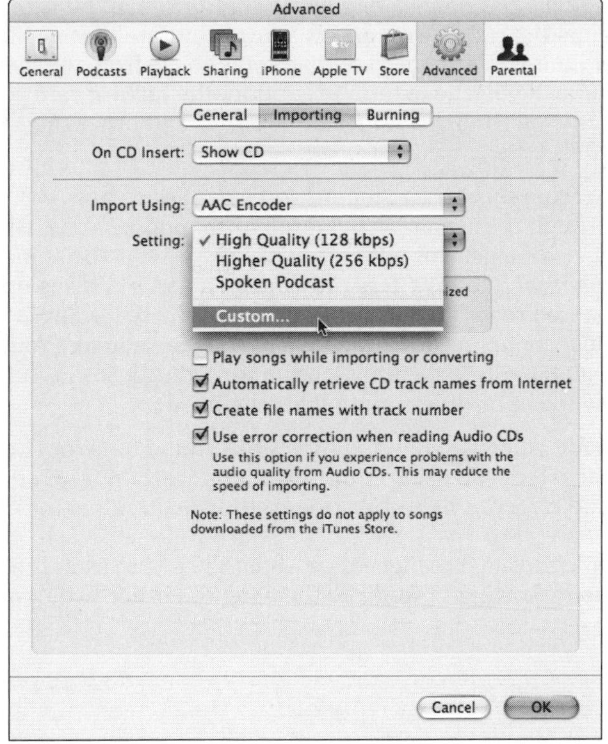

Figure 19-1: Choose custom settings for an AAC encoder.

The custom settings for AAC (see Figure 19-2) allow you to change the following:

- **Stereo Bit Rate:** This pop-up menu allows you to select the bit rate, which is measured in kilobits per second (Kbps). Using a higher bit rate gives you higher quality but also increases file size. The highest-quality setting for this format is 320 Kbps; 256 Kbps, considered higher quality, is the bit rate for the unprotected songs that Apple provides in its iTunes Plus store.
- **Sample Rate:** This pop-up menu enables you to select the *sample rate,* which is the number of times per second that the sound waveform is captured digitally *(sampled).* Higher sample rates yield higher-quality sound and larger file sizes. However, never use a higher sample rate than the rate used for the source. CDs use a 44.1 kilohertz (kHz) rate.
- **Use Variable Bit Rate Encoding (VBR):** This option helps keep down file size, but quality might be affected. VBR varies the number of bits used to store the music depending on the complexity of the sound. iTunes encodes up to the maximum bit rate of 320 Kbps in sections of songs

where the sound is complex enough to require a high bit rate. Meanwhile, iTunes keeps the rest of the song at a lower bit rate to save file space. The lower limit is set by the rate that you choose from the Stereo Bit Rate pop-up menu. If you chose the VBR option, the highest rate you can set (which is the lower limit of VBR) is 256 Kbps, and other rates that don't work with VBR are grayed out.

- **Channels:** From this pop-up menu, you can choose how you want music to play through the speakers: in stereo or in mono. *Stereo,* which offers two channels of music for left and right speakers, is the standard for music. *Monaural* (mono) offers only one channel but takes up half the space of stereo recordings when digitized. If the recording is in stereo, don't choose mono because you lose part of the sound. (You might lose vocals or guitar riffs, depending on the recording.) Select Auto to have iTunes use the appropriate setting for the music.
- **Optimize for Voice:** This option filters the sound to favor the human voice. Podcasters can use this option, along with the AAC encoder, to convert audio recordings into a podcast format optimal for iTunes.

We recommend choosing the highest bit rate (320 Kbps) from the Stereo Bit Rate pop-up menu, leaving VBR off, and leaving the other two pop-up menus set to Auto.

Figure 19-2: Set the AAC encoder to import with the highest bit rate and with automatic detection of sample rate and channels.

AAC Encoder
Stereo Bit Rate: 192 kbps
Sample Rate: Auto
Channels: Auto
Use Variable Bit Rate Encoding (VBR)
Optimize for voice
Default Settings
Cancel
OK

Changing MP3 encoder settings

We prefer using AAC encoding for music that we play on our iPods, but as of this writing, many MP3 players don't support AAC. The iPod supports both AAC and MP3 formats. You might want to use MP3 encoding for other reasons, such as acquiring more control over the compression parameters and gaining compatibility with other applications and players that support MP3.

The MP3 encoder offers four choices for the Setting pop-up menu on the Importing preferences tab:

- **Good Quality (128 Kbps):** This bit rate is certainly fine for audio books, comedy records, and scratchy records. You might even want to use a lower bit rate for voice recordings.
- **High Quality (160 Kbps):** Most people consider this bit rate high enough for most popular music, but we go higher for our music.
- **Higher Quality (192 Kbps):** This bit rate is high enough for just about all types of music.
- **Custom:** To fine-tune MP3 encoder settings, select the Custom setting. Customizing your MP3 settings increases the sound quality and keeps the file size small.

The MP3 encoder offers many choices in its custom settings dialog (see Figure 19-3).

Figure 19-3: Customize the settings for the MP3 encoder.

- **Stereo Bit Rate:** This pop-up's menu choices are measured in Kbps. Choosing a higher bit rate gives you higher quality but also increases file size. The most common bit rate for MP3 files that you find on the Web is 128 Kbps. Lower bit rates are more appropriate for voice recordings or sound effects.

  We recommend at least 192 Kbps for most music. We use 320 Kbps, the maximum setting, for songs that we play on our iPods.

- **Use Variable Bit Rate Encoding (VBR):** This option helps keep down file size, but quality might be affected. VBR varies the number of bits used to store the music depending on the complexity of the sound. For MP3, the VBR option includes a Quality pop-up menu right below the option.

If you choose Highest from the Quality pop-up menu for VBR, iTunes encodes up to the maximum bit rate of 320 Kbps in sections of songs where the sound is complex enough to require a high bit rate. Meanwhile, iTunes keeps the rest of the song at a lower bit rate to save file space. The lower limit is set by the rate that you choose from the Stereo Bit Rate pop-up menu.

Some audiophiles swear by VBR, but others don't ever use it. We use it only when importing at low bit rates, and we set VBR to its highest-quality setting.

Your iPod can play VBR-encoded MP3 music, but other MP3 players might not support VBR.

- **Sample Rate:** From this pop-up menu, you can choose the *sample rate* (how many times per second the sound waveform is captured digitally). Higher sample rates yield higher-quality sound and larger file sizes. However, never use a higher sample rate than the rate used for the source: For example, CDs use a 44.1 kHz rate.
- **Channels:** From this pop-up menu, choose how you want music to play through the speakers: in stereo or in mono. *Stereo,* which offers two channels of music for left and right speakers, is the standard for music. *Mono* recordings take up half the space of stereo recordings when digitized. Choose Auto to have iTunes use the appropriate setting for the music.
- **Stereo Mode:** From this pop-up menu, choose Normal or Joint Stereo. *Normal mode* is just what you think it is — normal stereo. Choose the Joint Stereo setting to make the file smaller by removing information that's identical in both channels of a stereo recording, using only one channel for that information while the other channel carries unique information. At bit rates of 128 Kbps and lower, this mode can actually improve the sound quality. However, we typically don't use Joint Stereo mode when using a high-quality bit rate.
- **Smart Encoding Adjustments:** Selecting this option tells iTunes to analyze your MP3 encoding settings and music source, changing your settings as needed to maximize the quality of the encoded files.
- **Filter Frequencies Below 10 Hz:** Selecting this option filters low frequencies. Frequencies lower than 10 hertz (Hz) are difficult to hear, and most people don't notice that they're missing. Filtering inaudible frequencies helps reduce the file size with little or no perceived loss in quality. However, we think that selecting this option and removing the low-frequencies detracts from the overall feeling of the music; thus, we prefer not to filter frequencies.

Changing AIFF, WAV, and Apple Lossless encoder settings

We recommend using AIFF, WAV, or Apple Lossless encoders for songs from audio CDs that you intend to burn. You get the best possible quality with these encoders because the music isn't compressed with a lossy algorithm. The Apple Lossless encoder (which is automatic and offers no settings to change) reduces the file size to about 60 to 70 percent of the AIFF or WAV versions. However, AIFF or WAV files are preferable for use with digital sound-editing programs, and they offer settings that you can change, such as the number of channels (stereo or mono) and the sampling rate.

Although AIFF and WAV formats have technical differences, here's the only major difference in storing and playing music: AIFF is the standard for Macs and their applications, and WAV is the standard for PCs and their applications.

You can import music with an AIFF or a WAV encoder at the highest-possible quality and then convert the music files to a lesser-quality format for use on your iPod.

AIFF- and WAV-encoded files take up huge amounts of hard drive space (about 10MB per minute). Although you can play these file types on an iPod, they take up way too much space and battery power to be convenient for anyone but the most discerning audiophile who can afford multiple iPods. You can handle these large files by adding another hard drive or by backing up portions of your music library onto other media, such as DVD-R (which can hold 4.38GB). The high quality of AIFF- and WAV-encoded files ensures an excellent listening experience through a home stereo. However, if multiple hard drives and backup scenarios sound like unwanted hassles, use AAC or MP3 encoding to compress files so that they take up less space on your hard drive.

The AIFF and WAV encoder dialogs offer similar custom settings; the AIFF Encoder dialog is shown in Figure 19-4. The pop-up menus offer settings for Sample Rate, Sample Size, and Channels. If you choose Auto for all three, iTunes automatically detects the proper sample rate, size, and channels from the source. If you choose a specific setting — such as Stereo, from the Channels pop-up menu — iTunes imports the music in stereo, regardless of the source. Audio CDs typically sample at a rate of 44.1 kHz, with a sample size of 16 bits, and with stereo channels.

The Sample Rate pop-up menu for AIFF and WAV encoders offers more choices than AAC, down to a very low sample rate of 8 kHz, which is suitable only for voice recordings.

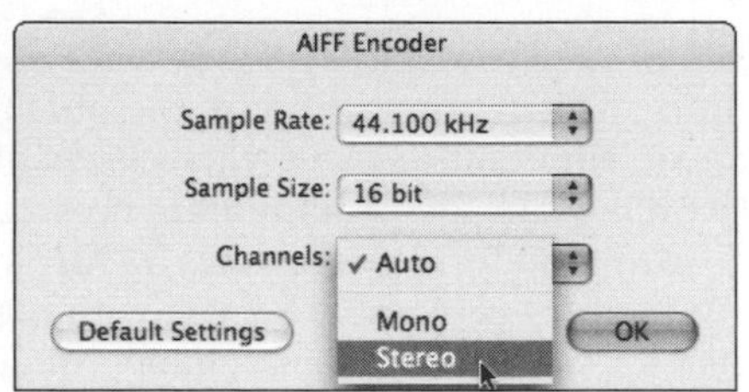

Figure 19-4: The Channels pop-up menu in the AIFF encoder custom settings allows you to import regardless of the source.

Importing Voice and Sound Effects in iTunes

Audio books from Audible (`www.audible.com`) and from the iTunes Store are available in a special format that doesn't require any further compression. However, you can also import audio books, spoken-word titles, comedy CDs, and other voice recordings in MP3 format.

If the recording has any music or requires close listening to stereo channels (such as a Firesign Theatre or Monty Python CD), treat the entire recording as music and skip this section. ("Nudge, nudge. Wink, wink. Sorry! Everything you know is wrong!")

By fine-tuning the import settings for voice recordings and sound effects, you can save a significant amount of space without reducing quality. We recommend the following settings, depending on your choice of encoder:

- **AAC:** AAC allows you to get away with an even lower bit rate than MP3 to achieve the same quality, thereby saving more space. We recommend using a bit rate as low as 80 Kbps for sound effects and voice recordings. Use the Optimize for Voice option to filter the sound to favor the human voice.
- **MP3:** Use a low bit rate (such as 96 Kbps). You might also want to reduce the sample rate to 22.05 kHz for voice recordings. Filter frequencies lower than 10 Hz because voice recordings don't need such frequencies.

Converting Songs to a Different Encoder Format in iTunes

Converting a song from one format to another is useful if you want to use one format for one purpose (such as burning the song to a CD) and a second format for another task (such as playing the song on your iPod). Changing formats is also useful for converting uncompressed songs or podcasts that were created in GarageBand (or a similar audio-editing application) and exported or copied to iTunes.

Converting a song from one compressed format to another is possible (say, from AAC to MP3), but you might not like the results. When you convert a compressed file to another compressed format, you are compressing further an already-compressed file, reducing the quality of the sound. You get the best results by starting with an uncompressed song that was imported in AIFF or WAV format and then converting that song to compressed AAC or MP3 format.

You can tell the format of a song by selecting it, choosing File➪Get Info, and then clicking the Summary tab. You might want to keep track of formats by creating version-specific playlists — say, a CD-AIFF–version playlist and an iPod-MP3–version playlist.

To convert a song to a different encoding format, follow these steps:

1. **Choose iTunes➪Preferences (Mac) or Edit➪Preferences (Windows), click the Advanced tab, and then click the Importing tab.**

   The Importing preferences appear, allowing you to make changes to the encoding format and its settings.

2. **From the Import Using pop-up menu, choose the encoding format into which that you want to convert the song.**

3. **In the Custom Settings dialog that appears, select the settings for that encoder.**

   For example, if you're converting songs in the AIFF format to the MP3 format, choose MP3 Encoder from the Import Using pop-up menu and then select the settings that you want in the MP3 Encoder dialog that appears.

4. **Click OK to accept the settings for your chosen format.**

5. **In the iTunes window, select the song(s) that you want to convert and then choose Advanced➪Convert Selection to *encoder*.**

   The encoding format that you choose in Step 2 (MP3, AAC, AIFF, Lossless, or WAV) appears in place of *encoder* on the menu.

   When the conversion is complete, a new version of the song appears in your iTunes library (with the same artist and song name, so it's easy to find). iTunes doesn't delete the original version — both are stored in your music library.

If you convert songs obtained from the Internet, you might find MP3 songs with bit rates as low as 128 Kbps. Choosing a higher stereo bit rate doesn't improve the quality — it only wastes space.

The automatic copy-and-convert operation can be useful for converting an entire music library to another format. Press Option (Mac) or Alt (Windows) and choose Advanced➪Convert Selection to encoder. All the songs copy and convert automatically. If you have a library of AIFF tunes, you can quickly copy and convert them to AAC or MP3 in one step and then assign the AIFF songs to the AIFF-associated playlists for burning CDs, and MP3 or AAC songs to MP3 or AAC playlists that you intend to copy to your iPod.

Part V
Have iPod, Will Travel

"It's a fully furnished, 3-bedroom house that's designed to fit perfectly over your iPod."

In this part . . .

This part explains how you can use your iPod the same way people often use PDAs — to take care of personal business. It also covers how to troubleshoot your iPod.

- Chapter 20 helps you listen to tunes whenever you head out on the highway or stay at the "Heartbreak Hotel."
- Chapter 21 covers managing your life on the road — setting the time and date, waking up with the alarm clock, sorting your contacts, recording memos, setting the combination lock, and customizing the iPod menu and display settings.
- Chapter 22 is about using your iPod as a hard drive. Here you can find how to transfer folders and files, store notes and text, and adding guides, books, and news feeds.
- Chapter 23 describes automatically synchronizing your iPod or iPhone with personal information via iTunes. Here you can also find out about adding information manually so that you don't miss any appointments or forget someone's name, address, or phone number.
- Chapter 24 gets into the nitty-gritty of troubleshooting your iPod, including how to use iTunes to update or restore your iPod or iPhone.

Chapter 20

Going Mobile

In This Chapter

- Connecting headphones and using portable speakers
- Using adapters and mounts to play your iPod in a car
- Using an integrated iPod car stereo interface
- Playing your iPod on FM radios by using wireless adapters
- Protecting your iPod with carrying cases
- Using power accessories on the road

You can truly go anywhere with an iPod. If you can't plug your iPod into a power source while it's playing, you can use the battery for quite a while before having to recharge. You can find all the accessories that you need to travel with an iPod in the Apple Store at `www.apple.com`.

Put on "Eight Miles High" by the Byrds while cruising in a plane at 40,000 feet. Watch the "Lust for Life" music video by Iggy Pop on a bus heading out of Detroit. Ride the rails listening to "All Aboard" by Muddy Waters, followed by "Peavine" by John Lee Hooker. Or cruise on the Autobahn in Germany with Kraftwerk. The iPod provides high-quality sound and excellent picture quality no matter how turbulent the environment.

In addition to their hard drives, iPods use a memory cache. The cache is made up of solid-state memory, with no mechanical or moving parts, so movement doesn't affect playback. The iPod plays sound from the memory cache rather than the hard drive. The iPod nano and iPod shuffle are entirely solid-state memory, which completely eliminates skipping. With skip protection, you don't have to worry about tremors, potholes, or strenuous exercise causing the audio to skip. Skip protection works by preloading up to 20 minutes of sound to the cache at a time (depending on the iPod model).

Connecting Headphones and Portable Speakers

Apple designed the iPod to provide excellent sound through headphones. From the headphone/line-out connection, though, the iPod can also play music through portable speaker systems. The speaker systems must be self-powered or able to work with very little power (like headphones) and allow audio to be input via a 3.5mm, stereo mini-plug connection.

The iPod includes a small amplifier powerful enough to deliver audio through the headphone/line-out connection. All current models, including the iPod shuffle, have a frequency response of 20 to 20,000 Hz (hertz), which provides distortion-free music at the lowest or highest pitches. (In this case, Hertz has nothing to do with rental cars. A *hertz* is a unit of frequency equal to one cycle per second.) At pitches that produce frequencies of 20 cycles per second or 20,000 cycles per second, the iPod responds with distortion-free sound.

If headphones aren't your thing, you can even wear an iPod shuffle inside a headband (and keep it relatively dry no matter how much you, um, create your own moisture). Thanko (`www.thanko.jp`) offers the Vonia sports headband that uses *bone conduction* — a hearing aid technology that conducts "Good Vibrations" through the bones of your skull, directly into your inner ear. The sound can be surprisingly clear and crisp although it won't be in stereo because the sound seems to come from inside your head.

Portable speaker systems typically include built-in amplifiers and a volume control, and they offer a stereo mini-plug that you can attach directly to the iPod headphone/line-out connection or to the dock headphone/line-out connection. To place the external speakers farther away from the iPod, use a stereo mini-plug extension cable, which are available at most consumer electronics stores. These cables have a stereo mini-plug on one end and a stereo mini-socket on the other.

Portable speaker systems typically have volume controls. Set your iPod volume to half and then raise or lower the volume of your speaker system.

When you travel, take an extra pair of headphones (or earbuds) and a splitter cable, which are available in any consumer electronics store. The Monster iSplitter is available in the Apple Store. That way, you can share music with someone on the road.

Portable speaker systems, such as the iBoom from DLO (`www.dlo.com`), and the Bose iPod Speaker Dock (`www.bose.com`), provide a dock connection for playing audio. For a portable stereo system that offers big sound on a rechargeable battery and is perfect for environments like the beach or a boat, check out the i-Fusion from Sonic Impact (`www.si-technologies.com`). (See Figure 20-1.) It includes universal adapters for all dockable iPod models and an audio input connection for connecting your computer or an audio player. The double-duty case is a durable cover that acts as a speaker cabinet to give the speakers better bass response.

Figure 20-1: The i-Fusion from Sonic Impact provides a dock and speakers for the road.

Playing Car Tunes

We always wanted a car that we could fill up with music just as easily as filling it up with gasoline, without having to carry dozens of cassettes or CDs. With an iPod, an auto-charger to save on battery power, and a way to connect the iPod to your car's stereo system, you're ready to pump music. (Start your engine and queue up "Getting in Tune" and then "Going Mobile" by The Who.) You can even go one step further and get a new BMW, Toyota, or similarly equipped car that offers an iPod dock cable installed and integrated into the car's stereo system so that you can control the iPod from your car stereo — including controls on the steering wheel.

Here's how to link your iPod to a car stereo:

- **Buy a car that offers an iPod-ready stereo.** BMW, Mercedes-Benz, Toyota, Honda, and many other auto companies offer models that are iPod ready.
- **Use your cassette player.** Use a standard cassette adapter and an iPod power adapter for your car's lighter socket. This method works even with rental cars (as long as they're supplied with cassette players). For a semi-permanent installation, you can add a car mount to keep your iPod secure. Cassette adapters offer medium quality that's usually better than wireless adapters.
- **Use your radio and a wireless adapter.** Use a wireless adapter that plays your iPod as if it were a station on your FM radio dial. Some car mounts offer built-in wireless adapters. This might be your only inexpensive choice if you don't have a cassette deck. ***Note:*** Wireless adapters might not work well in cities where FM stations crowd the radio dial.
- **Install an iPod interface.** Install an iPod interface for your car stereo that offers high-quality, line-in audio input and power. After you install this interface, thread the iPod cable into the glove box so that you can plug the cable into your iPod, hide the iPod in the glove box, and control the iPod from your car stereo's head unit. This method offers the best sound quality. As of this writing, Toyota is rolling out an integration kit for plugging an iPod into the car glove box and using either the steering wheel or usual audio system controls.

Unfortunately, not many car stereos offer a mini-socket for audio input. As of this writing, the few accessories that integrate directly with car stereos require custom car installations. Most connection standards are based on specific car models or stereo models. But stay iTuned, though, because standard car docks are on the horizon.

Using cassette and power adapters for your car

Until you get an iPod-ready car, a car stereo with a mini-socket for stereo audio input (also called *stereo-in connection*), or an iPod connection — or get one installed — you can use a cassette-player adapter to connect with your car stereo or a wireless device. We describe wireless connectivity later in the section, "Connecting by Wireless Radio." These solutions provide lower sound quality than iPod interface installations or stereo-in connections but are inexpensive and work with most cars.

Many car stereos have a cassette player, and you can buy a cassette adapter from most consumer electronics stores or from the Apple Store (such as the Sony CPA-9C Car Cassette Adapter). The cassette-player adapter looks like a tape cassette with a mini-plug cable (which sticks out through the slot when you're using the adapter).

You can connect the mini-plug cable directly to the iPod, to the auto-charger if a mini-socket is offered, or to the Apple Remote that in turn is connected to the iPod. Then insert the adapter into the cassette player, being careful not to get the cable tangled up inside the player.

One inherent problem with this approach is that the cable that dangles from your cassette player looks unsightly. You also might have some trouble ejecting the adapter if the cable gets wedged in the cassette player door. Overall, though, this method is the best for most cars because it provides the best sound quality.

Although some new vehicles (particularly SUVs and cars such as the Toyota Matrix mini-station wagon) offer 110-volt power outlets you can use with your Apple-supplied battery charger, most cars offer only a lighter/power socket that requires a power adapter to use with your iPod. Be careful to pick the right type of power adapter for your car's lighter/power socket.

Belkin (`www.belkin.com`) offers the Auto Kit for $49.95, and it includes a car power adapter with a convenient socket for a stereo mini-plug cable (which can connect directly to a car stereo if the stereo has a mini-socket for audio input). The adapter includes a volume-adjustable amplifier to boost the sound coming from the iPod before it goes into the cassette adapter or car stereo.

Even with a cassette adapter and power adapter, you have at best a clumsy solution that uses one cable (power) from a power adapter to the iPod and another cable (audio) to your car stereo cassette adapter. Attached to these wires, your iPod needs a secure place to sit while your car moves because you don't want it bouncing around.

You can fit your iPod securely in position in a car without getting a custom installation. The TuneDok ($29.95) from Belkin (`www.belkin.com`) holds your iPod securely and fits into your car's cup-holder. The TuneDok ratcheting neck and height-adjustment feature lets you reposition the iPod to your liking. The cable-management clip eliminates loose and tangled cables, and the large and small rubber base and cup fits most cup holders.

MARWARE (`www.marware.com`) offers an inexpensive solution for both car use and personal use. The $5.95 Car Holder, available when you select a MARWARE Sportsuit case, attaches to the dashboard of your car and lets you attach an iPod that's wearing one of the MARWARE Sportsuit covering cases. (See "Dressing Up Your iPod for Travel," later in this chapter.) The clip on the back attaches to the Car Holder.

ProClip (`www.proclipusa.com`) offers mounting brackets for clip-on devices. The brackets attach to the dashboard and can be installed in seconds. After you install the bracket, you can use different custom holders for the iPod models or for cell phones and other portable devices.

Integrating an iPod with your car stereo

Premium car manufacturers are introducing cars that are *iPod-ready:* including an iPod interface for the car stereo system. For example, BMW offers such a model with audio controls on the steering wheel. Mercedes-Benz, Volvo, Mini-Cooper, Nissan, Alfa Romeo, and Ferrari all also offer iPod-ready models. In addition, car stereo manufacturers (such as Alpine and Clarion) offer car audio systems with integrated iPod interfaces; see Figure 20-2. Many of these installations use the multiple CD changer interface of the car stereo for attaching separate CD changer units, substituting the iPod for the CD changer unit.

Figure 20-2: An iPod-integrated car stereo installation.

If you can't afford an iPod-ready car, you can opt for a custom installation of an iPod interface for your existing car stereo and car power (such as using a custom cable interface for a CD changer, which a skilled car audio specialist can install into your dashboard). For example, you can order a professional installation with the Dension ICE-Link, which adds line-level audio output and recharging capability to almost any vehicle. It uses the CD-changer connections in car CD players to directly connect your iPod into the car's audio system. Dension (`www.dension.com`) assumes that the buyer is a professional installer. Although you can install it yourself (especially if you already have a CD changer unit in your trunk), most installations require taking apart the dashboard and installing the ICE-Link behind your CD stereo. ICE-Link can be combined with almost any iPod mount.

If your car stereo doesn't offer a CD changer interface, you might want to have a new car stereo professionally installed that offers a CD changer interface or iPod capability — such as the Alpine CDA-9887 (`www.alpine-usa.com/driveyouripod`). With an integrated iPod setup, you can control the iPod from the car stereo's head unit or steering wheel controls. The car stereo provides power to the iPod to keep it fully charged.

Connecting by Wireless Radio

A wireless music adapter lets you play music from your iPod on an FM radio with no connection or cable although the sound quality might suffer a bit from interference. We always take a wireless adapter with us whenever we rent a car because even if a rental car has no cassette player (ruling out the use of our cassette adapter), it probably has an FM radio.

You can use a wireless adapter in a car, on a boat, on the beach with a portable radio, or even in your home with a stereo system and tuner. We even use it in hotel rooms with a clock radio.

To use a wireless adapter, follow these steps:

1. **Set the wireless adapter to an unused FM radio frequency.**

   Some adapters offer only one frequency (typically 87.9 MHz). Others offer you a choice of several frequencies: typically 88.1, 88.3, 88.5, and 88.7 MHz. Some even let you pick any FM frequency. If given a choice, choose the frequency and set the adapter according to its instructions. Avoid FM stations at specific frequencies that would interfere with your iPod signal.

2. **Connect the wireless adapter to the iPod headphone/line-out connector or to the line-out connector on the iPod dock.**

   The wireless adapter acts like a miniature radio station, broadcasting to a nearby FM radio. (Sorry, you can't go much farther than a few feet, so no one else can hear your Wolfman Jack impersonation.)

3. **Tune to the appropriate frequency on the FM dial.**

   Tune any nearby radio to the same FM frequency that you choose in Step 1.

You need to set the adapter close enough to the radio's antenna to work, making it impractical for home stereos. You can get better quality sound by connecting to a home stereo with a cable.

Don't be surprised if the wireless adapter doesn't work as well in cities because other radio stations might cause too much interference.

Here are a few wireless adapters that we recommend:

- **TRAFFICJamz** ($34.99) from Newer Technology (`www.newertech.com`) is both a charger and a transmitter that works with all model iPods.
- **iTrip** ($49.95) from Griffin Technology (`www.griffintechnology.com`) offers selectable LX or DX modes of broadcasting. Even in large cities with lots of radio stations crowding the dial, iTrip DX Mode delivers a background noise level below that of a cassette tape adapter.
- **TuneCast II Mobile FM Transmitter** ($39.99) from Belkin (`www.belkin.com`) is particularly convenient in a car because it includes a 14-inch cable that delivers power when used with the Belkin Mobile Power Cord for iPod. That way, you can preserve your batteries for when you're not near an alternate source. It offers four programmable memory slots for saving the clearest radio frequency wherever you go.
- **Monster iCarPlay Wireless** ($69.95) from Monster Cable (`www.monstercable.com`) offers a power adapter as well as excellent quality playback for a wireless radio unit. You can select radio frequencies of 88.1, 88.3, 88.5, 88.7, 88.9, 89.1, 89.3, or 89.5 MHz. Although a bit more expensive, we prefer it for its sound quality.
- **DLO TransPod FM** ($49.99) from Digital Lifestyle Outfitters (`www.dlo.com`) is an excellent all-in-one wireless FM transmitter, mounting system, and power adapter for using your iPod in a car. It also costs less than purchasing all three items separately.

Dressing Up Your iPod for Travel

The simple protective carrying case supplied with some iPod models is just not as stylin' as the myriad accessories that you can get for dressing up your iPod for travel. You can find different types of protective gear, from leather jackets to aluminum cases, in many different styles and colors. Apple offers access to hundreds of products from other suppliers on its accessories pages (`www.apple.com/ipod/accessories.html`). Some are designed primarily for protecting your iPod from harm; others are designed to provide some measure of protection while also providing access to controls.

On the extreme end of the spectrum are hardened cases that are ready for battlefields in deserts or jungles — the Humvees of iPod protective gear, if you will. Matias Armor ($39.95) by Matias Corporation (`http://matias.ca/armor`) is a sturdy case that fits all iPod models and offers possibly the best protection against physical trauma on the market. Your iPod rests within a hard, resilient metal exoskeleton that can withstand the abuse of bouncing down a flight of metal stairs without letting your iPod pop out. Of course, the very same feature that prevents your iPod from popping out also makes the iPod Armor difficult to open to get access to your iPod. This is not a case to use while listening to music.

Business travelers can combine personal items into one carrying case. The iPod Leather Organizer (about $15) from Belkin (`www.belkin.com`) is made from fine-grain leather that even Ricardo Montalban would rave about. The case holds personal essentials, such as business and credit cards, in four convenient slots. A handy mesh pocket keeps earphones easily accessible, and a billfold holds money and receipts.

On the sporty side, MARWARE (`www.marware.com`) offers the Sportsuit Convertible case ($34.95) with a patented belt-clip system, offering interchangeable clip options for use with the MARWARE Car Holder or with an armband or belt. The neoprene case has vulcanized rubber grips on each side and bottom for a no-slip grip as well as plastic inserts for impact protection, offering full access to all iPod controls and connections while the iPod is in the case. There's even space inside the lid to store earbuds.

If you like to carry a backpack with everything in it, consider getting the very first backpack ever designed to control an iPod within it: The Burton Amp Pack (`http://lonelyplanet.altrec.com/shop/detail/24004`), priced at $199.95, lets you switch songs on your iPod by pressing a button on the shoulder strap. Constructed from ballistic nylon, the Amp Pack offers a secure iPod storage pocket, a headphone port located on a shoulder strap, an easy-access side entry laptop compartment, and padded ergonomic shoulder straps with a soft, flexible control pad built in to a strap. It's perfect for listening to Lou Reed while hanging on to a pole in a subway car, or the

Hollies while navigating your way to the back of the bus. Other backpacks that can host iPods include the Thundervolt from JanSport (www.jansport.com) and the aptly named G-Tech Psycho (www.g-techworld.com).

Using Power Accessories

If you want to charge your iPod battery when you travel abroad, you can't count on finding the same voltage as in your home country. However, you still need to use your Apple power adapter to recharge your iPod. Fortunately, power adapters are available in most airports, but the worldly traveler might want to consider saving time and money by getting a travel kit of power accessories.

We found several varieties of power kits for world travel in our local international airport. Most kits include a set of AC plugs with prongs that fit different electrical outlets around the world. You can connect your iPod power adapter to these adapters. The AC plugs typically support outlets in North America, Japan, China, the United Kingdom, Continental Europe, Korea, Australia, and Hong Kong. You should also include at least one power accessory for use with a standard car lighter, such as car chargers from Belkin (www.belkin.com), Kensington (www.kensington.com), or Newer Technology (www.newertech.com).

One way to mitigate the battery blues is to get an accessory that lets you use replaceable alkaline batteries — the kind that you can find in any convenience store. The TunePower Rechargeable Battery Pack for iPod ($79.99) from Belkin (www.belkin.com) lets you power your iPod with standard AA alkaline replaceable batteries even when your internal iPod battery is drained.

Another way to supply power to your iPod on the road is to use your FireWire-equipped or USB 2.0–equipped laptop to supply the power (make sure that you use FireWire or USB 2.0 hardware that provides power; see Chapter 1) and then use a power adapter with your laptop. You can use, for example, the Kensington Universal Car/Air Adapter for Apple to plug a Mac PowerBook or iBook into any car cigarette lighter or EmPower-equipped airline seat. (The EmPower in-seat power system can provide either 110-volt AC or 15-volt DC power in an aircraft seat for passenger use.) Then connect the iPod to the laptop with a FireWire cable.

Chapter 21

Sleeping with Your iPod or iPhone

In This Chapter

- Setting the time, date, clock, alarm, and sleep functions
- Locking your iPod or iPhone with a combination lock
- Changing the iPod display settings
- Checking your calendar and sorting your contacts
- Recording voice memos on your iPod
- Customizing your iPod menus and settings

Even if you purchased an iPod simply to listen to music or watch videos, those thoughtful engineers at Apple put a lot more into this device.

Your iPod also keeps time.

Not only that, but the iPod and iPhone models provide you with a timekeeper that enables you to navigate your personal life, such as checking your calendar and To-Do list and setting alarms to wake up to music. You even have a stopwatch for timing; think jogging or commuting. You can look up contact names, addresses, and phone numbers. You can even record dictation, conversations, or oral notes on full-size iPods. This chapter also shows you how to customize the iPod menu to make your iPod more convenient when you're traveling.

Using the Clock

Older iPods (updated to use iPod software 2.0) include a clock and allow you to set the time and date, an alarm, and a sleep timer. Fifth- and sixth-generation iPods and iPod nano let you set multiple clocks for different time zones as well as set alarms for each clock, and also include a stopwatch along with the sleep timer. The iPod touch and iPhone offer the Clock application.

To look at the clock on a sixth- or fifth-generation iPod or iPod nano, choose Extras⇨Clocks from the main menu. To look at the clock on an iPod touch or iPhone, select Clock from the main menu.

To set the date and time with an iPod touch or iPhone, follow these steps:

1. **Choose Settings from the main menu.**

   The Settings menu appears.

2. **Choose General from the Settings menu.**

   The General menu appears.

3. **Choose Date & Time from the General menu.**

   The Date & Time menu appears with options to set the date and time and calendar time zone. The Set Automatically option is turned on by default to set the time and date automatically using the Internet. If this is OK with you, skip the next steps.

4. **(Optional) Touch the On button to turn the Set Automatically off in order to set the time and date manually.**

   After turning off the Set Automatically option, two new options appear: Time Zone and Set Date & Time.

5. **(Optional) Touch the Time Zone option to set the time zone.**

   The virtual keyboard appears; type the name of the city and touch the Return button on the keyboard, and your iPod touch or iPhone looks up the time zone for you.

6. **(Optional) Touch the Set Date & Time option to set the date and time manually.**

   Touch the date to set the date manually, and slide your finger over the slot-machine-style number wheel to select the month, day, and year. Touch the time and slide your finger over the wheel to set the hour, minutes, and AM or PM.

7. **Touch the Date & Time button in the upper left corner of the display to finish and return to the General menu.**

To set the date and time with a sixth-generation iPod or iPod nano, follow these steps:

1. **Press the Menu button until you see the iPod main menu.**
2. **Choose Settings⇨Date & Time.**

   The Date & Time menu appears with selections for setting the date, time, time zone, DST (daylight savings time), 24 hour clock, and the time in the title.

3. **Choose Time Zone.**

   A map appears with a red dot set to your time zone on the map.

4. **Scroll to choose a time zone and press Select.**

   Move the red dot to another zone by scrolling the click wheel — the red dot jumps from one region of the map to another, and the time zone appears below the map. Press the Select button to choose a zone. After selecting it, the Date & Time menu appears again.

5. **Choose Date from the Date & Time menu.**

   The Date display appears with the month field highlighted.

6. **Change the field setting by scrolling the click wheel.**

   Scroll clockwise to go forward and counterclockwise to go backward.

7. **Press the Select button after scrolling to the appropriate setting.**

   The next field is now highlighted.

8. **Repeat Steps 6 and 7 for the day and year.**

   After finishing the year field, the Date & Time menu appears again.

9. **Choose Time from the Date & Time menu.**

   The Time display appears with the hour field highlighted.

10. **Change the field setting by scrolling the click wheel.**

    Scroll clockwise to go forward and counterclockwise to go backward.

11. **Press the Select button after scrolling to the appropriate setting.**

    The next field is now highlighted.

12. **Repeat Steps 10 and 11 for minutes and AM/PM.**

    After finishing the AM/PM field, the Date & Time menu appears again.

To set the date and time with a fifth-generation iPod, follow these steps:

1. **Press the Menu button until you see the iPod main menu.**

2. **Choose Settings⇨Date & Time.**

   A menu appears with selections for setting the time zone, the date and time, the time format, and the time in the title.

3. **Choose Set Time Zone.**

   A list of time zones (actually geographical regions) appears in time zone order, starting with Eniwetok and Midway Island (near the International Date Line) and heading east toward Hawaii, Alaska, the Pacific coast of the United States, and so on around the world to Auckland, just west of the International Date Line. Each region offers a Daylight Saving Time (DST) setting.

4. **Scroll the Time Zone list and choose a time zone.**

   Press the Select button to choose the time zone (DST or standard time) that's right for you. After selecting it, the Date & Time menu appears again.

5. **Choose Set Date & Time.**

   The Date & Time display appears with up and down arrow indicators over the hour field, which is now highlighted.

   To show the military time, choose Time and press the Select button. The option changes from 12-hour to *24-hour* (military style). With 24-hour display, 11 p.m. is displayed as 23:00:00 and not 11:00:00. To switch back to 12-hour, press the Select button again with the Time option highlighted.

6. **Change the hour field setting by using the scroll wheel.**

   Scroll clockwise to go forward and counterclockwise to go backward.

7. **Press the Select button after scrolling to the appropriate setting.**

   The up and down arrow indicators move over to the minutes field, which is now highlighted.

8. **Repeat Steps 6 and 7 for each field of the date and time: minutes, AM/PM, the calendar date, calendar month, and year.**

9. **Press the Select button after setting the year.**

   The Date & Time menu appears again.

To display the time in the menu title, scroll to the Time in Title option in the Date & Time menu and then press the Select button to turn this option On. To stop showing the time in the menu title, press the Select button again to toggle it to Off.

To show the military time, choose the 24 Hour Clock option in the Date & Time menu and press the Select button to turn it on. The option changes from 12-hour to *24-hour* (military style). With 24-hour display, 11 p.m. is displayed as 23:00:00 and not 11:00:00. To switch back to 12-hour, choose the 24 Hour Clock option again and press the Select button to turn it off.

Displaying multiple clocks

With the iPod touch and iPhone, fifth- and sixth-generation iPods, and the iPod nano, you can display clocks with different time zones, which is useful if you traverse time zones or simply want to keep track of time in another time zone. (Maybe you like to know the time in Paris if you're calling from New York.) The initial clock and any clocks you add sport a daytime face (white background and black hands) from 6 a.m. to 5:59 p.m. and a nighttime face (black background with white hands) from 6 p.m. to 5:59 a.m.

To create clocks on an iPod touch or iPhone, select Clock from the main menu and touch the World Clock button along the bottom of the display. To add a clock, touch the plus (+) button in the upper right corner of the display, then type a city name on the virtual keyboard and touch Return, and your iPod touch or iPhone looks up the city's time zone to display the clock. To remove a clock, touch the Edit button in the upper left corner of the display, and touch the minus (-) button next to the clock to delete.

To create more clocks, edit the clocks, or delete additional clocks with fifth- and sixth-generation iPods and the iPod nano, follow these steps:

1. **Press the Menu button until you see the iPod main menu.**
2. **Choose Extras⇨Clocks and highlight a clock.**

   One or more clocks appear (depending on how many you have created), showing the present time and location. If you have more than one clock and you want to edit that clock, scroll the click wheel to highlight the clock to edit.
3. **Press the Select button on the iPod to select the clock.**

   The Add and Edit options appear, along with a Delete option if there is more than one clock.
4. **Scroll the click wheel to select Add, Edit, or Delete and press the Select button.**

   If you select Add or Edit, a list of geographical regions appears in alphabetical order, from Africa to South America. If you select Delete, the clock is deleted and you can skip any more steps.
5. **Scroll the Region list, choose a region, and press the Select button.**

   The City menu appears with a list of cities in the region in alphabetical order.
6. **Scroll the City list, choose a city, and then press the Select button.**

   You return to the list of clocks. You now have added a new clock (or edited a clock if you selected the Edit option).

Setting the alarm clock

Time is on your side with your iPod or iPhone. You can set a beep alarm or playlist to play for your alarm in third-, fourth-, fifth-, and sixth-generation iPod models and the iPhone. You can also connect your iPod or iPhone to speakers and wake up to music. You can set *multiple* alarms with sixth-generation iPods including the iPod nano, iPod touch, and iPhone.

To set an alarm on an iPod touch or iPhone, follow these steps:

1. **Select Clock from the main menu and touch the Alarm button along the bottom of the display.**
2. **To add an alarm, touch the plus (+) button in the upper right corner of the display.**

   The Add Alarm menu appears with options and a slot-machine-style wheel for setting the alarm time.
3. **(Optional) Touch the Repeat option to set the alarm to repeat on other days.**

   You can set it to repeat every Monday, Tuesday, Wednesday, and so on.
4. **(Optional) Touch Sound to select a sound for the alarm.**

   A list of sounds appear; touch a sound to set it for the alarm.
5. **(Optional) Touch Label to enter a text label for the alarm.**

   The label helps you identify the alarm in the Alarm list.
6. **Touch Save in the upper right corner of the display to save the alarm.**

To delete an alarm on an iPod touch or iPhone, select Clock from the main menu and touch the Alarm button along the bottom of the display. Touch the alarm, and touch the Edit button in the upper left corner of the display. The alarm appears with a minus (-) button next to it. Touch the minus (-) button, and then touch the red Delete button that appears, to delete the alarm.

To set an alarm on a sixth-generation iPod classic or iPod nano, follow these steps:

1. **Choose Extras⇨Alarms from the main menu.**

   The options Create Alarm and Sleep Timer appear.
2. **Choose Create Alarm and press the Select button.**

   The Alarms menu appears with options.
3. **Highlight the Alarm option and press the Select button to turn it on.**
4. **Choose Date from the Alarms menu.**

   The Date display appears with the month field highlighted.
5. **Change the field setting by scrolling the click wheel.**

   Scroll clockwise to go forward and counterclockwise to go backward.
6. **Press the Select button after scrolling to the appropriate setting.**

   The next field is now highlighted.

7. **Repeat Steps 5 and 6 for the day and year.**

   After finishing the year field, the Alarms menu appears again.

8. **Choose Time from the Alarms menu.**

   The Time display appears with the hour field highlighted.

9. **Change the field setting by scrolling the click wheel.**

   Scroll clockwise to go forward and counterclockwise to go backward.

10. **Press the Select button after scrolling to the appropriate setting.**

    The next field is now highlighted.

11. **Repeat Steps 9 and 10 for minutes and AM/PM.**

    After finishing the AM/PM field, the Alarms menu appears again.

12. **Choose Repeat from the Alarms menu, and choose a repeat multiple.**

    You can choose to set the alarm to go off once, every day, weekdays, weekends, every week, every month, or every year. After choosing a repeat multiple, the Alarms menu appears again.

13. **Choose Sounds from the Alarms menu and choose a tone or a playlist.**

    The Tones and Playlists options appear. Choose Tones to select a beep or set the alarm to none (no sound). Choose Playlists to select a playlist. After choosing a tone or a playlist, the Alarms menu appears again.

14. **Choose Label from the Alarms menu to set a label to identify this alarm.**

    You can set labels for your alarms so that you can identify them easily in the Alarms menu. Select a label from the prepared list, which includes labels such as Wake up, Work, Class, Appointment, and so on. After choosing a label, the Alarms menu of settings appears again.

15. **Press Menu to return to the Alarms menu that displays your new alarm with its label.**

You can create as many alarms, at different dates and times, as you need. To delete an alarm, select the alarm and choose Delete from the Alarms menu.

When the alarm goes off, the iPod displays the message "You have an alarm" (along with the date and time), and the Dismiss or Snooze options. The playlist (or beep tone) plays until you stop the alarm by selecting the Dismiss or Snooze options. Choose one or the other by scrolling the click wheel and select it by pressing the Select button.

With fifth-generation iPod models, you can set an alarm for each clock. (To create multiple clocks, see “Displaying multiple clocks,” earlier in this chapter.) To set an alarm for a fifth-generation iPod, follow these steps:

1. **Choose Extras⇨Clock from the main menu.**

   In current fifth-generation iPods and iPod nano, the clock has a face with hands. You see any multiple clocks you created and a New Clock.

   In third- and fourth-generation models, the clock is digital, and a menu appears with Alarm Clock, Sleep Timer, and Date & Time options.

2. **In fifth-generation iPods, select a clock and then choose Alarm Clock from the clock’s menu; in older iPods, choose Alarm Clock from the clock’s menu.**

   The Alarm Clock menu appears.

3. **Highlight the Alarm option and press the Select button.**

   `Off` changes to `On`.

4. **Choose Time.**

   The Alarm Time menu appears with up- and down-arrow indicators.

5. **Change the time by scrolling the click wheel.**

   Scroll clockwise to go forward and counterclockwise to go backward. See the description on how to set the time in “Using the Clock,” earlier in this chapter.

6. **Press the Select button after scrolling to the appropriate alarm time.**

   The Alarm Clock menu appears again.

7. **Choose Sound from the Alarm Clock menu.**

   A list appears. The Beep option is at the top of the list, followed by playlists on your iPod, in alphabetical order.

8. **Choose your alarm sound and then press the Select button.**

   If you choose Beep, the alarm beeps without the need for any headphones or speakers. If you choose a playlist, the playlist plays when the alarm goes off, and you do need speakers or headphones to hear the music.

9. **Return to the main menu (press Menu until you see the main menu).**

   A bell icon appears next to any clock that has its alarm set. You can turn off an alarm by performing Steps 1–3; when you select the Alarm option, On toggles to Off.

When the alarm goes off, the playlist (or beep tone) plays until you stop the alarm by pressing the Play/Pause button.

If you set an alarm for a new clock you created (see "Displaying multiple clocks" earlier in this chapter), the alarm goes off at the proper time for that time zone (based on the time kept by your iPod).

For example, you can keep your iPod set to Eastern U.S. time while you're in Los Angeles but use the Los Angeles clock to set your morning alarm.

Setting the sleep timer

Just like when using a clock radio sleep timer, you can set your iPod or iPhone to play music for a while before going to sleep. Although you can display multiple clocks on the iPhone, iPod touch, sixth- and fifth-generation iPods and iPod nano, you can set only one sleep timer.

To set the timer on the iPhone or iPod touch, select Clock from the main menu and touch the Timer button along the bottom of the display. The timer wheel appears with the Start button. Use your finger to scroll the timer wheel to set the timer in hours and minutes. Then touch the When Timer Ends button, and touch Sleep iPod to put the iPod touch or iPhone to sleep when the timer ends (you can also choose to play a sound). Touch Set in the upper right corner of the display to set the Sleep iPod option (or Cancel in the upper left corner to cancel). Finally, touch Start to start the timer.

To set the sleep timer on an iPod classic or iPod nano, choose Extras from the main menu, then select Alarms–Sleep Timer. To set the sleep timer on a fifth-generation iPod, select a clock and then choose Sleep Timer from the clock's menu.

A list of intervals appears, from 0 (Off) up to 120 minutes (2 hours). You can select a time amount or the Off setting (at the top of the list) to turn off the sleep timer. After the iPod shuts itself off or you turn it off, the preference for the Sleep Timer is reset to the default status, Off.

To turn off the iPod, press the Pause button. If you don't press Pause, it remains idle for a few minutes and then shuts itself off.

Using the stopwatch

Sixth- and fifth-generation iPods, iPod nano, iPod touch, and iPhone models feature a stopwatch with a lap timer, which is useful when timing exercises, jogging, race laps, how long it takes the bus to travel across town, or how long your friend takes to recognize the song you're playing. Whatever you want to measure with time, the stopwatch is ready for you.

You can use the iPod's menus, and also play music, audio books, and podcasts, while running the stopwatch. When you play video, the stopwatch continues to count as usual; when you press Menu to switch to the stopwatch display, the video automatically pauses.

To use the stopwatch on an iPod touch or iPhone, follow these steps:

1. **Select Clock from the main menu and touch the Stopwatch button along the bottom of the display.**

   A stopwatch appears with Start and Reset buttons and 00:00.00 (minutes, seconds, and fractions of second) as the stopwatch counter.

2. **Touch the Start button to start counting.**

   The stopwatch starts counting immediately, the left button changes to Stop, and the right button changes to Lap.

3. **(Optional) Touch the Lap button to mark each lap.**

   Touch the Lap button to record each lap. Repeat this step for each lap.

4. **Touch the Stop button to stop counting.**

   The counter stops counting. The left button changes to Start, and the right button changes to Reset. You can resume the count from where you left off by touching Start, or start the count again from zero by touching Reset.

To use the stopwatch on a sixth-generation iPod or iPod nano, follow these steps:

1. **Choose Extras⇨Stopwatch from the main menu.**

   A stopwatch appears with the play/pause icon.

2. **Press the Select button to start counting.**

   The stopwatch starts counting immediately.

3. **(Optional) Press the Select button to mark each lap.**

   Press the Select button to record the current lap time while counting resumes accurately for the next lap. Repeat this step for each lap.

4. **Press the Play/Pause button to stop counting.**

   The counter stops counting and the Stopwatch menu appears. The menu now includes the Current Log option to show the lap timings for the stopwatch session. Also included are previous stopwatch session logs. The iPod saves the stopwatch results in a session log for convenience, so you don't have to write them down.

5. **Select Resume to resume counting, or New Timer to start a new stopwatch session.**

   You can resume the stopwatch session from where you left off, or start a new stopwatch session.

6. **(Optional) Read your stopwatch logs by choosing Current Log or the date of a previous log in the Stopwatch menu.**

7. **(Optional) Delete your stopwatch logs by choosing Clear Logs in the Stopwatch menu.**

To use the stopwatch on a fifth-generation iPod, follow these steps:

1. **Choose Extras⇨Stopwatch⇨Timer from the main menu.**

   A stopwatch appears with Start and Clear buttons and 00:00:00.00 (hours, minutes, seconds, and fractions of second) as the stopwatch counter. Underneath is a lap counter with its own time in smaller digits.

2. **Scroll to highlight the Start button and then press the Select button to push the Start button.**

   The stopwatch starts counting immediately with both the main and lap counters. After these counters begin, the left button changes to Pause, and the right button changes to Lap.

   The stopwatch stops if the counter reaches 24 hours, you connect your iPod to your computer, or you allow your iPod to lapse into hibernation.

3. **(Optional) Enable the Lap button to mark each lap.**

   Scroll to highlight the Lap button and then press the Select button. The current lap time is recorded, the lap time is reset to zero, and counting resumes accurately. However, your iPod displays the total lap time for about five seconds so that you can quickly view it before it changes to reflect the actual count. Repeat this step for each lap.

4. **Select Pause to pause.**

   Scroll to highlight the Pause button and press Select to push the Pause button. Both the main counter and the lap counter stop counting. The left button changes to Resume, and the right button changes to Done.

5. **Click Resume to resume counting, or click Done to finish counting.**

   The iPod saves the main counter and lap counter results in a session log for convenience, so you don't have to write them down. You can read how to retrieve these logs in the following set of steps.

   After clicking Done, the stopwatch display still shows the final results. The buttons revert to Start and Clear.

6. **To reset the stopwatch counters, select the Clear button.**

   Scroll to highlight the Clear button and then press the Select button.

Each time you click the Done button, the stopwatch saves the results of the counters in a session log. Your iPod can store up to five session logs, but it deletes the oldest log when it records a sixth session. To view your session logs, follow these steps:

1. **Choose Extras⇨Stopwatch to see the list of session logs under the Timer option.**
2. **Scroll to highlight the session log you want to see and then press the Select button to see it.**

   The session log includes the date and time of the session, the total time, the shortest and longest lap times, the average lap time, and a list of each individual lap time. You can scroll the session log to see all of it.

To delete a session log, select it and choose Delete.

Choosing Display Settings

Your future might be so bright that you gotta wear shades, but your iPod or iPhone display might not be bright enough. From the Settings menu you can change the timer for the backlight on iPod classic and iPod nano models, set the brightness of the display on all models, and also set the contrast of black-and-white displays. (Color-display iPod models such as the sixth-generation iPod classic, iPod touch, iPod nano, and iPhone offer only a brightness control.) Choose the Settings menu from the main menu.

Backlight timer

An iPod display's backlight turns on when you press a button or use the scroll wheel, and then it turns off after a short amount of time (on iPod touch and iPhone models the display itself turns on when you press a button, and turns off after a short period of time.) On third-generation iPods, the backlight also lights up the iPod buttons.

You can set the backlight on iPods (except the iPod touch) to remain on for a certain interval of time. Choose Settings⇨Backlight from the main menu. A menu appears, giving you the options of 2 seconds, 5 seconds, 10 seconds, 15 seconds, 20 seconds, 30 seconds, and Always On. Select one by scrolling to highlight the selection and then press the Select button.

Using the backlight drains an iPod battery; the longer you set the interval, the more frequently you need to recharge the battery.

To set the backlight to *always* be on, choose Always On. If you want the backlight to *always* be off, choose Always Off. If you set it to always be off, the backlight doesn't turn on automatically when you press any button or use the scroll wheel.

Don't be alarmed if your backlight turns itself on at midnight for a brief flash. The iPod is just setting its internal clock. If you find this annoying, turn off the Backlight Timer.

Brightness and contrast

To adjust the brightness for an iPod or iPhone, choose Settings⇨Brightness from the main menu. The Brightness screen appears with a slider that shows the brightness setting, which ranges from low (a quarter-moon icon on an iPod nano or iPod classic, or a dim sun on an iPhone or iPod touch or older iPod model) to high (a bright sun icon).

On an iPod nano or iPod classic (or older iPod), scroll clockwise to increase the brightness (toward the bright sun) and counterclockwise to decrease the brightness (toward the moon or dim sun).

On an iPod touch or iPhone, slide the brightness slider's knob with your finger to the right to increase the brightness (toward the bright sun) and to the left to decrease the brightness (toward the dim sun).

You can also set the contrast of black-and-white iPod displays to make the black characters appear sharper against the display background. (This feature isn't provided in color-display iPod models.)

To adjust the contrast, choose Settings⇨Contrast from the main menu. The Contrast screen appears with a slider that shows the contrast setting, which ranges from low contrast (a black-and-white dot) to high contrast (a full black dot). Scroll clockwise to increase the contrast (toward the black dot) and counterclockwise to decrease the contrast (toward the black-and-white dot).

You might need to adjust the contrast of a black-and-white iPod if a sharp temperature difference freezes or bakes your iPod. If you leave your iPod in your car overnight in the cold or in direct sunlight, the contrast can change so much that you can't see your iPod display. Slowly, allow the iPod to warm up (don't use the oven or microwave) or cool down. Then adjust the contrast.

If you accidentally set the contrast too dark or too light, you can reset it to the halfway point between too dark and too light by pressing and holding the Menu button for at least four seconds.

Checking Your Calendar

Your iPod or iPhone can accept calendars from calendar applications, such as iCal (Mac) or Outlook (Windows). You can view these calendars (or a blank calendar if you haven't updated your iPod or iPhone with your calendar files). Choose Calendar from the main menu on an iPhone or iPod touch, or choose Extras⇨Calendars on an iPod classic, iPod nano, or older iPod.

The iPhone and iPod touch merge all your specific synchronized calendars into one calendar. Touch the Today button in the upper left corner of the display to see the calendar for today. Touch the List, Day, or Month buttons to change the calendar view to a list, a full day, or a month respectively. Touch any day to see the events on that day, and touch the plus (+) button in the upper right corner of the display to add a new event.

On an iPod classic, iPod nano, or older iPod, you can choose a specific calendar by name or choose All for a merged view of all your calendars. Select a calendar and then scroll the click wheel to go through the days of the calendar. Select an event to see its details. Press the Next and Previous buttons to skip to the next or previous month. To see your To-Do list, choose Extras⇨Calendars⇨To Do's.

If your calendar events use alarms, you can turn on your iPod calendar alarms. Choose Extras⇨Calendars⇨Alarms. Select Alarms once to set the alarm to Beep, select Alarms twice to set it to None (so that only the message for the alarm appears), or select it a third time to set it to Off. (The Alarms choices cycle from Beep to None to Off and then back to Beep.)

Calendars on your iPod or iPhone are far more useful if you synchronize your personal information; turn to Chapter 23 to see how.

Sorting Your Contacts

The bits of information that you're most likely to need on the road are phone numbers and addresses. An iPod or iPhone can store contacts right alongside your music. To see how to put your personal contacts into your iPod or iPhone, check out Chapter 23.

The contact list is sorted automatically, and the iPod or iPhone displays contact names in alphabetical order. You can change how the contacts sort so that you don't have to look up people by their first names (which can be time-consuming with so many friends named Elvis). The sort operation uses the entire name, but you decide whether to use the first name or the surname first.

On sixth-generation iPod classic and iPod nano models and the iPod touch, choose Settings⇨Sort By. (On fifth-generation and older iPods, choose Settings⇨Contacts⇨Sort.) Press the Select button in the scrolling pad (or use your finger with an iPod touch) for each option:

- **First (First Last on older iPods):** Sorts the contact list by first name, followed by the last name, so that *Mick Jagger* sorts under *Mick* (after *Mick Abrahams* but before *Mick Taylor*).
- **Last (Last, First on older iPods):** Sorts the contacts by last name, followed by the first name, so that *Brian Jones* sorts under *Jones.* (*Jones, Brian* appears after *Jones, Alice* but before *Jones, Norah.*)

On iPhone models, choose Settings⇨Phone⇨Sort Order, then touch one of these options:

- **First, Last:** Sorts the contact list by first name, followed by the last name.
- **Last, First:** Sorts the contacts by last name, followed by the first name.

On fifth-generation and older iPod models and the iPhone, you can display contacts by last or first name. On a fifth-generation or older iPod, choose Settings⇨Contacts⇨Display and then press the Select button in the scrolling pad for each option; on an iPhone, choose Settings⇨Phone⇨Display Order, then touch one of these options:

- **First Last:** Displays the contacts list by first name and then last name, as in *Ringo Starr.*
- **Last, First:** Displays the contacts list by last name followed by a comma and the first name, as in *McCartney, Paul.*

Setting the Combination Lock

If you think your iPod or iPhone might fall into the wrong hands, consider setting a combination lock, which is available in sixth- and fifth-generation iPods, the iPod nano, the iPod touch, and the iPhone. You can set a four-digit combination that locks the navigation controls, preventing anyone else from selecting content. ***Note:*** The lock works only when your iPod or iPhone is not attached to a computer.

If you're playing music when you lock your iPod or iPhone, the music continues playing — and you can even use the Play/Pause button to pause and resume playback — but you can't navigate the iPod or iPhone until you provide the combination. You also can't change the volume.

To conserve power, you can force your iPod to go to sleep by pressing the Play/Pause button, but it won't unlock. When it awakes, it remembers everything — including its combination.

To set a combination lock for your iPhone or iPod touch, follow these steps:

1. **Choose Settings⇨General⇨Passcode Lock from the main menu.**

   The Set Passcode display appears.

2. **Enter a four-number passcode by touching numbers in the calculator-style keypad.**

   You can touch the Cancel button to cancel, or enter the four numbers to set the passcode.

3. **Enter the same passcode number again to confirm the passcode.**

   After entering the passcode again, the Passcode Lock menu appears with the Turn Passcode Off, Change Passcode, and Require Passcode options.

4. **Touch General to return to the General menu.**

   Before doing so, you can turn the passcode off, change it, or set the Require Passcode option to Immediately, After 1 minute, or after several minutes.

To set a combination lock for your sixth-generation iPod or iPod nano, follow these steps:

1. **Choose Extras⇨Screen Lock.**

   The Screen Lock icon appears with your combination lock set to zeros.

2. **Select the first number of the combination by scrolling the click wheel.**

   While you scroll with your iPod, the first digit of the combination changes. You can also press the Previous/Rewind or Next/Fast-Forward button to scroll through numbers.

3. **Press the Select button to pick a number.**

   This sets your choice for the first number and moves on to the next number of the combination.

4. **Scroll to select each number of the combination and then press the Select button to set the number.**

   Repeat this step for each number of the combination. When you pick the last number, the message "Confirm Combination" appears. Repeat steps 2 and 3 for each number of the combination to confirm it. When you finish confirming the combination, the Lock and Reset options appear.

5. **Choose Lock or Reset.**

   Select Lock to lock the iPod, or Reset to reset the combination to zeros and return to Step 2. To unlock the iPod after locking it, press any button and then repeat steps 2 and 3 to enter each number of the combination.

Don't forget this combination! Use a four-digit number that is easy to commit to memory.

To lock your iPod with this combination, follow these steps:

1. **(Optional) Start playing music before locking the iPod.**
2. **Choose Extras⇨Screen Lock.**

   The iPod displays the Lock or Reset options.

3. **Choose Lock.**

When it's locked, a lock icon appears on your iPod even while music is playing.

To unlock a locked iPod or iPhone, you must do one of the following:

- **Enter the same combination.** After correctly entering the combination, the iPod unlocks and returns to the last viewed screen.
- **Attach the iPod to the computer you used to update the iPod with iTunes.** When you disconnect it after iTunes updating, the iPod is no longer locked.
- **Restore your iPod to its original factory settings.** As we describe in Chapter 24, this erases everything in the process. This is, of course, a measure of last resort.

Don't bother to call Apple to see whether the company can unlock your iPod for you. If you can't attach it to the proper computer or enter the correct combination, your only recourse is to restore the iPod to its factory conditions.

To set the combination lock on fifth-generation iPod models, follow these steps:

1. **Choose Extras⇨Screen Lock.**

   The Screen Lock menu appears.

2. **From the Screen Lock menu that appears, choose Set Combination.**

   The Enter New Code display appears.

3. **Select the first number of the combination by scrolling the click wheel.**

   While you scroll with your iPod, the first digit of the combination changes in the Enter New Code display. You can also press the Previous/Rewind or Next/Fast-Forward button to scroll through numbers.

4. **Press the Select button to confirm.**

   This confirms your choice for the first number and moves on to the next number of the combination.

5. **Scroll to select each number of the combination and then press the Select button to confirm.**

   Repeat this step for each number of the combination. When you confirm the last digit, the iPod displays the Screen Lock menu.

To lock your fifth-generation iPod with this combination, follow these steps:

1. **(Optional) Start playing music before locking the iPod.**
2. **Choose Extras⇨Screen Lock⇨Turn Screen Lock On.**

   The iPod displays this message:

   ```
   If you forget the code, connect iPod to your computer
   to unlock it.
   ```

   Underneath the message are the Lock and Cancel choices.

3. **Choose Lock.**

When it's locked, an Enter Code display appears on your iPod even while music is playing. A key in the upper-right corner indicates that your iPod is locked.

To change the combination lock for a fifth-generation iPod, choose Extras⇨Screen Lock⇨Change Combination. The Enter Old Code display appears for you to enter the original combination. After entering it correctly, the Enter New Code display appears, and you can enter a new combination.

If you frequently turn your Screen Lock on and off, you might want to add it to your iPod main menu for fast access. See "Customizing the Menu and Settings," later in this chapter.

Speaking into Your iPod

If you record conversations and interviews on the road, throw out your antiquated tape recorder. Your iPod can record hundreds of hours of voice-quality memos, meetings, notes, and interviews with a touch of a button. All you need is an accessory for your iPod model designed for voice recording, such as the MicroMemo from XtremeMac ($59.95; `www.xtrememac.com`) for sixth- and fifth-generation iPods. For third- and fourth-generation iPod models, check out the tiny Belkin iPod Voice Recorder (about $30; `www.belkin.com`) or the Griffin iTalk Voice Recorder (about $40; `www.griffintechnology.com`).

The voice memos are stored on your iPod, where you can review them immediately via the built-in speaker of the accessory, headphones, or speakers. Even better, the voice memos are automatically transferred to your iTunes library for archiving or reviewing on your computer.

The MicroMemo plugs in to the dock connector on your sixth- or fifth-generation iPod and includes a flexible, detachable microphone (you can also use any other input device with a 3.5mm connector) and a built-in speaker.

The Belkin iPod Voice Recorder and the Griffin iTalk Voice Recorder attach to the remote connector on the top of full-size third- and fourth-generation iPods (updated by version 2.1 of the iPod software or newer). Sorry, you can't use voice recorders with the iPod nano, iPod mini, or iPod shuffle.

Recording voice memos

To record voice memos, connect the voice recorder to the iPod and choose Extras⇨Voice Memos⇨Record Now. The iPod displays the Record screen. Press the Play/Pause button to begin recording and then point the voice recorder microphone toward the sound source. (With the Belkin iPod Voice Recorder, a green LED turns on when recording.) Pause the recording by pressing the Play/Pause button again.

When you finish recording, press the Menu button. The audio files for voice memos are stored on your iPod in the Recordings folder, using the date and time of the recording as the filename.

Playing back voice memos

To play a voice memo, choose Extras⇨Voice Memos and choose the voice memo from the list. (The Voice Memos menu doesn't appear unless the voice recorder is connected.) Then choose Play or press the Play/Pause button.

The voice memo plays just like any other song on your iPod: Press Play/Pause to pause playback and press it again to resume. You can hear the playback in the voice recorder's tiny speaker; attach headphones to your iPod; or connect your iPod to a home stereo, car stereo, or self-powered speakers.

You can play music through the voice recorder speaker by connecting the accessory to your iPod and playing. This trick comes in handy if you set your iPod as an alarm clock to play a music playlist; you can hear music when you wake up without having to connect the iPod to speakers. See the earlier section, "Setting the alarm clock."

Managing voice memos in iTunes

Just like your music, your voice memos synchronize automatically with your iTunes library if you set your iPod to update automatically. (See Chapter 12 to find out how to set your iPod to update automatically.) iTunes stores the voice memos in the library and creates a Voice Memos playlist so that you can find them easily.

If you update your iPod manually, you can drag voice memo files directly from the Recordings folder to your hard drive or drag and drop them over the iTunes window. ***Note:*** The iPod must already be enabled as a hard drive. (Check out Chapter 22 to see how to enable your iPod as a hard drive.)

Voice memos are stored as WAV files. If you want to archive them in a format that takes up less hard drive space, convert them by using an AAC or MP3 encoder, as we describe in Chapter 19.

Customizing the Menu and Settings

When traveling or using your iPod in situations or environments where portability is important, you might want to customize your iPod menu and display to make doing things easier, such as selecting certain albums, displaying the time, setting the screen lock, displaying menus with backlighting turned on longer than usual, and so on.

The Settings menu in the iPod main menu offers ways to customize your iPod experience by changing the main menu to have more choices. Choose Settings⇨Main Menu from the main menu. The iPod displays a list of menus; each menu is set to either On or Off. *On* means that the menu appears in the iPod main menu; *Off* means that the menu doesn't appear in the main menu.

Don't worry; the menus are still where they are supposed to be. Turning one to On simply adds it to the main menu as well.

For example, to put the Screen Lock option on the iPod main menu, choose Settings⇨Main Menu, scroll to the Screen Lock option, and select it to add it to the main menu. Select it again to remove it from the main menu.

Other ways to customize your experience include setting the Clicker sound and setting the language to use for the menus. The options in the Settings menu are

- **About:** This option displays information about the iPod, including the number of songs, videos, and photos; how much space is used; how much space is available; the software version in use; and the serial and model numbers.
- **Main Menu:** This option allows you to customize the main menu on iPods that use iPod software 2.0 or newer. For example, you can add items from other menus, such as Artists or Songs from the Music menu (Browse menu in older iPods) to the main menu.
- **Backlight:** Use this option to set the backlight to remain on for a certain amount of time by pressing a button or using the scroll wheel. Specify 2 seconds, 5 seconds, and so on. You can also set it to always be On.

  Using backlight drains an iPod battery. The longer you set the interval, the more you need to recharge the battery.

- **Audiobooks:** Use this option to set audio books to play at normal speed, slower, or faster.
- **Clicker:** When this setting is On, you hear a click when you press a button; when it's Off, you don't hear a click. With color-display, fourth-generation iPod models, the Clicker can be set to Speaker (the iPod speaker), Headphones, Both, or Off.
- **Language:** This option sets the language used in all the menus. See Chapter 1 for how to set the language.
- **Legal:** This option displays the legal message that accompanies Apple products.
- **Reset All Settings:** This option resets all the items on the Settings menu in your iPod, returning them to their original state. However, your music and data files on the iPod are not disturbed. This is not the same as resetting (and restarting) the iPod software itself; choosing Reset All Settings simply returns all settings to their defaults. See Chapter 24 for how to reset the iPod itself.

Chapter 22

Using Your iPod as a Hard Drive

In This Chapter

- Enabling your iPod to work as a hard drive
- Opening and copying files to iPod folders
- Copying notes and text files to your iPod
- Adding text guides, news feeds, and electronic books to your iPod

You have a device in your pocket that can play music and videos, sort your contacts, remind you of events, wake you up in the morning, and tuck you in at night. Did you also know that you can use your iPod to keep a safe backup of your most important files?

You read that right. Windows and Mac users can put their most important files on an iPod and use it just like a hard drive. You can also copy applications and utility programs or even copy your entire User folder to your iPod (if you have enough room after putting music on it). The handy iPod shuffle, which plugs directly into a USB connection, is designed to double as a USB flash memory drive for portable file storage.

You can also use software such as Jax from JoeSoft (`www.joesoft.com`) to add travel directions, weather forecasts, stock quotes, movie listings, and even gas prices to your iPod as text — as well as local news from selected news readers.

To learn more about backing up data on your iPod, including putting versions of the Mac OS X or Linux on your iPod, visit this book's companion Web site.

Enabling an iPod as a Hard Drive

You can use any iPod, including an iPod shuffle, as an external hard drive (or in the case of iPod shuffle or iPod nano, as a flash memory drive). And like any hard drive, you can transfer files and applications from your computer to your iPod and take them with you. An iPod is smart enough to keep your files separate from your content libraries so that you don't accidentally erase them when you update your iTunes library and photo library. And because your iPod is *with you,* it's as safe as you are.

As shipped, an iPod is formatted as a Macintosh hard drive and can be connected to any Mac. When you connect it to Windows, an iPod is reformatted as a Windows hard drive. You can then connect it to any Windows PC or any Mac.

If you format an iPod for Windows first, you can transfer files between Mac and Windows computers. A Mac can use Windows-formatted hard drives, but Windows can't use Mac-formatted hard drives. To reformat an iPod, restore it to its original factory conditions (which erases all content and data), and then reconnect it on a Windows computer to set it up, as described in Chapter 2.

We don't recommend using an iPod regularly as a hard drive to launch applications because iPods are designed for sustained playback of music and video. You can eventually burn out the device by using it to launch applications. Instead, use its external hard drive capabilities for backing up and copying files. Copy applications to a hard drive before launching them.

To use your iPod shuffle as an external flash memory hard drive and manage space on the iPod shuffle (allocating music and data space), see Chapter 12.

To use your full-size iPod, iPod mini, or iPod nano as an external hard drive, follow these steps:

1. **Connect your iPod to your computer.**
2. **Select the iPod name in the iTunes Source pane.**

   The iPod summary page appears, as shown in Figure 22-1.
3. **Select the Enable Disk Use option and then click Apply.**

   The Enable Disk Use option is available if your iPod is set to automatically synchronize music or videos with your iTunes library. If you already set your iPod to manually manage music and videos (see Chapter 12), this option is grayed out because it isn't needed, as setting the iPod to manually manage content already enables you to use it as a hard drive.

After enabling your iPod for disk use, you must always remember to properly eject your iPod before disconnecting it from your computer. Click the Eject button next to the iPod name in the iTunes Source pane to eject the iPod.

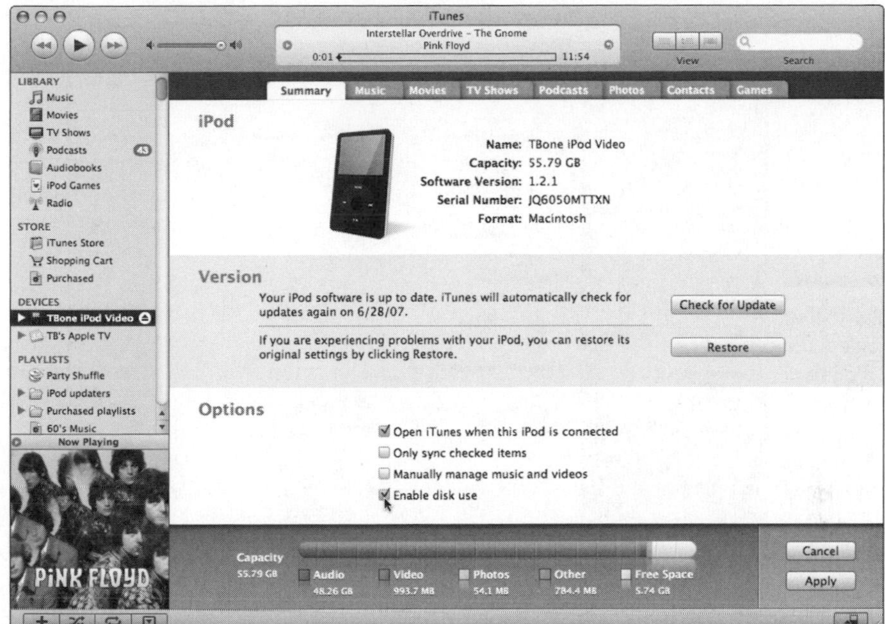

Figure 22-1: Enable an iPod as a hard drive.

If iTunes isn't running, an alternate way to eject a disk-enabled iPod on a Mac is to use the Finder to drag the iPod icon to the Trash icon, which turns into an Eject button when you drag the iPod icon onto it. Or, just right-click the iPod name or icon and then choose Eject from the shortcut menu.

An alternate way to eject a disk-enabled iPod on a Windows PC is to right-click the iPod name or icon and then choose Eject from the shortcut menu.

After ejecting an iPod, wait until its display shows either the `OK to disconnect` message on older models or the main menu on newer models. You can then disconnect the iPod from its dock or disconnect the dock from the computer. Don't ever disconnect an iPod before ejecting it. You might have to reset your iPod.

Opening iPod Folders

On a Windows PC, you can use My Computer or Windows Explorer to open iPod folders, view their contents, and transfer data to and from the iPod. If you open the My Computer window, the iPod appears as an external hard drive, as shown in Figure 22-2. Windows automatically assigns the iPod hard drive to a Windows drive letter. (The iPod in the figure is named *Journeyman* and is assigned to Drive E.)

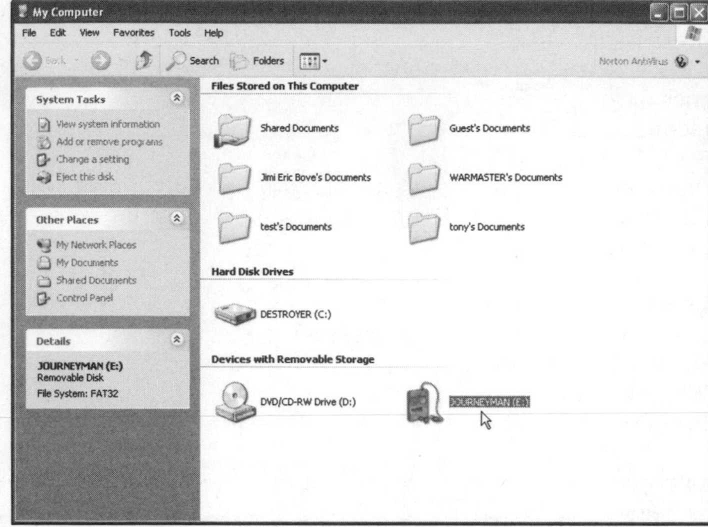

Figure 22-2: Select the iPod hard drive in the My Computer window.

The iPod hard drive opens up to show several folders, including Calendars, Contacts, and Notes (see Figure 22-3). You might also have other folders, depending on the iPod model; for example, a fifth- or sixth-generation video iPod includes a Photos folder. You can add new folders, rename your new folders, and generally use the iPod as a hard drive.

Don't rename the folders already provided on your iPod because they link directly to functions on the iPod. For example, the Calendars folder links to the Calendar menu on the iPod.

You can drag files or folders to the iPod window. To keep data organized, create new folders on your iPod and then copy files and folders to the newly created folders. To copy files and folders in Windows, use the drag-and-drop method in the My Computer window or Windows Explorer, or copy and paste the files or folders. On a Mac, use the Finder to drag files and folders to the newly created folders on your iPod.

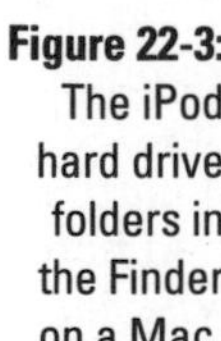

Figure 22-3: The iPod hard drive folders in the Finder on a Mac.

To delete files and folders from an iPod, select the filenames or folders and then press Backspace or choose File⇨Delete from the Windows Explorer menu, just like you do with your internal hard drive. On a Mac, select the filenames or folders and choose File⇨Move to Trash, or drag them to the Trash icon.

Don't use a hard drive reformatting utility to erase or format your iPod's hard drive. If you erase your iPod's hard drive this way, it might be unable to play music and videos.

Here how to see how much free space is left on your iPod. On a Mac, use the Finder to select the iPod icon on the Desktop and then choose File⇨Show Info. You can also choose Settings⇨About from the iPod main menu. Use your Windows PC to select the iPod icon in My Computer and then choose File⇨Properties.

We don't recommend using an iPod regularly as a hard drive to launch applications because iPods are designed for sustained playback of music and video. You can eventually burn out the device by using it to launch applications. Instead, use its external hard drive capabilities for backing up and copying files. Copy applications to a hard drive before launching them.

Adding Notes and Text

You can add text notes to your iPod so that you can view them on the iPod display — all sorts of notes, such as driving directions, weather, or even news. If you use your iPod only for music, you might want notes about the music. This feature works with iPods that run iPod software 2.0 or newer (including iPod mini and all iPods that use the dock connector).

Using the Notes folder

In a perfect world, you could rip audio CDs and also capture all the information in the *liner notes* — the descriptions of who played which instruments, where the CD was produced, and other details. Then, while sharing your iPod music with others, you could view the liner notes on the iPod screen whenever a question arises about the music.

You can almost achieve the same result by typing some of the liner notes (or any text you want) into a word-processing program, such as TextEdit (Mac) or Notepad (Windows). You can then save the document as a text-only file (with the `.txt` filename extension) and drag it to the Notes folder of your iPod.

You must save documents as text-only files to view them on an iPod. If you use a word processor, such as Microsoft Word, choose File⇨Save As and choose Text Only (or Text Only with Line Breaks) from the Save As Type pop-up menu in Windows or from the Format pop-up menu on a Mac. Notes text files can be up to 4K in size — roughly two or three printed pages of information. You can transfer up to 1,000 notes.

Text files in the Notes folder are organized by filename. You can view these notes files by choosing Extras⇨Notes. Make sure that your notes have descriptive filenames so that you can easily scroll the list of notes files to find the notes you want.

Your iPod can also display a folder hierarchy in the Notes folder, allowing you to organize your notes by creating folders (using the Finder with your iPod mounted as a hard drive) and putting notes files within the folders in the Notes folder.

Notes can include basic HTML tags (used on Web pages), such as paragraph markers (`<P>` and `</P>`) and line breaks (`<BR>`). HTML tags can define links to other notes text files and to audio files. Software companies, such as Talking Panda (`http://talkingpanda.com`), have created textual guides you can install in the iPod Notes folder that use these tags and links to present text on the iPod screen and play audio files. You can find out how to develop your own HTML tags by downloading Using iPod as a Tour Guide from the following site:

```
http://developer.apple.com/hardwaredrivers/ipod/iPodNoteReaderGuide.pdf
```

To navigate the Notes section of your iPod, use the iPod controls as follows:

- Press the Select button to open a note from its folder, just like playing a song in an album.
- Use the scroll wheel to navigate the list of notes in a folder as well as text in a note.
- When you scroll through text, iPod jumps from link to link, highlighting each link. When a link is already highlighted, press the Select button to follow the link. To go back to the previous link, press the Menu button.
- To go up to the folder that contains the note text file, press the Menu button to go back through the links until the iPod displays the folder.

Adding guides, books, and news feeds

Do you want the latest news, weather, sports scores, or driving directions available at the touch of a button of your iPod? How about lessons on speaking French, German, Italian, Spanish, or other languages? Enterprising software entrepreneurs have filled the vacuum left by Apple with accessories that provide displayable text on your iPod screen, such as the following:

- **VoodooPad** (www.flyingmeat.com/voodoopad) for Mac OS X lets you save linked pages as Word documents, Rich Text Format (RTF) files, or HTML to view in a Web browser. After you're inside iPod Notes, VoodooPad-linked words show up for you to click, and you can go from page to page just like you were using VoodooPad — only with an iPod scroll wheel instead of a mouse.
- **Jax for iPod** (www.joesoft.com) for Mac OS X offers synchronized feeds for news, weather forecasts, movie listings, stock quotes, horoscopes, sections of Web pages, and directions.
- **NewsLife** (www.thinkmac.co.uk/newslife), also for Mac OS X, lets you keep tabs on world news Web sites and blogs and also lets you transfer entire Web pages.
- **iLingo** (http://talkingpanda.com/ilingo.php) for Mac or Windows offers language lessons, with over 400 essential words and phrases of your chosen language, organized as Notes folders and files. It also includes audio files created by native speakers that provide proper pronunciation for all included phrases.
- **iBar** (http://talkingpanda.com/ibar.php) for Mac or Windows offers drink recipes with ingredients, instructions for mixing and proper garnishing, and advice on appropriate serving glassware. Many recipes are linked to audio anecdotes about the origin of specific cocktails as well as instructions on how to mix them.
- **EphPod 2** (www.ephpod.com) for Windows lets you update your iPod with news, weather, and other information updates.
- **Book2Pod** (www.tomsci.com/book2pod) is a shareware program for a Mac that allows you to read entire books on your iPod display. **iPodLibrary** (www.sturm.net.nz) is a similar shareware program for Windows.
- Mac users can also take advantage of the Notes folder and other iPod features by using some of the handy **AppleScripts** provided for iTunes and the iPod, which you can download from the Apple site (www.apple.com/applescript/ipod).

Chapter 23

Synchronizing Personal Info with Your iPod or iPhone

In This Chapter

- Synchronizing iPod and iPhone calendars and contacts automatically
- Copying calendar and contact files manually
- Exporting calendars and contact information
- Using utilities to copy content

We chose iPods for music and videos, but we also find it useful while traveling for viewing the personal information — contacts, appointments, events, and To-Do tasks — that we manage on our computers. And of course, an iPhone lets you dial your contact phone numbers as well as keep track of your personal info. The big difference with an iPhone is that you can add personal info on-the-go, and synchronize that information back with your computer.

iPods accepts industry-standard iCalendar and vCalendar files for calendars and To-Do lists, which you can export from most applications that offer calendars and To-Do lists. It also accepts industry-standard *vCards* (virtual business cards), which are records containing contact information for people, including street and e-mail addresses, phone numbers, and so on.

If you're a Mac user, you have it easy: You can use the free iCal and Address Book applications that come with Mac OS X. If you're a Windows user, you can choose between Microsoft Outlook (and its accompanying Address Book) and Outlook Express. In either case, you can automatically synchronize the information with your iPod or iPhone calendar and contact list with iTunes. iPods offer one-way synchronization from computer to iPod, while the iPhone offers two-way synchronization so that information you add to your iPhone is copied back to your computer.

If you don't mind updating your iPod manually with contacts and calendar information, you have even more choices in applications as long as you use standard formats that work with the iPod. You also have choices of third-party utilities for putting the information on an iPod as well as the tried-and-true technique of exporting (or dragging) information to your iPod.

You probably already know how to manage your calendar activities and your contacts on your computer. In fact, you're probably knee-deep in *vCards* (virtual business cards) for your Address Book, and the calendars in your vCalendar files look like they were drawn up in the West Wing. If not, visit this book's companion Web site to learn more about adding and editing contacts and calendar information on your Mac or Windows computer.

Synchronizing Contacts and Calendars

To synchronize your iPod or iPhone with contacts and calendars, follow these steps:

1. **Connect your iPod or iPhone to your computer.**

   iTunes launches automatically (if it isn't running already).

2. **Select the iPod or iPhone name in the iTunes Source pane in the Devices section.**

   If iTunes launched automatically, the iPod or iPhone should already be selected; if it isn't, select it. The iPod or iPhone summary page appears to the right of the Source pane.

3. **Click the Contacts tab for an iPod or the Info tab for an iPhone.**

   The Contacts and Calendars synchronization options page appears for an iPod, as shown in Figure 23-1. The Info page appears for an iPhone, as shown in Figure 23-2, offering not only Contacts and Calendars but also, if you scroll the page, Mail Accounts, Web Browser information, and Advanced sync options.

4. **Select the option to synchronize contacts.**

   On a Mac, select the Sync Address Book Contacts check box (refer to Figure 23-1 for an iPod or Figure 23-2 for an iPhone). For color-display iPods you can also select the option to Include Contacts' Photos (these are copied automatically with the iPhone). The iPhone Info page also lets you sync with Yahoo! Address Book contacts.

   On a Windows PC, select the Sync Contents From option and choose Windows Address Book or Microsoft Outlook from the drop-down menu, as shown in Figure 23-3.

5. **Select the All Contacts option. (Alternatively, select the Selected Groups option and choose which groups to synchronize.)**

   You can synchronize all contacts (as in Figure 23-2 and Figure 23-3) or just selected groups of contacts (such as the iPod_contacts group, as shown in Figure 23-1). To choose groups, select the check box next to each group in the list; scroll the list to see more groups.

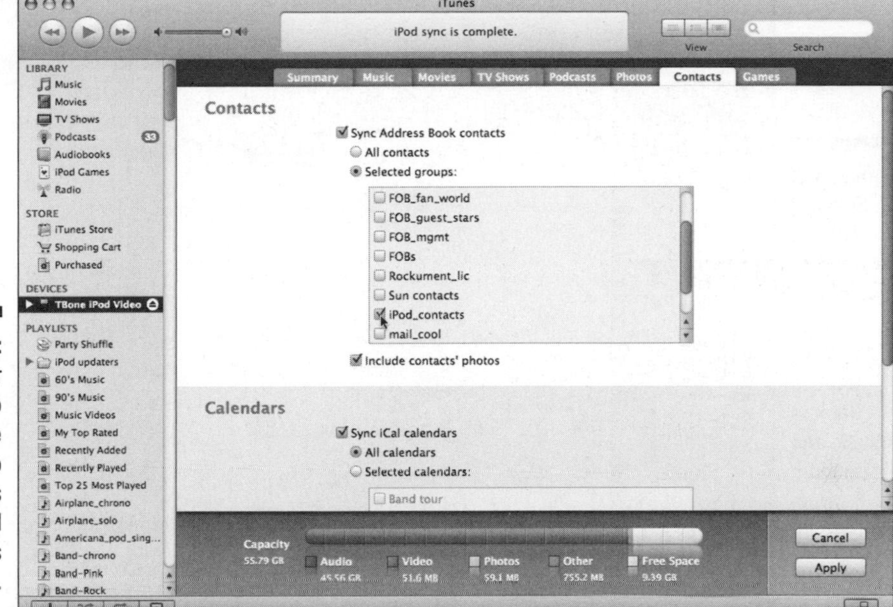

Figure 23-1: Set your iPod to synchronize with a group of contacts and all calendars on a Mac.

Figure 23-2: Set your iPhone to synchronize all contacts and calendars on a Mac.

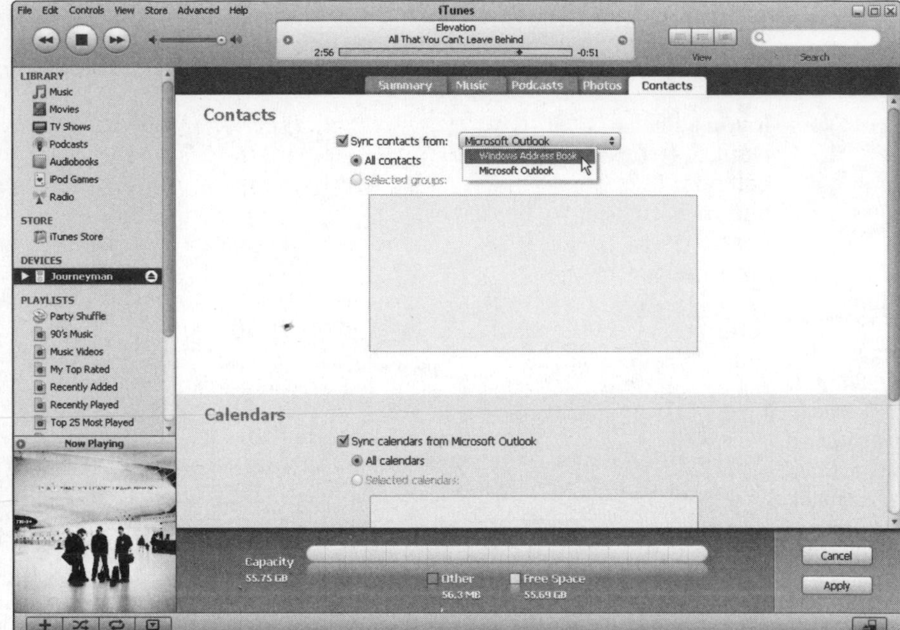

Figure 23-3: Set your iPod to synchronize contacts with Windows Address Book or Outlook, and all calendars from Outlook, on a Windows PC.

6. **To synchronize calendars, scroll the page and select the Sync iCal Calendars option (Mac) or the Sync Calendars from Microsoft Outlook option (Windows PC).**

7. **Select the All Calendars option. (Alternatively, select the Selected Calendars option and choose the calendars to synchronize.)**

   You can synchronize all calendars or just those you select. To choose specific calendars, select the check box next to each calendar in the list. The iPhone provides the Do Not Sync Events Older Than *xx* Days option, in which you can set the *xx* number of days.

8. **Click Apply to apply the changes. (Alternatively, click Cancel to cancel the changes.)**

   iTunes starts to synchronize your iPod or iPhone. Wait until it finishes synchronization before ejecting and disconnecting your iPod or iPhone. The iTunes status pane (at the top) displays the message `Sync is Complete`.

9. **After iTunes finishes synchronizing, eject the iPod or iPhone by clicking the Eject button, and then disconnect your iPod or iPhone.**

   Remember to wait for the `OK to disconnect` message or the iPod main menu before disconnecting your iPod.

After setting the synchronization options, every time you connect your iPod or iPhone, iTunes automatically synchronizes your device with your calendars and contacts.

If you select a calendar or a group of contacts to be synchronized and later want to remove that particular calendar or group of contacts, deselect the calendar (see the preceding Step 7) or the group (see the preceding Step 5) and then click Apply to resynchronize. iTunes synchronizes only the group of contacts and calendars selected, removing from an iPod or iPhone any that aren't selected.

After you synchronize and otherwise finish using your iPod with your computer, be sure to eject the device. If you forget this, the iPod hard drive might become unresponsive, and you might need to reset the device.

Adding Calendars Manually to an iPod

If you use an iPod as a hard drive, you can copy calendar files directly to the Calendars folder on your iPod (you can't copy manually to an iPhone). You can copy industry-standard iCalendar or vCalendar files, which many applications (including Microsoft Entourage, Outlook, and Palm Desktop) can export.

In most cases, you can drag an iCalendar file (with an `.ics` filename extension) or a vCalendar file (with a `.vcs` filename extension) to your iPod Calendars folder. To save calendar information in the iCalendar format from Outlook, you must save each appointment separately as an ICS (iCalendar) file. Follow these steps:

1. **Select the appointment in the calendar view or open the appointment by double-clicking it.**
2. **Choose File⇨Save As.**
3. **Choose iCalendar from the Save As Type pop-up menu and then choose a destination for the ICS file.**

   The destination can be either a folder on your hard drive or the iPod Calendars folder. If you choose a folder on your hard drive, be sure to copy the files to the iPod Calendars folder.
4. **Click Save.**

View your calendars on an iPod by choosing Extras⇨Calendars⇨All. Select a calendar and then use the scroll wheel to scroll through the days of the calendar, or select an event to see its details. Press the Next and Previous buttons to skip to the next or previous month. To see your To Do list, choose Extras⇨Calendars⇨To Do.

Although using automatic synchronization removes any calendar that isn't set to be synchronized, you can also remove a calendar manually. To remove a calendar from your iPod, connect the iPod to your computer and enable the iPod as a hard drive (see Chapter 22). You can then open the Calendars folder on the iPod and delete the calendar file. You can also copy calendar files from the iPod to your hard drive.

Adding Contacts Manually to an iPod

If you use an iPod as a hard drive, you can copy contacts in vCard files directly to the Contacts folder on your iPod (you can't copy manually to an iPhone).

A vCard, or *virtual business card,* is a standard format for exchanging personal information. An iPod sorts and displays contacts in the vCard format, and you can use separate vCard files for each person or use a group vCard file that contains records for many people.

After enabling your iPod as a hard drive (see Chapter 22), you can export your contacts as vCards directly into the Contacts folder of your iPod. In most cases, you can drag vCard-formatted contacts from the application's address book to an iPod Contacts folder.

You can copy one card, a group of cards, or even the entire list as a vCard file (with a `.vcf` filename extension) by dragging the vCard file into the Contacts folder. Contacts must be in the vCard format to use with an iPod.

You can use address book applications such as Outlook to export vCard files directly to your iPod. For example, in Outlook, you can export a vCard file for a contact directly into your iPod Contacts folder by following these steps:

1. **Choose File⇨Export to vCard.**
2. **Choose the iPod as the destination drive from the Save In pop-up menu.**
3. **Select the Contacts folder to save the contacts file.**

Using Utilities to Copy Files and Music

The iPod and iPhone have spawned a thriving industry of third-party accessories and products. Some of the most useful products are utility programs that expand the capabilities of an iPod or your ability to synchronize or otherwise copy information to (and from) an iPod. Full-featured programs have even been designed as replacements for iTunes. With so many programs to check out, you might be overwhelmed. We selected some of the best programs for Mac and Windows (as of this writing).

Keep in mind that with programs that allow music copying functions, copying copyrighted material to other computers without permission is illegal. Don't steal music (or anything else, for that matter).

Mac utilities

Third-party offerings for Mac have focused on extending the capabilities of an iPod, such as copying music from an iPod to a computer and updating an iPod with contacts and calendar information. Take a glance at the following examples:

- **iPDA (`www.zapptek.com/ipda`):** With this software, you can transfer personal information to your iPod from Entourage, Mail, Address Book, and iCal. You can even download weather forecasts and news headlines directly to your iPod.
- **iPod Access (`www.findleydesigns.com/ipodaccess`):** This comprehensive utility lets you transfer songs from an iPod to a Mac (Windows version also available) with song information and iTunes ratings. Loaded with features, iPod Access supports On-The-Go playlists and playing music and video directly from an iPod. It's available for $19.99 from Findley Designs, Inc.
- **Senuti (`www.fadingred.org/senuti`):** This program lets you copy songs to your computer from your iPod. You can search for songs and even play songs directly from your iPod with the program. Senuti reads the playlists on your iPod and lets you to transfer them to your computer. You can also automatically add songs to your iTunes library.
- **iPodRip (`www.thelittleappfactory.com/application.php?app=iPodRip`):** This third-party utility, available from The Little App Factory for $14.95, lets you transfer music from your iPod to your iTunes library and listen to music on your iPod through your computer (saving hard drive space). It supports all iPod song formats, including MP3, AAC, Protected AAC, and Audible.com books.
- **YamiPod (`www.yamipod.com/main/modules/home`):** Yet Another Manager for iPod (YAMiPod, get it?) is a freeware application that lets you copy music files from your iPod to your computer and vice versa. It can copy playlists, really simple syndication (RSS) news feeds, and podcasts; and synchronize your iPod with computers running Mac OS X, Windows, or Linux. You can run it directly from your iPod.

Windows utilities

Many third-party programs exist for Windows, and they do everything from extending the capabilities of an iPod and updating contacts and calendar information to replacing the need for MusicMatch Jukebox and iTunes.

- **iPodSync (`www.ipod-sync.com`):** Keep Outlook calendars, contacts, tasks, and notes synchronized between Windows and an iPod. iPodSync exports industry standard vCards for contacts and uses the iCalendar format for appointment information. iPodSync can even synchronize Outlook notes and tasks.
- **EphPod 2 (`www.ephpod.com`):** This utility lets you update your iPod with contacts from Outlook. It's a full-featured Windows application that you can use in place of MusicMatch Jukebox or iTunes. It supports standard Winamp (M3U) playlists and can synchronize an iPod with a library of music files. It imports Outlook contacts and also lets you create and edit your own contacts. EphPod can also download the latest news, weather, eBooks, and movie listings to an iPod.
- **Outpod (`http://outpod.stoer.de`):**This utility lets you export contact and calendar information in bulk from Microsoft Outlook to vCard and vCalendar files, which you can then drag to an iPod, as we describe in the earlier sections, "Adding Calendars Manually to an iPod" and "Adding Contacts Manually to an iPod."
- **Winamp ipod plug-in (`http://mlipod.sourceforge.net`):** Also known as `ml_ipod`, this plug-in for Winamp lets you manage your iPod from within the Winamp media library. It supports all iPod models, from the classic first generation to the iPod mini, photo, nano, and shuffle. Because iPod support is built into Winamp version 5.2 and newer, `ml_ipod` is an alternative for older versions of Winamp.
- **XPlay 2 (`www.mediafour.com/products/xplay`):** This utility, from Mediafour Corp., provides read and write access to your iPod hard drive for documents and data files, plus the ability to organize your music from the Explorer-based XPlay interface or from Windows Media Player. It's an alternative to MusicMatch Jukebox or iTunes. XPlay makes your iPod appear as a normal drive under Windows for sharing data files. It also makes your songs, playlists, artists, and albums appear in custom folders in Explorer so they're easy to access and manipulate as well as organized similarly to how an iPod organizes them.
- **YamiPod (`www.yamipod.com/main/modules/home`):** Yet Another Manager for iPod (YAMiPod, get it?) is a freeware application that lets you copy music files freely from your iPod to your computer and vice versa. It can copy playlists, RSS news feeds, and podcasts; and synchronize your iPod with computers running Mac OS X, Windows, or Linux. You can run it directly from your iPod.

Chapter 24

Updating and Troubleshooting

In This Chapter

- Troubleshooting iPod and iPhone problems
- Resetting your iPod or iPhone
- Updating iPod and iPhone software
- Restoring an iPod or iPhone to its factory condition
- Updating Apple TV software

This chapter describes some of the problems that you might encounter with your iPod or iPhone and how to fix them. If your iPod or iPhone fails to turn on or your computer fails to recognize it, you can most likely find a solution here.

This chapter also covers updating the firmware and software on your iPod or iPhone and restoring your iPod or iPhone to its factory default condition. (*Firmware* is software encoded in hardware.) That last option is a drastic measure that erases any music or information on the device, but it usually solves the problem if nothing else does.

Taking Your First Troubleshooting Steps

Problems can arise with electronics and software that can prevent an iPod or iPhone from turning on at all or from turning on properly with all its content and playlists. You can also have problems in the connection between your iPod or iPhone and your computer.

Checking the Hold switch

If your iPod refuses to turn on, check the position of the Hold switch on top of the iPod. The Hold switch locks the iPod buttons so that you don't accidentally activate them. Slide the Hold switch away from the headphone connection, hiding the orange layer, to unlock the buttons. (If you see the orange layer underneath one end of the Hold switch, the switch is still in the locked position.)

Checking the power

Got power? The battery might not be charged enough. If the battery is too low for normal operation, the iPod or iPhone doesn't turn on. Instead, a low battery screen appears for about three seconds and then disappears. At that point, your only choice is to connect the iPod or iPhone to an AC power source, wait for a moment, and then turn the power on by pushing any button on the iPod or the Home button on the iPhone. If your source of AC power is your computer, make sure that the computer is on and not set to go to sleep. The battery icon in the upper right of the display indicates whether the iPod or iPhone battery is full or recharging. For more information about maintaining a healthy battery, see Chapter 1.

If your iPod shuffle doesn't turn on or respond, recharge its battery by connecting it to the USB connection on your computer.

Resetting an iPod

This operation resets the operating system of an iPod and restarts the system. Sometimes when your iPod gets confused or refuses to turn on, you can fix it by resetting it.

For fifth- or sixth-generation video iPods, iPod nano, fourth-generation iPods, iPod mini, iPod U2 Special Edition, and color-display iPods, follow these steps:

1. **(Optional) Connect the iPod to a power outlet by using the AC power adapter.**

   You can reset your iPod without connecting it to power if it has enough juice in its battery. However, if you have access to power, it makes sense to use it because the reset operation uses power.

2. **Toggle the Hold switch.**

   Push the Hold switch to hold (lock) and then set it back to unlock.

3. **Press the Menu and Select buttons simultaneously and hold for at least six seconds or until the Apple logo appears; then release the buttons when you see the Apple logo.**

   The appearance of the Apple logo signals that your iPod is resetting itself, so you no longer have to hold down the buttons.

Release the Menu and Select buttons as soon as you see the Apple logo. If you continue to press the buttons after the logo appears, the iPod displays the low battery icon, and you must connect it to a power source before using it again.

For first-, second-, and third-generation iPod models, follow these steps:

1. **(Optional) Connect the iPod to a power outlet by using the AC power adapter.**
2. **Toggle the Hold switch.**

   Push the Hold switch to hold (lock) and then set it back to unlock.
3. **Press the Menu and Play/Pause buttons simultaneously and hold for at least five seconds until the Apple logo appears; then release the buttons when you see the Apple logo.**

   The appearance of the Apple logo signals that your iPod is resetting itself, so you no longer have to hold down the buttons.

To reset your iPod shuffle, disconnect it from a computer and switch the slider on the back to the Off position. The green stripe under the switch should not be visible. Wait five seconds and then switch the slider back to the Shuffle Songs or Play in Order position.

After resetting, everything should be back to normal, including your music and data files.

Resetting an iPhone or iPod touch

Sometimes when your iPhone or iPod touch gets confused or refuses to turn on, you can fix it by resetting it and restarting the system.

The iPhone and iPod touch run applications. If your iPhone or iPod touch freezes while running an application (such as Safari), press and hold the Home button below the screen for at least six seconds, until the application quits. If the iPhone or iPod touch still doesn't respond, turn it off by pressing the Sleep/Wake (On/Off) button on the top, and then press the same button again to turn it back on.

If that doesn't work, press and hold the Sleep/Wake button on the top for a few seconds until a red slider appears on the screen, and then slide the slider with your finger. Then press and hold the Sleep/Wake button until the Apple logo appears.

Finally, if none of these options work, reset the iPhone or iPod touch by pressing and holding the Sleep/Wake button and the Home button at the same time for at least ten seconds, until the Apple logo appears.

After resetting, everything should be back to normal, including your music and data files.

You can get more information, updated troubleshooting instructions, and links to the iPhone repair site by visiting the Apple support site for the iPhone (`www.apple.com/support/iphone`).

Draining the battery

Certain types of battery-powered devices sometimes run into problems if the battery hasn't drained in a while. In rare cases, an iPod or iPhone might go dark. Try resetting the iPod or iPhone first. If the device still doesn't work, disconnect it from any power source and leave it disconnected for approximately 24 hours. After this period, connect it to power and reset.

Try to keep your iPod or iPhone at room temperature — generally near 68° Fahrenheit (F)/20° Celsius (C). However, you can use the iPod or iPhone anywhere between 50–95° F (10–35° C). If you left the iPod or iPhone in the cold, let it warm up to room temperature before waking it from sleep. Otherwise, a low-battery icon might appear, and the iPod or iPhone won't wake up properly. If the iPod or iPhone doesn't wake from sleep after warming up, reset the device as we describe in the preceding section.

Hitting the iPod panic button (Disk Mode)

Hitting the panic button, even if there is one, is never a good idea. However, if all you see on your iPod display is the Apple logo and iPod name, and the device seems to be restarting over and over, try force-enabling your iPod as a hard drive. (This is also known as putting your iPod into Disk Mode, which works for iPods only — not iPhones.)

For current fifth- or sixth-generation video iPods, iPod nano, fourth-generation iPods, iPod mini, iPod U2 Special Edition, and color-display iPods, follow these steps:

1. **Be sure your iPod is charged with power.**

   If your iPod needs to be recharged, connect it to a power source as described in Chapter 1.

2. **Reset the iPod.**

   If you don't know how to reset your iPod, see the "Resetting an iPod" section, earlier in this chapter.

3. **When the Apple icon appears on the display, immediately press and hold the Select and Play/Pause buttons until `OK to disconnect` and `Disk Mode` appears on the iPod display.**

4. **If your iPod isn't connected to your computer, disconnect the iPod from the power adapter and connect it to your computer.**

   You can now use iTunes to update the iPod software or restore the iPod. See "Updating Your iPod, iPhone, or Apple TV," later in this chapter.

If the `OK to disconnect` and `Disk Mode` messages don't appear, repeat Steps 2 and 3. (You might need to press the buttons more quickly.) If the message still doesn't appear after repeating these steps, the iPod might need to be repaired.

For first-, second-, and third-generation iPod models, follow these steps:

1. **Connect the iPod to your computer's FireWire or powered USB connection, or to an AC power adapter.**

   This procedure doesn't work with older USB connections that don't provide power. Make sure the computer is on and isn't set to go to sleep.

2. **Reset the iPod.**

   If you're not sure how to reset your iPod, see the "Resetting an iPod" section earlier in this chapter.

3. **When the Apple icon appears on the display, immediately press and hold the Previous and Next buttons until the `Do not disconnect` message or FireWire icon appears.**

4. **If your iPod isn't connected to your computer, disconnect the iPod from the power adapter and connect it to your computer.**

   Some iPods show the message `OK to Disconnect` before you connect it to the computer. This changes to the `Do not disconnect` message after you connect it.

   You can now use iTunes to update the iPod software or restore the iPod. See "Updating Your iPod, iPhone, or Apple TV," later in this chapter.

If the `Do not disconnect` message or FireWire icon doesn't appear, repeat Steps 2 and 3. (You might need to press the buttons more quickly.) If the message or FireWire icon still doesn't appear, the iPod might need to be repaired.

After using the iPod in Disk Mode, you need to reset the iPod (as described in "Resetting an iPod" earlier in this chapter) to return your iPod to normal operation.

You can get more information, updated troubleshooting instructions, and links to the iPod repair site by visiting the Apple support site for the iPod (`www.apple.com/support/ipod`).

Updating Your iPod, iPhone, or Apple TV

When you turn on your iPod or iPhone, built-in startup diagnostic software checks the device's software for problems and attempts to repair the software if necessary. If the iPod or iPhone finds an issue while it's on, it automatically uses internal diagnostics to repair any damage. You might see a disk scan icon on your iPod or iPhone screen after turning it on, indicating that a problem was fixed. If you see this indicator, update your iPod or iPhone software with iTunes.

iTunes updates the software that controls the iPod or iPhone without affecting the music or data stored on an iPod drive.

If you use MusicMatch Jukebox rather than iTunes on your Windows PC, skip this section and see this book's companion Web site.

Make sure that you use the newest version of iTunes. To check for the availability of an updated version for Windows, choose Help➪Check for iTunes Updates.

If you use a Mac and you enabled the Software Update option in your System Preferences, Apple automatically informs you of updates to your Apple software for the Mac, including iTunes, iCal, and Address Book. All you need to do is select which updates to download and then click the Install button to download them. iTunes includes updates for all generations of iPods and can detect which model iPod you have.

Checking the software version

To determine which version of iPod software is installed on your iPod, choose Settings➪About from the iPod main menu. (With first- and second-generation iPods, choose Settings➪Info.) Similarly, on an iPhone, choose Settings from the Home menu, then General from the Settings menu, and then About from the General menu. Next to the word `Version` is information that describes the software version installed.

You can also determine the software version on your iPod or iPhone by using iTunes. Connect the iPod or iPhone to your computer and select the iPod or iPhone in the iTunes Source pane (in the Devices section). The device's summary page appears to the right of the Source pane, and the software version appears next to the Software Version heading at the top of the page.

Updating with newer software

iTunes tells you whether your iPod or iPhone has the newest software installed. Connect the iPod or iPhone to your computer and select it in the iTunes Source pane (in the Devices section). The iPod or iPhone summary page appears to the right of the Source pane, and the Version section of the page tells you whether your iPod or iPhone software is up to date and when iTunes will check for new software. (See Figure 24-1.) You can check for new software at any time by clicking the Check for Update button on the Summary page.

Some iPod models need to be disconnected from the computer temporarily and connected to a power source to finish the process of updating the software. Follow the instructions to disconnect your iPod and connect it to an AC power adapter, if required.

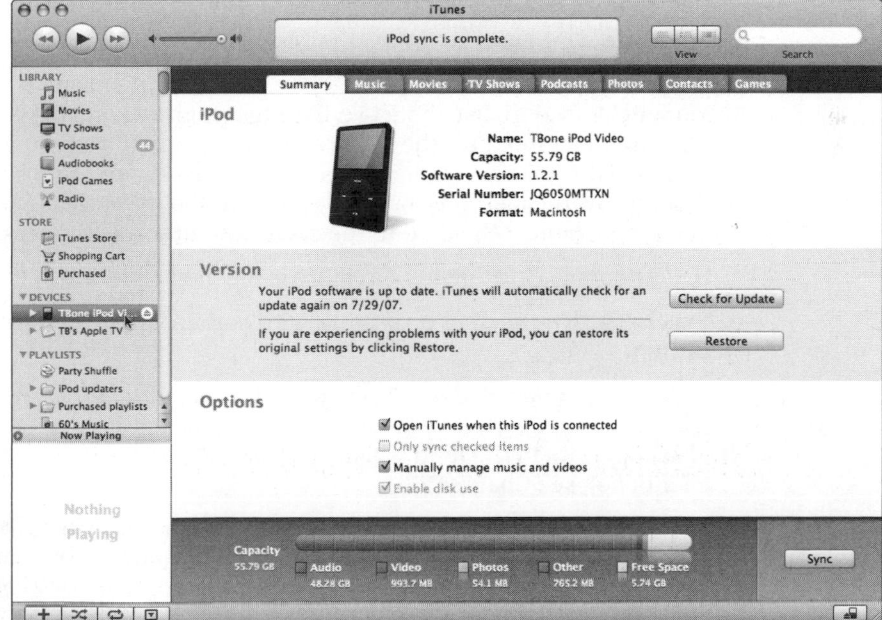

Figure 24-1: Use iTunes to update or restore your iPod.

Restoring to factory conditions

Restoring an iPod or iPhone erases the hard drive and returns the device to its factory settings, so make sure that you back up any important data that you keep stored on the device. To replace content that was erased by the restore operation, synchronize your iPod or iPhone from your computer's iTunes library, as we describe in Chapter 12.

To restore an iPod or iPhone, follow these steps for both the Mac and Windows versions of iTunes:

1. **Connect the iPod or iPhone to your computer.**

   iTunes opens automatically.

2. **Select the iPod or iPhone in the Source pane in the Devices section.**

   The device's Summary page appears to the right of the Source pane, replacing the browse/list view.

3. **Click the Restore button.**

   An alert dialog appears to confirm that you want to restore the device.

4. **Click the Restore button again to confirm the restore operation.**

   A progress bar appears, indicating the progress of the restore operation.

5. **For some iPod models, follow the instructions to disconnect your iPod and connect it to an AC power adapter, if required.**

   You might need to disconnect an iPod temporarily and connect it to an AC power adapter after the restore operation and during the process of updating the software. If you see a message asking you to disconnect the iPod, follow the instructions displayed with the message. You might also need to reconnect the iPod to the computer after this process.

   iTunes notifies you when the restore is finished.

6. **Synchronize your iPod or iPhone with content from your iTunes library.**

   Synchronize your iPod or iPhone with the content in your library, or manually manage your content, as we describe in Chapter 12. You can also copy data to the iPod while it's mounted as a hard drive (but not to an iPhone); see Chapter 22.

7. **When you finish synchronizing the iPod or iPhone with content and data, eject the device by clicking the Eject button.**

Updating an Apple TV

Apple TV can access the Internet through your wireless or Ethernet network, so the device can automatically check whether new software is available. Apple TV checks the Apple update server on a weekly schedule. When Apple TV detects an update, it downloads the update automatically and displays on your TV the message "An update is available for your Apple TV, do you want to install it now?" Apple TV then displays on your TV two choices: Update Now, or for you procrastinators out there, Update Later. Choose either option using your Apple Remote.

You don't have to wait for Apple TV to check for an update. You can update Apple TV at any time by choosing Settings⇨Update Software from the Apple TV main menu using your Apple Remote. To check the software version running in Apple TV, choose Settings⇨About.

Part VI
The Part of Tens

"It's like any other pacemaker, but it comes with an internal iPod docking accessory."

In this part . . .

In this part, you find two chapters chock full of information.

- Chapter 25 offers ten common iPod problems and their solutions.
- Chapter 26 provides 11 tips on using the equalizer.

Chapter 25

Ten iPod Problems and Solutions

In This Chapter

- Waking up your iPod
- Keeping your battery juiced
- Restoring your iPod to factory condition
- Helping your computer recognize your iPod

Unfortunately, humans — as well as the machines that they make — are not perfect. Even though we think that the iPod comes as close to perfection as possible, at some point, your iPod isn't going to work like you expect it to. When that happens, turn to this chapter. Here, we show you how to fix the most common iPod problems.

How Do I Get My iPod to Wake Up?

If your iPod doesn't turn on, don't panic — at least not yet. Try the following suggestions to get your iPod to respond:

- **Check the Hold switch position on top of the iPod.** The *Hold switch* locks the iPod buttons so you don't accidentally activate them. Slide the Hold switch away from the headphone connection, hiding the orange layer, to unlock the buttons.
- **See whether the iPod has enough juice.** Is the battery charged? Connect the iPod to a power source and see whether it works.
- **Reset your iPod if the iPod still doesn't turn on.** See Chapter 24 for resetting instructions.

If your iPod shuffle doesn't turn on or respond, recharge its battery by connecting it to the USB connection on your computer. If the iPod shuffle status light blinks orange when you press a button, the buttons are disabled. Press and hold the Play/Pause button for at least three seconds or until the status light blinks green.

How Do I Get My Battery to Last Longer?

You can do a lot to keep your battery going longer (much to the envy of your friends), including the following:

- **Press the Play/Pause button to pause (stop) playback.** Don't just turn off your car or home stereo or remove your headphones because if you don't also pause playback, your iPod continues playing until the playlist or album ends. When playback is paused, the power-save feature turns off the iPod after two minutes of inactivity.
- **Press and hold the Play/Pause button to turn off the iPod when you're not using it.** Rather than waiting for two minutes of inactivity for the power-save feature to turn off the iPod, turn it off yourself to save battery time.
- **Turn off backlighting.** If you don't need to use backlighting, turn it off because it drains battery power if the iPod is not plugged into a power source.
- **Set the Hold switch to lock when you're not using your iPod.** Keep your iPod controls locked so that they don't accidentally get turned on when you're not using your iPod.
- **Avoid changing tracks by pressing the Previous/Rewind or Next/Fast-Forward buttons.** The iPod uses a memory cache to load and play songs. If you frequently change tracks by pressing the Previous or Next buttons, the cache has to turn on the hard drive to load and play the songs, which drains the battery.
- **Use compressed AAC or MP3 files.** Playing larger, uncompressed AIFF or WAV files takes more power because the hard drive inside the iPod has to refresh its memory buffers more frequently to process more information as the song plays. Playing Apple Lossless files, even though they're compressed, also depletes battery power a bit more than playing AAC or MP3 files.

How Do I Keep My Scroll Wheel from Going Crazy?

Occasionally, an iPod scroll wheel stops working properly. If the scroll wheel doesn't scroll, try resetting the iPod, as described in Chapter 24. ***Remember:*** Resetting the iPod doesn't change an iPod's contents. After resetting, the iPod should work properly.

Second- and third-generation iPods use a nonmoving scroll wheel that works like a *trackpad* (also sometimes called a *touchpad*) of a laptop computer. Although the trackpad-style scroll wheel is far better than the first-generation moving wheel (which could be hampered by sand or dirt, and had moving parts that could be damaged), it has problems of its own: It goes crazy sometimes, and it can be very sensitive (not necessarily to criticism, but to the touch of your finger).

The trackpad-style scroll wheel translates the electrical charge from your finger into movement on the iPod display. If you accidentally use more than one finger, the scroll wheel might misread the signal and skip over selections or go backward while scrolling forward, and so on. ***Maintenance tip:*** If the scroll wheel has excessive moisture on it from humidity or a wet hand, wipe the wheel with a soft, dry cloth.

Don't use pencil erasers, pen caps, or other types of pointers to scroll the scroll wheel. (They won't work with trackpad-style scroll wheels, and using these might damage other types of scroll wheels.) And don't scroll with fingers sporting rings or a hand with a heavy bracelet or similar jewelry because these metals can throw off the sensors in the scroll wheel.

How Do I Get My Computer to Recognize My iPod?

If you can't get your computer to recognize your iPod, follow the first troubleshooting steps outlined in Chapter 24. If these steps don't fix the problem, make sure that your iPod is securely connected to your computer's USB connection (or FireWire connection in older models), and that it is the *only* device using that connection. (If you use a hub to share devices, try not using the hub to see whether it works without the hub.)

If you're using MusicMatch Jukebox, go to this book's companion Web site for more troubleshooting tips.

Also, make sure that your USB or FireWire cable is in good condition for connecting to your computer. For iPods that work with either FireWire or USB, try one type of connection or the other; if one connection type works but not the other, the problem is probably not in your iPod. Try connecting your iPod to another computer by using the same type of connection to see whether the same problem occurs. (Your computer might be to blame.)

If the same type of connection (FireWire or USB) to the other computer works, the problem is most likely your computer's connection or software. If the same type of connection doesn't work, the problem is most likely your cable or connection. You can try a new cable to see whether that works, or try the same type of connection with a different computer. Even if these suggestions seem obvious, doing them in the correct order can help you diagnose the problem.

What Are These Strange Icons on My iPod?

If you see an icon of a circle with a diagonal line across it, you should also see the words `Do not disconnect`. Don't do anything until the iPod finishes its update and displays the main menu or the `OK to disconnect` message. If this symbol stays on for a very, very long time (like, 20 minutes), try resetting the iPod, as described in Chapter 24.

Other strange icons might appear. When you turn on your iPod, built-in diagnostic software checks the iPod hard drive. If the iPod finds a problem when it's turned on, it automatically uses internal diagnostics to check for and repair any damage. You might see a disk folder icon on your iPod screen after turning it on, indicating that a problem was fixed. If this happens, restore your iPod to its factory condition (see Chapter 24) and reload content into it.

If the iPod displays any other strange icon, such as a backward Apple logo, a disk icon with a flashing question mark, or the dreaded disk-with-magnifying glass icon, the device might need to be repaired. If you get the "sad iPod" icon (with a frown and asterisks for eyes) or the folder icon with an exclamation point, try the troubleshooting steps in Chapter 24. If nothing seems to work, the iPod probably needs to be repaired. You can arrange for repair by visiting the Apple support site for the iPod (`www.apple.com/support/ipod`).

How Do I Restore My iPod to Its Factory Condition?

Restoring an iPod erases its hard drive and returns the device to its factory condition. Accordingly, make sure that you back up any important data stored on your iPod. You can use iTunes to restore your iPod, as we describe in Chapter 24. When finished, add music back to your iPod from the iTunes library or from your MusicMatch Jukebox library and then resynchronize your iPod with calendar and contact information.

If you're using MusicMatch Jukebox, check out this book's companion Web site to find out how to fill your iPod with music.

How Do I Update My iPod Software?

To determine which software version is installed on your iPod, press the Menu button until you see the iPod main menu. Then choose Settings⇨About; in earlier versions, choose Settings⇨Info. Look at the version number that describes the software version installed on your iPod. You can use iTunes to check which software version you're using and to update or restore your iPod (see Chapter 26).

How Do I Synchronize My iPod When My Library Is Larger Than My iPod's Capacity?

If you have less space on your iPod than content in your iTunes library, you can synchronize selected content only, or manually manage music and videos on your iPod. You can also select specific photo albums or videos, or select to specific playlists, rather than copying everything.

When you synchronize by playlist, you can create playlists exclusively for your iPod. You can also limit a smart playlist to a certain size: for example, 3.7GB (for a 4GB iPod nano).

By combining the features of smart playlists (Chapter 10) and synchronizing by playlist (Chapter 12), you can control how much of your iTunes library content is copied to and deleted from your iPod. You can even create multiple iTunes libraries — including sublibraries, based on your complete library — that you can set up for automatically synchronizing different iPods, as we describe in Chapter 13.

You can also keep your iPod synchronized to a subset of your library based on ratings. iTunes creates a new playlist specially designed for updating your iPod automatically — a smart playlist named "*your iPod name* Selection." iTunes decides which songs and albums to include in this playlist by using the ratings that you can set for each song in the iTunes song information, as we describe in Chapter 9.

How Do I Cross-Fade Music Playback with My iPod?

You can fade the ending of one song into the beginning of the next one to slightly overlap songs, just like a radio DJ, when you use iTunes. The *cross-fade setting* is the amount of time between the end of the fade-out from the first song and the start of the fade-in to the second song.

To cross-fade songs on your iPod, you have to play your iPod songs through iTunes on your computer. Connect your iPod to your computer and then connect your computer to a stereo or connect speakers (or headphones) to your computer. Press ⌘-Option (Mac) or Ctrl-Alt (Windows) when you launch iTunes; then select iPod in the iTunes Source pane.

If you're playing songs on an iPod that's connected to your computer and also playing songs from your iTunes library (or even on a second iPod, both connected to your computer), your songs cross-fade automatically.

You can change this cross-fade setting by choosing iTunes⇨Preferences (Mac) or Edit⇨Preferences (Windows) and then clicking the Playback tab. You can then increase or decrease the amount of the cross-fade with the Crossfade Playback option.

How Do I Decrease Distortion or Set a Lower Volume?

iPod models designed for the United States have a powerful 60-milliwatt amplifier to deliver audio signals through the headphone connection. The amplifier has a frequency response of 20 hertz (Hz) to 20 kilohertz (kHz), which provides distortion-free music at the lowest or highest pitches, but the amplifier might cause distortion at maximum volume depending on the recorded material — and potential ear drum damage.

For optimal sound quality, set the iPod volume to no more than three-quarters of the maximum volume and adjust your listening volume by using the volume control or equivalent on your car stereo or portable speaker system. (If no volume control exists, you have no choice but to control the volume from the iPod.) By lowering the iPod from maximum volume, you give your ears a break and also prevent over-amplification, which can cause distortion and reduce audio quality. See Chapter 15 for details on how to set the iPod volume limit and adjust the iPod volume.

Chapter 26

Eleven Tips for the Equalizer

In This Chapter

- Adjusting the equalizer on your home stereo
- Taking advantage of the iPod equalizer preset
- Getting rid of unwanted noise

You play your iPod in many environments, but the song that sounds like music to your ears in your car might sound like screeching hyenas when you're on a plane. In this chapter, we show you how to fix most sound problems that occur with iPods. Soon, you'll be cruising to the beat all the time — no matter where you are.

Setting the Volume to the Right Level

Before using the iPod equalizer to refine the sound, make sure the volume of the iPod is set to no more than about half or three-quarters of its max so you don't introduce distortion. (See Chapter 15 for details on how to set the volume limit and also adjust volume.) Then set your speaker system or home stereo volume before trying to refine the sound with equalizers.

Adjusting Another Equalizer

When you have the iPod connected to another system with an equalizer, try adjusting that equalizer:

- **Home stereo system:** Refine the sound with your home stereo equalizer because that might offer more flexibility and can be set precisely for the listening environment.
- **Car stereos:** The same rule applies as with your home stereo: Adjust the car stereo equalizer when you begin to listen to music on your iPod — before adjusting your iPod equalizer.

Setting Booster Presets

When playing music with your iPod through a home stereo or speakers (without a built-in equalizer) in a heavily draped and furnished room, try using the iPod Treble Booster equalizer preset or create your own equalizer preset (see Chapter 17) that raises the frequencies above 1 kilohertz (kHz). Boosting these higher frequencies makes the music sound naturally alive.

Reducing High Frequencies

When using your iPod to play music through a home stereo (without a built-in equalizer) in a room with smooth, hard walls and concrete floors, you might want to use the iPod Treble Reducer equalizer preset, which reduces the high frequencies to make the sound less brittle.

Increasing Low Frequencies

If you use high-quality, acoustic-suspension compact speakers, you might need to add a boost to the low frequencies (bass) with the Bass Booster equalizer preset so that you can boogie with the beat a little better. The Small Speakers equalizer preset also boosts the low frequencies and lowers the high frequencies to give you a fuller sound.

Setting Presets for Trucks and SUVs

We use our iPods in different types of cars: a sedan and a 4-wheel-drive truck. Trucks need more bass and treble, and the Rock equalizer preset sounds good for most of the music that we listen to. We also recommend using the Bass Booster equalizer preset when using your iPod in a truck if the Rock preset doesn't boost the bass enough. In a sedan, the iPod sounds fine without any equalizer adjustment.

Setting Presets When You're Eight Miles High

When using your iPod on an airplane where jet noise is a factor, try using the Bass Booster equalizer preset to hear the lower frequencies in your headphones and compensate for the deficiencies of headphones in loud environments. You might want to use the Classical equalizer preset, which boosts both the high and low frequencies for extra treble and bass. Try the Bose QuietComfort 3 Acoustic Noise Canceling headphones (`www.bose.com`) for plane travel — they work great!

If you're in an unpressurized environment at or above 10,000 feet — such as on a mountain peak — don't try to use a full-size iPod. Leave it turned off. Like many laptops, iPods that use hard drives can fail if operated at altitudes above 10,000 feet. The drive heads float above the recording surface on a small cushion of air produced by the spinning platters. If the air is too thin to create this cushion, the heads may contact the surface, possibly even damaging it.

Reducing Tape Noise and Scratch Sounds

To reduce the hiss of an old recording or the scratchy sound of songs recorded from a record, reduce the highest frequencies with the Treble Reducer equalizer preset.

Reducing Turntable Rumble and Hum

To reduce the low-frequency rumble in songs recorded from a turntable or recorded with a hum pickup, choose the Bass Reducer equalizer preset.

Reducing Off-Frequency Harshness and Nasal Vocals

To reduce a particularly nasal vocal sound reminiscent of Donald Duck (caused by off-frequency recording of the song source, making the song more harsh-sounding), try using the R&B equalizer preset, which reduces the midrange frequencies while boosting all the other frequencies.

Cranking Up the Volume to Eleven

If you want that larger-than-life sound, use the Loudness preset and then jack up the Preamp slider to the max, turn your stereo all the way up, and put your fingers in your ears to protect them. Then consult the DVD *This Is Spinal Tap* or the Spinal Tap fan site at `http://spinaltapfan.com`.

Index

• Numerics •

1-Click, iTunes Store, 71–72
first-generation iPods
  Disk Mode, 371
  troubleshooting resetting, 369
second-generation iPods
  Disk Mode, 371
  troubleshooting resetting, 369
third-generation iPods
  backlight timer, 340
  Disk Mode, 371
  overview, 11–12
  troubleshooting resetting, 369
fourth-generation iPods
  Disk Mode, 370–371
  overview, 11–12
  troubleshooting resetting, 368
fifth-generation iPods
  creating clocks, 333
  Disk Mode, 370–371
  locking, 346
  overview, 11–12
  playing movies, 254–256
  playing TV shows, 254–256
  playing videos, 254–256
  setting alarms, 336
  setting combination locks, 345–346
  setting date and time, 331–332
  sorting contacts, 343
  stopwatch, 339
  troubleshooting resetting, 368
  Videos menu, 255
sixth-generation iPods
  creating clocks, 333
  Disk Mode, 370–371
  locating songs by cover art, 242–243
  overview, 11–13
  playing games, 256–257
  playing movies, 254–256
  playing TV shows, 254–256
  playing videos, 254–256
  setting alarms, 334–335
  setting combination locks, 344–345
  setting date and time, 330–331
  sorting contacts, 343
  stopwatch, 338–339
  troubleshooting resetting, 368

• A •

AAC (Advanced Audio Coding)
  custom settings, 309–310
  encoders, 85, 301, 308–314
  formats, 300–301
  import settings, 314
  unprotected files, 123
accessing, shared libraries, 126–127
accessories, iPod, 18–19, 278–279, 327–328
account management, iTunes Store, 76–80
adapters
  cassette, 322–324
  power, 322–324
  wireless, 326
adding
  audio books to iTunes Library, 91–92
  books, 356–357
  calendars to iPods, 363–364
  contacts to iPods, 364
  cover art to iTunes, 164–166
  guides to iPods, 356–357
  music files to iTunes, 89–91
  news feeds to iPods, 356–357
  notes to iPods, 355–357
  podcasts to iTunes Library, 92–96
  radio stations to iTunes, 112
  song ratings to iTunes, 164
  text to iPods, 355–357
  videos to iTunes Library, 44, 96–97

address book
  adding manually to iPods, 364
  sorting, 342–343
  synchronizing, 360–363
adjusting
  brightness in iPhones, 341
  brightness in iPods, 341
  computer output volume, 100–102
  equalizers, 385
  frequencies in iTunes, 289
  preamp volume in iTunes, 288
  sound in iTunes, 284–287
  sound on Macs, 100–101
  sound in Windows, 102
  volume in iPhones, 269–270
  volume in iPods, 269–270
Adobe Photoshop Elements 4, 178
Advanced Audio Coding (AAC)
  custom settings, 309–310
  encoders, 85, 301, 308–314
  formats, 300–301
  import settings, 314
  unprotected files, 123
Aerolink, 279
AIFF (Audio Interchange File Format)
  changing encoder settings in iTunes, 313–314
  encoder, 85, 229–230, 301
  overview, 301
AirPort Express, 103
AirPort Express Base Station, 103
AirPort Extreme, 12
AirTunes, wireless stereo playback, 103–105
alarm clock
  deleting, 334
  setting, 333–337
album
  creating playlists, 169–170
  defined, 179
  locating songs by title, 245–246
  printing information, 234–237
Album view, 145
allowance account, iTunes Store, 78
Alpine CDA-9887, 325
amplitude, 289
AOL Wallet feature, 60
Apple
  iPod Web site, 12
  support page, 25
Apple Lossless
  changing encoder settings in iTunes, 313–314
  encoder, 85, 229–230, 300–301, 304
Apple menu, 19, 101
Apple Remote, 279
Apple SuperDrive, 227
Apple TV
  choosing iTunes libraries, 129–131
  choosing a network, 129–130
  language, 129
  sharing content, 127–131
  specifications, 128
  synchronizing, 190–191
  updating, 372–375
Apple Universal Dock, 18, 272, 276, 279
AppleCare warranties, 25
AppleScripts, 357
applications, Terminal, 135
artist name, locating songs by, 244–245
Artwork tab, 163
ascending order, 148
assigning
  equalizer presets to iPods, 294
  equalizer presets in iTunes, 291–293
  iTunes equalizer presets, 294
attaching, files to e-mail messages, 133
audio books
  adding to iTunes Library, 91–92
  browsing, 144
  deleting, 152
  displaying in List view, 146
  playing on iPods, 253–254
  playing in iTunes, 115
Audio CD, disc format, 232
Audio Devices Properties dialog, 102
Audio Interchange File Format (AIFF)
  changing encoder settings in iTunes, 313–314
  encoder, 85, 229–230, 301
  overview, 301
Audiobooks link, iTunes Store, 65–68

Aurius, 276
authorizing, computers, 80
Auto Kit, 323
AutoFill, 209–210

• B •

backing up
  to CD-R/RW, 222–223
  to DVD-R/RW, 222–223
  to hard drives, 223
  iTunes Library, 222–224
  between Mac and PC, 224
backups, incremental, 222
Bass Booster, 294
batteries. *See also* power
  calibrating, 23
  charging, 328
  checking status on iPod shuffle, 22
  maintaining life, 23
  overview, 21–22
  replacing, 24–25
  saving power, 24
  troubleshooting, 370, 380
Belkin Tunesync, 278
bit rate, 300
Blaze Media Pro, 124
bone conduction, 320
book
  conventions in this, 3
  icons in this, 6
  organization of this, 4–6
Book2Pod, 357
books, adding, 356–357
Booster presets, setting, 386
Bose iPod Speaker Dock, 321
Bove, Tony, *iLife '04 All-in-One Desk Reference For Dummies,* 134
Brick and Parachute, iPod game, 258
Browse button, iTunes, 47
Browse pane, iTunes, 46
Browse view
  customizing options, 148
  Library, 140–141
  overview, 145
browser, Cover Flow, 243
browsing
  audio books, 144
  charts, 63
  by cover art, 142–143
  iPod games, 146
  Library content overview, 140–141
  movies, 145
  playlists, 63–64
  podcasts, 68
  songs by artist and album, 143–144
  TV shows, 145
  videos, 145
burn playlist
  calculating duration, 228–229
  creating, 227–230
  importing music, 229–230
burning
  defined, 225
  discs, 233
  playlists, 227–230
  setting preferences, 230–232
  troubleshooting, 237–238
Burton Amp Pack, iPod case, 327–328
buying, content in iTunes Store, 71–76

• C •

cable, mini-plug, 272–273, 323
cache, 24
calculating, burn playlist duration, 228–229
calendar
  adding manually to iPod, 363–364
  overview, 342
  synchronizing, 360–363
calibrating, batteries, 23
car chargers, 328
Car Holder, 323
car stereos, as equalizers, 385
cassette adapters, 322–324
CD, playing tracks in iTunes, 48–53
CD Database (CDDB), 157
CD Info dialog (iTunes), 86
CD-R
  backing up to, 222–223
  drive overview, 19
  ejecting, 50

CD-R *(continued)*
- importing for, 229–230
- overview, 226
- ripping, 44, 82, 88–89
- selecting recordable, 226
- specifications, 226–227

CD-RW
- backing up to, 222–223
- drive overview, 19
- ejecting, 50
- importing for, 229–230
- overview, 226
- ripping, 44, 82, 88–89
- selecting recordable, 226–227
- specifications, 226–227

CD Spin Doctor, 91
CD Text, 231
CDDB (CD Database), 157
Chambers, Mark, *Mac OS X Tiger All-in-One Desk Reference For Dummies,* 4, 103, 119, 134–135
changing
- AAC encoder settings, 308–310
- AIFF encoder settings in iTunes, 313–314
- Apple Lossless encoder settings in iTunes, 313–314
- iTunes Library locations, 218–219
- MP3 encoder settings in iTunes, 310–312
- WAV encoder settings in iTunes, 313–314

Channels
- AAC custom setting, 310
- MP3 encoder setting, 312

charging, batteries, 328
charts, browsing, 63
checking
- battery status on iPod shuffles, 22
- software versions, 372–373
- sound on iPods, 287
- sound on iTunes, 286–287

classic. *See* iPod classic
clearing, On-The-Go playlists, 265–266
click wheel. *See* scroll wheel
client, FTP, 134–135
clocks, displaying multiple, 332–333
collection, 179
color-display iPods
- Disk Mode, 370–371
- troubleshooting resetting, 368

combination lock, setting, 343–346
Compact Disc-Digital Audio (CD-DA) format Mode 2 Form 2 (Red Book), 227
compression
- choices, 300
- overview, 304
- power consumption, 300

computers, authorizing, 80
connections
- headphones, 320–321
- home stereo, 273–274
- portable speakers, 320–321
- S-video, 118–119, 275–276
- stereo-in, 322
- types overview, 271–273
- wireless radio, 325–326

conserving, power, 344
consolidating, Library media files, 217
contacts
- adding manually to iPods, 364
- sorting, 342–343
- synchronizing, 360–363

content
- copying automatically, 186–192
- copying to iPod manually, 204–208
- copying selectively, 192–204
- deleting automatically, 186–192
- deleting selectively, 192–204
- editing information, 158–164, 208
- entering information, 157–158
- media file, 151
- modifying iTunes, 295–297
- searching for, 149–150
- sharing on a network, 124–127
- sharing with your Apple TV, 127–131
- storing remotely, 186

content indicators, 146–147
content link, iTunes, 57
Contextual menu, 164, 170
conventions, in this book, 3
converting
- files to iPod-ready format, 183
- songs to a different encoder format in iTunes, 315–316
- videos for iPods, 183

copying
- content automatically, 186–192
- content to iPod manually, 204–208

content selectively, 192–204
files between Macs and PCs, 133–135
iPod items, 205–206
iPod shuffle items, 210–211
media files, 132
cover art
adding, 164–166
locating songs by, 242–244
Cover browser, iTunes, 46
Cover Flow
browser, 243
locating songs with, 242–244
view, 142–143, 145
Cover Version, 53
Create Collection dialog (Photoshop Album), 181
creating
album playlists, 169–170
burn playlists, 227–230
clocks, 333
iMix, 176
iTunes Library on other hard drives, 221–222
libraries on other hard drives, 221–222
On-The-Go playlists, 262–267
playlists on an iPod, 207
playlists in iTunes, 168–173
podcast playlists, 170–172
radio station playlists, 111–112
smart albums, 181
smart playlists, 174–175
sub-libraries, 221
video playlists, 172
cross-fade
settings, 384
songs, 108–109
troubleshooting, 384
Crossfade Playback, iTunes, 87
Custom, MP3 encoder setting, 311
custom mix, 225
customizing
Browse view options, 148
encoder settings in iTunes, 308–314
iPod menu, 348–349
iPod settings, 348–349
List view options, 147–148

• D •

data, organizing iPod, 354
Data CD/DVD, disc format, 232
date, setting, 330–332
Date Added, 173
decibels, 288
deleting
alarms, 334
audio books, 152
content automatically on iPods, 186–192
content in iTunes, 151–153
content selectively on iPods, 192–204
iPod items, 206–207, 355
On-The-Go playlist items, 264–265
playlist items, 173
podcasts, 152
songs, 152
TV shows, 152
videos, 152
descending order, 148
development, iTunes, 2
dialog
Audio Devices Properties, 102
Get Info, 132
iTunes Preferences, 95–96, 287
Make Preset, 291
Multiple Item Information, 87, 160
New Album, 180
Open Stream, 112
Preferences, 52, 110
Smart Playlist, 174
Subscribe to Podcast, 93
Visualizer Options, 51
digital music, evolution, 303
digital photo album, 178
digital rights management (DRM), 122
Digital Video Interface (DVI), 128
disable playback, feature, 256
disabling
Apple TV device synchronization, 191
playback, 256
podcast synchronization, 192
disc
burning, 233
formats, 232

Disc Format, 231
Disk Mode, troubleshooting, 370–372
display
  iPhone, 25–28
  iPod classic, 28–29
  iPod nano, 28–29
  iPod touch, 25–28
  settings, 340–341
display settings
  backlight timer, 340–341
  brightness, 341
  contrast, 341
  overview, 340
displaying
  content in List view, 146–148
  multiple clocks, 332–333
  videos on an iPod, 183
  visuals in iTunes, 51–53
DLO TransPod FM, wireless adapter, 326
dock connector, 272–273
docking, 13, 272
downloading
  content in iTunes Store, 71–76
  interrupted, 74–75
  software upgrades, 41–42
drive, flash memory, 10–11, 15, 18, 57, 205, 351
DRM (digital rights management), 122
drop-down menu, 58
duration, limiting song, 174
DVD-audio, 303
DVD-R
  backing up to, 222–223
  drive overview, 19
  overview, 226
  selecting recordable, 226
  specifications, 226–227
DVD-RW
  backing up to, 222–223
  drive overview, 19
  overview, 226
  selecting recordable, 226
  specifications, 226–227
DVI (Digital Video Interface), 128

• E •

e-mail messages, attaching files to, 133
editing
  content information, 158–164, 208
  smart playlists, 175–176
  video software, 182
Eject button, iTunes, 48
ejecting
  CDs, 50
  iPods, 41
enabling
  Apple TV device synchronization, 191
  iPods as hard drives, 351–353
  Sound Check, 287
encoder
  Apple Lossless, 300–301
  changing, WAV settings, 313–314
  changing AIFF settings, 313–314
  changing Apple Lossless settings, 313–314
  converting songs to different formats, 315–316
  customizing settings in iTunes, 308–314
  import to MP3 CD-R, 230
  iTunes, 300–302
  overview, 85, 229–230
enhancing, sound in iTunes, 285–286
entering, content information, 157–158
EphPod 2, 357, 366
EQ (equalizer). *See* equalizer (EQ)
equalizer (EQ)
  adjusting other, 385
  assigning presets in iTunes, 291–293
  choosing iPod presets, 293–294
  defined, 289
  tips, 385–388
equalizing
  in iPods, 293–294
  in iTunes, 288–293
Ethernet, 119, 121, 128–129, 190
exporting
  iTunes playlists, 219–220
  videos, 182–183

• F •

factory settings
  restoring, 374
  troubleshooting, 382–383
FairPlay, DRM, 123
Fetch 5, 134
fifth-generation iPods
  creating clocks, 333
  Disk Mode, 370–371
  locking, 346
  overview, 11–12
  playing movies, 254–256
  playing TV shows, 254–256
  playing videos, 254–256
  setting alarms, 336
  setting combination locks, 345–346
  setting date and time, 331–332
  sorting contacts, 343
  stopwatch, 339
  troubleshooting resetting, 368
  Videos menu, 255
file formats, video, 182
File Transfer Protocol (FTP), 134
files
  adding music, 89–91
  attaching to e-mail messages, 133
  converting to iPod-ready format, 183
  copying between Macs and PCs, 133–135
  copying media, 132
  deleting iPod, 355
  importing M3U playlist, 220
  iTunes Music Library, 224
  locating media, 216–217
  organizing, 215–216
  storage settings in iTunes Library, 215–216
  unprotected AAC, 123
  using utilities to copy, 364–365
  video formats, 182
  zip, 135
Filter Frequencies Below 10 Hz, MP3 encoder settings, 312
finding, iTunes Library, 214
FireWire
  connection, 21, 273
  dock connector, 272
  external, 133
  six pin connection, 273
firmware, 367
first-generation iPods
  Disk Mode, 371
  troubleshooting resetting, 369
flash memory drive, 10–11, 15, 18, 57, 205, 351
folders
  Notes, 355–356
  opening iPod, 353–355
formats
  disc, 232
  recording sound, 303
fourth-generation iPods
  Disk Mode, 370–371
  overview, 11–12
  troubleshooting resetting, 368
frequencies
  adjusting in iTunes, 289
  defined, 289
  increasing low, 386
  reducing high, 386
FTP client, 134–135
FTP Explorer, 134
FTP (File Transfer Protocol), 134
full-screen, playing videos, 117–119
functions, iPod playback, 29–31

• G •

G-Tech Psycho, iPod backpack, 328
games
  iTunes Store, 258
  playing on iPods, 256–258
Gapless Album option, iTunes, 86–87
GarageBand, 91
Get Info dialog, 132
gift certificates
  iTunes Store, 76
  sending iTunes, 78–79

Good Quality, MP3 encoder setting, 311
Gookin, Dan, *PCs For Dummies,* 102
Gracenote CDDB, iTunes, 49, 157
guides, adding, 356–357

• H •

hard drives
  backing up to, 223
  enabling iPods as, 351–353
HDMI (High-Definition Multimedia Interface), 128
headphone connections, 272–273, 320–321
hertz, 320
Hide Artwork button, iTunes, 48
High-Definition Multimedia Interface (HDMI), 128
High Quality, MP3 encoder setting, 311
Higher Quality, MP3 encoder setting, 311
Hold switch
  overview, 21, 379
  troubleshooting, 367–368
home stereo, connections, 273–274
hum, reducing, 387

• I •

i-Fusion, 321
iBar, 357
iBoom, 278, 321
iCal, 342
ICE-Link, 325
icons
  in this book, 6
  troubleshooting, 382
iDisk, 223
iLife '04 All-in-One Desk Reference For Dummies (Bove and Rhodes), 134
iLingo, 357
iMix, creating, 176
import settings, selecting, 304–305
importing
  burn playlists, 229–230
  for CD-R/RW, 229–230
  iTunes preferences, 82–85
  M3U playlist files, 220
  voice and sound effects in iTunes, 314
increasing
  low frequencies, 386
  volume, 387–388
incremental backups, 222
Info tab, 161
inserts, printing, 234–235
installing
  iTunes on a Mac, 36–38
  iTunes on a Windows PC, 33–36
  software upgrades, 41–42
Internet
  connection, 19
  retrieving song information, 156–157
iPDA, Mac utility, 365
iPhone
  adjusting brightness, 341
  adjusting volume, 269–270
  AppleCare warranties, 25
  backlight timer, 340
  calendar, 342
  clearing On-The-Go playlists, 265–266
  deleting alarms, 334
  deleting items from On-The-Go playlists, 265
  display, 25–28
  limiting volume, 269–270
  locating songs by album title, 246
  locating songs by artist name, 244–245
  locating songs by cover art, 242–243
  locating songs by playlist, 247
  locking, 345
  playing movies, TV shows, and videos, 254–256
  playing On-The-Go playlists, 263–264
  power, 19–21
  repeating songs, 248–250
  setting alarm clocks, 334
  setting combination locks, 344
  setting date and time, 330
  setting up slide shows, 261
  shuffling song order, 250–252
  sleep timer, 337
  sorting contacts, 343
  specifications, 16–18
  stopwatch, 338
  support page, 25
  synchronizing calendars, 360–363

synchronizing contacts, 360–363
synchronizing overview, 188–189
troubleshooting resetting, 369–370
updating, 372–374
viewing photos, 259
iPhoto
organizing photos, 179–181
overview, 178
iPod. *See also specific iPod models*
accessories, 18–19, 178–179
adding calendars manually, 363–364
adding contacts manually, 364
adjusting brightness, 341
adjusting volume, 269–270
AppleCare warranties, 25
assigning iTunes equalizer presets, 294
clock overview, 329
connections, 271–276
converting videos for, 183
copying content to manually, 204–208
creating On-The-Go playlists, 262–267
creating playlists, 207
customizing menus, 348–349
customizing settings, 348–349
deleting items, 206–207
displaying videos, 183
editing content information, 208
ejecting, 41
enabling as a hard drive, 351–353
equalizing in an, 293–294
games, 71, 146
integrating with car stereos, 324–325
limiting volume, 269–270
locating songs by album title, 245–246
locating songs by artist name, 244–245
locating songs by cover art, 242–244
locating songs by playlist, 246–247
locking, 345–346
menus, 25–29
models, 11–18
opening folders, 353–355
overview, 9–11
playback functions, 29–31
playing, TV shows, 254–256
playing audio books, 253–254
playing games, 256–258
playing movies, 254–256
playing podcasts, 252–253
playing songs, 247–252
playing through car stereos, 321–322
playing through iTunes, 276–277
playing videos, 254–256
power, 19–21
power accessories, 328
repeating songs, 248–250
setting the language, 31–32
setting up iTunes, 38–41
shuffling song order, 250–252
slide show, 259–262
sound-checking, 287
synchronizing calendars, 360–363
synchronizing contacts, 360–363
travel accessories, 327–328
troubleshooting, 379–384
TunePower Rechargeable Battery Pack, 328
unlocking, 345
updating, 372–374
viewing photos, 259–262
iPod Access, Mac utility, 365
iPod AV Cable, 275
iPod classic
adjusting brightness, 341
adjusting volume, 269
calendar, 342
clearing On-The-Go playlists, 265–266
Cover Flow browser, 243
deleting items from On-The-Go playlists, 264–265
display, 28–29
limiting volume, 269–270
locating songs by album title, 245–246
locating songs by artist name, 244–245
locating songs my playlist, 247
overview, 13
playing On-The-Go playlists, 263
playing songs, 247–252
repeating songs, 248
saving On-The-Go playlists, 266
setting alarms, 334–335
setting up slide shows, 260–261
shuffling song order, 250–252
sleep timer, 337
sorting contacts, 343

iPod classic *(continued)*
Videos menu, 255
viewing photos, 259
iPod games, browsing, 146
iPod Hi-Fi, 278
iPod Leather Organizer, iPod case, 327
iPod mini
Disk Mode, 370–371
troubleshooting resetting, 368
using as a hard drive, 352
iPod nano
adjusting volume, 269
calendar, 342
clearing On-The-Go playlists, 265–266
Cover Flow browser, 243
creating clocks, 333
deleting items from On-The-Go playlists, 264–265
Disk Mode, 370–371
display, 28–29
limiting volume, 269–270
locating songs by album title, 245–246
locating songs by artist name, 244–245
locating songs by cover art, 242–243
locating songs by playlist, 247
overview, 13
playing games, 256–257
playing movies, 254–256
playing On-The-Go playlists, 263
playing songs, 247–252
playing TV shows, 254–256
playing videos, 254–256
repeating songs, 248
saving On-The-Go playlists, 266
setting alarms, 334–335
setting combination locks, 344–345
setting date and time, 330–331
setting up slide shows, 260–261
shuffling song order, 250–252
sleep timer, 337
sorting contacts, 343
specifications, 14–15
stopwatch, 338–339
troubleshooting resetting, 368
using as a hard drive, 352
Videos menu, 255
viewing photos, 259
iPod-ready, 324
iPod shuffle
checking battery status, 22
overview, 13
playing, 267–268
resetting, 369
space management, 211–212
specifications, 15–16
synchronizing, 208–212
iPod Software 1.0, 278
iPod touch
adjusting brightness, 341
adjusting volume, 269
backlight timer, 340
calendar, 342
clearing On-The-Go playlists, 265–266
deleting alarms, 334
deleting items from On-The-Go playlists, 265
display, 25–28
limiting volume, 270
locating songs by album title, 245
locating songs by artist name, 244–245
locating songs by cover art, 242–243
locating songs by playlist, 247
overview, 12
playing movies, 254–256
playing On-The-Go playlists, 263–264
playing songs, 247–252
playing TV shows, 254–256
playing videos, 254–256
repeating songs, 248–250
setting alarm clocks, 334
setting combination locks, 344
setting date and time, 330
setting up slide shows, 261
shuffling song order, 250–252
sleep timer, 337
sorting contacts, 343
specifications, 13–14
stopwatch, 338
troubleshooting resetting, 369–370
iPod U2 Special Edition
Disk Mode, 370–371
troubleshooting resetting, 368
iPod Voice Recorder, 346
iPodRip, Mac utility, 365

iPodSync, Windows utility, 366
iQuiz, iPod game, 257
iTalk Voice Recorder, 346
iTrip, wireless adapter, 326
iTunes
  adding radio stations, 112
  adjusting frequencies, 289
  adjusting preamp volume, 288
  adjusting sound, 284–287
  assigning equalizer presets to iPods, 294
  assigning equalizer presets to iTunes, 291–293
  changing AAC encoder settings, 308–310
  changing AIFF encoder settings, 313–314
  changing Apple Lossless encoder settings, 313–314
  changing MP3 encoder settings, 310–312
  changing WAV encoder settings, 313–314
  converting songs to a different encoder format, 315–316
  customizing encoder settings, 308–314
  development, 2
  displaying visuals, 51–53
  encoders, 300–302
  enhancing sound, 285–286
  Equalizer, 288
  equalizing, 288–293
  Gapless Album option, 86–87
  Gracenote CDDB, 49
  importing voice and sound effects, 314
  installing on a Mac, 36–38
  installing on a Windows PC, 33–36
  library, 44
  managing voice memos, 348
  MiniStore, 53
  modifying content, 295–297
  opening, 45–48
  overview, 19, 43
  playing CD tracks, 48–53
  playing iPods through, 276–277
  plug-ins, 53
  podcasts, 68–70
  repeating song lists, 50
  saving presets, 290–291
  setting start and stop points, 295–296
  setting up, 38–41
  setting volume, 284–285
  shuffle button, 50
  sizing components, 48
  sound-checking, 286–287
  splitting tracks, 296–297
  transferring On-The-Go playlists to, 266–267
  uses, 44–45
  using presets, 289–290
iTunes Library. *See* Library (iTunes)
iTunes Music Library file, 224
iTunes Preferences dialog, 95–96, 287
iTunes Store. *See* Store (iTunes)

• J •

Jax, 351, 357
jewel case, 234
Jobs, Steve, 55, 100, 122
Joint Stereo Mode, 312
Jukebox Station, 279

• K •

Kincaid, Bill, 2
Klondike (solitaire), iPod game, 257

• L •

LAN (local area network), 133
language
  choosing in Apple TV, 129
  setting iPod, 31–32
Leonhard, Woody, *Windows Vista All-in-One Desk Reference For Dummies,* 4
library
  accessing a shared, 126–127
  computer, 124
  sharing on a network, 124–125
Library (iTunes)
  adding audio books, 91–92
  adding music, 82–91
  adding podcasts, 92–96
  adding videos, 96–97
  backing up, 222–224
  browsing audio books, 144
  browsing content overview, 140–141

Library (iTunes) *(continued)*
browsing by cover art, 142–143
browsing iPod games, 146
browsing movies, 145
browsing TV shows, 145
browsing videos, 145
changing locations, 218–219
choosing for Apple TV, 129–131
consolidating media files, 217
content indicators), 146–147
creating on other hard drives, 221–222
creating a sub-library, 221
customizing Browse view options, 148
customizing List view options, 147–148
displaying content, 146–148
file storage settings, 215–216
finding, 214
importing preferences, 82–85
managing multiple, 220–222
manipulating, 217–220
moving hard drives, 219
overview, 81
searching for content, 149–150
sorting content, 148–149
sound-checking, 286–287
limiting
iPhone volume, 269–270
iPod volume, 269–270
song duration, 174
line-out connection, 272–273
liner notes, 355
linking, iPod and car stereos, 322
List pane, iTunes, 45
List view
customizing options, 147–148
displaying content, 146–148
Library, 140
listening, to radio stations, 110–111
Live Updating, 175
local area network (LAN), 133
locating
with Cover Flow, 242–244
media files, 216–217
MP3 broadcasts, 112
by playlist, 246–247
songs by album title, 245–246
songs by artist name, 244–245
songs by cover art, 242–243
songs on an iPod, 241–247
locking, iPods, 345
locks, setting combination, 343–346
lossy-style compression, 304
Lyrics tab, 163

• M •

M3U playlist files, importing, 220
Mac
adjusting sound, 100–101
backing up from/to PC, 224
connecting to a television, 118
installing iTunes, 36–38
overview, 18–19
utilities, 365
Mac OS X, 133–134
Mac OS X Tiger All-in-One Desk Reference For Dummies, Chambers, 4, 103, 119, 134–135
Macs, copying files between PCs and, 133–135
Make Preset dialog, 291
managing
media content, 177–183
multiple iTunes Libraries, 220–222
voice memos, 348
MARWARE, iPod cases, 23
Matias Armor, iPod case, 327
media content, managing, 177–183
media files
consolidating, 217
content, 151
copying, 132
locating, 216–217
menu(s)
Apple, 19, 101
Contextual, 164, 170
customizing iPod, 348–349
iPod, 25–29, 348–349
pop-up, 58
Settings, 24, 31–32, 40
Videos, 255
MicroMemo, 346–347
military time, showing, 332
mini-plug cable, 272–273, 323

MiniStore, iTunes, 47, 53
mixing, 225
mobility, 319
modifying, iTunes content, 295–297
mono (monaural), 310
Monster iCarPlay Wireless, wireless adapter, 326
Morris, Tee, *Podcasting For Dummies,* 70
movies
  browsing, 145
  iTunes Store, 65–68
  playing on iPods, 254–256
  synchronizing, 196–198
Moving Picture Experts Group (MPEG), 301
MP3
  encoders, 85, 300, 310–312
  import settings, 314
  locating broadcasts, 112
MP3 CD, disc format, 232
MP3 encoder
  changing settings in iTunes, 310–312
  formats, 300–302
  iTunes, 85
MP3 (MPEG-1, Layer 3), format, 302
MPEG (Moving Picture Experts Group), 301
Multiple Item Information dialog, 87, 160
music. *See also* songs
  adding to iTunes Library, 82–91
  importing for a burn playlist, 229–230
  ripping CDs, 88–89
  using utilities to copy, 364–365
music files, adding, 89–91
Music Quiz, iPod game, 258
music videos, displaying in List view, 146

• N •

nano. *See* iPod nano
network
  choosing for Apple TV, 129–130
  sharing content, 124–127
New Album dialog (iPhoto), 180
news feeds, adding, 356–357
NewsLife, 357
Newsweek, 122
Normal Stereo Mode, 312
Notepad, 355
notes, adding, 355–357
Notes folder, 355–356

• O •

Ohga, Norio, 227
On-The-Go playlists, creating, 262–267
1-Click, iTunes Store, 71–72
Open Stream dialog, 112
opening
  iPod folders, 353–355
  iTunes, 45–48
  iTunes Store, 56–58
Optimize for Voice, AAC custom setting, 310
Options tab, 162
organization, of this book, 4–6
organizing
  files, 215–216
  iPod data, 354
  photos, 178–183
  playlists, 170
Outlook, 342
Outpod, Windows utility, 366
output volume, adjusting computer, 100–102

• P •

parental controls, iTunes Store, 79
Party Shuffle, 106–108
PC
  backing up from/to Mac, 224
  copying files between Mac and, 133–135
  overview, 18–19
PCM (Pulse Code Modulation)
  algorithm, 301
  defined, 227
PCs For Dummies (Gookin), 102
Photo Library software, 178
photos
  organizing, 178–183
  synchronizing albums, 201–204
  viewing on iPods, 259–262
Photoshop Album
  organizing photos, 181
  overview, 178

Photoshop Elements 4 (Adobe), 178
Play Count, 173
playback
  disabling, 256
  functions, 29–31
  wireless stereo, 103–105
Player buttons, iTunes, 48
playing
  audio books on iPods, 253–254
  audio books in iTunes, 115
  CD tracks in iTunes, 48–53
  games on iPods, 256–258
  iPod shuffle, 267–268
  iPod slide shows, 261–262
  iPods through iTunes, 276–277
  movies on iPods, 254–256
  On-The-Go playlist items, 263–264
  podcasts on iPods, 252–253
  podcasts in iTunes, 112–114
  songs on an iPod, 247–252
  songs on iPods through car stereos, 321–322
  songs in iTunes, 106–109
  streaming radio in iTunes, 109–112
  TV shows on iPods, 254–256
  videos on iPods, 254–256
  videos in iTunes, 115–119
Playlist buttons, iTunes, 48
playlists
  album, 169–170
  browsing, 63–64
  burn, 227–230
  creating on an iPod, 207
  creating in iTunes, 168–173
  creating On-The-Go, 262–267
  defined, 223
  deleting items, 173
  exporting, 219–220
  locating songs by, 246–247
  organizing, 170
  podcast, 170–172
  radio stations, 111–112
  renaming, 170
  smart, 173–176
  song, 168–169
  synchronizing, 194–195
  video, 172
plug-ins, iTunes, 53
Podcasting For Dummies (Morris and Terra), 70
podcast(s)
  adding to iTunes Library, 92–96
  browsing in iTunes, 68
  defined, 44, 68, 92
  deleting, 152
  displaying in List view, 146
  playing on iPods, 252–253
  playing in iTunes, 112–113
  playlists, 170–172
podcasts, scheduling updates, 95–96
podcast(s)
  subscribing, 93–95
  subscribing to in iTunes, 69–70
  synchronizing, 192, 200–201
  updating, 95–96
pop-up menu, 58
Portable Folding Speaker System, 278
power. *See also* batteries
  accessories (iPod), 328
  adapters, 322–324
  conserving, 344
  consumption and compression, 300
  iPod, 19–21
  searching, 63
  troubleshooting, 368, 379
preamp, 288
preferences
  iTunes importing, 82–85
  iTunes Store, 73–74
  setting burning, 230–232
Preferences dialog, 52, 110
Preferred Speed, 232
prepaid cards, iTunes Store, 76
presets
  assigning equalizer, 291–293
  assigning iTunes equalizer, 294
  choosing equalizer, 293–294
  defined, 289
  saving iTunes, 290–291
  setting for airplanes, 386–387
  setting Booster, 386
  setting for trucks and SUVs, 386
  using iTunes, 289–290
printing
  album/song information, 234–237
  inserts, 234–235

ProClip, 324
Pulse Code Modulation (PCM)
  algorithm, 301
  defined, 227

• Q •

quality, space versus, 299–300
queuing, songs, 106–108
Quick Links panel, iTunes Store, 61, 63, 65, 76–79
QuickTime
  overview, 19, 34
  video technology, 182
QuietComfort 3 Acoustic Noise Canceling headphones, 387

• R •

radio. *See also* radio stations
  playing streaming, 109–112
  wireless connection, 325–326
radio stations. *See also* radio
  adding to iTunes, 112
  creating playlists, 111–112
  listening, 110–111
ratings, adding song, 164
RBrowser 4, 134
Really Simple Syndication (RSS) feeds, 92
rearranging, tracks in iTunes, 50
receiver, 273
recording
  sound, 346–348
  sound formats, 303
  voice memos, 347
Red Book (Compact Disc-Digital Audio (CD-DA) format Mode 2 Form 2), 227
reducing
  high frequencies, 386
  hum, 387
  nasal vocals, 387
  off-frequency harshness, 387
  scratch sounds, 387
  tape noise, 387
  turntable rumble, 387
renaming, playlists, 170
repeating
  song lists in iTunes, 50
  songs on iPhones, 248–250
  songs on the iPod, 248–250
  tracks in iTunes, 50
resetting
  iPod shuffle, 369
  troubleshooting iPod, 368–369
restoring, factory settings, 374
Rhodes, Cheryl, *iLife '04 All-in-One Desk Reference For Dummies,* 134
ripping
  CDs, 82
  defined, 44
  music CDs, 88–89
Robbin, Jeff, 2
Roxio, 91, 303
RSS (Really Simple Syndication) feeds, 92

• S •

S-video connection, 118–119, 275–276
SACD (Super Audio CD), 303
Sample Rate
  AAC custom setting, 309
  defined, 305
  MP3 encoder setting, 312
saving
  battery power, 24
  iTunes presets, 290–291
  On-The-Go playlists, 266
scheduling, podcast updates, 95–96
scratch sounds, reducing, 387
scroll pad. *See* scroll wheel
scroll wheel, troubleshooting, 380–381
Search field, iTunes, 48
searching
  for content, 149–150
  power, 63
second-generation iPods
  Disk Mode, 371
  troubleshooting resetting, 369
selecting
  import settings, 304–305
  On-The-Go playlist items, 263–264
  recordable CDs/DVDs, 226–227
Senuti, Mac utility, 365

setting(s)
alarm clocks, 333–337
burning preferences, 230–232
changing AAC encoder, 308–314
changing MP3 encoder, 310–312
combination locks, 343–346
customizing encoder, 308–314
customizing iPod, 348–349
date and time, 330–332
display, 340–341
equalizer volume, 385
presets for airplanes, 386–387
presets for vehicles, 386
selecting import, 304–305
sleep timer, 337
start and stop points in iTunes, 295–296
synchronization, 188
volume in iTunes, 284–285
Settings menu, 24, 31–32, 40
sharing
content on a network, 124–127
content with your Apple TV, 127–131
iTunes Store content, 122–124
Sharing dialog, 124–126
shopping cart, iTunes, 72–73
Show Artwork button, iTunes, 48
showing
duplicate items, 151
military time, 332
shuffle. *See also* iPod shuffle
song order on iPods, 250–252
Shuffle button, iTunes, 50
sixth-generation iPods
creating clocks, 333
Disk Mode, 370–371
locating songs by cover art, 242–243
overview, 11–13
playing games, 256–257
playing movies, 254–256
playing TV shows, 254–256
playing videos, 254–256
setting alarms, 334–335
setting combination locks, 344–345
setting date and time, 330–331
sorting contacts, 343
stopwatch, 338–339
troubleshooting resetting, 368
sizing, iTunes components, 48
Skip Count, 149
skipping, tracks in iTunes, 50
sleep timer, setting, 337
slide show, iPod, 259–262
slide to unlock, message, 25
smart albums
creating, 181
defined, 180
Smart Encoding Adjustments, MP3 encoder setting, 312
Smart Playlist dialog, 174
smart playlists
creating, 174–175
defined, 167, 207
editing, 175–176
overview, 173
software
checking versions, 372–373
downloading and installing upgrades, 41–42
Jax, 351
updating, 373, 388
video-editing, 182
software updates, troubleshooting, 383
song information
printing, 234–237
retrieving automatically, 156
retrieving manually, 156–157
song lists
printing, 235–237
repeating in iTunes, 50
songs. *See also* music
adding ratings, 164
browsing by artist and album, 143–144
converting to a different encoder format in iTunes, 315–316
cross-fading, 108–109
deleting from playlists, 152
deleting versions, 152
displaying in List view, 146
iTunes Store, 61–64
limiting duration, 174
locating by album title, 245–246
locating by artist name, 244–245
locating by cover art, 242–244
locating with Cover Flow, 242–244
locating on the iPod, 241–247
locating by playlist, 246–247

Party shuffle, 106–108
playing on the iPod, 247–252
playing in iTunes, 106–109
playlists, 168–169
queuing, 106–108
repeating on the iPod, 248–250
retrieving information, 156–157
shuffling order on ipods, 250–252
sorting
contacts, 342–343
Library content, 148–149
Sorting tab, 161
sound
adjusting iTunes, 284–287
enhancing in iTunes, 285–286
importing effects in iTunes, 314
overview, 283–284
recording, 303, 346–348
recording formats, 303
troubleshooting distortion, 384
Sound Check
enabling, 287
overview, 231
sound-checking
iPods, 287
iTunes Library, 286–287
sound distortion, troubleshooting, 384
Sound Enhancer, 285
Sound Studio 3, 91
Source pane, iTunes, 45
space
management on the iPod shuffle, 211–212
quality versus, 299–300
speakers, connecting portable, 320–321
specifications
Apple TV, 128
CD-R, 226–227
DVD-R, 226–227
iPhone, 16–18
iPod nano, 14–15
iPod shuffle, 15–16
iPod touch, 13–14
Spectrograph, 53
splitting, tracks in iTunes, 296–297
Sportsuit Convertible case, iPod case, 327
Status pane, iTunes, 48
stereo, 310
Stereo Bit Rate
AAC custom setting, 309
MP3 encoder setting, 311
stereo-in connection, 322
Stereo Mode, MP3 encoder setting, 312
stereo system, as an equalizer, 385
stopwatch, iPod, 337–340
Store (iTunes)
1-Click, 71–72
account management, 76–80
account set-up, 59–61
audiobooks, 65–68
buying content, 71–76
downloading content, 71–76
games, 258
gift certificates, 76
iPod games, 71
movies, 65–68
opening, 56–58
overview, 55–56
parental controls, 79
preferences, 73–74
prepaid cards, 76
Quick Links panel, 61, 63, 65, 76–79
sharing content, 122–124
shopping cart, 72–73
songs, 61–64
TV shows, 65–68
videos, 65–68
streamed, 124
streaming broadcast. *See* radio
streaming radio, playing, 109–112
Subscribe to Podcast dialog (iTunes), 93
subscribing
defined, 93
podcasts, 93–95
Summary tab, 161
Super Audio CD (SACD), 303
synchronizing
Apple TV, 190–191
automatically, 186–191
calendars, 360–363
contacts, 360–363
disabling Apple TV device, 191
enabling Apple TV device, 191
iPhone, 188–189
iPod shuffle, 208–212

synchronizing *(continued)*
movies, 196–198
overview, 20, 359–360
photo albums, 201–204
playlists, 194–195
podcasts, 200–201
selectively, 192–204
settings, 188
troubleshooting, 383
TV shows, 198–199
System Preferences, 19, 36, 41, 101

• T •

tape noise, reducing, 387
television, connecting a Mac to a, 118
Terminal applications, 135
Terra, Evo, *Podcasting For Dummies,* 70
text, adding, 355–357
TextEdit, 355
third-generation iPods
backlight timer, 340
Disk Mode, 371
overview, 11–12
troubleshooting resetting, 369
This Is Spinal Tap, DVD, 387
thumbnails, 178
Thundervolt, iPod backpack, 328
time, setting, 330–332
tips
equalizer, 385–388
power saving, 24
touch. *See* iPod touch
touch wheel. *See* scroll wheel
tracks
rearranging in iTunes, 50
repeating in iTunes, 50
skipping in iTunes, 50
splitting in iTunes, 296–297
TRAFFICJamz, wireless adapter, 326
transferring, On-The-Go playlists to iTunes, 266–267
Treble Booster, 294
troubleshooting
batteries, 370, 380
battery drainage, 370
burning, 237–238
cross-fading, 384
Disk Mode, 370–372
factory settings, 382–383
Hold switch, 367–368
icons, 382
iPod, 379–384
iPod and computer recognition, 381–382
iPod touch resetting, 369–370
power, 368, 379
resetting iPhone, 369–370
resetting iPods, 368–369
scroll wheel, 380–381
software updates, 383
sound distortion, 384
synchronizing, 383
video playback, 119
volume, 384
TuneCast II Mobile FM Transmitter, wireless adapter, 326
TuneDok, 323
TunePower Rechargeable Battery Pack, iPod, 328
turntable rumble, reducing, 387
TV, iPod connections, 275–276
TV shows
browsing, 145
deleting, 152
displaying in List view, 146
iTunes Store, 65–68
playing on iPods, 254–256
synchronizing, 198–199

• U •

Uniform Resource Locator (URL), 112
Universal Dock, 18, 272, 276, 279
unlocking, iPods, 345
unpinching, 25
updating
Apple TV, 372–375
iPhone, 372–374
iPod, 372–374
Live, 175
podcasts, 95–96
software, 373, 388

upgrades, downloading and installing software, 41–42
URL (Uniform Resource Locator), 112
USB connection, overview, 19, 21, 272
USB hard drive, 133
utilities
  Mac, 365
  using to copy files and music, 364–365
  Windows, 366

• V •

Variable Bit Rate (VBR)
  AAC custom encoder setting, 309–310
  MP3 encoder setting, 311–312
  overview, 305
VBR (Variable Bit Rate)
  AAC custom encoder setting, 309–310
  MP3 encoder setting, 311–312
  overview, 305
vCard (virtual business card), 364
Video Input, iPod connections, 275–276
video playlists, creating, 172
Video tab, 161
VideoLAN Client, 220
video(s)
  adding files to iTunes library, 44
  adding to iTunes Library, 96–97
  browsing, 145
  converting for iPods, 183
  deleting, 152
  displaying on an iPod, 183
  editing software, 182
  exporting, 182–183
  file formats, 182
  iTunes Store, 65–68
  playing, 115–119
  playing on iPods, 254–256
  playlists, 172
  preparing for iTunes and iPods, 182–183
  troubleshooting playback, 119
Videos menu, 255
View buttons, iTunes, 47
virtual business card (vCard), 364
Visualizer Options dialog, iTunes, 51
visuals, displaying in iTunes, 51–53
voice
  importing effects in iTunes, 314
  memos, 347–348
  playback, 347
  recording, 346–347
voice memos
  managing, 348
  playback, 347
  recording, 347
volume
  adjusting computer output, 100–102
  adjusting iPod, 269–270
  adjusting preamp, 288
  increasing, 387–388
  limiting iPod, 269–270
  setting equalizer, 385
  setting in iTunes, 284–285
  troubleshooting, 384
Volume control, iTunes, 48
VoodooPad, 357
Vortex, iPod game, 257

• W •

warranties, AppleCare, 25
WAV (Waveform Audio File)
  changing encoder settings in iTunes, 313–314
  encoder, 85, 229–230
  format, 302
Waveform Audio File (WAV)
  changing encoder settings in iTunes, 313–314
  encoder, 85, 229–230
  format, 302
Web sites (Accessories)
  Alpine, 325
  Apple online store, 18
  Apple travel accessories, 327
  Belkin, 275, 323, 326–328, 346
  Bose, 321, 387
  Dension, 325
  Digital Lifestyle Outfitters, 278, 326
  DLO, 321
  Engineered Audio, 176, 279
  Griffin Technology, 326, 346

Web sites (Accessories) *(continued)*
JanSport, 328
Kensington, 328
MARWARE, 23, 323, 327
Matias Corporation, 327
Monster Cable, 326
Newer Technology, 326, 328
Overstock, 278
PluginsWorld, 53
ProClip, 324
Saffire-USA, 279
Sonic Impact, 321
Thanko, 320
XtremeMac, 346
Web sites (Content)
Audible, 115, 314
Elgato Systems, 44
Freeverse, 91
Live365.com, 112
Rockument, 70
Roxio, 91
SHOUTcast, 112
Spinal Tap fan site, 387
Web sites (Information)
Apple iPod, 12
AppleScripts, 357
Book2Pod, 357
EphPod 2, 357, 366
Gracenote, 157
iBar, 357
iLingo, 357
iPDA, 365
iPod Access, 365
iPodLibrary, 357
iPodRip, 365
iPodSync, 366
Jax, 357
NewsLife, 357
Outpod, 366
Senuti, 365
VideoLAN Client, 220
VoodooPad, 357
Winamp, 220, 366
XPlay 2, 366
YamiPod, 365–366
Web sites (Software)
Jax, 357
JoeSoft, 351
Web sites (Support)
Apple Lithium-ion Batteries, 23
Apple support page, 25
iPhone support page, 25
Weverka, Peter, *Windows XP GigaBook For Dummies,* 4
Wi-Fi wireless networking, 103
Winamp, 220, 366
Windows
adjusting sound, 102
utilities, 366
Windows PC, installing iTunes, 33–36
Windows Vista All-in-One Desk Reference For Dummies (Leonhard), 4
Windows XP GigaBook For Dummies (Weverka), 4
WinZip, 135
wireless adapters, recommended, 326
wireless radio, connection, 325–326
wireless stereo playback, 103–105
WireTap Pro, 124

• X •

XPlay 2, Windows utility, 366

• Y •

YamiPod
Mac utility, 365
Windows utility, 366

• Z •

zip, files, 135

BUSINESS, CAREERS & PERSONAL FINANCE

0-7645-9847-3

0-7645-2431-3

Also available:

- Business Plans Kit For Dummies 0-7645-9794-9
- Economics For Dummies 0-7645-5726-2
- Grant Writing For Dummies 0-7645-8416-2
- Home Buying For Dummies 0-7645-5331-3
- Managing For Dummies 0-7645-1771-6
- Marketing For Dummies 0-7645-5600-2
- Personal Finance For Dummies 0-7645-2590-5*
- Resumes For Dummies 0-7645-5471-9
- Selling For Dummies 0-7645-5363-1
- Six Sigma For Dummies 0-7645-6798-5
- Small Business Kit For Dummies 0-7645-5984-2
- Starting an eBay Business For Dummies 0-7645-6924-4
- Your Dream Career For Dummies 0-7645-9795-7

HOME & BUSINESS COMPUTER BASICS

0-470-05432-8

0-471-75421-8

Also available:

- Cleaning Windows Vista For Dummies 0-471-78293-9
- Excel 2007 For Dummies 0-470-03737-7
- Mac OS X Tiger For Dummies 0-7645-7675-5
- MacBook For Dummies 0-470-04859-X
- Macs For Dummies 0-470-04849-2
- Office 2007 For Dummies 0-470-00923-3
- Outlook 2007 For Dummies 0-470-03830-6
- PCs For Dummies 0-7645-8958-X
- Salesforce.com For Dummies 0-470-04893-X
- Upgrading & Fixing Laptops For Dummies 0-7645-8959-8
- Word 2007 For Dummies 0-470-03658-3
- Quicken 2007 For Dummies 0-470-04600-7

FOOD, HOME, GARDEN, HOBBIES, MUSIC & PETS

0-7645-8404-9

0-7645-9904-6

Also available:

- Candy Making For Dummies 0-7645-9734-5
- Card Games For Dummies 0-7645-9910-0
- Crocheting For Dummies 0-7645-4151-X
- Dog Training For Dummies 0-7645-8418-9
- Healthy Carb Cookbook For Dummies 0-7645-8476-6
- Home Maintenance For Dummies 0-7645-5215-5
- Horses For Dummies 0-7645-9797-3
- Jewelry Making & Beading For Dummies 0-7645-2571-9
- Orchids For Dummies 0-7645-6759-4
- Puppies For Dummies 0-7645-5255-4
- Rock Guitar For Dummies 0-7645-5356-9
- Sewing For Dummies 0-7645-6847-7
- Singing For Dummies 0-7645-2475-5

INTERNET & DIGITAL MEDIA

0-470-04529-9

0-470-04894-8

Also available:

- Blogging For Dummies 0-471-77084-1
- Digital Photography For Dummies 0-7645-9802-3
- Digital Photography All-in-One Desk Reference For Dummies 0-470-03743-1
- Digital SLR Cameras and Photography For Dummies 0-7645-9803-1
- eBay Business All-in-One Desk Reference For Dummies 0-7645-8438-3
- HDTV For Dummies 0-470-09673-X
- Home Entertainment PCs For Dummies 0-470-05523-5
- MySpace For Dummies 0-470-09529-6
- Search Engine Optimization For Dummies 0-471-97998-8
- Skype For Dummies 0-470-04891-3
- The Internet For Dummies 0-7645-8996-2
- Wiring Your Digital Home For Dummies 0-471-91830-X

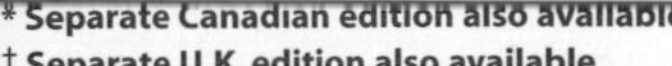

*** Separate Canadian edition also available**
† Separate U.K. edition also available

Available wherever books are sold. For more information or to order direct: U.S. customers visit www.dummies.com or call 1-877-762-2974. U.K. customers visit www.wileyeurope.com or call 0800 243407. Canadian customers visit www.wiley.ca or call 1-800-567-4797.

SPORTS, FITNESS, PARENTING, RELIGION & SPIRITUALITY

0-471-76871-5

0-7645-7841-3

Also available:

- Catholicism For Dummies 0-7645-5391-7
- Exercise Balls For Dummies 0-7645-5623-1
- Fitness For Dummies 0-7645-7851-0
- Football For Dummies 0-7645-3936-1
- Judaism For Dummies 0-7645-5299-6
- Potty Training For Dummies 0-7645-5417-4
- Buddhism For Dummies 0-7645-5359-3
- Pregnancy For Dummies 0-7645-4483-7 †
- Ten Minute Tone-Ups For Dummies 0-7645-7207-5
- NASCAR For Dummies 0-7645-7681-X
- Religion For Dummies 0-7645-5264-3
- Soccer For Dummies 0-7645-5229-5
- Women in the Bible For Dummies 0-7645-8475-8

TRAVEL

0-7645-7749-2

0-7645-6945-7

Also available:

- Alaska For Dummies 0-7645-7746-8
- Cruise Vacations For Dummies 0-7645-6941-4
- England For Dummies 0-7645-4276-1
- Europe For Dummies 0-7645-7529-5
- Germany For Dummies 0-7645-7823-5
- Hawaii For Dummies 0-7645-7402-7
- Italy For Dummies 0-7645-7386-1
- Las Vegas For Dummies 0-7645-7382-9
- London For Dummies 0-7645-4277-X
- Paris For Dummies 0-7645-7630-5
- RV Vacations For Dummies 0-7645-4442-X
- Walt Disney World & Orlando For Dummies 0-7645-9660-8

GRAPHICS, DESIGN & WEB DEVELOPMENT

0-7645-8815-X

0-7645-9571-7

Also available:

- 3D Game Animation For Dummies 0-7645-8789-7
- AutoCAD 2006 For Dummies 0-7645-8925-3
- Building a Web Site For Dummies 0-7645-7144-3
- Creating Web Pages For Dummies 0-470-08030-2
- Creating Web Pages All-in-One Desk Reference For Dummies 0-7645-4345-8
- Dreamweaver 8 For Dummies 0-7645-9649-7
- InDesign CS2 For Dummies 0-7645-9572-5
- Macromedia Flash 8 For Dummies 0-7645-9691-8
- Photoshop CS2 and Digital Photography For Dummies 0-7645-9580-6
- Photoshop Elements 4 For Dummies 0-471-77483-9
- Syndicating Web Sites with RSS Feeds For Dummies 0-7645-8848-6
- Yahoo! SiteBuilder For Dummies 0-7645-9800-7

NETWORKING, SECURITY, PROGRAMMING & DATABASES

0-7645-7728-X

0-471-74940-0

Also available:

- Access 2007 For Dummies 0-470-04612-0
- ASP.NET 2 For Dummies 0-7645-7907-X
- C# 2005 For Dummies 0-7645-9704-3
- Hacking For Dummies 0-470-05235-X
- Hacking Wireless Networks For Dummies 0-7645-9730-2
- Java For Dummies 0-470-08716-1
- Microsoft SQL Server 2005 For Dummies 0-7645-7755-7
- Networking All-in-One Desk Reference For Dummies 0-7645-9939-9
- Preventing Identity Theft For Dummies 0-7645-7336-5
- Telecom For Dummies 0-471-77085-X
- Visual Studio 2005 All-in-One Desk Reference For Dummies 0-7645-9775-2
- XML For Dummies 0-7645-8845-1